AUG 20
4

D1222459

RECONSIDERING REAGAN

RECONSIDERING
REAGAN

RACISM, REPUBLICANS, AND THE ROAD TO TRUMP

DANIEL S. LUCKS

SHOREWOOD-TROY LIBRARY
650 DEERWOOD DRIVE
SHOREWOOD, IL 60404

BEACON PRESS ▪ BOSTON

BEACON PRESS
Boston, Massachusetts
www.beacon.org

Beacon Press books
are published under the auspices of
the Unitarian Universalist Association of Congregations.

© 2020 by Daniel S. Lucks

All rights reserved
Printed in the United States of America

23 22 21 20   8 7 6 5 4 3 2 1

This book is printed on acid-free paper that meets the uncoated paper
ANSI/NISO specifications for permanence as revised in 1992.

Text design and composition by Kim Arney

Library of Congress Cataloging-in-Publication Data

Names: Lucks, Daniel S., author.
Title: Reconsidering Reagan : Racism, Republicans, and the Road to Trump /
    Daniel S. Lucks.
Description: Boston : Beacon Press, 2020. | Includes bibliographical
    references and index.
Identifiers: LCCN 2019059280 (print) | LCCN 2019059281 (ebook) |
    ISBN 9780807029572 (hardcover) | ISBN 9780807029985 (ebook)
Subjects: LCSH: Reagan, Ronald—Political and social views. | Racism—United
    States—Political aspects. | Republican Party (U.S. : 1854–)—History—20th
    century. United States—Politics and government—1989–
Classification: LCC E877.2 .L83 2020 (print) | LCC E877.2 (ebook) |
    DDC 973.927092—dc23
LC record available at https://lccn.loc.gov/2019059280
LC ebook record available at https://lccn.loc.gov/2019059281

To Drs. Deborah and Lee Meisel

CONTENTS

INTRODUCTION

*Ronald Reagan ran on practically the same platform I ran on in
1948. . . . I'm very pleasantly surprised. I didn't think it would
happen in my lifetime.*
　　　　　　　—Strom Thurmond boasting to a reporter (1981)[1]

*Nothing has frustrated me more in this job than the false image
of bigotry that has been fastened upon me.*
　　　　　　　—Ronald Reagan to a constituent (1984)[2]

Ronald Reagan's sunny demeanor, charisma, and old-fashioned patriotism captured the imagination of the American electorate, catapult-
ing him to two consecutive presidential landslide victories in 1980 and
1984.[3] Despite his polarizing policies and his administration's multiple
scandals, millions of white Americans revered the avuncular Reagan for
restoring American pride and confidence after the national traumas of
the Vietnam War and Watergate. Most significantly, Reagan personified
the triumph of an optimistic brand of conservatism, which made him
the most consequential president of the postwar era. Over the years,
journalists and scholars across the political spectrum have described an
"Age of Reagan" that cast a long shadow on American life and dominated
an era in American history much like Franklin Roosevelt and his New
Deal had in the decades after 1945. In 2008, for example, even Senator
Barack Obama spoke of his goal of becoming a transformational president like Reagan who changed "the trajectory of America" in a way both
Richard Nixon and Bill Clinton failed to do.[4]

In an effort to score political points to help perpetuate a robust future for conservatism, conservatives launched the Ronald Reagan Legacy Project during the Clinton presidency, which sanitized Reagan and

succeeded in distorting his legacy beyond recognition.[5] Namely, the project's success in mythologizing Reagan has obscured his longstanding hostility to the civil rights movement, skill in exploiting white racism for political gain without appearing racist, and his efforts to turn the clock back on civil rights during his presidency. It has also whitewashed most Blacks' unremitting disdain for Reagan and his racist politics and policies that festered throughout the entirety of Reagan's political career. *Reconsidering Reagan* documents how Reagan's woeful legacy on race contradicts conservatives' view of Reagan as a national saint and constitutes a blight on his legacy.

President Donald Trump's barrage of blatantly racist statements has propelled race to the forefront of American political life, thereby providing a timely opportunity to reappraise Reagan's record on race and civil rights. While Trump was more overt in his racism, *Reconsidering Reagan* demonstrates that Reagan's record on civil rights was just as racist as Trump's. Most tellingly, Nobel Peace Prize recipients Martin Luther King Jr. and Archbishop Desmond Tutu both branded Reagan as a racist for his support of the white supremacist South in the 1960s and the white supremacist South African regime. Days after Reagan's 1966 landslide victory in the gubernatorial election in California, a distraught King decried Reagan's "scarcely disguised appeals to bigotry."[6] Nearly two decades later, Tutu called Reagan "a racist pure and simple."[7] When forced to choose sides, Reagan always sided with the white supremacists striving to uphold the racial caste system while indicting King, and other combatants, for racial justice as Communist pawns. Reagan's tarring of the civil rights movement with a red brush had been a staple of Southern racists' long campaign to discredit the civil rights movement as a Communist plot.[8] By any conceivable standard, close political alliances with white supremacists exceeded King's remote links with Communists, a claim that Reagan repeated in October 1983 after reluctantly signing the bill making King's birthday a national holiday.

Given Reagan's stature as a transformative political figure, books on virtually all aspects of Reagan's life and presidency abound.[9] While there have been a spate of articles, book chapters, and references to Reagan's civil rights record, particularly his racist War on Drugs, surprisingly, none of the previous biographies of Reagan have focused exclusively on Reagan and race. Accordingly, *Reconsidering Reagan* is the first full-length book study of Reagan's life and presidency devoted to the topic of Reagan and race.[10] It also demonstrates the extent to which Reagan was on the wrong side of history in a civil rights movement that forced the nation to reckon with its original sin of slavery and explains why African Americans overwhelmingly viewed him with contempt.

Indeed, Blacks' distrust of Reagan began from the moment he entered the political arena as a Barry Goldwater states' rights conservative opposing the landmark Civil Rights Act of 1964. This coincided with Goldwater's conservative movement's success in making inroads with the Democratic South by opposing federal intervention to topple Jim Crow, the racial caste system that operated primarily in the South. In his 1966 campaign for governor, which occurred not long after the August 1965 Watts riots, Reagan made the explosive issue of race a centerpiece of his campaign while distancing himself from segregationists. Against the backdrop of the carnage of the Watts riots, he deployed the racially freighted term "law and order," blamed the riots on liberal politicians coddling lawless criminals, and the liberal notion that government policies are the answer to poverty. At virtually every campaign stop, he stoked white middle-class fears of residential integration by excoriating California's controversial and far-reaching Fair Housing Act.[11] His reluctance to repudiate the conspiracist John Birch Society confirmed the view that he sympathized with right-wing extremists. From the outset, Blacks perceived Reagan as an existential threat. Baseball legend Jackie Robinson, a moderate Republican who often criticized the tactics of more militant Blacks, castigated Reagan as a "Hollywood Style" Goldwater and called Reagan's victory in the California gubernatorial primary a "tragedy."[12] Likewise, on the eve of Reagan's 1966 gubernatorial election against his racially liberal foe, incumbent Democratic governor Edmund G. "Pat" Brown, the Black-owned *Los Angeles Sentinel*, warned that "no greater catastrophe could overcome the Negroes of this state . . . than the election of Ronald Reagan."[13] Reagan's victory over Brown was the first major triumph of the white backlash against the civil rights movement, as millions of middle-class white Democrats voted Republican for the first time, largely over concerns of riots, residential integration, and the influx of Black people to California. Over the years, the enmity of Blacks deepened as Reagan and Nixon became the avatars of the Republican Party's Southern strategy.

Reconsidering Reagan is a corrective to Reagan's inflated reputation and legacy that belied his racially reactionary policies and his offensive rhetoric. The Ronald Reagan Legacy Project's success in canonizing Reagan as a great president and a role model for future presidents reaped immense dividends. Within a few years after its creation in 1997, Reagan's conservative acolytes had succeeded in divorcing Reagan's legacy from reality. They lauded Reagan as a heroic president who restored America to greatness after the ravages of the 1960s, and endlessly touted the myth that he singlehandedly won the Cold War without firing a shot. As the efforts to chisel Reagan's face on Mt. Rushmore, replace the profile of Franklin Roosevelt on the dime with that of Reagan, and erect a Reagan memorial near the National Mall in Washington, DC, gained momentum by the late 1990s, criticism of Reagan had virtually receded from mainstream public discourse. Such mythmaking obscures the fact that during his presidency Reagan was a polarizing political presence, and his approval ratings were often lower than his immediate predecessors. In particular, the deification of Reagan into a national saint has prevented the country from having a frank discussion on Reagan's divisive racial legacy and his failure to even recognize, let alone reconcile, what Gunnar Myrdal called the "American Dilemma"—the disparity between American ideals and its racial practices.

In July 2019, the National Archives released an October 1971 audio clip between then governor Reagan and President Nixon in which Reagan called African diplomats "monkeys" still "uncomfortable wearing shoes," which has brought new interest to Reagan's troubling record on race. These revelations of Reagan's racism, coming in the middle of the Trump era, have made the investigation of Reagan and race more urgent. In the popular imagination, it is not Reagan's civil rights policies but his reassuring persona, militant anti-Communism, and calls to roll-back government that define Reagan's legacy. Yet, Reagan's subtle skill in stoking white resentments over race was a mainstay of his political success and needs to be taken into account in assessing his overall legacy.

Like many conservatives, Reagan never honestly confronted America's racist legacy.[14] In his 1980 debate with President Jimmy Carter, for example, Reagan commented on the great progress that was made from the time he was young when "the nation did not realize it had a racial problem."[15] This grossly insensitive remark revealed Reagan's obliviousness to America's original sin of slavery. Yet, it is not so shocking given that Reagan's political success was in large part fueled by his skill in crafting an idyllic narrative of the past that resonated with white Americans reeling from the racial, cultural, and economic dislocations of the 1960s and 1970s. He spoke of America as "a shining city on a hill whose beacon light guides freedom-loving people everywhere," and, echoing Lincoln, as the "last, best hope on Earth." However, whereas Lincoln's political career and legacy was defined by his collision with slavery, in Reagan's America, that original sin of slavery was indiscernible. After a generation of wrenching turmoil, Reagan revived an American exceptionalism, which had always overlooked the baneful legacy of slavery, Jim Crow, and structural racism embedded in the fabric of every institution. For African Americans, this American exceptionalism was tragic and humiliating. James Baldwin, the poet of the civil rights movement, best encapsulated Blacks' views of American exceptionalism:

> The American Negro has the great advantage of having never believed the collection of myths to which white Americans cling: that their ancestors were all freedom-loving heroes, that they were born in the greatest country the world has ever seen, or that Americans are invincible in battle and wise in peace, that Americans have always dealt honorably with Mexicans and Indians and all other neighbors or inferiors.[16]

Reagan never fathomed how American experience was a nightmare for Blacks. His 1980 campaign slogan, "Let's Make America Great Again," which Donald Trump copied in 2016, and his iconic 1984 campaign slogan, "It's Morning Again in America," reflected his veneration of a mythical country where racism never existed. In light of America's history of slavery, Jim Crow, and structural racism, Blacks resented Reagan's myopic vision of American greatness. Nevertheless, the civil rights gains of the 1960s, a decade Reagan abhorred and vilified, gave hope for a better future. For African Americans, the Reagan years did not represent a "morning in America" but a "nightmare," because it was yet another betrayal of the long quest to achieve racial equality.

Reagan's death in June 2004 prompted a weeklong display of grief across the nation.[17] The funeral's careful orchestration and fawning, nonstop coverage preempted reporting of other events, including his racially polarizing policies. Political leaders from both political parties hailed Reagan as a great leader and patriot and praised his trademark optimism for restoring American pride in the 1980s. The lionization of Reagan that largely omitted references to his controversial decisions prompted Thomas Kunkel, dean of the University of Maryland's school of Journalism, to assail the effusive coverage for depicting Reagan as "a cross between Abe Lincoln and Mother Theresa, with an overlay of Mister Rogers."[18] At the end of the day, the Reagan funeral was the capstone of the Reagan Legacy Project.

Many commentators noted how Blacks were noticeably absent from the long list of mourners who gathered in Washington, DC, and at the Reagan Presidential Library in Simi Valley, California, where he was laid to rest.[19] In Washington, where the population was more than 70 percent Black at the time, of the thousands who stood in line to pay their respects to Reagan, African Americans represented approximately one out of each eight hundred mourners. Amadi Boone, a DC resident, said he had "no reason whatsoever to mourn Ronald Reagan's death." After a few moments of reflection, Boone added, "In my opinion, the man should have died in jail."[20]

Amid all the paeans to Reagan for rejuvenating a sense of national pride and presiding over the end of the Cold War, Blacks perceived Reagan as an anti–civil rights leader who had little compassion for the poor, dismantled social welfare programs, and ratcheted up a racist War on Drugs that targeted Blacks, within a few years leading to the mass incarceration of people of color.[21] As a consequence of the misguided War on Drugs, by 2004, the year of Reagan's death, approximately one-third of young Black men under thirty were in prison, on parole, or on probation.[22] Kenneth Nunn, a law professor at the University of Florida, summed it up best: "I think Ronald Reagan was a president that made racism fashionable again. And he could do it with a smile. The face of racism was no longer George Wallace. Who can't like Ronald Reagan?"[23]

Notwithstanding Reagan's abysmal record on race, he remained especially sensitive to the implication that opposition against him grew out of some personal racial animus. Nancy Davis, Reagan's second wife, once shared that "the only thing that got Ronnie steamed up was the occasional allegation that he was a bigot."[24] Many people resent being called a racist but on several occasions, the smooth, unruffled actor-turned-politician lost his composure when pressed on the racist implications of his civil rights policies. In the early weeks of his 1966 gubernatorial primary campaign, for example, Reagan angrily stormed out of a National Negro Republican Assembly in Santa Monica when he was criticized for opposing the Civil Rights Act. A few years later, Reagan got into a verbal altercation with an African American woman in Miami who accused the Florida GOP of being run on a "for-whites-only basis."[25] These are just a couple of examples; there were many others.

To rebut the flurry of accusations that he was a bigot, Reagan resorted to shopworn anecdotes—some genuine, others apocryphal. In what his aides called the "Jackie Robinson" story, Reagan claimed that as a young radio announcer in the 1930s he had worked to rescind an official bylaw of Major League Baseball that stated, "Baseball is a game for Caucasian gentlemen only." In fact, such a bylaw never existed, and yet Reagan trotted out this story time and again to prove his commitment to equality. His closest political aide, Michael Deaver, once remarked that Reagan never got beyond the story of Robinson, who broke baseball's "color line," which was ironic since the sports legend loathed Reagan.[26]

Reagan also often dredged up his upbringing in a racially tolerant home and stressed that both of his parents instilled in him and his older brother, Neil, an abhorrence of racism and anti-Semitism. The fact that Reagan was imbued with a dose of antiracism in his childhood renders his racist politics and policies more troubling. Unlike US senators Strom Thurmond and Jesse Helms, two key political allies who were raised with the racist mores of their native South, and other of his racist collaborators across the country, Reagan apparently knew better. Though he denigrated the civil rights movement throughout his political career, he often claimed he was for civil rights "before there was a civil rights movement."[27] This may explain his acute prickliness when reporters, political opponents, or Blacks called out the racist effects of his policies.

The 1971 conversation between California governor Reagan and President Nixon, in which racial slurs were cast on African diplomats, is a revealing glimpse into Reagan's soul. His openly racist statement shocked many Americans. An examination of his policies indicates that Reagan's words were not an aberration.[28] While Reagan usually cloaked his racism in terms of states' rights, rather than overt racist rhetoric, racial politics were at the root of his appeal and success. Furthermore, the "monkey" statement he made is consistent with his support of the white racist governments in Rhodesia and South Africa. While he justified his support for these majority-white countries on the grounds that they were bulwarks against Communist penetration of sub-Saharan Africa, his private comments suggest that he did not believe Black Africans were capable of self-government. In this respect, his views echoed those of his mentor William F. Buckley Jr. and other conservative intellectuals who articulated the belief that both the civil rights movement and the African decolonization movement were threats to Western civilization. To substantiate their white supremacist beliefs in opposing Black independence movements in Africa, they flirted with scientific racist assumptions that white supremacy was rooted in biology.[29] (Donald Trump echoes these sentiments in referring to African nations as "shitholes.")

Reagan's habitual use of the racially coded story of the "welfare queen," his embrace of "law and order," and his states' rights speech at the Neshoba County Fair in Philadelphia, Mississippi, are only a few examples of how he ran against the civil rights movement and practiced the politics of racism. Still, Reagan and his conservative supporters overlooked these "dog whistles" and claimed that they came from not racists but instead "color-blind" conservatives who were merely opposed to quotas, busing, and affirmative action. Nonetheless, "color-blind" conservatism emerged as an effective means of thwarting Black demands in the early years of the twentieth century.[30] Reagan's embrace of "color blindness" was a subtle and effective diversion—a tool of "polite" racism that furnished a cloak of deniability with regard to the discriminating effects of his policies.[31] In his successful appeal to white working-class Democrats, he sidelined the importance of the struggle for racial justice by laying the blame for racial inequity on the shoulders of Blacks themselves. His belief that Blacks were lazy welfare chiselers and that Democrats were using the government to addict and incapacitate Blacks by giving them "free things" is just one illustration of his tendency to blame Blacks, rather than structural racism, for the racial divide that worsened under his presidency. In the end, Reagan's substantive policies on civil rights during his long political career were virtually indistinguishable from the most extreme racial conservatives like Alabama governor George Wallace, Helms, and Thurmond.

Prior to the 2019 release of the National Archives clip, Reagan's supporters cited Reagan's lack of explicit personal bigotry in vehemently denying Reagan was a racist. But this is immaterial given Reagan's staunch opposition to every significant piece of civil rights legislation since he entered public life. Reagan's justification for his views, on the ostensible grounds that civil rights legislation violated his belief in limited government, was congenial to many of his supporters and powerful political allies who harbored invidious views on race.[32] Reagan's fundamental political strategy was to position himself as the heir to Barry Goldwater's states' rights conservatism, which had long sought to incorporate the Democratic South into the Republican Party's conservative wing by appealing to Southern racial prejudices.[33] Whatever his private sentiments toward individual African Americans, Reagan always sided with the most racially conservative elements—even white supremacists—and he prospered politically by these alliances.

At certain points, *Reconsidering Reagan* examines the broader historical currents of Reagan's conservative movement and its hostility to the civil rights movement, from its neo-Confederate origins defending segregation in the 1950s to the rise of Donald Trump in the 2010s. Particular attention is paid to the indispensable role of one of Reagan's mentors, William F. Buckley Jr., and the racist views of Buckley's magazine, *National Review*, during the height of the civil rights movement.[34] While the term "civil rights" encompasses the quest to achieve equality and dignity for all people regardless of sex, race, age, religion, orientation, ability, or other characteristics, the focus here is on Reagan and his little-recognized legacy of racism toward African Americans. In other civil rights matters, Reagan was similarly wanting. For example, his silence and inaction on the AIDS crisis was so callous that activist Larry Kramer of ACTUP (the AIDS Coalition to Unleash Power) accused Reagan of being a "monster."[35]

Prior to the advent of the Ronald Reagan Legacy Project, perhaps no single individual was more influential in molding Reagan's legacy than the journalist Lou Cannon, who covered Reagan's entire political career, from Sacramento to Washington, DC, and wrote four voluminous biographies on Reagan over a span of three decades. Despite their vast scope, Cannon's pioneering studies contained scant references to Reagan's attitudes toward Black America and his racial policies.[36] When pressed on the matter, Cannon acknowledges Reagan's record on race was wanting, but like Reagan's hagiographers, Cannon exculpates him for an apparent absence of personal racism.[37]

This lacuna about Reagan and his racial policies is even more striking in the era of Donald Trump. In order to fully understand Reagan's legacy, a serious consideration of his views, pronouncements, and policies on race is imperative. It is also indispensable for understanding the rise of Trump, who took over the Republican Party by making verbal attacks on nonwhites central to his political messaging. *Reconsidering Reagan's* analysis of Reagan's and the conservative movement's racial policies leads to the conclusion that Trump is not *sui generis* but a culmination of where the Republican Party and the conservative movement have gone since Goldwater's nomination in 1964, the year Reagan launched his political career. For good reason, Reagan's racial legacy is something the framers of the Ronald Reagan Legacy Project refuse to acknowledge.[38]

Reconsidering Reagan is divided into three parts. Part I, "Up from Racial Liberalism," traces Reagan's early years before he entered electoral politics. Its two chapters trace his abandonment of the racial liberalism of his upbringing. Chapter 1 narrates how amid the Hollywood labor strife of the 1940s, Reagan underwent a profound midlife conversion from liberal to staunch anti-Communist and FBI informant, which informed his perception of the civil rights movement and leadership through a red prism. Chapter 2 lays out Reagan's embrace of the modern conservative movement, which was laced with racism from the outset and had long sought to incorporate the Old South into its anti–New Deal coalition by defending the South's white supremacist culture as a redoubt against Communism. Reagan's fidelity to this conservative movement, particularly his messianic anti-Communism, caused him to jettison all vestiges of the racial liberalism he grew up with in his youth and choose states' rights over civil rights.

The four chapters of part II, "Riding the Wave of the White Backlash, 1966–1980," detail how Reagan facilitated his long, twisting path to the presidency by deftly riding the wave of the white backlash with a genial smile. In Reagan's 1966 California gubernatorial campaign against civil rights stalwart incumbent Governor Edmund (Pat) Brown, race was central to his meteoric political rise from Hollywood actor to chief executive of the nation's most populous state. Against the anxious backdrop of the Watts riots, and white middle-class fears that California's controversial Fair Housing Act would result in hordes of Blacks moving into their neighborhoods, Reagan crisscrossed California, excoriating fair housing, claiming, "If an individual wants to discriminate against Negroes and others in selling their house, it is his right to do so."[39] Referring to urban areas as "jungles" and ascribing the causes of the Watts riots to "lawless rioters and looters" made him a master of the racially coded "law and order" politics that undermined the reigning New Deal order on the treacherous shoals of race.

Reagan followed his playbook on race in his three races for the presidency, in 1968, 1976, and 1980. Chapter 4 examines Reagan's oft-overlooked quest for the Republican nomination in 1968.[40] Even though Reagan did not campaign in any of the primaries, he ran a spirited—albeit quixotic—campaign to deny Richard Nixon a first-ballot victory by focusing his attention on the powerful Republican Southern power barons. Amidst the cataclysmic events of 1968—the assassinations of Martin Luther King Jr. and Robert Kennedy, protests over the Vietnam War, and a surge in racial uprisings that shook the nation—Reagan pursued what is known as the Southern strategy, thrilling crowds across the Old South by appealing to George Wallace voters with his scorching attacks on civil rights leaders as dangerous Communists fomenting the riots. In the tense days after King's assassination, in a revealing comment, Reagan even blamed the martyred civil rights leader for planting the seeds of his own destruction by adopting nonviolent civil disobedience. Though Reagan failed in his quest to secure the Republican nomination, his Southern appeal anticipated the region becoming the heart of Reagan country.

Reagan's racially polarizing policies continued unabated throughout his pre-presidential years. After his bid for the 1968 Republican nomination failed, Reagan returned to Sacramento to govern California and bolster his presidential prospects targeting Black radicals like Angela Davis, Eldridge Cleaver, members of the Black Panther Party, and Black student protestors clamoring for the creation of Black studies programs at colleges and universities throughout the state. Seeking the mantle of conservative reformer for a future presidential bid, Reagan also made the racially charged issue of welfare reform the linchpin of both his successful 1970 gubernatorial reelection campaign and his second-term agenda. Speaking before white audiences who associated welfare recipients with Blacks, Reagan blasted the beneficiaries of social programs as "rats," "moochers," "chiselers," and "parasites."

In 1976, Reagan mounted an insurgent primary bid for the Republican presidential nomination against incumbent Gerald Ford, running to the right on the hot-button racial issues of the day. He campaigned before white audiences across the country with a stump speech featuring the racist trope of a Black Chicago "welfare queen" benefiting from the sweat of hard-working white taxpayers. Once again, Reagan pursued a Southern strategy, soliciting Southern support by touting the region as a repository of conservative values and fulminating against the Voting Rights Act as "humiliating to the South."[41] After a string of early defeats, Senator Jesse Helms of North Carolina, the last of the Southern segregationists, seized control of Reagan's campaign in the crucial state of North Carolina, and rescued Reagan's political career from the abyss, propelling him to a series of primary victories in the South with the help of Democratic George Wallace voters who crossed party lines to vote for Reagan. Some of Reagan's momentum was staunched after Reagan's statement that he would send US troops to preserve the white supremacist Rhodesian government created an uproar. Though Ford narrowly prevailed over Reagan, Reagan's successful Southern strategy kept his candidacy alive until the Republican convention in Kansas City, and it underscored the ascendancy of the anti–civil rights Southern wing of the Republican Party and the eclipse of the Rockefeller wing of the party of Lincoln.[42]

In 1980, in a reprise of his 1968 and 1976 campaigns, Reagan's campaign centrally featured racial appeals to Southern whites and white working-class Northerners. In his bid to wrest the South from the embattled incumbent, Jimmy Carter, Reagan successfully courted a burgeoning bloc of Evangelical voters seething over the Internal Revenue Service's decision to deny tax-exempt status to the private segregated Christian academies that had burgeoned across the South, as a means of circumventing *Brown v. Board of Education*. Reagan also received one of the most enthusiastic receptions of his campaign during an appearance at the historically racist Bob Jones University in Greenville, South Carolina. In his first campaign appearance since he accepted the Republican nomination in 1980, Reagan flew to Philadelphia, Mississippi (where the Ku Klux Klan murdered three civil rights workers in 1964), and told an all-white crowd that he believed in states' rights, a term associated with Southerners' defense of slavery and invoked as a euphemism for preventing the federal government from interfering with the racial mores of the South. Though the 1980 presidential election was largely a referendum on the "malaise" of the Carter administration, Reagan's victory buoyed the hopes of racial conservatives bent on remaking the federal judiciary and reversing the landmark civil rights precedents of the Warren Court. As the sixty-nine-year-old Reagan took the oath of office on January 20, 1981, the common prediction about the incoming Reagan administration was the notion of an imminent assault on the civil rights gains of the 1960s.[43]

The five chapters of part III, "Rolling Back the Civil Rights Revolution," examine Reagan's two-term presidency as a "new nadir" for Black America. In his effort to reverse the gains of the civil rights revolution, Reagan compiled the worst civil rights record of any president in the modern era. He weakened the enforcement of civil rights laws, attempted to dilute the Voting Rights Act (the "crown jewel" of the civil rights movement), gutted the US Commission on Civil Rights (known as the nation's conscience on civil rights), and tried to revoke the tax-exempt status for Bob Jones University. In an unprecedented move, he adhered to judicial conservatism as an ideological litmus test in his crusade to transform the federal judiciary by appointing young, conservative judges who he hoped would reverse the landmark civil rights jurisprudence of the Warren Court. As a result of Reagan's civil rights policies, morale plummeted among the career attorneys in the Civil Rights Division of the Department of Justice, many of whom resigned in disgust. A *New York Times*/CBS News poll taken in January 1982 found that *0 percent* of Blacks thought he cared about their problems.[44] If the Reagan administration's policies were not bad enough, Education Secretary Terrel Bell noted in his memoirs that racial slurs were commonplace in the White House, such as references to "Martin Lucifer Coon" and "sand niggers."[45]

Reagan further enraged Black America—and many others throughout the world—by his appeasement of the brutal, racist apartheid government of South Africa. His belief that imposing economic sanctions on South Africa was not necessary to change the regime's racist policies was an extension of his belief that federal power was not appropriate to end racial apartheid in the American South in the 1960s. Instead of

siding with Nelson Mandela, Reagan maligned the anti-apartheid movement as another Communist pawn and looked on South African Blacks'
racist oppressors as "more civilized" fellow travelers in the fight against
Communism. By the end of 1984, Blacks' pent-up anger over Reagan's
racial policies found expression in their leadership of the Free South Africa Movement (FSAM), a broad coalition of civil right leaders, and in
demonstrations across the United States calling for the dismantling of
apartheid in South Africa. By virtue of the FSAM's unstinting grassroots
mobilization, the Congressional Black Caucus (CBC) spearheaded the
overriding of Reagan's 1986 veto of a bill imposing economic sanctions
on the South Africa regime. Blacks' leadership in passing the sanctions
bill was a catalyst for the toppling of apartheid in South Africa by 1990.

Most ominously, Reagan's presidency witnessed the ratcheting-up of
the racist War on Drugs, which spurred the current epidemic of mass
incarceration. Though the United States makes up less than 5 percent of
the world's population, it holds 25 percent of the world's known prison
population.[46] In the fifteen years after 1985, every month, a new federal
or state prison was created to cope with the flood of new inmates.[47] Racial disparities in imprisonment are the most salient consequence of the
ill-conceived War on Drugs.[48]

While Reagan and his administration were not solely culpable for
the War on Drugs, Reagan expended his vast political capital by making
his War on Drugs a centerpiece of his domestic agenda, even though
only 2 percent of Americans' polled regarded drugs as the nation's most
pressing problem.[49] Like Reagan's racially freighted attacks on crime,
welfare, and taxes, the War on Drugs was infused with racist assumptions of Black criminality, and had been used by the Nixon administration to bludgeon Blacks and the antiwar Left.[50] Seizing on fears of a
"crack" cocaine epidemic, Reagan signed a series of hastily drafted laws
that targeted Blacks. The most grievous was the imposition of disparate
sentences punishing crack cocaine use at a hundred times more than the
use of powder cocaine—crack was most often used in Black and poor
urban communities of color. Furthermore, the drug laws imposed mandatory minimum sentencing, ending judicial discretion in punishment,
and initiated the military surveillance of the ghettos. Within a few years,
incarceration rates skyrocketed and devastated Black communities. By
2005, Blacks constituted 12.8 percent of the population but nearly half

of the country's total prison population and 42 percent of death row inmates. Blacks are currently imprisoned at more than five times the rate of their white counterparts. Since Congress enacted the Reagan-era draconian drug laws, Blacks were languishing in prison, often for committing the same nonviolent drug offenses as their white counterparts, who were not prosecuted.[51] The devastating impact of Reagan's War on Drugs was a logical outcome of the "law and order" and tough-on-crime rhetoric that Reagan, Nixon, and other conservatives launched in the 1960s to appeal to the biases of anxious white Southerners and northern working-class whites.

Despite the success of the civil rights community in thwarting many of Reagan's civil rights initiatives by preventing the evisceration of the Voting Rights Act, preserving affirmative action, and working to deny Judge Robert Bork a seat on the Supreme Court, one of the greatest tragedies of the Reagan administration was that its policies forced the nation to refight many of the key civil rights battles that had been won in the 1960s and 1970s. Mary Frances Berry, the former chair of the US Commission on Civil Rights, whom Reagan tried to fire over her denunciations of his civil rights policies, spoke about how the civil rights struggle in the Reagan era "followed a pattern of winning while losing."[52] Civil rights organizations were forced to divert an inordinate amount of precious time, energy, and resources away from the unfinished work of the civil rights revolution: the fight for economic justice. Moreover, Reagan's fiscal policies—dubbed Reaganomics—consisted of tax cuts for the very wealthy and the slashing of social programs for the poor, which exacerbated socioeconomic disparities and broadened the racial divide.

By the end of Reagan's presidency, the cumulative impact of his incessant attacks on civil rights laws and their remedies increasingly fostered negative attitudes with respect to race in the United States. This hostile climate was instrumental in Vice President George H. W. Bush's successful utilization of the racist Willie Horton ad, during his run for the presidency, that smeared Democratic nominee Michael Dukakis as being soft on crime and stoked racial stereotypes by thrusting the time-honored whites' psychosexual fear of Black men to the forefront of the 1988 presidential race. The racial demagoguery of Bush's campaign was a fitting coda to Reagan's presidency. On the eve of Reagan's departure, veteran *Washington Post* journalist Mary McGrory inveighed, "In his eight years in office he has taken actions that suggest that if he is not a bigot, he might as well have been as far as blacks were concerned."[53] In 1989, Reagan left office as a beloved figure among large swaths of white America, but progressives and many people of color harbored disdain for his anti-civil rights agenda, his racial insensitivity, and widening socioeconomic disparities.

Donald Trump began his takeover of the party of Reagan by spouting racist conspiracy theories about President Barack Obama, branding Mexicans as rapists and criminals, and calling for a ban on all Muslims entering the country. Before Trump, Reagan "was the most successful backlash politician in American history," who cultivated an image as a white man's president and, in the process, exacerbated the nation's racial divide.[54] Although Reagan differed from Donald Trump in terms of personality and temperament, and though he did not demonize Mexicans and immigrants, *Reconsidering Reagan* will show that Reagan's racially coded "dog whistles," such as "law and order," "welfare queens," and attacks on affirmative action, contributed to the second white backlash and helped pave the way for the Republican Party's white ethnonationalism of the Trump era.[55] In 2018, Catherine Lhamon, chair of the US Commission on Civil Rights, said it best when she observed that she thought the Reagan administration was "the nadir for civil rights" but now worried that the "Trump administration is taking a page out of the Reagan playbook and consolidating it."[56]

Given how deeply embedded racism is in American history and in our institutions—particularly in the era of Donald Trump—an honest reckoning of Reagan's record on race is in order.

PART I

UP FROM RACIAL LIBERALISM

CHAPTER 1

EARLY REAGAN

The Unmaking of a Racial Liberal

What Ronald Reagan inherited from his childhood is an astounding ability to turn away from any reality which is too harsh and paint one that is softer and gentler to the eyes.

—Patti Davis, on her father (1992)[1]

My father's greatest fault was his stubbornness about facing up to unpleasant realities, particularly concerning America. It was difficult for him to grapple with national shames—slavery, the treatment of Native Americans, and Vietnam.

—Ron Reagan Jr. on his father (2011)[2]

Ronald Reagan's tangled views on race originated in his turbulent childhood. In 1965, as he entered politics, Reagan described his all-American Midwestern childhood as "one of those rare Huck Finn idylls,"[3] but the reality was not idyllic. He was born on February 6, 1911, in Tampico, Illinois, one in a series of small towns through which his father, Jack, a restless, itinerant shoe salesman, had moved his young family. Between the ages of six and ten, Ronald and his older brother, Neil, attended a different school every year. Ronald's childhood was marred not only by the loneliness and trauma that accompanied the perpetual moving but also by his father's alcoholism. Reagan described a cold, wintry night when he was eleven years old and, trudging home through the snow, tripped over his father on the front porch, who was passed out "drunk, dead to the world," as one of the most profound memories of his childhood.[4] Jack Reagan's alcoholism strained his marriage and exacerbated the Reagans' chronic financial woes. The Reagan family never owned a home, and Jack often spent his earnings at the tavern. Indeed, grinding poverty was a constant of Reagan's youth. "We didn't live on the wrong side of the tracks, but we lived so close to them we could hear the whistle real loud," he recalled.[5]

Jack Reagan's alcoholism profoundly affected Reagan's personal and political life, and those close to him, contributing to his aloofness, difficulty forging friendships, and propensity to live in a world of fantasy.[6] Throughout his life, Reagan erected a veil between himself and the world. Even as a boy, he developed his trademark badinage as a defensive mechanism. Stuart Spencer, Reagan's longtime campaign manager, ascribed Reagan's preference for "happy endings" to Reagan's childhood as the second son of an alcoholic father.[7] Reagan's apparent obliviousness to the ongoing legacy of racism and avoidance of the AIDS scourge is a perfect illustration of his propensity to filter out not only the darker aspects of life but of the America he revered. Reagan's description of his childhood as a "rare Huck Finn idyll" is telling, given that Twain's great American novel concerned itself so fundamentally with the themes of racism and slavery.

In his memoirs, Reagan recalled how his childhood in Dixon, Illinois, where the family finally settled when he was nine, shaped his "body and mind for all the years to come after."[8] When the Reagans moved to Dixon, in December 1920, the population was 8,191, but that included only twelve Black families. Blacks were not allowed to stay at the local hotel, get their hair done at the salon, or join the local golf club.[9] Reagan's childhood coincided with the "second coming" of the Ku Klux Klan, and one of Reagan's contemporaries even recalled seeing Klan parades and cross burnings in Dixon.[10] And yet, despite these evident public displays of racism, Reagan emphasized an idealized vision of Dixon as the backdrop for his 1980 campaign pledge "Let's Make America Great Again."

Throughout his political career, both Reagan and his supporters were quick to bristle over any criticism over his racial policies. In their efforts to deflect such criticisms, Reagan and his supporters were quick to point out that Reagan's parents had instilled a strong dose of racial open-mindedness in young Ronald and his brother. For their time, Reagan's parents were unusually progressive on racial issues, so much so that the details of his upbringing and early political orientation might well have suggested that Reagan would grow up to become a zealous advocate for civil rights and not, as it happened, an opponent who sided with racists.

Other than the privations of their hardscrabble prairie childhoods and their abhorrence of racism, Reagan's parents were an unlikely union. Jack Reagan, orphaned at six, was a raffish, garrulous Irish Catholic salesman. He despised the Klan and any semblance of racism or anti-Semitism. Reagan recounted, on more than one occasion, his father's anguish growing up in an era when many stores still had signs on their doors saying "No Dogs or Irishmen Allowed."[11] When the racist movie *The Birth of a Nation* was rereleased and shown in Dixon's whites-only theatre, Jack forbade Ronald and Neil from seeing it. Reagan recalled his father saying that no son of his "was going to sit through their shenanigans."[12] Over the years, Reagan proudly repeated a story about how his father refused to stay at a hotel after the clerk told him that Jews were not allowed and instead spent a frigid night in his car, to the detriment of his health.[13] In addition to his skill as a raconteur and love of sports, Reagan inherited his father's passion for politics and early allegiance to the Democratic Party.

His mother, Nelle, was an abstemious, devout Scots-Irish Protestant with literary aspirations and a theatrical flair. The stabilizing force in the family, Nelle had a bigger influence on Ronald than on Neil, who was closer to Jack. A saintly pillar of Dixon's Church of Disciples, Nelle was revered for her charitable deeds. Ronald regularly accompanied her to church, where he cleaned, began his acting career in skits alongside his mother, and fell in love with the pastor's daughter, Margaret Cleaver. The pastor, Ben Cleaver, treated Reagan like a son, leading Garry Wills to observe that Reagan was "close to being a minister's kid without moving into the rectory."[14]

Like her husband, Nelle infused young Ronald with a strong dose of racial liberalism. According to Reagan, Nelle "was absolutely color blind" and instructed her sons to "judge everyone by how they act, not what they are."[15] Nelle's beloved Church of Disciples stressed "the brotherhood of man" and had an abolitionist heritage. In early 1928 she proclaimed her racial liberalism to her Dixon Sunday school class in a sermon called "Negro Disciples and Their Contribution," though at least a few members of the congregation belonged to the Ku Klux Klan.[16]

After graduating from Dixon High School in 1928, Reagan, along with his girlfriend, Margaret, matriculated at nearby Eureka College, a small school affiliated with the Church of Disciples. Founded by abolitionists who had fled Kentucky in 1848, Eureka had a long, noble record of racial integration. It was also the first college in Illinois (and only the third in the nation) to admit women on an equal basis.[17] Only a fraction of high school graduates attended college in the 1920s, and doing so was a testament to Reagan's drive and ambition. The onset of the Great Depression at the beginning of his sophomore year strained the Reagan family's already precarious finances, but by dint of his savings from his years working as a lifeguard in Dixon, Ronald was able to stay at Eureka. He later gave his meager earnings to his parents, which enabled his older brother to attend Eureka as well.

A lackluster student, Reagan relied on his prodigious memory to pass his classes and immersed himself in a host of extracurricular activities. He pledged a fraternity, served three years as a basketball cheerleader, joined the drama club, and was elected student body president, as he had been at Dixon High. He experienced his first, thrilling brush with politics when he delivered an impassioned speech in support of a student strike over Eureka's proposed faculty cuts.

In spite of his poor eyesight, Reagan was the starting offensive guard on Eureka's football team. There, he developed a long friendship with William Franklin Burghardt, one of the few Blacks at Eureka. In a 1981 interview with the *Washington Post*, Burghardt said, "I just don't think he was conscious of race at all."[18]

During one of the Eureka College football team's road trips, a hotel refused to admit Burghardt and the one other Black player. The coach decided that the entire team should sleep in the bus. Reagan suggested that the two Black players stay at his parents' home, which was only fifteen miles from the hotel. The Reagans graciously welcomed the two young men into their home, which was unusual by the standards of the early 1930s but another instance of the Reagan family's decency and racial progressivism. Years later, Reagan responded to Blacks' criticisms of his racial policies by saying that he had been "fighting for civil rights before they called it civil rights."[19]

The election of Democrat Franklin D. Roosevelt in November 1932 that year buoyed the sprits of a nation wracked by joblessness, starvation, and despair. Jack Reagan, who had campaigned hard for FDR, was re-warded for his efforts by receiving a job as a clerk for the Federal Emergency Relief Administration. Later, as a conservative politician, Reagan would excoriate such welfare programs and their recipients, but, despite the contradiction, he continued to revere Roosevelt for providing his father and other Americans with a sense of purpose during the dark days of the Great Depression.

Reagan graduated from Eureka at the height of the Great Depression. With over fifteen million Americans unemployed (more than 20 percent of the population at the time), his job prospects were bleak. Unable to find employment in Chicago, Reagan landed a job as a radio announcer at a small radio station in Davenport, Iowa, where he honed his public-speaking skills. His smooth, resonant voice combined with a crackling delivery beguiled his audience, and the following year he was transferred to a larger station in Des Moines. There, as a sportscaster, he deftly recreated Chicago Cubs baseball and Big Ten football games via telegraph and made his broadcasting reputation. A talented, charming, and glib radio announcer, Reagan quickly earned notoriety in Iowa, but he harbored dreams of becoming a movie star. In the spring of 1937, Reagan arranged a trip to cover the Chicago Cubs' spring training on Catalina Island with the intention of exploring a film career. There, he met a Hollywood agent who got him a screen test with Warner Brothers. The studio was impressed by Reagan's presence and offered him a seven-year contract, with a starting salary of a whopping $200 a week, equivalent to $3,500 today. On May 22, 1937, Reagan left Des Moines in, as he put it, "a cloud of dust."[20]

EARLY YEARS IN HOLLYWOOD: A "HEMOPHILIAC" LIBERAL

Reagan never fulfilled his dream of becoming a movie star, but he worked steadily and achieved a string of small successes playing lead roles in thirty-one B movies between 1937 and 1943. Warner Brothers packaged Reagan's Midwest wholesomeness and boyish charm with such skill that he famously referred to himself as "the Errol Flynn of the B's."[21] Six months after his arrival in Hollywood, he moved his parents to the West Coast, affording them a comfortable middle-class existence after a lifetime of struggle. In 1939, during the filming of *Brother Rat*, Reagan met the actress Jane Wyman, and the two began a highly publicized romance that excited the gossip columnists. They married in January 1940 and had two children.

During his early years in Hollywood, Reagan's fidelity to the racial liberalism of his youth remained intact. Soon after he arrived, Reagan was admitted to the Lakeside Country Club, but he refused to join after he found out that they had denied admission to his boss, Jack Warner, because he was Jewish. Instead, Reagan joined the Hillcrest Country Club, a Jewish country club in Los Angeles.[22] In his early years in Hollywood, Reagan associated with a number of organizations that had sterling antiracist credentials, such as the Mobilization for Democracy, the American Veterans Committee, and the Hollywood Independent Citizens Committee of the Arts, Sciences and Professions (HICCASP). And he was a contract actor for Warner Brothers, known as one of the more liberal studios for its staunch support of Franklin Roosevelt's New Deal.[23] Reagan impressed many of his contemporaries in Hollywood with not only his knowledge of politics but also his passion for social and racial justice.

From the outset of his movie career, Reagan ingratiated himself with wealthy and powerful men such as studio mogul Jack Warner, and Reagan's agent, Lew Wasserman, whom Reagan would help make the most powerful man in Hollywood. Shortly after the United States entered World War II, Jack Warner enlisted William Guthrie, a former FBI agent and Warner Brothers' emissary to the military, to secure two deferments for the near-sighted Reagan. Warner and Guthrie also convinced the Army Air Corps to create a special movie detail, under Warner's supervision, at the Hal Roach Studios, in Culver City.[24] While other movie stars, such as Jimmy Stewart, Henry Fonda, Douglas Fairbanks Jr., and Clark Gable, served and fought in World War II, Reagan spent the war just thirteen miles from his home, narrating films for the Army Air Corps. He made the most of his exposure in uniform though. One of Reagan's biographers noted, "No twentieth century president with the exception of Dwight D. Eisenhower had been seen in uniform by more people."[25]

Reagan's critically acclaimed performance in the 1942 film Kings Row propelled him to the brink of stardom, but the wartime service derailed his career. Yet, his work for the Army Air Corps would serve him well in his future work as a political propagandist. Toward the end of the war, Reagan narrated the short film Wings for This Man for the Army Air Corps. The film lauded the courage of the Black Tuskegee pilots and called for greater tolerance of African Americans. "You can't judge a man by the color of his eyes or the shape of his nose," Reagan said. "You judge him by how he performs in combat."[26]

The wartime years and his stint for the Army Air Corps deepened Reagan's interest in politics. After the war, Reagan's determination to become an A-list movie star was stymied by his wartime absence from the screen and the emergence of a new generation of actors, so he increasingly devoted his attention to liberal politics. A self-professed "hemophiliac liberal," Reagan recalled in his 1965 memoir, "I was blindly and busily joining every organization I could find that would guarantee to save the world."[27] After the horrors of the US bombings of Hiroshima and Nagasaki, in 1945, Reagan became an early proponent of the abolition of nuclear weapons and the internationalization of atomic energy. In March 1946, he joined the Black entertainer and Communist sympathizer Paul Robeson at a dinner for the left-leaning Los Angeles Committee for a Democratic Far Eastern Policy, a group opposed to President Harry Truman's support of the Chinese leader Chiang Kai-shek.[28] In April 1946, Reagan was the toastmaster at the state convention for the liberal American Veterans Committee, which maintained racially integrated chapters in the South and called for the end of racially restrictive housing covenants. The following month, Reagan joined the star-studded executive council of HICCASP, a progressive organization that fought for civil rights and sought the abolition of lynching, poll taxes, and segregation.[29]

The culmination of Reagan's progressive political activism was his narration of *Operation Terror*, a thirteen-part radio program aired in 1946 about the spike of Ku Klux Klan activity in Southern California and Jim Crow Georgia. The program was sponsored by the Mobilization for Democracy and the Hollywood Writers Organization, two popular front organizations that had formed a coalition with a broad array of leftist groups to fight fascism. In an emotional address, Reagan likened the Klan to terrorists that had to be stopped. "I have to stand and speak," he said, "to lift my face and shout that this must end, to fill my lungs bursting with clean air, and so cry out 'stop the flogging, stop the terror, stop the murder!'"[30] These Hollywood popular front organizations were primarily concerned with fighting fascism, but they also mobilized against racist portrayals in film and sought roles for Black actors.[31]

Reagan's participation in the *Operation Terror* radio broadcast garnered plaudits from civil rights advocates, but it was not without controversy. Los Angeles mayor Fletcher Bowron blasted the broadcast as the work of "misguided leftist motion picture actors" and called for the investigation of the "Mobilization of Democracy."[32] The California Committee on Un-American Activity branded the Mobilization of Democracy "a vicious, potentially dangerous Communist front" composed of "left wing movie people" committed to "fomenting racial prejudice."[33] But, more importantly, the broadcast aroused the interest of FBI director J. Edgar Hoover, who was obsessed by what he viewed as a Communist infiltration of the film industry.

THE RED SCARE AND THE MAKING OF A RACIAL CONSERVATIVE

As Hoover fixated his gaze on extirpating alleged Communists from Hollywood, he noticed Reagan and his political activities showing up in reports from the FBI's Los Angeles field office.[34] Late one evening in 1946, three of Hoover's agents knocked on the front door of the Hollywood Hills house Reagan shared with his wife, Jane Wyman. They told the actor that they had "some information which might be useful" to him and thought he might, in turn, have the same for them.[35] Hoover was eager to cultivate more informers in Hollywood,[36] and he was aware that Reagan's brother, Neil, a conservative advertising executive in Los Angeles, was working as an informer in the FBI's investigation of the entertainment industry.[37] Hoover also knew that Guthrie, the former FBI agent had helped secure Reagan's comfortable job at the Hal Roach Studio in Culver City, and he thought that Reagan's image as a wholesome all-American man might make him a good prospect in the quest to ferret out Communists in the film colony.[38]

Despite Reagan's initial hesitation to get involved in informing, he changed his mind after the agents told him that the Communists in Hollywood despised him and had just held a meeting where someone said, "What are we going to do about that son-of-a-bitching bastard Reagan?"[39] Later, he came to believe that the Soviets were not only intent on gaining control of Hollywood but also striving to influence the content of its films."[40] Before the agents departed, Reagan consented to meeting regularly with them to discuss some of the things that were going on in Hollywood. His contacts with the FBI would become regular enough that Reagan earned the informer's number T-10. Over the years, Reagan's relationship with the FBI deepened; during the 1960s, Hoover would lend his power to aid Reagan's political rise in California.[41] Hoover's loathing of the Left and his inveterate racism led him to wage counter-intelligence programs (known as COINTELPRO) to discredit, undermine, and disrupt African American organizations and their leaders.[42] In the ensuing years, under the guise of rooting out suspected Communists, COINTELPRO was responsible for some of the most devastating incidents of government repression in United States history. On racial matters, Hoover's FBI would wiretap, harass, and intimidate civil rights leaders such as Martin Luther King Jr. and disrupt, infiltrate, and discredit civil rights organizations such as the Black Panther Party and other leftist organizations it deemed subversive. Reagan's nighttime encounter with the FBI was the beginning of a long, fruitful symbiotic relationship with Hoover's terrorist regime.

Around the time of Reagan's nighttime encounter with the FBI agents, he was becoming concerned over the increasing accusations that HICCASP and other Hollywood organizations he was affiliated with were rife with Communists. Reagan was not the only concerned liberal. At a HICCASP board meeting, James Roosevelt, the son of FDR, proposed a resolution declaring that HICCASP must be "vigilant against being used by Communist sympathizers."[43] Reagan, a relative newcomer to the board, was outraged when he saw that this apparently rather innocuous proposal fomented so much rancor among board members. After the meeting, Reagan, along with a few other anti-Communist members, penned another resolution to be voted on at the next meeting: "We reaffirm our belief in the free enterprise and the democratic system and repudiate Communism as desirable for the United States."[44] On July 5, 1946, HICCASP debated the measure at James Roosevelt's home while undercover FBI agents patrolled the premises and took down the license plate numbers of the attendees. The majority of HICCASP members voted down Reagan's proposal on the grounds that it was unnecessary and divisive. Never one for nuance, Reagan took the sinister, Manichean view that HICCASP and the other popular front organizations were doing Moscow's bidding. As a consequence, he resigned his membership, but not before he ran off with the group's records and turned them over to his brother, Neil, a staunch anti-Communist and FBI informer, who had warned Reagan that the people in HICCASP could cause him real trouble.[45] The contretemps over the resolution was a crucial turning point for Reagan because it convinced him that liberals were dangerously naïve to the imminent Communist threat.[46]

Reagan's epiphanous experience with HICCASP, however, was merely a prelude to his much deeper involvement with Hollywood politics. It sparked his conviction that the Soviets were not only intent on gaining control of Hollywood but also striving to influence the content of its films, and he vowed to stop it.[47] Through his leadership roles in the Screen Actors Guild (SAG), Reagan, though a B movie actor, would emerge as a central, powerful figure in the labor strife that convulsed Hollywood from 1945 through 1947.

The Hollywood strikes that thrust Reagan into the center of the political maelstrom were part of the larger "strike wave" of 1945–1946 that gripped the entire nation during the postwar period.[48] Despite Reagan's unshakeable certainty that an international Communist brigade was directing the Hollywood strikes, the origins were far more complex. The Hollywood strikes were rooted in a complex and ferocious jurisdictional dispute that predated Reagan's arrival and had nothing to do with the Soviet Union. It involved a bitter struggle over control of the film industry pitting the newly formed Conference of Studio Unions (CSU) against the corrupt, Mafia-infested International Alliance of Theatrical Stage Employees (IATSE), one of the oldest and most powerful unions in the movie business. Since the 1930s IATSE had become increasingly corrupt, rarely went on strike, and reached sweetheart deals with management that left their members angry.[49] The Hollywood producers supported IATSE because of its control over the projectionists, who had the power to shut down the movie theatres, and because IATSE served the interests of the moguls, rather than the workers whose wages remained stagnant. On the other hand, HICCASP, the Screen Writers Guild, and most of the thousands of painters, carpenters, electricians, stagehands, and other set directors supported the CSU because they were convinced it was an honest union devoted to improve their lot after the Depression and war.

Beginning in the early 1940s, under the leadership of Herbert K. Sorrell, the CSU had been waging a bitter struggle to organize a broad coalition of set directors to overtake the corrupt IATSE. A fearless former boxer, the pugnacious Sorrell had a zest for militancy. He once said, "I love to hear the crack of bones in a scab's legs."[50] On March 12, 1945, an estimated 10,500 CSU workers broke the "no strike" wartime pledge claiming exclusive jurisdiction on behalf of the set decorators.[51] The IATSE contested the strike on the grounds that they, not the CSU, represented the set decorators and dispatched Roy E. Brewer, a militant anti-Communist and one of Reagan's future mentors, to reassert IATSE's dominion over studio labor and force out the CSU.

CSU defied the National War Labor Board's order directing that the strike be terminated immediately. The strike continued for the next six months paralyzing the studios, resulting in periodic episodes of violence on the picket lines.[52] On October 5, 1945, tensions climaxed when a bloody melee erupted at the Warner Brothers studio entrance in Burbank after Reagan's boss, Jack Warner, unleashed private security guards on the strikers resulting in smashed windows, cars being overturned, and strikers being knifed, clubbed, and gassed before studio police used fire hoses to restore order.[53] The national exposure of the mayhem at Warner Brothers, known as "Hollywood Black Friday," forced the parties back to the negotiating table. A few weeks later, the six-month strike was temporarily resolved after the executive council of the American Federation of Labor (AFL), with which both IATSE and CSU were affiliated, ordered the workers to return to work and empowered a three-person committee to resolve the outstanding jurisdictional issues between the two competing unions.[54] In the interim, the AFL awarded the CSU the right to represent most of the set workers. Brewer, who had just become leader of IATSE, blamed the violence on Communists trying to gain a foothold in Hollywood.[55]

Despite the AFL's attempt to arbitrate the bitter jurisdictional dispute between its two affiliates, the struggle between the IATSE and CSU continued to roil the film industry. In September 1946, the CSU led another strike, and the studios retaliated by firing CSU workers. Sorrell's militancy, dogged determination, and past association with Harry Bridges, a leader of the International Longshoremen's Union, convinced the FBI that Sorrell was a Communist.[56] Accordingly, IATSE under the leadership of Brewer, and the studio bosses launched a scorching attack against Sorrell and the CSU, smearing them as Communist pawns. Unbowed, Sorrell vehemently denied the allegation. In fact, Sorrell was not a Communist but a fiercely independent, patriotic American trade unionist who believed in the power of organized labor to raise the living standards for the working class. In fact, Sorrell had violated the no-strike pledge during the United States' wartime alliance with the Soviet Union and openly critiqued the Soviet Union.[57] As for the CSU rank and file, it is indisputable that it had some active Communists, but the overwhelming majority of CSU workers joined the union because they were livid over the corrupt IATSE's cozy relationship with the studio bosses and its failure to improve the harsh working conditions of its members.

During this time, as a leader of SAG entrusted with resolving the ongoing union dispute, Reagan entered the fray, which was becoming increasingly violent and posed a threat to his livelihood. SAG's role was pivotal because if the actors honored the picket line, they could close the studios, and the strike would be resolved within twenty-four hours. Reagan desperately wanted to resume his acting career, which had been disrupted when he was at the brink of stardom. In the throes of his political conversion, Reagan never grasped the economic motives of the striking workers and readily accepted Brewer and the FBI's erroneous assessment that Sorrell's CSU was a "perfidious Communist front" organization bent on gaining a Soviet foothold in Hollywood, and he vowed to destroy the CSU.[58]

A month after CSU's second strike, Reagan delivered a powerful address before a tumultuous crowd of SAG members at the Hollywood Legion Stadium in which he presented the board's recommendation against supporting the strike.[59] Reagan's captivating speech helped sway SAG members to vote to cross the picket line. Shortly thereafter, violence and mayhem flared again on the Warner Brothers lot in Burbank as pitched battles between the police and union members resulted in property damage and bodily injury. Reagan, a recipient of anonymous threats, began to carry a .32 Smith & Wesson. The strike went on for months and led to the largest mass arrest in California history after strikers violated a court order limiting the number of pickets outside studio gates. By the end of 1947, however, without SAG's support, the CSU "dissolved like sugar in hot water."[60]

The impact of Reagan's real-life performance in helping to crush the CSU far exceeded any of his film performances. It garnered him the praise that had been missing from the mostly lackluster reviews of his acting and boosted his self-esteem in a challenging period when his act-ing career was in decline and his marriage was strained. His wife's career was skyrocketing. In 1948, Wyman earned an Academy Award for her portrayal of a young deaf woman in *Johnny Belinda*. That same year, she filed for divorce, in part from her weariness with Reagan's incessant talk about and obsession with union politics.[61] In keeping with his lifelong tendency to evade distressing facts, Reagan claimed he was never di-vorced because he was not the one who'd initiated it.[62]

Reagan's acting career may have been in the doldrums, but his stub-born certainty and resolve endeared him to the powerful studio bar-ons whose fortunes had been jeopardized by the labor strife grinding their studios to a halt. Reagan's longtime boss Jack Warner applauded Reagan as "a tower of strength, not only for actors but for the whole industry."[63] While Reagan would earn the lasting enmity of Hollywood liberals and labor sympathizers, many SAG members remained grate-ful for his pivotal role in keeping them working. In the spring of 1947, SAG's board elected Reagan as president, a post he would hold for the next five years, making him one of the most powerful figures in Holly-wood. His newfound status exhilarated him, and around this time he confessed to actress Patricia Neal that he dreamed of being president of the United States.[64]

Charges that Reagan was an opportunistic, company stooge were rampant and made him disliked by many in the entertainment indus-try. As a result of the crushing of the CSU, former union members had lost their livelihoods and even their homes, and many never recovered from the ordeal. A particularly damning indictment of Reagan's charac-ter came from Father George Dunne, a Jesuit priest and an outspoken advocate for civil rights causes who would march with Martin Luther King Jr. Dunne had reported on the Hollywood strike for the Catholic newspaper, *Commonweal*.[65] In an effort to break the impasse between IASTE and CSU, Dunne met with Reagan and other SAG leaders for three hours in early 1947. Dunne told the group that Sorrell was an hon-est labor leader, not a Communist. Dunne further contended that IATSE leaders and film producers had exploited the nationwide Red Scare in an effort to destroy the CSU. According to Dunne, Reagan refused to listen, and he concluded that Reagan was not speaking for the SAG members but rather was doing the bidding of the producers still aligned with the corrupt IATSE gangsters. Dunne found Reagan "articulate and sharp" but also "dangerous" and "ignorant," because "he interpreted everything in terms of the Communist threat."[66]

Reagan was also vengeful against his critics. Take the case of the Canadian actor Alexander Knox. At a SAG mass meeting, Knox urged members to honor the picket line and later mocked Reagan by saying that Reagan spoke fast "so that he could talk out of both sides of his mouth at once."[67] Knox's criticisms incensed Reagan, who later notified the FBI of the Canadian actor's leftist politics.[68] As a result, Knox became ensnared in the Hollywood blacklist and did not make another movie in the United States until 1967.[69] FBI documents prove that, despite his repeated denials, Reagan was complicit in implementing the Hollywood blacklist that barred suspected Communists from working in the movie industry. Journalist Seth Rosenfeld obtained FBI documents proving that Reagan lied when he denied he had ever informed on anybody during the years of the Red Scare in Hollywood in the 1940s and early 1950s.[70] While his highly publicized October 1947 testimony as a "friendly" witness before the House Un-American Activities Committee (HUAC) struck an overall tone of moderation, we now know that Reagan had privately provided names of suspected Communists to the FBI—and even told the FBI that he believed Congress should declare the US Communist Party illegal.[71] Later, after it became clear that many people had been unjustly ensnared in the blacklist, Reagan blithely concluded that HUAC "never accused anyone of being a Communist unless they had every last bit of evidence."[72]

The Hollywood blacklist not only targeted innocent people and damaged countless lives, but it also cast a dark shadow on earlier efforts to expose the scourge of racism in film and enhance the predicament of Black actors.[73] Many of the so-called Hollywood Ten, ten writers and directors who were cited for contempt for refusing to testify before HUAC, had been politically galvanized by the campaign against racial discrimination in the film industry. The fact that six of the Hollywood Ten were Jewish may explain their heightened sensitivity to racism and anti-Semitism. Dalton Trumbo, the Oscar-winning screenwriter and the most celebrated of the Hollywood Ten, had condemned Hollywood filmmakers for their racist caricatures of Black life.[74] At the very least, the smattering of Communists in Hollywood hardly posed a threat to

American institutions—many of them joined the Communist Party in the 1930s because that was the only major US political party to take a firm stand against fascism. Nonetheless, the crackdown of civil liberties severely tested the durability of the US Constitution. One of the many casualties of the Hollywood blacklist was the elimination of films that addressed the issue of racism endemic in American society.

Father Dunne's take on Reagan was prescient. Anti-Communism would become the animating cause of Reagan's life. A casualty of his myopic anti-Communism would be his youthful concern for racial justice. Henceforth, Reagan perceived courageous civil rights leaders, such as Martin Luther King Jr. and, later, Nelson Mandela, through a Red prism. Under the sway of his anti-Communism and extreme right-wing politics, Nelle and Jack Reagan's son became a fellow traveler with some of the most bitter racists and white supremacists in America, such as J. Edgar Hoover and Strom Thurmond.

Although Reagan retained his allegiance to the Democratic Party, considered himself a Cold War liberal, and campaigned for President Truman's reelection in 1948, by the early 1950s, Reagan's politics would drift precipitously rightward. Over the years, both Reagan and his supporters would use Reagan's youthful racial liberalism as a shield to parry the charges that Reagan's racist politics and policies evidenced his racism. Whatever youthful commitment Reagan harbored for the evil of racism vanished when he became an FBI informant and messianic anti-Communist amid the Hollywood labor strife of the 1940s. By the mid-1950s, Reagan would find common cause with a burgeoning movement of fellow conservatives that clashed with the onset of the modern phase of the civil rights movement. Until the end of his life, Reagan viewed the Black freedom struggle as part of a Red plot to undermine the American system and allied himself with white supremacists who shared his enduring anti-Communism and profited politically by these alliances at the expense of civil rights and anti-racism.

CHAPTER 2

ON THE WRONG SIDE OF HISTORY

States' Rights vs. Human Rights

*While not himself a racist, Mr. Goldwater articulates
a philosophy which gives aid and comfort to the racist.*

—Martin Luther King Jr. on
Barry Goldwater's candidacy (July 16, 1964)[1]

B y the mid-1950s, Reagan had found a political home in a new conservative movement that crystalized with the launch of William F. Buckley's magazine, *National Review.* Considered the bible of the conservative movement, *National Review* opposed the civil rights struggle and sided with the Southern segregationists.

In the throes of his zealous conversion to staunch anti-Communist, Reagan jettisoned his passion for racial justice. By the early 1960s, Reagan's view of liberalism as the opening wedge to totalitarianism had progressed so far to the right that he was accepting awards from fervent racists such as Mississippi governor Ross Barnett and Arkansas governor Orval Faubus.[2] Though Reagan's anti-Communism and fears of an omnipotent, centralized US government remained his paramount preoccupations, in 1964, the year the civil rights movement moved to the front pages of history, Reagan chose Barry Goldwater's brand of states' rights conservatism over human rights.

REAGAN IN THE 1950S: THE MAKING OF A RACIAL CONSERVATIVE

Although Reagan's acting career never returned to the level of his prewar success, by the early 1950s, his status as SAG president made him one of

the most commanding figures in Hollywood. His most significant relationship was with the powerful talent agency MCA (Music Corporation
of America). Early on, Reagan's agent, Lew Wasserman, and MCA cofounder Jules Stein had seen Reagan's potential to not only ensure labor
peace but also help MCA fulfill its quest to become the most dominant
force in Hollywood. They were right, as Reagan helped MCA become
what a federal judge termed an "octopus" with "tentacles reaching out
to all phases and grasping everything in show business."[3] By the same
token, Reagan's proximity to Hollywood power brokers, especially MCA,
increased his personal wealth and propelled his political career.

Nonetheless, Reagan's tenure as SAG president, from 1947 to 1952,
was controversial because of a series of deals that he and MCA brokered
to their mutual benefit.[4] In 1949, Wasserman persuaded Warner Brothers to release Reagan from half of his exclusive contract and would be
free to work with other studios. This unusual concession allowed Reagan to secure a new, lucrative deal with Universal Studios, a financial
windfall for an actor whose career was in decline. More significantly, a
few years later, the SAG board—which included Reagan, his new second
wife, Nancy, and four others—helped MCA obtain a "blanket waiver"
from the rule prohibiting talent agents from being producers. With this
unprecedented privilege, MCA became the only talent agency able to
move into the burgeoning television industry while also maintaining its
base as a premier talent agency. MCA went on to monopolize Hollywood television production.

Even after Reagan's tenure as SAG president ended in 1952, the deals
continued. In 1954, with Reagan's acting career in steep decline, MCA
secured him a lucrative contract with General Electric to become the
host of its *General Electric Theater*, the first major production of MCA's
new television unit, Revue Productions. MCA eventually gave Reagan
25 percent ownership in the show itself, which further increased his
wealth.[5] In another twist of the rules, Reagan, who was now officially a
producer, never quit SAG's executive board, and the union approved a
permanent extension of MCA's blanket waiver.

In 1959 SAG reelected Reagan as its president, a move that coincided
with a period of labor unrest involving television residuals. Even though
Reagan owned a stake in *General Electric Theater*, he was instrumental in resolving the strike. SAG agreed to receive a onetime payment

of $2.65 million for its approximately 13,500 members in exchange for surrendering its members' rights to any royalties from the over five thousand movies made prior to 1960. MCA had purchased Paramount Studio's film library and stood to benefit greatly from the deal.[6] Even though the $2.65 million seeded SAG's pension and welfare fund, for decades, the Hollywood acting community derided the agreement as "The Great Giveaway."[7] Even Reagan's fellow conservative Bob Hope grieved, "The pictures were sold down the river for a certain amount of money."[8] Over the years, Reagan's mutually beneficial relationship with MCA continued and perhaps peaked in 1966, when MCA's Jules Stein negotiated the sale of Reagan's Malibu property at a tremendous profit that made Reagan even more wealthy.[9]

The Justice Department would later investigate Reagan's dealings with MCA. Investigators subpoenaed his tax records and called him before a federal grand jury. During his 1962 testimony, Reagan failed to recall if SAG had granted him the waiver in exchange for residual fees.[10] The Justice Department eventually absolved Reagan of any illicit activities because investigators could find no corroborating evidence that Reagan had received a quid pro quo from the MCA waiver. Given Lew Wasserman's penchant for secrecy and his refusal to take notes, this result was not surprising.[11] Nonetheless, the investigation—especially Reagan's testimony—raised credible questions of cronyism.

Besides hosting the Sunday evening broadcast of GE Theater, Reagan served as a corporate pitchman and roving goodwill ambassador for GE, traveling at least sixteen weeks a year. It was this work that drove his metamorphosis from actor to politician.[12] He visited all of GE's 139 plants across the US and delivered thousands of speeches to approximately a quarter of a million employees. Afraid of flying at the time, Reagan traveled by train, and the long rides afforded him the opportunity to read right-wing fare, including the journals Human Events and Reader's Digest, books such as Whittaker Chambers's Witness and F. A. Hayek's The Road to Serfdom, and his favorite biweekly periodical, National Review. Reagan looked back on his GE years as a "postgraduate course in political science" and an "apprenticeship for public life."[13] Reagan distilled the talks he gave to GE employees into what become known as "The Speech," which became the basis for the one he gave in support of Barry Goldwater's 1964 presidential campaign, "A Time for Choosing."

Reagan's growing conservatism matched GE's corporate politics and culture. After the war, GE had also been beset by labor strife. Like many other corporations at the time, GE was closing plants in the industrial North and moving to the South, where labor costs were low and unions were weak.[14] However, under the leadership of Lemuel Ricketts Boulware, an ardent conservative who served a GE executive, none of GE's sixteen thousand workers went on strike.[15] GE took notice and promoted Boulware to vice president of labor and community relations. In this capacity, Boulware eliminated labor unrest among company workers by cultivating GE's image as a benevolent employer. He also hired Reagan, who had just resigned as SAG president, to spread the anti-union gospel to GE's many thousands of blue-collar workers that their interests were in harmony with the company's. Boulware also became a mentor to Reagan and a benefactor to *National Review* and other conservative causes.

Reagan's 1952 marriage to aspiring actress Nancy Davis was another step along his path from Cold War liberal to staunch right-wing conservative. By all accounts, without Nancy's ambition, devotion, love, and support, Reagan would not have become president. Reagan's second marriage was both a lifelong love affair and a political partnership. Nancy's preference for the society of wealthy people thrust Reagan closer to conservative friends such as the actors Richard Powell, William Holden, and Robert Taylor. Nancy shared Reagan's disdain for left-wing causes and never showed any interest in or sympathy for the civil rights movement.

Like her husband, Nancy had had a troubled, unsettled childhood. Her parents—a peripatetic stage actress named Edith Luckett and a used-car salesman named Kenneth Seymour Robbins—separated shortly after her birth. Nancy lived in Queens, New York, for her first two years. Busy with her acting career, Edith later sent young Nancy, an only child, to live with an aunt in Bethesda, Maryland. When she was eight years old, Nancy settled with her mother in Chicago, after Edith married a wealthy, esteemed, and archconservative Chicago neurosurgeon, Loyal Davis. Nancy revered her stepfather, who adopted her when she was fourteen, and embraced both his conservative politics and his meticulous dress. Loyal Davis developed an instant rapport with his future son-in-law Reagan and, after the Davises retired to Arizona, would introduce him to his Phoenix friend and neighbor Senator Barry Goldwater.

Nancy's parents harbored racist views that contrasted vividly with those of Nelle and the now deceased Jack Reagan. Edith had been reared in the slums of Washington, DC, though she claimed that she came from an elegant plantation background in Virginia. She was prone to indulge in racist banter. As for Nancy's stepfather, allegations of his virulent racism and anti-Semitism dogged him throughout his illustrious medical career. The medical interns who worked with Davis were so aghast at his racist views that when they delivered babies in Chicago's Black ghettos, they encouraged the mothers to name their sons "Loyal" as a way to privately taunt their boss.[16] Despite the explicit racism of Nancy's mother and stepfather, Reagan formed a warm relationship with his in-laws, and Dr. Davis became one of Reagan's mentors on political conservatism. His stature and overall comportment made him a personal role model for Reagan to emulate in a way the by now deceased Jack Reagan never could.

A MOVEMENT COALESCES: *NATIONAL REVIEW*

At the time Reagan underwent his political conversion, an organized conservative movement did not exist in the United States.[17] In 1950, the literary critic Lionel Trilling famously remarked, "In the United States at this time liberalism is not only the dominant but the sole intellectual tradition. . . . For it is the plain fact [that] there are no conservative or reactionary ideas in circulation but only irritable mental gestures which seem to resemble ideas."[18] Discontent stirred among the remnants of the America First Committee, composed of opponents of Roosevelt's New Deal, isolationists drawn to Ohio senator Robert Taft, and supporters of Senator Joseph McCarthy—all of whom vied to oppose the dominant postwar liberal consensus. But it wasn't until William F. Buckley Jr. launched *National Review* in 1955 that conservativism gained intellectual coherence. On racial issues, both Buckley and the *National Review* were infused with a virulent dose of racism that had infected the conservative movement since its inception.[19]

The magazine debuted only a few weeks before Martin Luther King Jr. assumed leadership of the Montgomery bus boycott and catapulted the Black freedom struggle to the forefront of the national consciousness. *National Review*'s inaugural issue included a mission statement stating that the magazine "stands athwart history, yelling Stop."[20] As part of this goal, of standing "athwart history" over the years, *National Review* favored legal segregation in accordance with "states' rights" and further argued that Black people's alleged backwardness justified the right of Southern whites to prevail over Blacks.[21] As proof of the need to preserve the racial status quo, a number of *National Review*'s contributors endorsed pseudoscientific racist opinions about Blacks' inherent racial inferiority. By fusing the disparate strands of militant anti-Communism, libertarianism, and traditionalism into a comprehensible, if unwieldy, intellectual movement, *National Review* founded modern conservatism.[22] Reagan was a charter subscriber of the *Review* and held dear the memory of picking up the first issue in its plain wrapper.[23] He, too, wanted to stand "athwart history."

Buckley and Reagan did not meet until 1961, but they quickly developed a warm relationship that lasted for the rest of Reagan's life.[24] Buckley's friendship with Reagan was a testament to Buckley's influence on Reagan, because the normally reserved Reagan had few intimates among his many political acquaintances. While Reagan was a disengaged father, Buckley took a paternal interest in Reagan's children and frequently dispensed advice to them. In the 1970s, Buckley regularly corresponded with Reagan's daughter Patti, who shared her poetry with Buckley.[25] In the late 1970s, when Ron Reagan Jr. dropped out of Yale to dance with the Joffrey Ballet, Reagan enlisted Buckley to persuade him to remain in college.[26]

With regard to political matters, Buckley played a pivotal role in making Reagan a conservative Republican. In a memorable speech at the thirtieth anniversary of *National Review* on December 5, 1985, then president Reagan gushed that he "was a Democrat when he picked up his first issue in a plain brown wrapper, and now as an occupant of public housing, he awaits as anxiously as ever his biweekly edition—without the wrapper." He then lauded Buckley and the *Review* not only for parting "the Red Sea" but also because they "rolled it back, dried it up, left it exposed, for all the world to see."[27] Reagan and Buckley were odd bedfellows. Unlike Reagan, the erudite Buckley was born to a cosmopolitan, wealthy family that vacationed on a lavish estate in South Carolina that was staffed with Black servants. His mother, Aloise Steiner, was from New Orleans and proudly described herself as a "daughter of the confederacy."[28] His father, Will Buckley, was a wealthy oil magnate who made a fortune in Mexico before being expelled from the country in 1921 for his role in organizing a coup against the Mexican government. In contrast to Jack Reagan, Buckley's father was an anti-Semite and racist who regarded Blacks and Native Americans as inferior and unworthy of the privileges of citizenship.[29] By the 1950s, Will Buckley had forged a friendship with Strom Thurmond, one of the last Jim Crow demagogues.[30]

As part of the conservative movement's broader goal of incorporating the South into its coalition, Buckley's *Review* was infused with a neo-Confederate mind-set.[31] *National Review* fused an adherence to free-market economics, messianic anti-Communism, and traditionalist conservatives, a variant of the political philosophy of Edmund Burke, who espoused a revival of traditional values, best embodied by the American South's adherence to order, stability, and the maintenance of racial hierarchy into the three-legged stool of the modern American conservative movement.[32] The traditionalist movement, which emerged after World War II, garnered the attention of the American public, and members were collectively referred to as the "new conservatives." They were an eclectic group of writers and thinkers, but they were united by their crusade to rid the world of the hedonism and moral relativism endemic in secular society and who urged a return to religious and absolute values. As such, new conservatives revered the hierarchal orders of the Catholic Church and of feudalistic societies that embodied the time-honored values of stability, order, and chivalry, and a reverence for the eternal. For all of these reasons, they romanticized the Confederacy.

For Reagan, a creature of Hollywood, galvanized by stemming the Communist contagion and curbing the growth of the state, reverence for a return to traditional values appeared incongruous. By the time Reagan became a full-fledged conservative, he was also a divorced actor and had stopped being a regular churchgoer. Though not a libertine by the standards of Hollywood in the late 1940s and early 1950s, he had slept around between marriages, preferring one-night stands or brief affairs with much younger women. He wed Nancy when she was a few months pregnant with their daughter Patti.[33]

The traditionalists laid much of the groundwork for the conservative movement's opposition to the Black freedom struggle. Traditionalists were a heterodox group, but many were untroubled by a racist ideology that continued to support segregation. Two of the most influential were *National Review* contributors Russell Kirk and Richard M. Weaver Jr.

Steeped with sympathy for the racist mores of the Old South, they were prominent writers who provided intellectual heft to the conservative movement. Kirk was enamored with Southern culture and Southern agrarian writers. As a graduate student at Duke University, he wrote his master's thesis extolling John Randolph of Roanoke, a member of Virginia's landed gentry who elevated the interests of slaveholders during his long political career in the early nineteenth century.[34] In 1953, Kirk published the groundbreaking book *The Conservative Mind: From Burke to Eliot.* Of its import, the historian of conservatism George Nash has written: "It is not too much to say that without this book, we, the conservative intellectual community, would not exist today."[35] *The Conservative Mind* examines a wide range of conservative thinkers, yet it is replete with paeans to the Old South. For Kirk, the South was "the citadel of tradition" and the front line of defense for "civilization." "The South," he told his readers, "need feel no shame for its defense of beliefs that were not concocted yesterday."[36] In conformity with the new conservatives, Kirk avoided any sustained look at the evil of slavery in his book.

Along with Kirk, the scholar Richard M. Weaver was the most prominent new conservative whose espousal of the virtues of tradition, particularly the Southern agrarian variety, would regularly appear in the *National Review.* A Southerner, Weaver spent his career as a literature professor at the University of Chicago, shuttling between Hyde Park and his beloved North Carolina farm. His passionate defense of the traditional values and community of the Old South was a recurring theme of his works. He praised the South's "traditions" of anticonsumerism and chivalry as the antidote to modernity. In a 1957 essay titled "Integration is Communization," Weaver argued that "integration" and "communization" were synonymous.[37] Opposed to granting Blacks full citizenship on the grounds that doing so would be a detriment to Western civilization, Weaver argued, "The Negro has shown that his tendency, when he was released from all constraining forces, was downward rather than upward."[38]

National Review debuted not long after the unanimous *Brown v. Board of Education* decision riled up the Old Confederacy. On January 25, 1956, the two-month-old *Review* called *Brown* "one of the most brazen acts of judicial usurpation in our history, patently counter to the intent of the Constitution, shoddy and illegal in analysis, and invalid in sociology."[39] Shortly thereafter, all but three Southern US senators signed a document called the *Declaration of Constitutional Principles* (known as the *Southern Manifesto*), which argued against racial integration and assailed the *Brown* decision as an abuse of judicial power. Fittingly, the *Review* endorsed Virginia's plan to resist the integration of its schools, known as the Gray Commission plan, pushed by the minions of former Klan member Senator Harry F. Byrd of Virginia.[40]

The frontal assault on *Brown* was merely the opening salvo in the *Review*'s long campaign to stand athwart history, more particularly, against the civil rights movement. On February 29, 1956, Buckley argued that support for segregation was not about racial matters but about states' rights. "Support for the Southern position rests not at all on the question of whether Negro and White children should, in fact, study geography side by side, but on whether a central or a local authority should make that decision," he wrote.[41] This was the rationale Buckley and, later, Reagan would use to justify their opposition to the Civil Rights Act of 1964. Buckley believed that the South would eventually change its racial caste system without federal intervention. But, despite his attempt to give resistance to integration some intellectual justification, Buckley laid bare *National Review*'s underlying racist position in a notorious editorial titled "Why the South Must Prevail." In the midst of the massive resistance crisis surrounding school integration at Arkansas' Little Rock High School in September 1957, Buckley wrote:

> The central question . . . is whether the White community in the South is entitled to take such measures as are necessary to prevail, politically and culturally, in areas in which it does not predominate numerically? The sobering answer is Yes—the White community is so entitled because, for the time being, it is the advanced race. . . . *National Review* believes the South's premises are correct . . . it is more important for any community, anywhere in the world, to affirm and live by civilized standards, than to bow to the demands of the numerical majority.[42]

Purporting to speak for Southern Blacks, Buckley continued: "The great majority of the Negroes in the South who do not vote do not care to vote, and would not know for what to vote if they could."[43] The *Review* published a rebuttal to the editorial, penned by Buckley's former

Yale debating partner and brother-in-law L. Brent Bozell Jr., contending that the *Review*'s editorial was "dead wrong."[44] But in a one-paragraph counter-rebuttal Buckley reiterated his position, insisting that the Fourteenth and Fifteenth Amendments were "inorganic accretions to the original document, grafted upon it by victors-at-war by force."[45] Here, Buckley echoed the prevailing view that Reconstruction was a colossal injustice foisted upon the South by an unruly band of opportunistic Northern carpetbaggers and corrupt, deviant Blacks ill-equipped for self-rule.

Soon thereafter, the *Review* went all out and hired the segregationist firebrand James J. "Jack" Kilpatrick and anointed him the magazine's authority on civil rights issues.[46] Kilpatrick, who described himself as "only a little to the South of John C. Calhoun," was the editor of the *Richmond News Leader* and one of the most vocal advocates for "massive resistance" to desegregation.[47] In 1957, Kilpatrick published *The Sovereign States: Notes of a Citizen of Virginia*, which resurrected John C. Calhoun's long discredited doctrine of "interposition." Calhoun, the nineteenth-century South Carolina politician and former US vice president, held that states had the right to interpose themselves between their citizens and the federal government in order to protect themselves from federal laws seen as unconstitutional.[48] According to his biographer, Kilpatrick refused to fraternize with Blacks and in his columns repeatedly referenced his belief in Blacks' innate inferiority.[49] He developed a warm rapport with Ronald and Nancy Reagan, who, upon Kilpatrick's death in 2010, issued a statement saying, "Jack was our dear friend for many years, and I have fond memories of our times together. . . . Jack brought a common sense wisdom to the discussions of the day."[50]

Along with Kilpatrick's opinions, sociologist and psychologist Ernest van den Haag's racially suspect views frequently appeared in *National Review*. On December 1, 1964, van den Haag's essay "Intelligence or Prejudice" graced the *Review*'s front cover. Cast as a series of questions and answers, van den Haag's essay tacked back and forth between agreement and agnosticism on whether innate difference existed between Blacks and whites. The article dismissed the accepted scientific evidence that there were no racial differences in intelligence and argued that there were differences and that they necessitated school segregation.[51] In 1966, van den Haag testified in support of the South African apartheid regime before the International Court of Justice, in The Hague.[52] Upon his death, Buckley lavished praise on van den Haag as a "tuning fork of reason in the cacophonous world of social science."[53] Buckley presided over van den Haag's 2002 memorial service and eulogized him as "most awfully learned."[54]

Buckley continued to package the *Review*'s suspect theories alongside more measured arguments for states' rights. In his memoir *Up from Liberalism*, Buckley responded to an African nationalist, saying, "You people are not ready for self-rule because in order for Democracies to be successful, it must be practiced by politically mature people among whom there is a consensus on the meaning of life within their society."[55] Frequently offensive, during the outbreak of the AIDS epidemic, in the 1980s, Buckley suggested that gay men should be tattooed on their buttocks to indicate whether they carried the disease.[56]

Notably, at the dawn of a new century, Buckley issued a rare apology—something Reagan never did—for having believed that "we could evolve our way out of Jim Crow, I was wrong: federal intervention was necessary."[57] Buckley's later confession was too little, too late. From his unwavering opposition to school desegregation, the Civil Rights Act of 1964, and the Voting Rights Act of 1965, to his persistent defense of South Africa's apartheid regime, Buckley embodied conservatism's presumption that white, Christian, Western civilization was superior to all others.[58] And so did Reagan.

THE 1964 GOLDWATER CAMPAIGN AND REAGAN'S POLITICAL DEBUT

As the 1950s drew to a close, Reagan was moving ever rightward. Although he never publicly endorsed the pro-segregationist views of *National Review*, the voluble Reagan was curiously silent on civil rights, despite its growing importance to American society. During the 1950s, Reagan made many trips throughout the South, where he spoke before Kiwanis Clubs, GE employees, and other groups railing against Communism, confiscatory taxes, and liberalism. Never once, however, did he speak out against the injustice and inhumanity of Jim Crow. And during one of his many trips to the South, he bonded with the bombastic, rabid segregationist from Raleigh, North Carolina, Jesse Helms.

At the same time, Reagan's anti-Communist rhetoric was becoming increasingly apocalyptic. Speaking before audiences of local businessmen from the Elks, Rotary Club, National Association of Manufacturers, and Chamber of Commerce, he chillingly warned of "the slow accretion of federal legislation that would jeopardize our freedom." Reagan also feared that the enactment of the Medicare program was an example of "creeping socialism" that would "invade every area of freedom in this country," and he predicted it would force Americans to spend their "sunset years telling our children and our children's children what it was like in America when men were free."[59]

Since the late 1940s, Reagan's anger over the exorbitant or confiscatory income taxes he paid also factored into his inexorable rightward tilt. Reagan's enmity over taxes arose after the IRS filed a lien in the amount of $24,911 for income he had deferred during the war.[60] His indictment of the progressive income tax as a disincentive to taking on additional acting roles would be a staple of his scorching attacks on big government and taxes.[61]

Notwithstanding his antipathy for a powerful federal government, in March 1960 Reagan used his connections with J. Edgar Hoover to have the FBI track down his estranged nineteen-year-old daughter Maureen, who had moved to Washington, DC, and was living with an older, married policeman. In 1965, just as Reagan was about to enter politics, the FBI assisted him once again in squelching news that his nineteen-year-old adopted son Michael was consorting with the son of a mobster. Of course, such private matters were beyond the FBI's ordinary jurisdiction, though Reagan willingly received special entitlements at taxpayer expense.[62]

Reagan's strong opinions eventually got him into trouble with GE. During one of his speeches, he lambasted the popular Tennessee Valley Authority (TVA) as a government boondoggle whose "annual interest on the TVA deal is five times as great as the flood damage it prevents."[63] GE had a $50-million-a-year contract with the TVA, and, going forward, GE demanded prior approval of his speeches. When Reagan refused to agree to this, GE terminated him.[64] Without the constraints of his employment with GE, Reagan's public comments became even more extreme. As late as 1961, he persisted in the erroneous belief that Communists were attempting to infiltrate the entertainment industry.[65] Reagan participated in a series of televised events organized by Frederick Schwarz, an Australian physician who espoused paranoid Communist conspiracy theories. In a speech before Schwarz's Southern California School of

Anti-Communism, Reagan warned the young students, saying, "You're a target. Communists will appeal to your rebellious nature."[66] Perhaps the most revealing example of Reagan's extremism was his August 30, 1962, keynote speech for Congressman John Rousselot of Southern California, a member of the far-right John Birch Society, in which he accused the centrist President Kennedy of leading the country to socialism.[67] Rumors swirled that Reagan was a "Bircher," and though never confirmed, many people considered Reagan a member of the John Birch Society because he sounded like one. And unlike Buckley, he never repudiated the conspiracist society.

The new conservative movement offered Reagan and fellow conservatives the hope of melding a conservative coalition between anti–New Deal Republicans and Southern Democrats to challenge the regnant New Deal consensus. Although *National Review* had laid the intellectual predicate for modern conservatism, the magazine struggled financially and had a relatively small readership. By the late 1950s, other outlets for right-wing discontent emerged, supported by various "messengers of the right," such as FBI agent Dan Smoot, *Chicago Tribune* publisher Robert McCormick, *Review* publisher William Rusher, and book publisher Henry Regnery.[68]

One of these conservative media figures, Clarence Manion, had risen to prominence in right-wing circles by hosting a weekly nationally syndicated radio show called the *Manion Forum of Opinion*, which offered a dystopian view of America occasioned by invectives against the *Brown v. Board of Education* ruling. As the 1960 presidential election loomed, Manion, who was also a member of the John Birch Society's national council, contemplated supporting segregationist Arkansas governor Orval Faubus to lead a states' rights bid for the presidency. As part of "Operation Dixie," South Carolina textile magnate Roger Milliken, a benefactor of *National Review* who despised unions, had invited US senator Barry Goldwater of Arizona to address the nascent South Carolina Republican Party in Greenville, on May 16, 1959. Manion and Goldwater had met a few times. In fact, Goldwater made his national debut on Manion's radio show in 1957. After hearing Goldwater's rousing speech in Greenville, in which he excoriated *Brown* as unconstitutional, Manion vowed to make Goldwater the leader of the conservative movement. When he was not doing his radio show, organizing for Goldwater became an obsession for Manion, who eventually convinced Goldwater to articulate his conservative principles in a book.[69]

By the late 1950s, Goldwater's fulminations against President Eisenhower's domestic agenda as a "dime store New Deal," his attacks on organized labor, and his calls to roll back Communism made him a darling of the burgeoning conservative movement. Manion and other conservatives thought Goldwater's stance on states' rights would help lure Southern white Democrats into the Republican Party and reject the national Democrats' growing affection for civil rights. In March 1960, after Goldwater made a stirring states' rights keynote address, South Carolina Republicans unanimously pledged their thirteen votes at the upcoming national convention to Goldwater.[70]

Like William F. Buckley Jr., Barry Goldwater was born into privilege. His father, Baron Goldwater, was a wealthy Jewish businessman and the proprietor of Goldwater's Department Store, a chain of stores, the largest of which was in Phoenix. Young Barry married Margaret (Peggy) Johnson, the daughter of the founder of Borg-Warner, one of the country's leading automotive-parts manufacturing corporations. Like many people born to privilege, Goldwater pretended that he was a self-made man.[71]

As his supporters have tirelessly argued, Goldwater's racially conservative policies were not based in any sort of personal bigotry. Goldwater's Department Store, they were quick to point out, was one of the first businesses in Phoenix to employ Blacks (though Blacks were not allowed to work as salesclerks except during the busy holiday season). As a US senator, Goldwater hired Blacks as part of his staff. Even though Goldwater supported the tepid 1957 Civil Rights Bill, when Strom Thurmond, a member of the Democratic Party's breakaway Dixiecrats, filibustered the bill, historian Rick Perlstein recounted, "Goldwater was the only senator who spelled Strom Thurmond for bathroom breaks."[72] Goldwater argued on the Senate floor that public school segregation was unjust and created feelings of inferiority among young Black students, but he still insisted, "I am not prepared, however, to impose that judgment of mine on the people of Mississippi or South Carolina. . . . That is their business, not mine."[73] Like Reagan, Goldwater's apparent lack of personal racism did not mitigate the fact that he favored racist policies and found common cause with segregationists and white supremacists.

Hoping to create a Goldwater groundswell at the 1960 Republican National Convention in Chicago, Manion convinced a reluctant Goldwater to write a conservative manifesto. Published in March 1960 and ghostwritten by L. Brent Bozell Jr., *The Conscience of a Conservative* was largely a distillation of the attacks on big government and calls for a "rollback" of the Soviet Union that *National Review* and other budding conservative outlets had been articulating for the past few years. Nevertheless, the slim volume exceeded all expectations. It debuted at number ten on the *New York Time*'s best-seller list and made Goldwater the face of the conservative movement.[74] *National Review*'s Frank S. Meyer raved that it placed "Goldwater in the first rank of American statesmen."[75]

Chapter 4 of *The Conscience of a Conservative*, titled "States' Rights," and chapter 5, titled "Civil Rights," were shorn of the *Review*'s allusions to Black inferiority but delighted segregationists with their deference to Southern racial customs. On the burning issue of school integration and the desegregation of public facilities, Goldwater argued that they were local matters best left to the people of the South, not the federal government. His views were plain and succinct: "I believe that the problem of race relations, like all social and cultural problems, is best handled by the people directly concerned . . . [and] should not be effected by engines of national power."[76] Like Reagan, Goldwater emphasized his repugnance at bigotry, but his constitutional proclamations ignored the persistence of racism, and African Americans and racial progressives justly perceived Goldwater as an apologist for segregation.

Goldwater's supporters hoped the senator's newfound notoriety would propel him to the Republican nomination in 1960 and rescue the party from the hold of its moderate Eastern establishment wing. At the Chicago convention, however, Goldwater's cadre of zealous supporters was outmanned, and the party nominated the frontrunner, Vice President Nixon. Before the nomination, Nixon had hammered out a secret agreement with liberal New York governor Nelson Rockefeller that enraged Goldwater's devoted constituency. Dubbed the Treaty of Fifth Avenue, Nixon and Rockefeller agreed to a Republican platform that rejected Goldwater's brand of conservatism by calling for the "removal of the last vestiges of segregation and discrimination in all areas of national life—voting and housing, schools and jobs, and pledged support for the objections of the sit-in demonstrators."[77] Appearing on the podium after losing the nomination, Goldwater exhorted his disappointed conservative supporters to "grow up." He continued: "If we want to take this Party back—and I think we can someday—let's get to work." Notably, as Goldwater addressed the delegates, some of his supporters marched around the hall to the sounds of "Dixie."[78]

John F. Kennedy's narrow defeat of Nixon has been attributed to a surge of support from Black voters in crucial northern states, who rewarded the young Massachusetts senator for telephoning Coretta Scott King in the final days of his campaign and helping to secure her husband's release from prison. Martin Luther King Jr. had been arrested during a sit-in in Atlanta and was kept in jail because he had violated the terms of his probation imposed earlier for driving without a driver's license. By contrast, Nixon, who was supportive of civil rights, had failed to intervene. Worse, Nixon's final campaign stop occurred at the South Carolina statehouse, where the Confederate flag would soon be raised to proclaim the Palmetto State's commitment to segregation.[79]

During the 1960 campaign, Reagan was not officially a Republican, but he was a member of Democrats for Nixon, and he was despondent over Kennedy's election. In a letter to Vice President Nixon in 1959, Reagan had mused, "Shouldn't one tag Mr. Kennedy's bold new imaginative program with its proper age? Under the tousled boyish hair cut it is still old Karl Marx."[80] Reagan blamed the Kennedy brothers for his firing from GE. Years later, Reagan's son Michael revealed that Reagan had said Attorney General Robert Kennedy had contacted GE's president, Ralph Cordiner, who reportedly remarked, "If you want government contracts, get Reagan off the air."[81] As a result, Reagan harbored a particular animosity against Robert Kennedy for investigating his work as SAG president.[82]

Conservative activists heeded Goldwater's summons to "grow up," and soon after Kennedy's election, conservatives launched a vigorous grassroots campaign to take over the Republican Party. Following Nixon's impressive showing in the Upper South states of Virginia, Tennessee, and Kentucky, officials with the Republican National Committee intensified Operation Dixie, an RNC initiative unveiled in 1957 to target white Southern voters. In a preview of the Southern strategy, Goldwater argued as early as 1961, "Republicans should stop trying to outbid the Democrats for the Negro vote," and pronounced his famous political dictum, that the Republican Party should "go hunting where the ducks are."[83]

As Goldwater was laying the groundwork for his 1964 presidential campaign, the high-profile Birmingham campaign shocked the conscience of many and finally forced the nation to reckon with the scourge of segregation. In May 1963, televised images from Birmingham, Alabama, of Public Safety Commissioner Bull Connor's troops unleashing dogs and high-powered water hoses on innocent men, women, and children provoked international outrage. Before Martin Luther King Jr.'s campaign to desegregate Birmingham, only 4 percent of the American public thought that civil rights was America's most vital issue; after the events in Birmingham, a Gallup poll showed that for the first time a majority of Americans regarded civil rights as the nation's most urgent issue.[84]

By 1963, the end of the Red Scare and the dreaded blacklist helped the civil rights movement engage the attention of Hollywood. Harry Belafonte enlisted a contingent of approximately sixty Hollywood stars to attend the March on Washington on August 28. Reagan was not in attendance.[85] Instead, Reagan was making an appearance at a rally for Members of Project Alert, an extreme right-wing organization that had called for the hanging of civil rights champion Supreme Court Chief Justice Earl Warren for treason.[86] As for the civil strife roiling the South, Reagan counseled Blacks to be patient, even though white Southern officials bedecked themselves with buttons saying "Never" and violently opposed efforts at desegregation.

By the spring of 1964, with a historic civil rights bill on the verge of passing Congress, Senator Goldwater was in the midst of a bitter primary battle for the Republican nomination against civil rights supporter New York governor Nelson Rockefeller. In the wake of the assassination of President Kennedy, his civil rights bill had been languishing in Congress, but his successor, Lyndon Johnson, a Southerner, surprised the civil rights community by deploying his masterful legislative skills to defeat another filibuster and keep it alive. On the eve of the vote, Goldwater sought the counsel of two young conservative legal thinkers: Robert Bork, a Yale University law professor, and William Rehnquist, a conservative local Phoenix attorney. Together, they wrote a seventy-page memo to Goldwater, advising him to oppose the Civil Rights Act because "individual men ought to be free to deal and associate with whom they please for whatever reasons appeal to them."[87] Armed with the memo, on June 18, 1964, only eight days after he narrowly defeated Rockefeller in the crucial California primary, Goldwater joined segregationist Southern Democrats and voted against the bill.[88] Standing on the floor of the Senate, Goldwater warned it would produce a "federal police force of mammoth proportions."[89] His Republican colleague Senate Minority Leader Everett Dirksen never directly named Goldwater but glowered at him when he thundered, "You can go ahead and talk about conscience! It is man's conscience that speaks in every generation."[90]

On July 2, 1964, with the support of twenty-seven of the thirty-three Senate Republicans, President Johnson signed the Civil Rights Act, effectively outlawing segregation in public accommodations. Speaking for many Republicans, Dirksen claimed, "No Army can withstand the strength of an idea whose time has come."[91] The night after LBJ signed the Civil Rights Act, his aide Bill Moyers was surprised when he saw the president looking so melancholy in his bedroom. When Moyers asked what was wrong, LBJ said, "We [Democrats] delivered the South to the Republican Party for a long time to come."[92]

Less than two weeks later, the Republican National Convention convened at the Cow Palace in San Francisco to nominate Goldwater for president. Outside the convention hall, the Republican delegates were subject to fifty thousand anti-Goldwater demonstrators including people from the Congress of Racial Equality (CORE), who held a coffin with a sign that said the Republican Party was born in 1860 and died in 1964.[93] In downtown San Francisco, an estimated forty thousand civil rights supporters demonstrated against Goldwater. James Farmer, the head of CORE and leader of the 1961 Freedom Rides, said Goldwater "provided the rallying point for bigots and extremists who once built their hopes on the late Senator Joseph R. McCarthy of Wisconsin."[94]

The day after Goldwater had cast his vote against cloture of the civil rights bill, William Scranton, the popular moderate Republican governor of Pennsylvania, was so enraged that he announced he would mount a challenge against Goldwater at the convention, but Goldwater was still nominated on the first ballot with an approving Reagan, now officially a Republican, attending the convention as an alternative California delegate. In Goldwater's acceptance speech he famously said, "Extremism in the defense of liberty is no vice" and "moderation in the pursuit of justice is no vice." The speech exhilarated conservatives and horrified the Rockefeller-Scranton wing of the party. Richard Nixon, for one, was sickened by Goldwater's strident speech and knew the senator had for-feited any chance of winning the general election.[95]

Goldwater's emphasis on states' rights was anathema to the handful of Black delegates in attendance, some of whom had been physically and verbally harassed during the convention.[96] Baseball legend Jackie Robinson was on the convention floor as a Rockefeller delegate and witnessed Goldwater supporters putting out their cigarettes on Black delegates. Afterward, Robinson lamented, "I had a better understand-ing of how it must have felt to be a Jew in Hitler's Germany,"[97] and, indeed, the *Chicago Defender* ran the headline "GOP Convention, Re-calls Germany, 1933."[98] The civil rights coalition was so fearful of Gold-water and his supporters that NAACP leader Roy Wilkins, A. Philip Randolph, and Martin Luther King Jr. called for a moratorium on all "mass marchers, mass picketing, and mass demonstrations" until after the presidential election.[99]

The only place Goldwater did well was in the South.[100] Traveling with the Goldwater campaign in seven states of the Old Confederacy, journal-ist Richard Rovere reported, "The Goldwater movement, whether or not it can command a majority, remains an enormous one in the South, and appears to be a racist movement and almost nothing else."[101] In contrast, when the First Lady, Lady Bird Johnson, toured eight Southern states later that year, she and her daughter Lynda Bird were frequently heckled and booed.[102] On September 16, 1964, former Dixiecrat and now Repub-lican senator Strom Thurmond pledged his support to Goldwater and switched parties, citing his belief that "the principles of our forefathers live on in the cause" of Goldwater.[103] Thurmond's pledge initiated a wave of Southern defections from their traditional home in the Democratic Party to the GOP. The following day, a frenzied crowd of twenty thou-sand came to the Greenville, South Carolina, airport to watch Thur-mond greet the arrival of Goldwater's Boeing 727. The pandemonium that accompanied the first day of Goldwater's campaigning alongside Thurmond was such that by the end of the day, forty-five people would require emergency first aid and two would suffer heart attacks. Accord-ing to a local paper, "The Beatles would have had a hard time eliciting the adoration that Barry Goldwater enjoyed in Winston-Salem."[104]

— — —

Since Reagan's firing from *General Electric Theater* in 1962, political activism for conservative causes had become the animating cause of his life, and he became a star surrogate for the Goldwater campaign. Whereas the news that Thurmond would be visiting California outraged California Republicans, Reagan and M. Phillip Davis, Reagan's co-chair of the California Citizens for Goldwater-Miller Committee, were delighted.[105] In the run-up to the June primary, Reagan campaigned alongside Goldwater and captivated conservatives with his spellbinding stump speeches in strip malls throughout Southern California, flaying liberal Republicans for "conducting the most vicious and venomous campaign against a candidate our party has ever seen."[106] Reagan's wholesome and amiable demeanor was a sharp contrast to Goldwater's edgy belligerence.

Seeing the popularity of Reagan's appearances, a group of wealthy, self-made California businessmen, who would later compose President Reagan's "Kitchen Cabinet," convinced Goldwater to have Reagan present a thirty minute prerecorded speech as a televised commercial for Goldwater a week before the election, October 27, 1964. The speech, "A Time for Choosing," was a reprise of the stump speech Reagan had delivered thousands of times as a traveling GE spokesman. Reagan's folksy address was replete with his stirring warnings about the growth of government and the danger of Communism. For all of his fears that liberal prescriptions for big government were imperiling liberty, he omitted any references to the raging civil rights revolution that was seeking to uphold the great promise of liberty enshrined in the Bill of Rights and the Fourteenth Amendment. In Reagan's time for choosing, he chose "states' rights" over human rights.

Reagan was initially worried that the speech hadn't gone well and that he had "let Barry down."[107] A few hours after going to sleep, though, he was awakened by someone calling from Citizens for Goldwater headquarters in Washington, DC, who was shouting, "The switchboard has been lit up ever since the broadcast. It's 3 A.M. and there's been no let up!"[108] Reagan's communication skills had evoked in viewers comparisons with his idol, FDR. Telegrams flooded to Reagan from across the country, hailing the speech as a political masterpiece. F. Clifton White, Goldwater's master delegate counter, was amazed at how the calls inundating the Citizens for Goldwater office were from newly energized conservatives.[109] According to David Broder and Stephen Hess, "It was the most electrifying political debut since William Jennings Bryan electrified the 1896 Democratic Convention with his Cross of Gold speech."[110]

Still, as expected, a week later Johnson and the Democratic Party won in a landslide. With an astounding 94 percent of the Black vote, Johnson carried Virginia, Florida, North Carolina, and Tennessee.[111] By contrast, Kennedy had received 70 percent of the Black vote in 1960.[112] Goldwater's triumph over LBJ in the solidly Democratic Deep South states of Alabama, Georgia, Louisiana, South Carolina, and Mississippi provided a morsel of solace to his demoralized supporters, and it portended a Republican ascendancy in Dixie. Years later, Mississippi senator Trent Lott observed that the Goldwater-Johnson race was "the first time [Southern Democrats] really started thinking, 'Gee maybe we are Republicans.'"[113] For the time being, at least, Goldwater's drubbing seemed to confirm the folly of nominating such an extremist candidate. Liberal historian Richard Hofstadter summed up the conventional wisdom: "When in all our history has anyone with ideas so bizarre, so archaic, so self-compounding, so remote from the basic American consensus, ever gone so far?"[114] Despite the outbreak of racial uprisings in Harlem, Philadelphia, New Jersey, Illinois, and Rochester in the summer of 1964, the scope of Johnson's victory temporarily defused the talk of a dreaded "white backlash" over the urban disorders that would cause frightened whites to flock to conservative politicians like Reagan who were preaching the virtues of "law and order."[115]

While the backlash had not yet materialized, the success of segregationist George Wallace in the 1964 Democratic primaries in Wisconsin, Indiana, and Maryland underscored white anxiety over the pace of the civil rights revolution and urban riots. In Reagan's California, the electorate approved Proposition 14, a state initiative that repealed the controversial and far-reaching Rumford Fair Housing Act signed by Governor Brown in 1963, which eliminated racial discrimination in the sale and rental of all residential properties with over five units. The bill had been the culmination of a long campaign to end discrimination in the sale and rental of public and private housing in California and paralleled efforts in Washington, Ohio, and Michigan. Fearing that the Rumford Act would lower their property values and result in increased crime in their suburban neighborhoods, whites from all socioeconomic and educational backgrounds voted overwhelmingly to approve Proposition 14. In fact, the margin of Proposition 14's victory far exceeded Johnson's lop-sided margin of victory in the Golden State, portending future fissures around issues of residential integration.[116] Civil rights leaders and their liberal allies were shocked by the rebuke. In the days before the 1964 election, Martin Luther King Jr. campaigned against Proposition 14 in Los Angeles, warning California voters that its passage would constitute a "tragic setback for integration throughout the country" and "the most shameful development in our nation's history."[117] Described by *Time* "as the most bitterly fought issue in the nation," the fierce opposition to the Rumford Fair Housing Act demonstrated the national scope of white anxieties over residential integration.[118]

Reagan's star performance with his "Time for Choosing" speech ignited a groundswell of hope among conservatives that the handsome fifty-three-year-old former actor would lead their nascent movement out of the political wilderness. Reagan's and Goldwater's politics were nearly identical, but Reagan's sunny demeanor blunted his extremism. Only days after the 1964 presidential election, Reagan was among five contributors who penned postmortems on the election for *National Review*. Writing like a prospective candidate for office, Reagan argued that Johnson's election was not a repudiation of conservatism but a resounding vote against a false and caricatured image of conservatism propagated by LBJ's campaign and the media. He said, "We represent the forgotten American," who works hard, pays his taxes, and "knows there just 'ain't no such thing as a free lunch.'"[119] Although Reagan personally admired Goldwater, he believed he would have fared much better in a matchup against LBJ.[120]

Reagan's Kitchen Cabinet, a small group of self-made Southern California millionaires, shared Reagan's abhorrence of socialism and his zealous anti-communism. They also believed Reagan would have been a smoother candidate than the mercurial Goldwater and were the most influential group urging him to run for governor of California in 1966 against the two-term incumbent, Pat Brown. Throughout 1965, Reagan tested the waters for a gubernatorial bid by traveling throughout the state, where he railed against the Rumford Act and delighted the conservative faithful with his calls to avenge Goldwater's defeat. By the end of the year, with financial assistance from the Kitchen Cabinet, Reagan hired the political consulting firm Spencer and Roberts to run his campaign. They helped transform Reagan from a right-wing Goldwater disciple into a seemingly innocuous, charming moderate able to attract California voters across the political spectrum.

Amid the unparalleled prosperity of mid-1960s California, an undercurrent of anxiety prevailed, particularly in the predominantly white suburbs of Southern California, over rising crime, taxes, and the civil rights revolution, which was best exemplified by the groundswell of support for Proposition 14. Though Goldwater had lost the state decisively, his passionate supporters were undaunted, and they were buoyed by Reagan's flirtation with politics.[121] As Reagan geared up for a possible run for governor, the combustible mix of fear of crime and erosion of authority, exacerbated by the Watts riots in August 1965, made working-class white Democrats susceptible to Reagan's appeals to "law and order" and traditional values. It is in this milieu that Reagan would tap into a rich vein of middle-class anxiety over the cultural and racial dislocations of the 1960s while on his way to the White House. The first step, however, would be the race to become the next governor of California.

PART II

RIDING THE WAVE OF THE WHITE BACKLASH

1966–1980

CHAPTER 3

REAGAN'S FIRST CAMPAIGN

Riots, the Rumford Act, and Backlash Politics

If an individual wants to discriminate against Negroes in selling or rent-
ing his house, he has the right to do so.

—Reagan on the Rumford Fair Housing Act (September 1966)[1]

The election of Mrs. Lurleen Wallace in Alabama, the conservative
Claude R. Kirk, in Florida, and Ronald Reagan in California . . . is in-
dicative that large segments of America still suffer from a repulsive moral
disease that must be cured before our moral health can be restored.

—Martin Luther King Jr. on Reagan's win (November 9, 1966)[2]

R eagan's emergence as a conservative star overlapped with the high
tide of the civil rights movement and the "liberal hour." In the first
seven months of 1965, a fierce gust of reform swept Washington. Under the stewardship of Lyndon Johnson, the Democratic-controlled
Eighty-Ninth Congress passed a raft of Great Society legislation, including Medicare, Medicaid, and a host of antipoverty programs that
provided relief to the poor. As Reagan's supporters sulked, African
Americans were exultant. For Black America, the crowning achievement
of the civil rights revolution was the passage of the Voting Rights Act on
August 6, 1965. Standing alongside President Johnson was John Lewis,
executive director of the Student Nonviolent Coordinating Committee
(SNCC), who proclaimed that the Voting Rights Act was a "milestone
and every bit as momentous . . . as the Emancipation Proclamation or the
1954 Supreme Court decision."[3] After decades of struggle, "the lock on
the ballot box for African Americans had been shattered."[4]

Calling the Voting Rights Act "unnecessary because the federal government already had constitutional authority to require registration of
Negro voters in the South," Reagan continued to refer to the landmark
civil rights legislation as "empty promises" and "a grandstand stunt."[5]
Reagan spent much of 1965 crisscrossing California, testing the waters
for a future gubernatorial bid and castigating the Rumford Fair Housing
Act. It was still a live issue because the NAACP, among other organizations, had filed suits contending that Proposition 14 violated the Fourteenth Amendment.[6]

Reagan's preternatural optimism lifted the spirits of disconsolate conservatives. He was adamant that Goldwater's "presentation" was the problem, not his policies, and reserved particular scorn for the Earl Warren
wing of the California Republican Party, such as California US senator
Thomas Kuchel, the co-manager in the Senate for civil rights legislation,
who had refused to endorse Goldwater. Speaking before the Los Angeles
County Young Republicans a week after the election, a defiant Reagan
jumped into the intraparty fray when he said that conservatives must not
"turn the Republican Party over to the traitors in the battle just ended."[7]

Amid the rubble of the Goldwater debacle, several indicators showed
promise for Reagan's future political prospects in the Golden State. First,
his friend and fellow actor George Murphy had prevailed in California's
senatorial campaign against Pierre Salinger, the former JFK press secretary, proving that a conservative could win a statewide campaign in California. As noted, the successful grassroots mobilization of thousands of
anxious white middle-class homeowners against the Rumford Act revealed the potential resonance of race to derail the ascendant liberal order in California. According to Hale Champion, an advisor to Governor
Brown, the Rumford Act was the most important issue in California in
1964 and cost Salinger the election.[8] Most dramatically, the smoldering
racial anxiety that flared in the wake of the Watts riots in August 1965
cemented Reagan's standing with white Californians, fearful of crime
and neighborhood desegregation. In the short time between Johnson's
landslide victory in November 1964 and Reagan's formal announcement
of his gubernatorial bid in January 1966, the political landscape in California had changed significantly.[9] The white backlash against civil rights
policies that benefited African Americans would become the dominant
political force. Reagan's facility for tapping into this backlash without

appearing angry or racist was a major contributing factor to his dazzling political rise.

WATTS AND FAIR HOUSING: FEAR AND LOATHING IN THE GOLDEN STATE

Only days after Johnson triumphantly signed the Voting Rights Act, the euphoria vanished in Southern California when the Watts riots broke out in South-Central Los Angeles. On the surface, the palm tree–lined streets of Watts, with their comely single-family cottages, seemed to validate the National Urban League's recently commissioned survey that ranked Los Angeles, of sixty-eight American cities, as the best place for African Americans to live. Watts's halcyon façade belied the reality that it was a segregated Black ghetto, which, though nearly twice the size of Manhattan, did not have a single hospital, bowling alley, movie theater, or skating rink.[10] More than two-thirds of its residents did not have a high school diploma, and approximately one-third of the families had incomes below the poverty level. The 1960 US Census reported that Los Angeles was "more segregated than any city in the South," and the Black-owned *California Eagle* noted, "More Negro children attend all-Negro schools in Los Angeles than attend such schools in Little Rock."[11]

To add to their plight, the Blacks of Watts chafed under the occupation of a brutally racist police force, headed by William H. Parker, that behaved like an occupying army.[12] The despair of Watts was testament to the need for remedies such as those set out in the Rumford Act, remedies that would end the prohibition of Blacks from residing in much of Los Angeles. The McCone Commission, created by Governor Brown to investigate the riots, cited the passage of Proposition 14 as one of three "aggravating events" that occurred in the year prior to the Watts uprising.[13]

Before the National Guard restored order in Watts, thirty-four people had died, more than one thousand were injured, and property damage was estimated at $200 million over six days of rioting.[14] From August 11 to 16, 1965, a shocked American public watched television clips of Black residents throwing debris at police; looting department, grocery, and liquor stores; and yelling, "Burn, baby, burn!" in rioting that far exceeded the violence of that in Harlem the previous summer. Nobody was more surprised by the detonation in Watts than Lyndon Johnson. Joseph A. Califano Jr., one of the president's top aides, recalled that a distraught Johnson was absolutely paralyzed and stunned by the Watts riots and withdrew "into the bosom of his family and friends" at his Texas ranch. He did not even return Califano's numerous phone calls—"the only time in the years I worked for Lyndon Johnson that this occurred," Califano said.[15] LBJ was fearful that the uprising would provoke white backlash, and he predicted that one of the political beneficiaries would be Ronald Reagan in his gubernatorial campaign.[16]

Once again, LBJ was right. In the predominantly white Los Angeles basin, pistol sales increased 250 percent in the days following the outbreak of violence.[17] Along with the protests at Berkeley, Watts eroded the credibility and popularity of Governor Brown. When the violence erupted, Brown was vacationing in Greece. By the time he arrived back in Los Angeles, on August 15, the Watts riots were at their peak, and sniper fire impeded his ability to tour the curfew zone. Speaking to reporters, a nonplussed Brown said the Watts riots were "unbelievable" and "beyond my comprehension."[18]

In the harrowing days after the riots, Brown's temporizing and confusion contrasted with the tough stance of the bombastic Los Angeles chief of police, William H. Parker. Parker had catapulted himself to national notoriety with his provocative and racist attacks on Black rioters as lawless deviants and his broadsides against civil rights leaders who "coddled criminals" and Blacks in general as "lazy, welfare cheats who were work-averse people."[19] As part of Governor Brown's blue-ribbon commission tasked with analyzing the causes of the Watts riots, Parker maintained, "Someone threw a rock, and like monkeys in a zoo, they all started throwing rocks."[20]

The potent combination of the Watts riots and the enduring anger over the Rumford Act helped shape the contours of Reagan's candidacy into a backlash-based campaign in which he would opportunistically stress the racially charged issues of "law and order," riots, and crime.[21] Reagan blamed the Watts riots on Blacks' dependence on government and the "philosophy that in any situation the public should turn to the government for answers."[22] Meanwhile, the racial issue continued to fester as Blacks continued to pour into the Golden State in search of jobs, opportunity, and the California dream, but many whites felt they were ruining the state. One white Hollywood electrician—a lifelong Democrat—planned to vote for Reagan because "these people [Blacks] burn and loot and get killed in riots and we give them money, . . . and they don't want to work."[23] By the end of 1965, it was becoming apparent that race was the wedge issue that facilitated Reagan's appeal to white working-class voters who had typically voted for the Democratic Party.[24] Having fled the crime of Los Angeles for the suburbs, these voters were resentful that Governor Brown and other liberals were quick to sympathize with the rioters and blame the police for the problems of the inner cities.[25]

Meanwhile, Governor Brown was bemused by Reagan's entrance into the political fray. He relished the possibility of facing Reagan, convinced he could easily portray the former actor as a political lightweight who consorted with Birchers. On racial issues, the contrast between Brown and Reagan was stark. Like Nelle and Jack Reagan, Brown's mother had inculcated in young Pat a strong sense of racial tolerance. Unlike Reagan, however, Brown never abandoned his commitment to racial equality. Only four months after his first gubernatorial inaugural, in 1959, Brown signed the Fair Employment Practices Act, which forbade businesses and labor unions from discriminating against employees and job applicants based on race.[26] A few months later, Brown signed the Unruh Civil Rights Act, named for Assembly Speaker Jesse Unruh, which went beyond other states' civil rights laws to outlaw racial discrimination in public accommodations and businesses.[27] In May 1961, Brown's donation of $100 to help fund the Freedom Riders sparked an uproar among his Southern colleagues at a governor's conference, but Brown remained unbowed and dedicated himself to making California the most racially progressive state in the nation.[28]

Brown perceived the passage of Proposition 14, which overturned the Rumford Fair Housing Act, as a personal rebuke. His signing of the Rumford Act, on June 21, 1963, had been the capstone of his civil rights legacy. Working closely with Black assemblyman William Byron Rumford, Brown expended considerable political capital fighting for the groundbreaking legislation. Brown, reminiscing about how hard he lobbied trying to end discrimination in housing, said, "I wanted to do the idealistic thing and I felt that blacks not being able to get houses . . . was an absolute disgrace. . . . I don't think I've lobbied for anything harder than I did for the Rumford bill."[29] Teeming with pride over its passage, he called it "one of the great victories of his career."[30]

When the Rumford Act was passed in 1963, a political firestorm immediately ensued. The mighty forty-thousand-member California Real

Estate Association (CREA) sprang into action, spearheading the drive to overturn the law.[31] Within months, CREA had marshaled enough signatures to put in place Proposition 14, the initiative to repeal the Rumford Act.[32] Brown campaigned against Proposition 14, decrying it as a "vicious" law designed by a "vigilante committee" that constituted a "blow to decency" and a victory for "prejudice and bigotry."[33] An increasing percentage of Northern whites were finally acknowledging the evil of Southern segregation, yet a 1963 Gallup poll found that 78 percent of white people would still leave their neighborhoods if many Black families moved in.[34] Not surprisingly, the campaign for Proposition 14 attracted support from hundreds of thousands of homeowners, many of them living in the path of the ghettos' expansion into neighboring blue-collar suburbs such as Southgate, Huntington Park, Lynwood, Walnut Park, and Bel Gardens.[35] One white blue-collar woman typified the overriding hostility when she angrily told an interviewer, "Don't ask me about civil rights . . . If I had a gun, I'd kill every nigger on this block."[36]

After California voters approved Proposition 14, citizens throughout the state flooded Reagan with letters about Brown's support of the Rumford Act. One Hollywood resident wrote:

> My family and our two sons and daughters in law all voted for Brown in the last two elections—(6 votes) all Demos.
>
> We are all voting for you this time. We expect no miracles, but Mr. Brown's stand on 14 finished him with us. There is one issue in the campaign—forced housing—if you can hammer on nullifying the Rumford Act—you will be elected, please push on that issue.
>
> Every Democrat that is turning to you is strictly for that reason, that is the ones I talk to.[37]

Reagan insisted that Proposition 14 had nothing to do with race and racism but maintained that it constituted an unwarranted infringement upon private property rights. The *Los Angeles Times* scoffed at Reagan's denial, writing, "Anyone who thinks that [Proposition 14] isn't about the racial issue just hasn't been paying attention."[38] James Flournoy, a prominent Los Angeles Black Republican, admonished Reagan, saying that every time he called for the repeal of the Rumford Act, "you are automatically slapping one million Negroes in the face."[39] Above all, the passionate opposition to fair housing and the fear of Black rioters enabled Reagan to invade traditional Democratic constituencies and reshuffle political loyalties in California.

Reagan also took advantage of the protracted turmoil accompanying the Free Speech Movement (FSM) at the University of California, Berkeley, as further evidence of Brown's incompetence. The issue of student unrest at the Berkeley campus highlighted Reagan's populist themes of attacking young student protestors and the overall liberal views of the Berkeley campus communities as "filthy," "radical" and "anti-American," who posed a grave threat to American values of patriotism, law and order, and morality. This line of attack riled up taxpayers, who funded the public university.[40] The FSM had grown out of the civil rights movement, which added a racial subtext to Reagan's fusillades against the university. Mario Savio, the founder of the FSM, had participated in civil rights activism in the Bay Area.[41] His political consciousness deepened after his firsthand experience with terror as a Freedom Summer volunteer in Mississippi in 1964, which spurred his turn to political activism on the college campus.

As the 1964 fall term began, Savio and other student veterans of the civil rights struggle staffed outdoor information tables along a twenty-six-foot-wide area known as the "Bancroft Strip." There they highlighted news from Mississippi and mobilized against Proposition 14. The Bancroft Strip became the spot where civil rights activists sought volunteers and donations. It was also where students and their allies had protested the racial agenda of Barry Goldwater and his delegates at the Republican convention held in nearby San Francisco the previous summer. In mid-September, after investigators from the conservative *Oakland Tribune* informed the university that the Strip was owned by the university and therefore could not be used for political purposes, university president Clark Kerr ordered its closure.[42]

The university's attempt to close down the Bancroft Strip created an immediate uproar. Having risked his life during Freedom Summer, Savio took the ban on free speech personally, and he and other young activists perceived it as an attempt to undermine the civil rights movement. For the rest of the fall semester, the FSM roiled the Berkeley campus, launching massive campus protests that helped define a generation of student activism across the US and around the world. By the end of the term, hundreds of students had been arrested for occupying the administration building. In addition, key administrators had been replaced and university rules were changed to establish an area, Sproul Plaza, where political activity could occur. Reagan would angrily tout the mess at Berkeley as emblematic of the failure of the liberal establishment to maintain law and order.

THE PRIMARY CAMPAIGN: REAGAN AND THE WHITE BACKLASH

By the time Reagan launched his campaign for governor, on January 4, 1966, white backlash had become a dominant force in American politics and a threat to the reigning liberal order. Reagan's announcement speech was taped at his home before a crackling fire and then distributed to reporters.[43] The gist of the speech concerned Reagan's standard talk about cutting taxes and warnings about the growth of big government. However, he saved his sharpest rhetoric for the issue of crime, affording him the opportunity to tout his "law and order" rhetoric. With the raw memory of the Watts riots gnawing at the California electorate, Reagan shrewdly incorporated racially coded language when he declared, "Our city streets are jungle paths after dark, with more crimes of violence than New York, Pennsylvania, and Massachusetts combined."[44]

In the early weeks of his campaign, Reagan was still plagued by controversy surrounding his support from the right-wing John Birch Society. He told reporters, "Any members of the society who support me will be buying my philosophy. I won't be buying theirs."[45] Reagan's unwillingness to repudiate the extremist organization that peddled conspiracy theories continued to bedevil his nascent campaign. California's Republican Party had been beset by bitter rifts between the Earl Warren pro–civil rights wing and the budding conservative wing of the party, which was centered in the booming suburban metropolis of Orange County. By the mid-1960s, Earl Warren, the former Republican governor of California, had been chief justice of the US Supreme Court for over a decade and had earned the wrath of Reagan and other conservatives for leading a judicial revolution on civil rights. In the California Republican primary, Reagan faced a challenge from former San Francisco Mayor George Christopher, an Earl Warren–style Republican. Like his fellow San Franciscan, Governor Pat Brown, Christopher had amassed a stellar record on civil rights as mayor of San Francisco. He had once even offered baseball star Willie

Mays the upstairs bedroom in his residence after a San Francisco realtor had refused to sell to Mays because he was Black.[46]

Reagan's incipient political career was nearly derailed when the usually even-tempered actor lost his composure while being pressed on his civil rights views. The revealing incident occurred the evening of March 5, 1966, at a debate before the California branch of the National Negro Republican Association (NNRA) in Santa Monica. Reagan appeared with Christopher and another primary opponent, William Patrick. The NNRA had been created in response to Black Republicans' revulsion over Goldwater's opposition to civil rights, and Reagan had been reluctant to accept the invitation.[47] Still recuperating from a severe viral infection, a weary Reagan's discomfort at appearing before such an unsympathetic audience was further exacerbated by Christopher's recent charges that Reagan was a right-wing extremist. Even though Reagan had abandoned any pretense of seeking support from Blacks, aides convinced an ailing Reagan to attend, because his absence would reinforce an impression that he was what his opponents said he was.[48]

From the outset of the debate, Christopher hammered Reagan on his civil rights record and stressed that *he*, Christopher, would have voted for the Civil Rights Act of 1964 and Voting Rights Act of 1965. A visibly irritated Reagan responded with a rambling statement that vaguely condemned racial bigotry but adding that he opposed the Civil Rights Act because, he said, it was poorly written. Once elected governor, Reagan went on, he would look to the private sector, not the government, for solutions to racial injustice. But drama ensued after Ben Peery, a Black Los Angeles businessman, rose from his seat and asked Reagan, "How are Negro Republicans going to encourage other Negros to vote for you after your statement that you would not have supported the civil rights bill?"[49] Taken aback, Reagan stammered and, flustered, denied he was a racist. As to the substance of the question, Reagan said he supported the goals of the Act but, without elaboration, criticized the Bill as a "bad piece of legislation." Reagan then defended Barry Goldwater as an outstanding human being, stating, "If I didn't know personally that Barry Goldwater was not a racist, I could not have supported him."[50] Patrick, waging a long-shot bid for governor, chimed in, calling Reagan's civil rights views "indefensible."[51]

Christopher then rose from his seat and contrasted his support for civil rights legislation with Reagan's embrace of "states' rights." For Christopher

and others who supported civil rights, Reagan's claims of personal decency were no substitute for federal legislation to dismantle Jim Crow.
The former San Francisco mayor, who headed Nelson Rockefeller's 1964
presidential campaign, accused Reagan of besmirching the Republican
Party by his unwillingness to disassociate himself from avowed racists
and the extreme John Birch Society. "The position taken by Goldwater
did more harm than any other thing to the Republican Party," Christopher charged, "and we're still paying for the defeat. . . . Unless we cast out
this image, we're going to suffer defeat now and in the future."[52]

In response, Reagan, his face flushed, angrily threw down his note
cards and stormed off the stage vowing to "get that S.O.B."[53] Watching
from the sidelines, Reagan's press secretary, Lyn Nofziger, was alarmed
and chased after Reagan, advising him to go home and settle down.
Nofziger later drove to Reagan's house and pleaded that he return to the
hotel where the NNRA delegates were having a cocktail party, insisting
that his failure to do so would send a message that he did not like Blacks.
Reagan agreed and, upon his return, summoned his usual charm and
met with delegates individually, apologizing for his behavior. He maintained that his irritation was not directed at Black people but at Christopher's implication that he was a racist.[54]

For about a week, Reagan's campaign advisors fretted that the outburst at the NNRA convention had derailed his political career in its
infancy. Fearing that Brown would do what LBJ had done to Goldwater—that is, paint Reagan as a temperamental political extremist unfit
for high office—Reagan's strategists, Stuart Spencer and Bill Rogers, ex-
peditiously moved to quell the brewing crisis. Nofziger issued a press
release explaining, as Reagan had to the delegates, that Reagan's walkout
was not directed at the NNRA but rather at "the insinuations of other
candidates that he was a bigot."[55] This did not stanch the flood of critical
press coverage. Paul Conrad, an editorial cartoonist for the *Los Angeles
Times*, drew a cartoon of a headless Reagan with the caption "Where's
the Rest of Me?," a reference to the title of Reagan's recent ghostwritten
autobiography. The cartoon so incensed Reagan that he contacted the
Times publisher, Dorothy Chandler, demanding that Conrad be fired.[56]
Hoping to keep Reagan's misstep in the news, Christopher provided the
transcripts of the debate to reporters and feigned sympathy for Reagan
calling him a "temperamental and emotionally upset candidate."[57] Polls

taken after the incident revealed that Reagan's lead over Christopher had eroded virtually overnight. Reagan's initial, contradictory efforts to explain the walkout had proved fruitless.[58]

The commotion, however, quickly vanished. On March 16, another outbreak of violence occurred in Watts, drawing attention away from Reagan's gaffe and back toward Governor Brown's problems. A turf war between Hispanic and Black youths sparked the latest bout of unrest, resulting in two deaths, approximately twenty injuries, and forty-nine arrests. The *Los Angeles Times* reported that fear gripped the region only seven months after the first riots.[59] Reagan denounced Governor Brown for leaving the state after having been notified about the possibility of trouble in Watts. Christopher, on the other hand, said, "It was wrong to blame all of society or all Negroes [for the riots]."[60]

As the June primary loomed, racial issues hovered over the political landscape. One of the most noteworthy developments was Reagan's surprising surge in popularity among white working-class Democratic voters who had previously supported both Brown and LBJ but who had also overwhelmingly voted for Proposition 14. Then, on May 10, 1966, the California Supreme Court ruled Proposition 14 unconstitutional and rejected the argument of Reagan's personal attorney and Kitchen Cabinet member, William French Smith, that the people of California had a right to discriminate.[61] The fact that five unelected justices overturned the votes of 4.5 million Californians reignited the issue just a month prior to the primary. Appearing at the Pomona Fairgrounds before a group of supporters, Reagan condemned the court's decision as contrary to the opinions "the people expressed in the 1964 election regarding the rights of property owners." He continued, "All of us are losers if we allow this precedent to be established."[62] Although Reagan's initial reaction may have been somewhat measured, a few weeks later, before an enthusiastic crowd of white voters, Reagan tied the ruling to the Watts riots, blaming the "arson and murder" on the architects of the Great Society. As for Proposition 14, Reagan said, "I have never believed that majority rule has the right to impose on an individual as to what he does with his property. It has nothing to do with discrimination. It has to do with our freedom, our basic freedom."[63] In the final days before the primary, Reagan's lead over Christopher widened as he continued to rail against the Rumford Act.

On June 8, 1966, Reagan routed George Christopher in the Republican primary, garnering a whopping 77 percent of the vote. Despite having received more votes than Governor Brown, who survived a primary challenge from conservative Los Angeles mayor Sam Yorty, the *New York Times* editorial page predicted California voters would come to their senses and grant Brown a third term.[64] On the whole, blacks were aghast that California Republicans, the party of the legendary former governor and chief justice Earl Warren, had chosen Reagan as their gubernatorial nominee. Jackie Robinson, a Rockefeller Republican, called Reagan's primary victory "a tragedy."[65] The *Baltimore Afro-American* excoriated Reagan for "having exploited to the full the so-called white backlash to win the California Republican gubernatorial nomination."[66]

Like many of Reagan's future political foes, Pat Brown had initially underestimated Reagan as a mere B movie actor. In an attempt to undermine Christopher's campaign, Brown's campaign leaked to the press news that Christopher, owner of a small dairy farm, had been convicted in 1940 of a misdemeanor for buying milk from Marin County farmers in violation of California's milk price-fixing laws. By the time Reagan vanquished Christopher in June, Brown's associates acknowledged that Reagan was a skillful campaigner who had tapped into the anxieties of a large swath of the electorate. It became apparent that Brown was vulnerable on social issues, especially race, and his political operatives worried that the governor had moved too far and too fast on civil rights.[67] To appease these concerns, Brown awkwardly, and suddenly, announced, "Law enforcement, not racism, had become the overriding issue in the campaign."[68] A month after the primary, Brown skipped the opening of the first movie theater in Watts, an event that his staff had arranged to highlight Brown's commitment to rebuilding Watts.[69]

In looking forward to the fall matchup against Reagan, the Brown campaign had ample cause for anxiety. Millions of white working-class voters in the sprawling suburbs of Southern California had voted for the Democratic Party because a large percentage of them had come from the traditionally Democratic South and the rural West, another Democratic stronghold, bringing with them small-town ideals, religious evangelicalism, and support of the racial status quo. The ferment of the 1960s was straining their allegiances.[70]

Much to the dismay of Pat Brown, Gallup polls indicated that most Americans thought that the Johnson administration was pushing too hard on civil rights.[71] Furthermore, the beginning of large-scale dissent over the Vietnam War was fracturing the unwieldy New Deal coalition. Less than two years after political pundits wrote conservatism's obituary, the *Saturday Evening Post* editorialized, "It seems like the air of unreality is settling over us all. For, very clearly things are not what they had seemed two years ago."[72]

THE FALL CAMPAIGN: THE TEST OF THE WHITE BACKLASH

Reagan's first campaign dovetailed with the advent of the Black Power movement, which reverberated across America in the summer of 1966. Its calls for Black autonomy, pride, and empowerment struck a chord with a restless generation of young Blacks mired in cycles of poverty, angry over the prospect of being sent to Vietnam, and impatient over the glacial pace of the nonviolent phase of the civil rights movement. Not long after the fiery and provocative Stokely Carmichael assumed the leadership of the Student Nonviolent Coordinating Committee (SNCC), the national press seized on Carmichael's defiant declaration of Black Power at the Meredith March in June as a new, even sinister Black militancy.[73] The *Times* indicted Black Power as a racist philosophy that preached segregation in reverse."[74] By the summer of 1966, polls showed that race riots and crime had supplanted the Vietnam War as the greatest concern of the American people, and public support for addressing the problems of Black America had waned.[75]

The rancorous debates in California over Proposition 14, beginning in 1963, were one among many harbingers of how difficult it would be to redress racism even outside the South. As W. E. B. Du Bois correctly noted, "The Negro Problem is not the sole property of the South."[76] Dilapidated housing in segregated ghettos, mass unemployment, and gross disparities in public education and employment all made a mockery of the term "equality." In January 1966, Martin Luther King Jr. launched a campaign in Chicago in hopes that nonviolent protest could succeed in eradicating slums in the North, as it had done in shattering Jim Crow in the South. King's campaign floundered in the Windy City in the face of opposition from Chicago mayor Richard J. Daley and his powerful urban political machine, resistant to change from outside agitators. Throughout the wrenching ordeal, King and his supporters came up against a wall of opposition when they marched in the all-white neighborhoods of Gage Park and Marquette Park and in the middle-class suburban neighborhood of Cicero. After someone in an angry mob hit King on the head with a rock, he remarked, "I think the people of Mississippi ought to come up to Chicago to learn to hate."[77]

This new phase of the Black freedom struggle offered an opportunity for conservatives to make a case against the movement without being forced to support Jim Crow segregation. The fervid opposition to King's campaign in Chicago, along with Reagan's passionate opposition to the Rumford Fair Housing Act, reflected middle-class whites' unwillingness to "sacrifice their neighborhoods" and tax dollars for further investment in Black America. In the fall of 1966, Reagan's ascendant gubernatorial campaign and the specter of white backlash was the big story in American politics—and a symbol of resurgent Republicanism. On October 3, 1966, Republican National Committee chair Ray Bliss said in a news conference that the party's slate of candidates would highlight the race issue, because polls demonstrated a large number of Americans were gravely concerned about urban uprisings.[78] Public opinion polls reflected the unstable mood in the country over civil rights. A Gallup poll conducted in September 1966 reported that white resistance to the pace of civil rights had reached its highest point in years, with 52 percent of all adults believing that the Johnson administration was pushing civil rights too hard.[79] In October, *Newsweek* revealed even more startling news: 70 percent of whites felt the cause of political equality was being pushed "too fast" in America.[80]

In California, the bloc of moderate Republicans who had rallied around George Christopher's candidacy was overmatched in its bid to prevent Reagan from overturning Earl Warren's civil rights legacy. After California Republicans bowed to Reagan's demand to oppose the Fair Housing Act, and at the same time voted down a plank condemning "extremism," the *Los Angeles Sentinel* retorted:

> Mr. Reagan is rapidly assuming the stature as the outstanding American spokesman for racism although he pleads he is not a racist. His private estimate of his own attitude is a matter of little concern to those

Americans who are interested in the achievement of equality for all Americans. What is important is what he says and how he acts when attempts are made to insure equality.

Judged by his actions alone, and discounting his words of self-praise, Mr. Reagan cannot be distinguished from Governor George Wallace of Alabama. If Governor Wallace is to be judged as a racist because of what he does (and it must be borne in mind that he denies he is a racist), then that same standard of judgment condemns Ronald Reagan.[81]

At the same time, a Harris poll conducted in August 1966 revealed that 46 percent of white Americans would be opposed to a Black family moving next door.[82] Reagan was clearly tapping into racism widespread in the electorate. During Reagan's mid-September campaign swing though the conservative Central Valley, resentment among the farmers over Brown's support of the Rumford Act was palpable. One of Reagan's ecstatic supporters was an elderly white woman who said, "Governor Brown has ruined the state" with his passing of the Rumford Act. "We had a nice home, but the Negroes come right next to you."[83]

Having defeated Richard Nixon for California governor in 1962, Brown was a tough politician, and he realized at this point that he was in for the fight of his political career. One of Brown's tactical retreats to the center on civil rights was signing a bill that toughened penalties for inciting a riot. He also announced that he would consider amendments to the Rumford Act.[84] For a brief period, this ploy appeared to reap some dividends. Just before Labor Day, Reagan's lead in the polls dwindled to only 3 points.[85] Then, a riot erupted in the predominantly Black Hunter's Point neighborhood in San Francisco on September 26, 1966, halting whatever momentum Brown had gained from his belated attempts to appear tough on crime. In a scene eerily reminiscent of the Watts riots, vandals broke windows, overturned cars, and looted stores after a white police officer shot and killed a Black youth suspected of stealing a car. Brown interrupted a campaign swing and flew to San Francisco to help calm the waters. Traveling with the governor on the plane, journalist Bill Boyarsky recalled Brown's despair as he lamented that he was now "disliked by Negroes as much as whites."[86]

The Hunter Point uprising subsided quickly, but it served as a reminder of the racial unrest that had engulfed the state during Brown's tenure. Once again, Reagan pilloried Brown for his lack of leadership, accusing him of having learned nothing from Watts and warning him not to "reward" the looters, while at the same time, Reagan castigated Black leaders for urging civil disobedience.[87] The beleaguered Brown disparaged Reagan "for speaking on something he had never dealt with his entire life."[88] A few days later, a beaming Reagan appeared on the cover of *Time*, and the magazine not only praised him for capitalizing on the public's desire for "law and order" but also touted him as a potential presidential candidate in 1968.[89] Polls taken after Hunters Point showed Reagan regaining his comfortable lead in the race.[90] In the final weeks of the campaign, a disciplined Reagan relentlessly pounded Brown for the spike in crime and the upsurge in race riots but denied that the white backlash was any part of his campaign.[91]

When Reagan heard that Black Power firebrand Stokely Carmichael was scheduled to speak at Berkeley, his campaign smelled blood. On October 18, Reagan wired Carmichael, urging him to cancel his appearance at the university, and issued a press release, demanding that Brown join him in insisting that Carmichael stay away.[92] Brown responded by denigrating Reagan's ploy as "cynical or stupid or both," and he accused Carmichael and his radical friends of being opposed to "peaceful progress," who are doing "everything they can to defeat me and elect Reagan." Speaking at a Republican rally, Reagan said, "We cannot have the university campus used as a base from which to foment riots."[93] Reagan's stunt aside, Carmichael presented his concept of Black Power on October 29 to approximately ten thousand people at the Greek Theatre, electrifying the crowd of Berkeley students as he bellowed against the Vietnam War.[94] Even though Carmichael's visit was without incident, the publicity Reagan brought to his appearance just days before the election helped to reinforce Reagan's message that Brown and the liberal administrators at Berkeley were on the side of Black militants and unable to maintain order on campus.

On November 8, 1966, Reagan crushed Brown by almost a million votes. Reagan's triumph was duplicated by Republican victories throughout the nation. In a striking comeback from its devastating defeat two years earlier, the GOP captured forty-seven seats in the House of Representatives, three in the Senate, and eight governorships. The electorate delivered a stinging rebuke to the Johnson administration's Great

Society, its handling of the Vietnam War, and the riots. Two days after the election, a disconsolate Lyndon Johnson held a press conference where he evaded the issue of white backlash, ascribing the Democratic Party's loss to three popular Republicans in the big states of Ohio, Michigan, and California.[95] In his private musings to aides, however, he struck a different chord, saying, "I don't think I lost the election. I think the Negroes lost it." He predicted that the backlash would "move beyond George Wallace and become respectable."[96]

In California, the Democratic Party's divisions over the Vietnam War, the electorate's frustration over Brown's handling of the "mess at Berkeley,"[97] anger over high taxes, and overall fatigue with Pat Brown all factored into Reagan's triumph. Reagan also proved to be a sensational campaigner. But the pivotal role that race played in Reagan's first political victory cannot be overstated. Polls indicated that three out of four people who voted for Reagan indicated that they'd done so to protest the racial unrest of the past few years. Polls also revealed that "crime, drugs, juvenile delinquency" were the most pressing problems confronting the state, with "racial problems" second.[98]

Only weeks after his bitter defeat, Brown remarked, "Whether we like it or not, the people want separation of the races."[99] Years later, he reflected, "People always felt that I was too friendly with blacks anyway. They just tarred me with it and said, 'Put a guy in there that'll put these colored guys in their place.'"[100] Brown's lamentations were confirmed by the fact that even though Reagan defeated Brown by nearly a million votes, Reagan won a mere 5 percent of the Black vote, far lower than Nixon had in 1962 when he lost to Brown.[101]

After all of his achievements in furthering California's postwar economic boom with his programs to construct freeways, install vast water systems, and expand the largest public university system in the world, Pat Brown was crestfallen over losing to Reagan, whom he'd derided as a mere actor. Of the flood of sympathetic letters and telegrams that poured in after the election, none consoled Brown more than the one that came from one of his Republican predecessors, Earl Warren, whom he revered. "Nina and I voted for you two weeks ago and since then have been praying that there would be enough thinking voters in California to ensure your reelection," Warren wrote. In a swipe at Reagan, the chief justice and former California governor said to Brown, "Someday the people of

California will comprehend how silly and shadowy was the campaign to unseat you."[102] Perhaps no other single person had been as responsible as Chief Justice Warren for ensuring that the Constitution's protections would be applied to African Americans. Little could Warren fathom that Reagan would soon lead the campaign to undermine the landmark civil rights precedents that he had recently established.

The scale, scope, and contours of Reagan's triumph in the trend-setting state of California signified the splintering of the reigning postwar liberal order on the treacherous shoals of race, the emergent counter-culture, and the escalating war in Vietnam.[103] The politically shrewd Richard Nixon, who had been humiliated in his bid to unseat Brown in 1962, beheld Reagan's successful thumping of his old rival with a mixture of awe and anxiety. In the throes of planning his own political comeback, Nixon was impressed by Reagan's success in virtually every white working-class suburb in Southern California, and it would provide the blueprint for Nixon's bid for the presidency. He also saw the charismatic Reagan as a formidable opponent for the Republican nomination. For Reagan, his die-hard supporters, and, most importantly, his wealthy Kitchen Cabinet, Reagan's gubernatorial campaign had ignited a "prairie fire" they hoped would sweep the nation and propel him to the presidency in 1968.

CHAPTER 4

REAGAN'S 1968 RACE FOR THE PRESIDENCY

"Law and Order" and the Southern Strategy

> *When a Hollywood performer, lacking distinction even*
> *as an actor, can become a leading warhawk candidate*
> *for the presidency, only irrationality induced by a war*
> *psychosis can explain such a melancholy turn of events.*
>
> —Martin Luther King Jr., on Reagan's
> presidential candidacy (November 11, 1967)[1]

R eagan's stunning victory over Pat Brown during the 1966 midterm elections was the most electrifying political story of the year. For millions of white Americans, Reagan's confidence, and tough "law and order" campaign rhetoric, including his stern attacks on unruly student protestors, radical hippies, and their Black radical allies, seemed to be the antidote to the tension and uncertainty gripping the nation. Days after his victory, the *New York Times* noted that the profusion of "Reagan for President" banners that filled his election headquarters "underscored his sudden injection into the national Republican picture." While Reagan dismissed talk of the presidency as premature, the *Times* mentioned that Reagan "conspicuously stopped short of any of the historical renunciations of presidential interest."[2]

For years, Reagan brimmed with optimism, convinced it was God's plan for him to be elected president and lead a conservative movement that would restore America's greatness. Reagan had always cast his sights beyond Sacramento. After all, his two abiding preoccupations—combating Communism and shrinking the federal government—were issues well beyond the purview of California state politics. Stanley Plog, an advisor to Reagan's gubernatorial campaign, recalled, "The primary thing was to educate him on the politics and issues of California because all along, that guy has been focused on national politics. He always wanted to be president, not governor."[3]

Only nine days after the election, Reagan convened a group of advisors at his Pacific Palisades home to discuss strategy for a possible bid for the 1968 Republican nomination. At the prodding of his campaign spokesman, Lyn Nofziger, and Thomas C. Reed, his Northern California campaign chair, Reagan approved the hiring of F. Clifton White, the brilliant political guru and delegate counter who had masterminded Barry Goldwater's capture of the Republican nomination in 1964.[4] White enthusiastically enlisted, because he sensed that Reagan's appealing personality and fresh face would pose the most formidable challenge to President Johnson in 1968.[5]

Reagan sanctioned the development of a meticulous strategy to capture the Republican nomination. Reed and White decided to schedule appearances in states where Nixon's support among delegates was weak and avoid states with upcoming primaries; this way, Reagan's presence would not convey the impression that he was actually running for president. Having just been elected as governor of California, Reagan had to avoid the appearance that he was hankering for higher office. In an appearance on the ABC news program *Issues and Answers*, he said, "I have a four-year contract with the people of California."[6] Still, he never issued an outright denial of his intention to run for president. In an interview just prior to the Western Governors' Conference in June 1967, Reagan said, "If the Republican Party comes knocking at my door, I won't say, 'Get lost, fellows.'"[7]

Despite his disavowals and his refusal to run in any primaries, Reagan ran a spirited "favorite son" campaign for the 1968 Republican nomination, hoping to win support from the party power brokers. Amid the racial turmoil and urban rebellions of the long, hot summer of 1967, in which there were dozens of riots, and through August 1968, Reagan campaigned throughout the country, thrilling loyal Republicans at $100-a-plate dinners by thundering against the welfare state and blaming the civil rights movement and radical Blacks for fomenting riots. In his effort to deny Nixon a victory on the first ballot, Reagan targeted Southern power barons such as Strom Thurmond, barnstorming throughout the South, where he electrified whites with his law-and-order rhetoric and comparisons of Black militants to Hitler Youth.[8]

Though Nixon eventually won the Republican nomination and the presidency, Reagan's oft-overlooked 1968 campaign anticipated his future appeal in the South, his inimitable skill in exploiting racial resentment without appearing racist, and the ascendancy of the Goldwater wing of the Republican Party anchored in the South and West.

1967: LAYING THE GROUNDWORK FOR A PRESIDENTIAL BID

Reagan's political inexperience and his lack of familiarity with California issues were repeatedly raised by the media and his political opponents. Seldom in the annals of American political history had a more inexperienced politician assumed such a difficult and complex task as governing the twenty million inhabitants of the Golden State. Not long after the election, Reagan was asked what kind of governor he would be. In response, he quipped, "I don't know! I've never played a governor."[9] Weeks into his administration, it became evident that Reagan was more interested in his national ambitions and bored by the mundane details of the job, which he turned over to his young aides. Consequently, there were rumblings in the halls of the capitol about "the acting governor," and some Republican legislators moaned, "He is a presence, not a Governor."[10]

Reagan's ascension to the governorship sent shockwaves throughout Sacramento. Other than a handful of archconservatives, most state officials had dismissed Reagan as a lightweight politician and resented his demonization of state government. Ever since World War II, under the aegis of the administrations of Republican governors Earl Warren and Goodwin Knight and Democrat Pat Brown, California state government was characterized by a bipartisan progressivism that helped spur its extraordinary postwar growth and development. Despite their different party affiliations, Democrats and Republicans united to construct a vast infrastructure of freeways, bridges, highways, aqueducts, and canals, as well as internationally renowned universities and colleges, that composed the backbone of California's booming economy. Sacramento's political culture of bipartisan cooperation was key to the creation of California's Golden Years.[11]

Reagan's meteoric political rise brought about a profound rupture in Sacramento. On the advice of Nancy Reagan's astrologer, Jeane Dixon, Reagan took the oath of office at precisely 12:01 a.m. on January 2, 1967.

In a symbolic move, Pat Brown, who had infuriated Reagan by appointing more than eighty judges in his waning days in office, was excluded from the inauguration.[12] In his early months as governor, Reagan continued to infuriate legislators with his antigovernment rhetoric. For Blacks and the poor, he offered no support whatsoever. At the same time, his Kitchen Cabinet had enormous sway over his staff's selections for key appointments. One of its members, the drugstore magnate Justin Dart, boasted he could get Reagan on the telephone any time he wanted.[13] After Nancy Reagan complained that the governor's mansion was "a wooden firetrap" and a "tinderbox" that was not up to her standards, the Kitchen Cabinet purchased a twelve-room Tudor manor home in one of Sacramento's fashionable neighborhoods that was more suitable for the Reagans, and then rented it to them at a bargain price.[14]

Although Reagan never jettisoned his harsh campaign rhetoric, his presidential ambitions forced him to govern in a moderate and pragmatic fashion. Without the support of the Democrats, who controlled both houses of the state legislature in Sacramento, Reagan would have no legislative accomplishments, and he would have nothing to talk about on the speaking tours Reed and White scheduled for him. His failure to achieve any tangible legislation would cast doubt on his fitness for the presidency.

Perhaps the most telling illustration of Reagan's pragmatism in his first year in Sacramento was his signing of the Therapeutic Abortion Act. Prior to the Supreme Court's 1973 decision in *Roe v. Wade*, abortion was not the galvanizing issue that it would become for the conservative movement. A July 1966 poll conducted by California pollster Mervin Field indicated that 72 percent of Californians favored liberalizing abortion laws.[15] After much vacillation and anguish, Reagan finally signed the bill on June 15, 1967. It gave women more reproductive rights than any other state, until the passage of *Roe v. Wade*.[16] A decade later, after the rise of the powerful anti-abortion movement to the forefront of conservative politics, Reagan issued a mea culpa about signing the bill and endorsed a constitutional amendment that banned abortions.

Futhermore, Reagan compromised on the most important challenge he confronted in the early days of his administration: passing a budget. Reagan had loathed "confiscatory" taxation since the 1940s, and his broadsides against "spendthrift" Democrats in Sacramento had been a staple of his campaign rhetoric against Pat Brown. When he assumed office, Reagan was confronted with the reality that Brown had left a massive budget deficit. But instead of cutting the budget in line with his stated economic agenda, Reagan approved a mammoth $1 billion tax increase, the largest tax hike by any governor in the history of the United States—and over four times larger than Brown's tax hike, in 1959.[17]

Within days of his inauguration, Reagan signaled his willingness to adhere to his campaign promise to repeal the Rumford Fair Housing Act when he appointed staunch conservative Burton E. Smith, the former president of the California Real Estate Association, to be the state's next real estate commissioner angering the civil rights community.[18] At an April 18, 1967, press conference, Reagan reiterated his intention to repeal the Rumford Act, stating, "If revision could solve the problems of [Proposition] Fourteen, I could go for revision," and adding, "If the legislature passed a bill to repeal the Rumford Act, I'll sign it."[19] But Reagan's hopes of repealing the Rumford Act suffered a fatal blow on May 29, 1967, when the US Supreme Court ruled in *Reitman v. Mulkey* that Proposition 14 was unconstitutional. In his concurring decision, Justice William O. Douglas proclaimed Proposition 14 was "a form of sophisticated discrimination whereby the people of California harness the energies of private groups to do indirectly what they cannot under our decisions allow their government to do."[20] Still, Reagan would not let the matter die. He declared, "It is now up to the legislature to change the Rumford housing act, in accord with the will of the people of California."[21]

Given Reagan's focus on the state budget and establishing a solid record to support his bid for the presidency, the fate of the Rumford Act became less of a priority after the *Reitman v. Mulkey* decision. Years later, Republican Assembly leader William T. Bagley, whose compromise bill on the Rumford Act had passed the Assembly, recalled that Reagan's chief of staff at the time, Phil Battaglia, had told him, "We wouldn't mind if you killed the repeal bill."[22] In the final hours before the 1967 California legislature recessed for a month, efforts to repeal the act collapsed after an Assembly–Senate conference committee was unable to reconcile the two competing bills.[23] Two days after the legislative session adjourned, Reagan announced that a special session to reconsider the revision of the Rumford Act was unlikely.

Reagan's handling of the matter pleased nobody. A week after the effort for repeal died in the legislature, six staunchly conservative legislators from Orange County told the *Los Angeles Times* that the "inability of the two houses to make any changes in the Rumford Fair Housing Act had so far been Reagan's greatest failure."[24] In late September, in a speech before the annual CREA convention, Reagan was still roiling the waters when he decried open housing laws as an infringement on a basic human right and renewed his vow to fight for the Rumford Act's repeal in the next legislative session.[25] Ultimately, however, Reagan failed to take the initiative in repealing the Rumford Act. In 1979 Reagan told an interviewer that he reversed his position after meeting with members of the Black community in March 1968, and he "realized the symbolism of [the act] . . . and how much it meant morale-wise to [Blacks]."[26] Reagan's sudden realization of the injustice of racial discrimination failed to assuage Blacks' anger over his months, even years, of barnstorming through the state, inveighing against the Rumford Act. Many viewed his volte-face as an insincere and politically motivated attempt to further his presidential prospects.

Reagan's pragmatism on policy matters did not impede him from maximizing the symbolic and politically beneficial issue of the "mess at Berkeley." With the assistance of Reagan's longtime supporter J. Edgar Hoover, the university's Board of Regents ousted the powerful University of California president, Clark Kerr.[27] The firing of Kerr, the architect of California's Master Plan for Higher Education of 1960, shocked the public. Days after Kerr's firing, 767 faculty members—about one half the total at the Berkeley campus—rebuked the Reagan administration and the Board of Regents for their "destructive political intervention" in university affairs. Following the faculty vote, thousands of students protested Kerr's dismissal.[28]

A few months later, Kerr presciently observed, "There was a serious possibility" that Reagan could be elected President of the United States because he "is excellent on television, a factor which is becoming more and more crucial in presidential elections."[29] Meanwhile, Reagan continued his stealth bid for the Republican nomination.

"LAW AND ORDER" AND REAGAN'S 1968 SOUTHERN STRATEGY

After the California legislature recessed in August, Reagan's compromise on the budget with the Democratic-controlled legislature led to a slew of effusive articles. In spite of the lawmakers' dislike of Reagan's amateurish grasp of governance and his regal demeanor, Democratic pollster Don Muchmore concluded that Reagan's legislative accomplishments were so impressive that "by Californians' judgment, Reagan's presidential possibilities are considered improved."[30]

Following Reed and White's timetable, Reagan barnstormed the country in the fall with high-profile speaking appearances in states where Nixon's delegate support was considered shaky. Reagan's bid was quixotic, because Nixon had already received commitments from a large number of political brokers, including the influential Strom Thurmond, but Reagan privately asked two powerful Southern Republicans, Senator John Tower and Governor Claude Kirk, to refrain from endorsing Nixon.[31] From the beginning, White and Reed stressed that Reagan should go "hunting where the ducks are," in the South. The combination of his gauzy patriotism, staunch militarism, "law and order" rhetoric, and attacks on Black militants struck a chord in the South, which would become the heart of Reagan's support.

The potency of Reagan's calls for "law and order" was enhanced by the spasm of racial unrest that convulsed Detroit, Newark, and more than one hundred other cities during the "Long, Hot Summer" of 1967. Like the Watts riots two years earlier, the Detroit and Newark uprisings shocked the nation, casting further doubt on the viability of liberalism. The riots seemed to vindicate the belief of opponents of residential integration that Blacks were not yet ready for the full perquisites of citizenship, and that future programs aimed at alleviating the conditions of the ghetto were pointless. By the time the uproar in the Motor City subsided, on July 28, more than forty people were dead, seven thousand had been arrested, and over $50 million in property damages had been sustained. The conflagrations prompted President Johnson to appoint the National Advisory Commission on Civil Disorders, known as the Kerner Commission, to investigate the causes of the riots.[32]

The causes of the riots in Detroit, Newark, and other Northern cities were rooted in decades of structural racism, which governments at the local, state, and federal levels had designed and sanctioned. In addition, redlining and other real estate practices kept neighborhoods segregated and reinforced the profound racial disparities in education, employment, and income levels.[33] As in the Watts uprising in 1965, the racial unrest was often sparked by profound rage over incidents of police brutality, which was endemic in the ghettos. As was his wont, Reagan ignored the institutional racism and anger over the conditions of the ghetto, characterizing the strife as simply "riots of lawbreakers" planned by "provocateurs."[34] Seventy-one percent of Americans agreed with Reagan's assertion that the riots were "mainly organized."[35] The riots further spurred the politics of the white backlash and corroborated the view that Black pathology, not structural racism, caused crime. In September, a Harris poll revealed that 82 percent of respondents endorsed Reagan's statements advocating a "firm hand" in dealing with the recent racial disturbances.[36] Martin Luther King Jr., however, brooked no sympathy for the white backlash, claiming it stemmed from either white racism or a lack of empathy from the "ache and anguish" of Blacks' daily struggles in the ghetto.[37]

Buoyed by the same Harris poll that showed Reagan had an 80 percent approval rating, on September 29, 1967, Reagan ventured to the friendly terrain of Columbia, South Carolina, to speak at a Republican Party fundraiser. Billed as the largest political fundraising event in state history, more than 3,500 white Southerners paid over $100 a plate to hear Reagan's speech, which television cameras beamed to homes throughout the South. After a fulsome introduction from Strom Thurmond, who called him "one of the leading figures in the world today," Reagan received an "enthusiastic reception" and further endeared himself to South Carolinians by clearing up their state Republican Party's debt. He skirted the issue of the South's segregationist history, stating, "There are those who feel that just passing laws is an answer to the problem, but to me it's not that simple." However, instead of elaborating on how segregation could have been outlawed, he attacked welfare moochers. Reagan, like Thurmond a former Democrat, said the Democratic Party "left us when it decided that a few men in Washington knew better than we do what is good for us."[38]

Reagan did not have to tell the South Carolina Republican convention the obvious: Thurmond left the Democratic Party in 1964 over LBJ's support of civil rights. Thurmond was the avatar of the Republican Party's Southern strategy and the most powerful Southern Republican kingpin, and his support was key to Reagan's presidential prospects. Even though Thurmond had informally pledged his support to Nixon, Thurmond's support of Nixon was not ironclad, and his slavish praise of Reagan was a testament to his infatuation with him.

To Blacks, Reagan's courtship of Thurmond reinforced their belief that Reagan was the foremost cultivator of the backlash. The *Baltimore Afro-American* denounced Reagan's embrace of the "bitter-ended segregationist Strom Thurmond" and slammed Reagan as another Goldwater who was "clearly not interested in the support of black voters."[39] While Thurmond and other Dixiecrats might have felt like welcomed newcomers to the Republican Party, Republican Edward Brooke of Massachusetts, the first Black senator since Reconstruction, deemed "law and order" a slogan with racist undertones that served as a reminder to white America to keep Blacks in their place. "You can't say that the Negro left the Republican Party," Brooke argued, adding, "I'm convinced that the Negro feels like he was evicted."[40]

Reagan was one of the most sensational stories of the 1966 election cycle, but the success of a slew of newly elected Republican moderates such as Senators Brooke, Charles Percy from Illinois, and Mark Hatfield of Oregon, and the newly reelected Governor George Romney of Michigan, spurred party officials to increase their outreach efforts to the African American electorate. The year 1967 was the peak of power for the moderate wing of the Republican Party since the Eisenhower presidency. On racial issues, the moderates were bent on preserving their heritage as the party of Lincoln and were determined to exorcise the ghost of Goldwater.[41] Many of them initially rallied around the candidacy of George Romney, a handsome, square-jawed former automobile executive who had just been elected to his third term in Michigan. Romney's supporters believed that his political appeal in Michigan could be replicated in the other crucial battleground states of the industrial Midwest and Northeast. A Harris poll taken two weeks after the 1966 midterms showed Romney defeating Lyndon Johnson by 54 percent to 46 percent, far outpacing any of his potential rivals for the Republican nomination.[42]

On civil rights, Romney and Reagan could not have been more different. A Mormon, Romney, the father of 2012 Republican presidential nominee Mitt Romney, had resisted an appeal from authorities in his church to oppose the Civil Rights Act of 1964. He addressed a Mormon congregation calling for "a stepped-up citizen campaign to eliminate social justice based on race and color," when the Church of Latter Day Saints forbade Blacks from entering the priesthood.[43] His appeal to African Americans was viewed as an antidote to the Goldwater fiasco—Romney had even written a twelve-page letter to Barry Goldwater, explaining that he had not "supported the national ticket because the Goldwater campaign had, by design, a 'Southern-rural white orientation.'"[44] After the Detroit riots, Romney embarked on a twenty-day, seventeen-city tour of the ghettos across the country, and he called for cuts in the space program and military spending, as well as a "drastic revision" of the budget, to finance a massive effort to combat "greater bloodshed and possible destruction of the nation."[45] The high hopes of Romney supporters were punctured after Romney returned from a fact-finding mission in Vietnam and fatally acknowledged that he had been "brainwashed."[46] The connotations of "brainwashing" raised questions about the Michigan governor's mental health and destroyed his once promising candidacy. Romney's early exodus left the Republican field barren of any civil rights supporters other than Nelson Rockefeller, but of all the remaining presidential hopefuls, Reagan occupied the most right-leaning plank on civil rights.

In December, Reagan spent four days at Yale University as the recipient of a Chubb fellowship. Despite the cool reception and spate of hostile questions from Ivy Leaguers fuming over Reagan's hawkish support of the Vietnam War, Reagan displayed his trademark wit and self-possession.[47] Michael C. Smith of the liberal Republican Ripon Society observed that the sole occasion Reagan became unruffled was when a student pressed him on civil rights. According to Smith, the student quietly said to Reagan that "whenever the Governor was asked about his position on civil rights, he would respond with stories about Jackie Robinson and Willie Mays, or about Negroes he had appointed to certain boards. But what substantive program," the student asked, "did the Governor recommend as a solution?" Reagan's response was so vague and evasive that it gave the listeners the impression he really had not given that too much thought."[48] Robert L. Coate, Northern California chair of the California Democratic Party, had a much harsher view of Reagan, stating, "Reagan handles racism in such a manner that racists understand exactly what he is saying, without his having to spell it out for them."[49]

Richard Nixon agreed with Pat Brown that Reagan was an extremist and intellectual lightweight, and he regarded the prospect of a Reagan presidency as calamitous for both the Republican Party and the nation.

Yet, at the same time, Nixon was awestruck at Reagan's rapid political ascent.[50] Ever since Reagan had vanquished Pat Brown, who had easily defeated Nixon for California governor in 1962, the former vice president had brooded privately that Reagan posed the gravest threat to his presidential nomination. Nixon's worst nightmare was that the combination of Rockefeller's strength among moderates in the industrial North, with Reagan's "favorite son" status in the California delegation, as well as his natural strength in the South would deprive Nixon of a victory on the first ballot, thereby creating a brokered convention and enabling the charismatic Reagan to win the nomination on the second ballot. In a campaign memo, Nixon conceded Reagan's personal charisma but stressed that he thought Reagan's strength was derived primarily from the "ideological fervor of the Right and the emotional distress of those who fear or resent the Negro and who expect Reagan somehow to keep him 'in his place'—or at least to echo their own anger and frustration."[51]

When Nixon declared his intention to campaign in the states that held primaries and Reagan refused, the notion of the former vice president's inevitability increased. For the time being, this decision dashed the hopes of Reagan's faithful supporters.[52] Political reporter David Broder described Reagan's damp prospects by noting his aides' "fatalistic" attitude "almost to the point of naiveté" over Reagan's refusal to declare his candidacy, because he believed that "events would order themselves." One Republican colleague of Reagan's told the *Washington Post*, "Ron honestly believes that God will arrange things for the best," but his supporters "who made him Governor are willing to give God a hand in making him President, and they're not too happy with the slowdown."[53]

1968: THE STEALTH CANDIDACY CONTINUES

Reagan's refusal to enter any of the Republican primaries did not signify the end of his presidential dreams. He continued to crisscross the country, addressing Republican audiences and holding frequent campaign meetings with staff, and his supporters geared up to snatch delegates in non-primary states. Nevertheless, he continued to deny he was a candidate. Reagan's elusive quest for the Republican nomination became more earnest after Senator Robert Kennedy, a man Reagan had loathed since the Kennedy-led Justice Department hauled him to testify before a grand jury in the anti-trust case against MCA, announced his candidacy

in March.[54] By then, Reagan was offering himself as the charismatic conservative counterpart to Kennedy, a man who petrified Reagan and other
conservatives with his skill in galvanizing Blacks, other people of color,
and the poor. Heeding the advice of Reed and White, Reagan staked out
the most conservative positions on the burning issues of the day—civil
rights and the Vietnam War—in hopes of winning over Strom Thurmond and other Southern party chieftains. A Harris poll conducted in
mid-January revealed just how effective Reagan's brand of racial conservatism was in the crucial states of the Old Confederacy.[55]

By the beginning of 1968, the civil rights movement had reached a
crossroads. Like the rest of the country, it was buffeted by internecine
debates over the Vietnam War. With the ghettos exploding with Black
nationalists vowing violence and the promises of the Great Society being "shot down on the battlefields of Vietnam," Martin Luther King Jr.
was depressed and exhausted.[56] Having been mercilessly vilified from all
sides for speaking out against the war, King and his Southern Christian
Leadership Conference decided to embark on the Poor People's Campaign and planned a march of a multiracial coalition of poor people to
Washington, DC, to dramatize their plight and demand anti-poverty
legislation.[57] Reagan dismissed the Poor People's Campaign as a "fraud"
and a "hoax," and after the protestors constructed a shantytown of tents
on the National Mall, Reagan insisted on its forcible removal if the leadership refused to close the encampment once its permit expired.[58]

In the meantime, the Kerner Commission released its blockbuster
report on February 29, 1968, in which it attributed the cause of the riots
to white racism, not Black anger. The report famously concluded, "Our
nation is moving toward two societies, one black, and one white—separate and unequal." In order to avert an imminent catastrophe, the commission urged "a commitment to national action on an unprecedented
scale," including a massive infusion of aid to cities across the nation, and
it recommended the passage of the Fair Housing Bill, which had been
languishing in Congress.[59] Reagan and other conservative apostles of law
and order were angry over the Kerner Commission. At a press conference a few days after the release of the report, Reagan lashed out at the
commission's finding that white racism was the cause of the riots and
accused the Kerner Commission of failing "to recognize the efforts that
have been made by millions of right-thinking people in this country."[60]

Reagan added fuel to the fire when he reiterated his view that the Rumford Act should be amended.

In early March, King diverted his attention from the Poor People's Campaign and came to Memphis to lead a strike on behalf of the city's sanitation workers, who were demanding a living wage. On April 4, 1968, an assassin's bullet felled King, sparking a new wave of racial disturbances in more than a hundred cities across the nation that left a trail of death and destruction in their wake. Not since the Civil War had the nation experienced such widespread domestic violence. President Johnson, who had recently announced the shocking news that he would not be seeking reelection, planned to address the nation and announce his intention to revive the stalled Fair Housing Act.[61]

On the afternoon of King's assassination, Reagan had flown to Washington, DC, where he was scheduled to deliver a speech the following day at a luncheon for the Women's National Press Club, at the Hilton Hotel.[62] His arrival coincided with the outbreak of rioting and looting that engulfed the nation's capital moments following the news of King's murder. In spite of the mayhem, Reagan refused to cancel the appearance and followed the example of other politicians like New York mayor John Lindsay and Robert Kennedy, who both urged calm and helped avert further rioting. As rioting went on in Washington, Reagan nonetheless spoke at the luncheon, where his introductory remarks sent the crowd into twitters of laughter with his jokes about movie stars and governors. Then, he moved to the issue of the spiraling costs of welfare. Reagan was twenty minutes into his talk before he mentioned King's assassination, saying, "The nation died a little Thursday night." Ward Just, a staff writer for the *Washington Post*, noted the irony of Reagan's light repartee at the luncheon against the looting and death transpiring only blocks away from the Hilton.[63] Back in Sacramento, Reagan's press secretary, Paul Beck, delivered a message from Reagan condemning King's murder, but added, "Dr. King's murder began with our first acceptance of compromise with the laws of the land," which implied that King was somehow responsible for his assassination by embracing civil disobedience to unjust laws.[64]

Reagan's conduct in the wake of King's assassination differed from the solemnity of his fellow presidential rivals. Citing security concerns, President Johnson did not attend King's funeral in Atlanta on April 9, 1968, though the president's anger over King's opposition to the Vietnam War also colored his decision. With the exception of Reagan and George Wallace, all of the other national political heavyweights were in attendance.[65] King's funeral, like that of President Kennedy, was a national spectacle broadcast live on all three major television networks and watched by 120 million Americans.[66] For the first time since its founding, in 1792, the New York Stock Exchange closed to honor the life of a private citizen. According to *Time*, the country had not "so deeply involved itself in mourning" since JFK's funeral, less than five years earlier.[67]

On the day of King's funeral, Reagan, the self-professed "noncandidate," continued politicking before an adoring all-white crowd at a Republican luncheon in Albuquerque, New Mexico.[68] Upon his arrival at the airport, Reagan spoke at a news conference and echoed the words of his press secretary in calling King's assassination "a great tragedy that began when we began compromising with law and order and people started choosing which laws they'd break." In a curious segue, he added, "It seems possible that [King] was betrayed because he wasn't traveling fast enough." In a follow-up question, reflecting that the assassin was not yet known, a reporter pressed whether Reagan was implying that Dr. King's murderer might have been Black. Reagan said no, that he meant the crime might have originated among "those who want dissent and insurrection."[69] In a similar vein, Strom Thurmond released the following statement to his South Carolina constituents: "We are now witnessing the whirlwind sowed years ago when some preachers and teachers began telling people that each man could be the judge of his own case."[70] Reagan's message was clear: he agreed with the 31 percent of Americans who felt King was a rabble-rousing, Communist liar who was responsible for his own assassination.[71]

While Reagan continued to campaign in the days after the assassination, his rivals' hiatus from politicking resumed. The *New York Times* reported Reagan's "noncandidacy" was gathering steam due to indications of renewed interest on the part of New York governor Nelson Rockefeller for a third presidential bid.[72] On April 30, Rockefeller recanted his recent decision not to join the race, citing King's assassination as the reason and stressing that he was the only Republican who could heal the nation.[73] The reentry of Rockefeller stoked Nixon's anxieties, which were intensified after Reagan traveled to New Orleans and Miami, Reagan's seventh extended political trip since September. In spite of his continuing

Southern charm offensive, Reagan's meeting in New Orleans with 334 delegates from twelve Southern states, half of what he needed to win the nomination, was disappointing because the delegations felt he was "protesting his candidacy too much" and preferred that he formally announce his candidacy.[74]

Regardless, word of Reagan's Southern solicitation prompted an anxious Nixon to swoop down to Atlanta to court the same contingent of Southern Republican Party chieftains, who had earlier agreed to vote for him as a bloc at the upcoming Miami convention. After realizing his entreaties were not well-received—many of the old Southern Democrats now voting as Republican were leery of Nixon for his early support of civil rights initiatives and were now besotted with Reagan. Nixon persuaded Strom Thurmond, who had earlier agreed to support him, to fly down to Atlanta for a face-to-face meeting in which the powerful senator agreed to deliver the crucial southern bloc in exchange for Nixon's promises to appoint strict "constructionist judges" to the federal court and to consult Thurmond on his vice presidential decision.[75] After the meeting, the previously neutral Georgia Republican chairman G. Paul Jones introduced a jubilant Nixon as the man "who could lead us to the White House." Other powerful Republican Party chairmen from Virginia, Mississippi, North Carolina, and Florida followed suit, affirming their support for Nixon even though their hearts longed for Reagan. Three weeks later, Thurmond gave Nixon his official, long-coveted endorsement.[76]

In the face of Nixon's apparent lock on the Republican nomination, an undaunted Reagan, still convinced his nomination was "God's will," continued his elusive bid. His views on civil rights endeared him to Southerners, but they did not play well with moderates. One of them, Republican governor John A. Love of Colorado, brooded that the surge in racial violence might hand the nomination to an unelectable Reagan.[77] At a luncheon in Miami on May 22, Reagan got in a shouting match with an African American woman who charged the Florida GOP was run on a "for-whites-only basis." When pressed on a racial issue, once again, Reagan lost his composure and snapped back, saying that by supporting liberals, Blacks were delivering themselves "to those who have no other intention than to create a Federal plantation."[78]

The assassination of Senator Robert F. Kennedy on June 5, moments after he declared victory in the California Democratic Primary, was another traumatic and shocking event in a year when the entire world seemed to be veering into chaos. Kennedy's campaign for the presidency galvanized Reagan, who loathed Kennedy and feared a reprise of the 1960 Nixon-Kennedy matchup.[79] Blacks, however, felt differently. Following King's assassination, African Americans transferred their hopes onto Robert Kennedy. According to journalist Jack Newfield, King's murder "enabled Kennedy to glimpse the deeper roots of America's internal disease," racism, and to "imagine himself as the healer of that disease."[80] On the evening of King's assassination, Kennedy's moving and impromptu speech in Indianapolis calling for unity between Blacks and whites helped avert a riot and offered the nation hope of healing the racial divide. Kennedy's political evolution from Joseph McCarthy protégé to champion of civil rights and the downtrodden was the inverse of Reagan's political trajectory of abdicating the racial liberalism of his youth by cozying up to George Wallace supporters.

THE MIAMI CONVENTION: HUNTING FOR DUCKS IN DIXIE

Given Reagan's visceral contempt for Kennedy, the assassination temporarily deflated Reagan's zeal for the nomination.[81] After a few weeks, however, he rededicated himself to the goal of denying Nixon a victory on the first ballot by attempting to unshackle the former vice president's hold on the Southern delegations. The only politician rivaling Reagan's support in the South was George Wallace. Only two weeks after George Wallace buried his forty-one-year-old wife, Lurleen, who had been elected Alabama governor as a placeholder for her husband, Wallace resumed his third-party presidential campaign. Many Blacks familiar with Reagan's ability to camouflage his racist policies, were alarmed by Reagan's political momentum. Writing in the *Los Angeles Sentinel*, for example, African American columnist A. S. "Doc" Young editorialized, "The truth of the matter is most Negroes would almost quickly vote for George Wallace, Alabama's bantam bigot, than for Gov. Reagan."[82] Wallace's foray into the 1968 presidential race presented Reagan with the knotty challenge of distancing himself from some of Wallace's noxious rhetoric without alienating the Alabamian's legion of loyal supporters and ideological soulmates whom Reagan hoped would propel him to the nomination.[83] While Reagan did not subscribe to Wallace's demagogic populism and his rhetoric was shorn of Wallace's racist epithets, Reagan rivaled Wallace as the foremost practitioner of the politics of white backlash. At a June 25, 1968, press conference, the normally glib Reagan struggled to walk this tightrope. In response to a question as to whether he agreed with Governor Rockefeller's characterization of Wallace as a racist, Reagan said he had never met Wallace and thus didn't "know what his attitudes are or [what] his feelings are."[84] Following Reagan's announcement on July 16, 1968, of a six-day swing through the South, a reporter asked him whether he could draw a distinction between himself and Wallace on racial issues. Again, Reagan stonewalled, saying the "best move" Wallace supporters could make was to switch their support to a Republican.[85] Reagan's response was clear: he was the Republican Party's answer to George Wallace.

The architects of Reagan's "noncandidacy" still harbored hopes that Reagan's star power and charisma could catapult him to the Republican nomination if a combination of Reagan's Southern support and Rockefeller's strength among moderates could only stop Nixon from winning on the first ballot.[86] Reagan decided to take his campaign through the South. He relished the opportunity to campaign in the Old South, which he would tout as the national repository of conservative values.[87]

On July 19, 1968, Reagan, along with a bevy of aides, boarded a plane to Amarillo, Texas, for a five-state swing through the heart of Dixie in a last-ditch effort to unshackle some of Nixon's soft support in the South. Traveling through Amarillo, Little Rock, Birmingham, Charlottesville, and Frankfort, Kentucky, Reagan spoke in front of enthusiastic crowds imploring Wallace supporters not to throw away their votes.[88] In his meetings with Southern delegates, Reagan was heartened by the number of times they told him they would abandon Nixon if Reagan were to officially declare himself a candidate.[89] Reports that Reagan's efforts had achieved measurable gains in the delegations of Alabama, Florida, and Texas, and that North Carolina Republican gubernatorial hopeful James Gardner had shifted from a pro-Nixon stance to one of public neutrality, occasioned House Minority Leader Gerald Ford to speculate on the possibility that the convention would go to a second or third ballot.[90] *Newsweek* reported Nixon's delegate count had slipped to 591, when he had 650 a month earlier and needed 667 to win.[91] On the eve of the convention, Reagan's charge through Dixie dispelled early predictions of a Nixon coronation.

On July 31, Reagan interrupted his Southern campaign swing and appeared at the Republican National Convention platform hearings in Miami. He elicited cheers from the usually staid committee when he blasted the findings of the Kerner Commission, stating, as he had in the past, "We must reject the idea that every time the law is broken, society is guilty rather than the law breaker."[92] Reagan's remarks incited a rare public rejoinder from Chief Justice Earl Warren, who chided those who viewed rising crime with "self-righteous indignation and oversimplification."[93]

With the convention set to convene the following Monday, rumors swirled over the weekend that Nixon was poised to offer the vice presidential nomination to a liberal like Rockefeller, New York mayor John Lindsay, Vietnam War critic Senator Mark Hatfield, or Senator Charles Percy, all of them anathema to Southerners. A Nixon supporter, the Mississippi power baron Clarke Reed, acknowledged that talk of Nixon naming a liberal running mate "scares the hell out of us," and "individual delegates are getting shaky."[94] David Broder, writing for the *Washington Post*, reported of Nixon's struggle "against increasing odds" to keep the Southern delegations from bolting to Reagan and pitting senior party officials against grassroots delegates.[95]

A palpable air of excitement pervaded the Republican National Convention in the sweltering Miami summer heat as House Minority Leader Ford called the proceedings to order. Hours later, the atmosphere became electric when the broad-shouldered Reagan strode up to the podium and formally announced he was a candidate for the presidency. Harry Dent, Strom Thurmond's political aide and an architect of the Southern strategy, recalled how "lightning struck. I have been in politics for I don't know how many years and I have never seen anything like it."[96] On the other hand, Reagan's official entrance was not a surprise since he had been running unofficially for months. Liberal New Mexico governor David Cargo wisecracked, "It's like a woman nine and a half months pregnant announcing she's going to have a baby."[97]

Like most Southerners, Strom Thurmond was awestruck by Reagan; Reagan spoke his language. But the old Dixiecrat feared a vote for Reagan would be tantamount to a vote for the despised Rockefeller, and he had grown exasperated by Reagan's coyness in failing to announce his candidacy. A newcomer to the Republican Party, Thurmond did not want to be marginalized in his new party like he had been in his old party. At sixty-five, Thurmond was done with "lost causes" and wanted an ally in the White House. Almost singlehandedly, Thurmond doused the flames kindled by Reagan's last-minute charge and acted with alacrity to hold the Southern line for Nixon.[98] By all accounts, Thurmond's Herculean efforts saved Nixon. Other conservative figures, such as Senators Barry Goldwater and John Tower of Texas, deemed Reagan unelectable and did not want to turn the convention into a bloodbath.[99]

Ultimately, Nixon's superior political machine overcame Reagan's late charge, enabling him to prevail on the first ballot with 697 votes and continuing his ongoing Lazarus-like resurrection from political oblivion after a razor-thin defeat for the presidency in 1960 and a humiliating loss to Pat Brown in 1962. Reagan finished third, with 182 votes, behind Nelson Rockefeller, who received 277 votes. Reagan's political guru, F. Clifton White, a political legend renowned for his ruthlessness in steering Goldwater's nomination in 1964, marveled at the great job "Nixon's forces did of organizing at the convention." Still, White called Reagan's efforts "a near miss" that almost cracked the Southern line.[100] Until the final hours before the vote, Reagan was relentlessly searching for delegates.[101] In defeat, Reagan was heartened by his faith: "The good Lord knows what He is doing. This wasn't our turn."[102]

After the national headiness and heady excitement of the Miami convention, an exhausted Reagan returned to Sacramento.[103] His disavowals that he ever campaigned for the presidency came quickly. At a press conference on August 13, 1968, Reagan incredibly said, "There was never a presidential bug in my system."[104] Over the years, both Ron and Nancy Reagan denied that Reagan ever ran for president in 1968. Writing to a supporter in 1976, Reagan claimed that his last-minute announcement was a "myth" and never did he believe that "a former actor who had only been a governor a matter of months could suddenly say he wanted to be President."[105] Reagan's protestations of his non-candidacy were certainly news to his political aide Thomas C. Reed, who had devoted nearly two years of his life tirelessly working behind the scenes to make Reagan president.[106]

Reagan's quest for the presidency in 1968 furnished important lessons for his future runs for the White House. He continued to consolidate his appeal in the South, and he continued to exploit hot-button issues such as campus unrest, busing, and affirmative action and to elevate the racially charged issue of welfare to the forefront of his agenda. Never again would he run a dilatory, half-hearted campaign. In his future runs, he would appear before the voters in all of the primaries, where he would deploy his charm and charisma to personally woo wavering delegates. His abortive bid in 1968 was his "dress rehearsal," laying the foundation for his "near miss" in 1976 and his ultimate victory in 1980.[107]

CHAPTER 5

THE PERFECT TARGETS

Black Radicals and Welfare Moochers

*Listening to Ronald Reagan it is possible to imagine that blacks
or Chicanos or Indians do not really exist in California—except
as welfare chiselers or threats to family and property.*
—*New York Times* (October 1970)[1]

Richard Nixon narrowly defeated the Democratic Party nominee, former vice president Hubert Humphrey, and George Wallace to win the
presidency in 1968. The likelihood that Nixon would seek a second term
in 1972 put the fifty-seven-year-old Reagan's presidential aspirations in
abeyance. Reagan returned to Sacramento having to settle for the less
glamorous task of governing California. From his perch as governor of
the nation's most populous state, the charismatic Reagan remained the
darling of the conservative movement. His standing among conservatives was burnished by a series of highly publicized contretemps with the
Black Panther Party (BPP) and other Black radicals who sought to purge
the deep-seated racism embedded in California's college campuses and
woven throughout the fabric of American society.

By 1968, along with hippies and Berkeley protestors, Black political
militants joined the ranks of Reagan's perfect political foils. While many
college students were drawn to the BPP, and a smattering of white liberals
regarded them as "radical chic," their strong appeal to college students
alarmed not only conservatives but also millions of middle-class whites,
who perceived the group as a dangerous gang of criminals. The salience
of the BPP gave Reagan an opportunity to deflect attention from his own

record on race by depicting campus protestors and leading BPP figures as violent extremists bent on revolution. To this end, Reagan and other "law and order" conservatives succeeded in obscuring the BPP's efforts to defend Black communities from systemic police violence and provide basic educational and health services to communities that government agencies had forsaken. In spite of Reagan's pragmatic governance in a period when the Democrats controlled both houses of the state legislature, his incendiary rhetoric against student protestors, radical Black militants, and racially charged attacks on supposed welfare chiselers helped propel him to a second term as governor of California and solidify his standing as a future presidential candidate.

REAGAN VERSUS THE BLACK PANTHERS, ELDRIDGE CLEAVER, AND ANGELA DAVIS

By the late 1960s and early 1970s, the struggle for racial justice had begun to lack the moral clarity it had once had. The turmoil within the civil rights movement over Black Power and the daunting task of addressing the intractable issues of residential, educational, and economic inequality in the urban centers of the North and West left the civil rights movement divided, uncertain, and groping for a new strategy. To say the least, King's assassination left a profound emotional and spiritual void, which partially sparked the growth of the BPP. The Black Panthers and their revolutionary rhetoric for a time captivated the imagination of millions while providing an outlet for Black pride, empowerment, and cultural expression.

A marriage of campus unrest with the demands of radical Blacks aligned with the BPP erupted at a number of California schools in the late 1960s. Prior to his reelection bid in 1970, Reagan would be ensnared in highly publicized confrontations over issues of academic freedom with Eldridge Cleaver and Angela Davis, two of the most controversial and outspoken radical Blacks furnishing the "law and order" Governor Reagan with political gold. The vast majority of Californians sympathized with Reagan's mantra that either students "obeyed the rules" or "they should get out."[2]

By the fall of 1968, Black students in California's sprawling higher-education system demanded more inclusion, more representation in managerial and administrative positions, and a revamping of the curriculum to include Black studies programs.[3] The previous year, Harry

Edwards, a part-time sociology and anthropology professor at San Jose State College and a former discus thrower, had filed a protest with the university over racial discrimination in housing, fraternities, and campus social life, and he threatened to disrupt the school's season-opening football game against the University of Texas at El Paso. Fearing violence, the president of San Jose State College cancelled the game—the first time a football game had been cancelled in the US because of fears of racial unrest.[4] In an angry response, Reagan called the cancellation "an appeasement of lawbreakers" and declared Edwards unfit to teach. Edwards, in turn, called Reagan "a petrified pig unfit to govern," and he shortly thereafter began a campaign to get Black athletes to boycott the upcoming Olympics in Mexico City. Although the boycott did not happen, Edwards's campaign led to US Olympians Tommie Smith's and John Carlos's clenched-fist salute on the medal podium. Although the athletes' protest eventually became an iconic moment in the civil rights struggle, when they returned from Mexico City they were suspended from the US track team and were the recipients of numerous death threats. Most Americans appeared to agree with Reagan's characterization of Smith and Carlos as traitors for failing to salute the flag.[5]

In the fall of 1968, Black students engineered a new wave of student protests on California campuses. This put Reagan on a collision course with Black students, university administrators, and faculty.[6] In October of that year, Black students occupied the computer center at the University of California at Santa Barbara, demanding that the head football coach be dismissed, a Black Studies Department be created, and racial discrimination on campus be brought to an end.[7] The following month, Black students occupied the president's office at San Fernando Valley State College in Northridge, holding him and about three dozen employees hostage for close to three hours, resulting in the largest arrest of college students in US history.[8] After the acting president of the college granted amnesty to the protestors under duress, Reagan remarked that the protestors "should have been taken out of there by the scruff of their neck."[9]

That same month, the Black Student Union at San Francisco State College called a student strike that lasted until the following March and remains the longest campus strike in US history.[10] For five months, the strike shook the San Francisco Bay Area and garnered national headlines pitting Reagan, the Black Panther Party, local politicians, students, and the college faculty, administrators, and Board of Trustees in a highly public and contentious clash. The students were protesting the drop in Black enrollment to a mere 3 percent and the delay in the creation of a much-anticipated Black Studies Department.[11] But the spark that lit the students' fuse was the suspension of English instructor George M. Murray, a BPP member who had called for a student strike for November 6 for "defending the BPP's policy of self-defense and carrying arms and urged students to join the fight" to protect themselves from what he called the "white racist administrators."[12] Murray had recently been hired to work with four hundred disadvantaged minority students as part of an experimental program to raise their educational level. After his suspension, more than one hundred Blacks gathered on campus and succeeded in getting the faculty to refuse to teach classes.[13] On November 13, San Francisco State College's president, Robert C. Smith, called in hundreds of police in full riot gear to enforce order, but when a handful of students began throwing rocks and bottles, Smith decided to close the campus indefinitely.[14] The police's excessive use of force shocked many otherwise ambivalent students and increased their support for the strikers on campus. Murray's suspension also provided strikers with a vehicle to protest and illustrate the racism and authoritarianism embedded not only at San Francisco State College but also woven into the fabric of American society.

While most of the faculty supported President Smith's decision to close the campus, Reagan, trumpeting "law and order," demanded that Smith reopen the campus and vowed to restore order.[15] Unable to deal with the escalating crisis, Smith, who had vacillated on suspending Murray, resigned on November 26.[16] Reagan offered the job to English professor S. I. Hayakawa, an iconoclastic, diminutive Japanese American who wore a tam-o'-shanter and reveled in his public persona as a hardline administrator. Hayakawa's parents had been interned during World War II, and he had been a forthright supporter of civil rights as a columnist for the Black-owned *Chicago Defender*, but he supported Reagan's tough policy against student protest. On December 2, 1968, Hayakawa reopened the campus.[17] The following day, known as "bloody Tuesday," Hayakawa confronted a howling mob of students and pulled the wires out from the loudspeakers on a protestor's van and ordered police to remove the assembled strikers. Along with Hayakawa and San Francisco mayor Joseph Alioto, Reagan held a press conference announcing the arrest warrants for seven of the strike leaders. Throughout the ordeal, Reagan vowed to crush the strike.[18] Hayakawa became a conservative folk hero, which later catapulted him to the United States Senate.

The strike, however, continued. The turmoil was a political boon for Reagan. He repudiated strikers in strident language, and his uncompromising public comments garnered headlines overshadowing the strikers' legitimate demands.[19] At an impromptu press conference on January 5, 1969, he declared, "Those who want to get an education, those who want to teach, should be protected by the point of the bayonet if necessary," and asked the California legislature to assist in ridding California campuses of "criminal anarchists and latter-day Fascists."[20] In one of his most outrageous comments, Reagan maintained that "thirty-five Negroes" at San Francisco State College had attacked a university dean "with switchblades at his throat," forcing him to admit them to courses.[21] Though an investigation failed to substantiate the story, Reagan's tale generated more press than reports of its falsity.

Reagan considered maintaining scrutiny on the working habits of college professors to determine which members of the faculty should be dismissed for participating in the strike. He also suggested that political attitudes should become a criterion in the hiring process at California state colleges and universities.[22] Although the resolution of the strike, on March 20, 1969, did include the creation of a Black Studies Department, Reagan's uncompromising stance against the strike helped his overall approval rating rise to 78 percent, its highest since he had assumed office.[23]

Reagan had earlier thrust himself into another controversy at his bête noire, the University of California at Berkeley, just across the bay from San Francisco. This one had flared up after Berkeley's decision in September 1968 to hire the BPP's notorious Minister of Information, Eldridge Cleaver, as a lecturer for an experimental course on racism in the US.[24] Cleaver, whose stirring memoir *Soul on Ice* had been published to much fanfare, had become a lightning rod for criticism of the Black rebellion. The *New York Times* named *Soul on Ice* as one of its top-ten books for 1968, and it became the manifesto of Black Power masculinity.[25] Cleaver was a spokesperson for what it meant to be Black in America, and many Berkeley students applauded the news of his hiring. That said, Cleaver was a deeply compromised leader. He had already served eight years in prison for rape and, at the time of the appointment, was out on bail awaiting trial after a shootout with police that left seventeen-year-old fellow BPP member Bobby Hutton dead. Cleaver's history notwithstanding, university officials failed to foresee the firestorm generated by news of his appointment.[26]

Immediately following the announcement, the university received a flood of irate letters and phone calls. Both Reagan and his likely opponent for reelection, the powerful Democratic Assembly Speaker, Jesse Unruh, saw no intellectual merit in Cleaver's appointment.[27] Reagan demanded that the Board of Regents rescind the appointment and declared, "If Eldridge Cleaver is allowed to teach our children, they may come home one night and slit our throats."[28] For his part, during the controversy, the voluble and often outrageous Cleaver called Reagan a "punk, a sissy, and a coward."[29] Cleaver continued: "I challenge the punk to a duel to the death and he can choose his own weapon: it could be a baseball bat, a gun, a knife, or a marshmallow. I'll beat him to death with a marshmallow." Throughout the ordeal, the FBI, Reagan's longtime ally, ratcheted up tensions by mailing Cleaver's obscene rants against Reagan to university officials, alumni associations, and Rotarians to sway public opinion against granting Cleaver a forum for his speeches and diatribes.[30]

The Board of Regents convened an emergency meeting and, hoping to quell the uproar, decided to reduce the number of Cleaver's lectures from ten to one, but they refused to rescind the invitation entirely.[31] The Regents' peremptory action precipitated a meeting of the entire Berkeley Academic Senate, which rebuked the Regents for "usurping the judgment of the faculty members."[32] The civil rights community charged Reagan and the Regents with racism. Carlton Goodlett, publisher of the San Francisco Black newspaper the *Sun-Reporter*, threatened to launch a campaign to disassociate the Black middle class from all UC programs.[33] Anger on campus over the Regents' actions provoked a sit-in at Sproul Hall, the main administrative building, resulting in 122 arrests and a wave of demonstrations during the first week of classes.[34] Meanwhile, the UC Berkeley Academic Senate voted 668 to 114 to overturn the Regents' decision and allow Cleaver to present all ten of his lectures.[35] Over one thousand students signed up to listen to Cleaver, even though enrollment was limited to one hundred. For all the hubbub, Cleaver's first lecture, on

October 8, 1968, which was covered in all the major national newspapers, proved anticlimactic, with one attendee describing it as "scholarly" and "boring."[36] The controversy subsided after Cleaver jumped bail and fled the country for Algeria.

Although only a very small fraction of Californians subscribed to Cleaver and the BPP's revolutionary policies—including ending police brutality, exempting Blacks from military service, and calling for full employment and decent housing for Blacks—a majority of Berkeley faculty and students were sympathetic to revamping the curriculum to include courses on Black history and racism, and to increase the enrollment of Black students. They also resented Reagan and the Regents' usurpation of the faculty's role in the shared governance of the university.

Many Black Americans saw Cleaver and the BPP as providing a program to combat racism and imperialism. But for the majority of Californians, however, hoary issues of academic freedom paled in comparison to their conviction that Cleaver was a dangerous criminal. They agreed with Reagan that their hard-earned tax dollars should not be funding a university coddling such people bent on revolution, and they agreed with his crackdown on unruly students and liberal educators.

Still seething over the Berkeley community's embrace of Cleaver and sensing another opportunity to showcase his tough "law and order" policies, Reagan refocused his energy on a new uproar that arose in May 1969 after the university decided to develop a derelict 2.8-acre area a few blocks from campus. Although the university owned the property, local activists had become accustomed to using it as a "People's Park." The university's decision pitted it against local activists, many of them veterans of the FSM, whose political activism stemmed from the civil rights movement. After a series of clashes between protestors and police, at approximately 4:30 a.m. on May 15, 1969, also known as "Bloody Thursday," Reagan dispatched the California Highway Patrol and the Berkeley police department into People's Park to secure it. The presence of hundreds of police officers in Berkeley fencing the park sparked a noontime rally at Sproul Hall that drew three thousand protestors. In the middle of the rally, though, police turned off the sound system, and thousands of angry protestors marched to the park chanting, "We want the park!"[37]

As they approached the park, the protestors were met by about seventy-five police officers in riot gear. Within minutes, chaos and violence erupted after somebody opened a fire hydrant. Under the direction of Edwin (Ed) Meese III, Reagan's chief of staff and future attorney general, officers indiscriminately fired tear gas and buckshot into the fleeing crowds. Approximately 128 people were admitted to the hospital mostly for gunshot wounds. James Rector, a Berkeley student, was mortally wounded when the police shot him. Journalist Robert Scheer said Meese later told him that Rector "deserved to die."[38]

The next day, Reagan ordered three thousand National Guard troops to occupy the Berkeley campus. The Guard's helicopters dispensed tear gas that the wind dispersed over the entire city, sending children and the elderly to hospitals, killing a protestor, and blinding another.[39] The outrage against Reagan's brutal tactics was overwhelming. Even the conservative *Oakland Tribune* called the action "a piece of arrant recklessness" and accused the Oakland Police Department of introducing "a kind of storm trooper philosophy into the Berkeley confrontation."[40] An unrepentant Reagan famously told a farmers' convention held at Yosemite National Park, "If it takes a bloodbath, let's get it over with. No more appeasement."[41] Despite the criticism, Reagan's firm line on student unrest continued to be a politically popular move with middle-class white Californians. As a matter of fact, Reagan's poll numbers peaked in the beginning of 1969 and reached their highest point during his tenure as California governor.[42]

Next up for Reagan was Angela Davis. Ten months after Cleaver sought sanctuary in Algeria, a graduate student working as an undercover FBI agent identified Angela Davis, a twenty-five-year-old Black philosophy professor at the University of California at Los Angeles, as a member of the US Communist Party. Under Reagan's lead, the Board of Regents invoked an archaic 1940 rule against employing Communists and voted 19–2 to fire her at the end of the school year.[43] Under Reagan's leadership, the Regents overlooked state and federal court precedents that membership in the Communist Party did not disqualify a professor from teaching at a state university. When asked how he reconciled firing Davis with the Regents' prohibition of "political tests" for faculty appointments, Reagan responded, "Advocacy of communism with a small 'c' is different from membership in the Communist Party." This prompted one of the dissenting Regents, William M. Roth of San Francisco, to deride Reagan's rejoinder as "sophistry."[44] Among the other dissenting Regents, Fred Dutton, a close associate of Pat Brown's, bluntly characterized the decision as having derived from "a bunch of old men raising old issues, saying they believe in law and order and doing illegal acts."[45] Reagan's willingness to sacrifice freedom of speech on the altar of anti-Communist hysteria was consistent with his conduct as an enforcer of the Hollywood Blacklist.

Davis's firing catapulted her into the public spotlight, and in her lawsuits against UCLA over her firing, she ascribed racism as much as her Communist affiliation as the reason for her termination.[46] Many agreed with her, and over two thousand students and faculty members flocked to Davis's first lecture on Frederick Douglass at Royce Hall—UCLA's largest auditorium—after her firing was overturned.[47] On October 20, 1969, Superior Court judge Jerry Pacht ruled in Davis's favor, saying that her party membership did not justify her dismissal and calling the Regents' decision "terrifying," because it could logically be extended to enable the Regents to outlaw membership in any party out of power.[48] In the meantime, Davis resumed her job, and Reagan and his allies schemed to find another way to terminate her. The following June, Reagan, an ex officio Regent, joined a 15–6 majority in voting to dismiss Davis on the vague grounds that she had engaged in "inflammatory" rhetoric, when she spoke in four off-campus speeches on behalf of the so-called Soledad Brothers, three Black inmates charged with murder in the death of a guard at Soledad State Prison. The Regents also cited Davis's reproach of UC Berkeley educational psychologist Arthur Jensen, who wrote a spate of articles that attributed lower IQ scores of Blacks to "genetics" and not "environmental factors."[49] The decision was hard-won, because the Regents also conceded that Davis had not used propaganda on her students and that her political activities had not interfered with her teaching duties.[50] A few weeks prior to the Regents' decision, Reagan's personal lawyer (and US attorney general during Reagan's presidency), William French Smith, presided over a meeting of the Regents on the Davis matter, but they had already decided to fire her. One Regent, William M. Roth, boycotted the meeting, calling the outcome "predetermined" and a "star court proceeding . . . not in accordance with the best traditions of the Board of Regents."[51] Reagan took pains to stress that the firing was based on Davis's "unprofessional conduct" and not her party membership. But Regent Dutton took issue with Reagan: "A 26-year-old bookish black girl is surely no threat to our state or the traditional values that the overwhelming majority of us believe in." He went on to call Davis's rhetoric "anemic" compared to Reagan's "bloodbath statements and other frequent, intentional, publicly reported language that provokes and prolongs turmoil on our campuses and in our state."[52]

Davis's firing was the culmination of Reagan's consolidation of power over the Regents through his appointment of new Regents and changes in views in some of the Regents from the Pat Brown era.[53] His skillful articulation of the public's hostility against the university system's embrace of radicals became an issue in his reelection bid.

A few weeks after the Regents' decision, Davis was indicted, without evidence, for allegedly purchasing firearms that were used in a raid of the Marin County courthouse to free the Soledad Brothers. The raid ended in the death of a judge, two prisoners, and the seventeen-year-old inmate who had engineered the failed escape. Davis made the cover of *Newsweek* and the FBI's ten-most-wanted list. She called the charges a "frameup."[54] On October 13, 1970, she was arrested in New York City, and her eighteen-month incarceration sparked the nationwide "Free Angela Davis" movement. After one of the longest, costliest, and most controversial criminal proceedings in California history, an all-white jury in conservative Santa Clara acquitted Davis of all charges. Although Reagan vowed that Davis would never again teach in the University of California system, Davis taught at UC Santa Cruz from 1991 to 2008. She also became an advocate for overhauling the prison-industrial complex, which boomed amid President Reagan's War on Drugs, in the 1980s.

WELFARE MOOCHERS

Governor Reagan's stances on a host of hot-button issues such as Supreme Court rulings, busing, welfare, and taxes continued to infuriate Blacks and the civil rights movement. By the mid-1960s, fellow Californian Earl Warren, revered by Blacks for his role in leading a judicial revolution as chief justice of the US Supreme Court around civil rights, became a bogeyman of Reagan's allies in the conservative movement. During his campaign for governor in 1966 and for the presidency in 1968, Reagan lambasted the Supreme Court under Warren's leadership.

After Warren's retirement from the court, in 1968, President Nixon nominated Warren Burger, the chief judge of the Fifth Circuit Court of Appeals, to succeed him. Burger had not endeared himself to Blacks after delivering a number of speeches supporting Nixon's views on law and order.[55] Three months later, Nixon had the opportunity to fill another Supreme Court seat following the resignation of Justice Abe Fortas, who initially earned his towering legal reputation for his opposition to the internment of Japanese Americans during World War II. Nixon kept his promise to Strom Thurmond to name a Southerner to the court and nominated South Carolinian Clement F. Haynsworth Jr. Like Thurmond, Haynsworth was a Dixie Democrat who had turned Republican after the nomination of Goldwater. The selection of the South Carolinian stirred immediate outrage and mobilization from Blacks and civil rights and labor organizations.[56] Andrew Young, one of Martin Luther King Jr.'s closest aides, fretted that Haynsworth's nomination would "serve to turn back the clock of our history."[57] After reports surfaced that Haynsworth was a member of the racially discriminatory Commonwealth Club in Richmond, Virginia, the *Baltimore Afro-American* editorialized that the judge was "an unworthy and dangerous nominee for the Supreme Court."[58] After a protracted and intense battle, on November 21, 1969, the Senate voted 55–45 against confirming Haynsworth. It was the first time since 1930 that the Senate had voted down a nominee to the Supreme Court.[59]

Reagan was aligned with Nixon's decision to undermine the Warren Court's civil rights jurisprudence and had endorsed Haynsworth's nomination. After the Senate vote, Reagan released a statement calling it "regrettable that some senators who objected to this distinguished man were not able to rise above narrow political considerations." Without elaboration, Reagan said, "It is obvious that a proper balance must be restored to the Supreme Court," and he expressed his assurance that the "President will nominate a successor to the court that shares Judge Haynsworth's constitutional approach to the court."[60] Nixon next nominated another Southerner, G. Harrold Carswell, but after reports surfaced that Carswell had expressed support for white supremacy, the Senate rejected him too. In the end, the Senate confirmed Nixon's third nominee for the open seat, Federal Court of Appeals judge Harry Blackmun from Minnesota.

Nixon's record on civil rights was complicated. Although Nixon devoted seventeen campaign speeches to law and order, he never addressed civil rights in a major speech. Privately, he derided Blacks as "niggers," "jigaboos," and "jungle bunnies."[61] Unlike Reagan, however, Nixon was a supporter of civil rights during the 1950s and knew that legal segregation was finished. A few years into his administration, Nixon agreed with the view of Daniel Patrick Moynihan, a Democrat whom he had named as his top advisor on urban issues, that the polarizing issue of race could benefit from a period of "benign neglect." Moynihan urged the administration to focus on jobs, not race.[62] As president, Nixon sought a middle ground on civil rights by moving very slowly on integration of the public schools and housing, and he embraced a "suburban strategy" driven by "color-blind" arguments of individualism and free-market consumerism.[63] Notwithstanding Nixon's moderate record, his divisive rhetoric, particularly about crime, solidified his political standing among white Southerners and northern working-class white voters and helped transform Johnson's War on Poverty to his War on Crime.

Meanwhile, the issue of busing became an explosive topic in the nation's struggle to implement *Brown v. Board of Education*. Reagan became directly embroiled in the issue in February 1970 after a Los Angeles County Superior Court judge ruled that the Los Angeles Unified School District practiced segregation and ordered the district to prepare a desegregation plan by September 1, 1971, that would include busing. The *Los Angeles Times* characterized the decision "as the most significant court decision on racial discrimination outside of the South."[64]

In response to the Los Angeles ruling, Reagan fatuously claimed that California schools "have always been racially integrated."[65] He also released a written statement with more strident language, blasting the decision as "utterly ridiculous" and criticizing mandatory busing as shattering "the concept of neighborhood schools as the cornerstone of the educational system."[66] Reagan's legal staff supported the school board's appeal of the ruling, which stayed the case for at least five years.[67] In the meantime, Reagan endorsed Assemblyman Floyd Wakefield's bill that prohibited busing to promote desegregation without parental consent, even though the California Attorney General's Office warned that the proposed bill would most likely be unconstitutional.[68] In September 1970, during the height of his reelection campaign, Reagan signed a bill prohibiting the busing of public school students without the written permission of their parents and blasted busing as "a ridiculous waste of time and public money." Multiple lawsuits were filed immediately after Reagan signed the bill.[69] Leonard H. Carter, the West Coast regional director of the NAACP, called it a "political bill" and grimly concluded, "The Reagan Southern Strategy is no secret. In 1966 the campaign issue was forced housing; today his campaign is forced busing."[70] (Carter expressed the sentiments of civil rights leaders when he lumped Reagan in with the governor of Mississippi, John Bell Williams.)

Amid the furor over busing and campus unrest, Reagan handily defeated the powerful Assembly Speaker Jesse Unruh in his 1970 bid for reelection, albeit with a margin of victory that was half of what it had been in 1966. The author of the bill that outlawed discrimination based on race in public accommodations in California, Unruh had also been instrumental in shepherding the Rumford Fair Housing Act through the state legislature. Unruh, known as "Big Daddy," who coined the phrase "money is the mother's milk of politics," was a charismatic figure who dominated the California legislature, but he had created many enemies in the Democratic Party.[71] He was no match for the telegenic and popular Reagan in a statewide race. Reagan's victory cemented his status as the leader of the Republican Party's conservative wing, and a presidential candidate in waiting.

As his presidential ambitions grew, Reagan staked out the most racially conservative positions on a host of other wedge issues. Along with Nixon, Reagan continued to be the foremost apostle of the policies of "law and order." Welfare reform, in particular, became the centerpiece of his agenda for his second term. Reagan's stereotyping of welfare recipients as cheats mooching off hard-working taxpayers had been a mainstay of his reelection campaign speeches. He famously used racially freighted caricatures of Black women as "welfare queens" to foster hostility and resentment toward nonwhites. Given that Reagan and his wife were beneficiaries of the financial largesse of his wealthy Kitchen Cabinet, his positions might seem a bit hypocritical. The California Welfare Rights Organization pointed out another type of hypocrisy. In 1971 they presented Reagan with an award as the "highest-paid welfare recipient in the state" after a student-run radio station at California State University confirmed that the millionaire Reagan had failed to pay any state income taxes in 1970.[72]

As early as July 1967, Reagan convened a panel to ascertain the extent of welfare fraud in California.[73] His preliminary steps to reform welfare in his first term never gained traction because of his preoccupation with his presidential ambitions, but it remained a volatile issue that he could use to rile up his base. Since becoming governor, Reagan had been besieged with angry letters from citizens decrying the burdens of earning a living in California while having to support people on welfare. After three years in office, many Democratic voters who crossed over to vote for Reagan out of anger over crime, the Rumford Act, and welfare "moochers" were disappointed that Reagan had not done anything about the "unreasonable handouts."[74] One constituent letter took the extreme position of saying that welfare recipients should be disenfranchised because they "contribute nothing to the economy."[75]

The profusion of such angry letters fortified Reagan's decision to make welfare the cornerstone of his successful 1970 reelection. Throughout the fall campaign, he barnstormed California railing against "self-seeking politicians" who defraud hard-working taxpayers by urging organized welfare groups to "make poverty a profession."[76] He was convinced that mothers on welfare, who in California happened to be disproportionately Black, were exploiting loopholes in the overlapping federal regulations to augment their incomes at the expense of hard-working taxpayers. His political opponents were often struck by how Reagan's kind and gentle demeanor masked a callousness for the needy. After the family of Patty Hearst provided food to the poor as partial ransom to her kidnappers, Reagan said, "It's just too bad we can't have an epidemic of botulism."[77] He went so far as to make the incredulous claim that welfare was the "greatest domestic problem facing the nation today."[78] Part of his political strategy was to stake out a position to the right of all the other likely future contenders to replace Nixon.

Flush from his reelection victory, Reagan's fifth State of the State address, on January 12, 1971, demonstrated his resolve to make welfare reform the linchpin of his second-term agenda. Calling welfare "a cancer eating at our vitals," Reagan proposed a sweeping overhaul of California's welfare program.[79] His chief bogeyman was the Aid to Families with Dependent Children (AFDC), a joint federal-state program that provided aid to single mothers and their children.[80] Created as part of the Social Security Act of 1935, the number of AFDC recipients nearly doubled throughout the nation in the 1960s as a result of an increase in single-parent families. In the popular imagination, the idea of the AFDC evoked images of irresponsible, predominantly Black single mothers and their illegitimate children.

On February 2, 1971, Reagan submitted a preliminary budget to the legislature with a $700 million reduction in welfare and indicated that most of the cuts would be aimed at the AFDC program.[81] News of Reagan's proposal to balance California's $6.7 billion budget by slicing programs for the indigent prompted a fellow Republican governor to muse, "You know, Ronald Reagan was first elected with all of that John Birch Society-type rhetoric. After he got in, he seemed to be learning. I was delighted with his progress. But that last budget of his goes back to all of that John Birch Society stuff."[82] The Democrats, weary of Reagan's proclivity to govern by press conference and resentful of his demagoguery over the welfare issue, denied his pro forma request to appear before a joint session of the California legislature.[83] Many Democrats, along with a number of moderate Republicans, saw Reagan's proposal as a ruse to scapegoat the poor, including many Black recipients of AFDC, and not to balance the budget. Phil Burton, a liberal who represented a Black district in San Francisco, derided Reagan for "talking about some women with eight kids from eight different fathers driving a Cadillac and having a color TV—just stupid stuff."[84] Democrats and moderate Republicans attributed the spike in the welfare rolls to the recent economic downturn, and not to the allegedly shiftless behavior of welfare recipients. Many legislators, such as moderate Republican assemblyman William T. Bagley, chair of the Welfare Committee, felt Reagan was once again "demagoguing" welfare, as he had done with the Rumford Act.[85]

On March 3, 1971, Reagan presented his comprehensive reform package at the Town Hall, a luncheon club at the fashionable Biltmore Hotel in Los Angeles. His speech received widespread national press. In addition to cutting $700 million from welfare spending, he proposed reducing medical benefits to the indigent, tightening welfare eligibility requirements, limiting the amount an individual can earn on welfare, and freezing welfare and medical aid loans. In his remarks, Reagan had nothing but scorn for welfare recipients and social workers, and he suggested that a careful scrutiny of the welfare rolls would "turn up thousands of persons who were illegally receiving checks."[86] Seeking the mantle of conservative reformer, Reagan directed his words at a national audience.

Democrats controlled the state legislature, and Reagan's plan ran into a wall of opposition in both Houses.[87] They objected to Reagan's grandstanding and accused him of targeting the poor and vulnerable, arguing that welfare required a federal solution similar to Nixon's Federal Assistance Plan (FAP), which would replace AFCD with a guaranteed annual income for poor working families with children under eighteen.[88] State senator Mervyn M. Dymally, the Black chair of the Democratic caucus, objected to the work program saying it "has the overtones of slave labor."[89] Others considered Reagan's remarks about welfare being a "cancer" that threatened "society itself" to be hyperbolic.[90] Republicans were critical too. William Bagley warned that "any widespread cuts in welfare grants," coupled with what he called Reagan's "welfare rhetoric of recent months, would generate class warfare. It would tear the state apart."[91] State Senator Anthony Beilenson, the liberal Democratic chair of the Committee on Health and Welfare, known for his seriousness and integrity, conducted more than two months of public hearings and concluded that the Reagan proposal was "a fraud and a hoax," and killed it in committee. Beilenson acknowledged that problems with fraud existed in California's welfare program, but he was convinced that Reagan was cynically exaggerating and manipulating the problem for political gain.[92] Instead, Beilenson introduced a bipartisan bill that included some of Reagan's provisions for job training for welfare recipients, as well as cost-of-living increases for welfare recipients, but it eliminated his more draconian cuts.

Just before the committee was to vote on the new bill, Reagan publicly denounced it. He attacked Beilenson for "being blatantly partisan" and said the new bill would not save taxpayers millions of dollars in savings, as Reagan's proposed bill would.[93] A. Allen Post, a highly respected nonpartisan legislative analyst, found that Reagan's original bill would only save $34 million, not the $89 million that Reagan touted.[94] By early June, Reagan and the legislature were hopelessly at loggerheads over both the budget and welfare proposals.

With the bills bottlenecked in the legislature, Democratic Assembly speaker Bob Moretti, an ambitious young Unruh protégé, became the Democratic point man for the bill. After eleven days of protracted negotiations, Moretti and Reagan produced a compromise bill—the California Welfare Reform Act of 1971. The CWRA tightened eligibility for

welfare recipients and included Reagan's much-touted one-year resi-
dency requirement, but, in the end, nearly two-thirds of eligible families
would receive more financial support.[95] The bill angered many Blacks,
such as Assemblyman John J. Miller, a Democrat, who said that the welfare bill "takes from the working poor to feed the nonworking poor."[96]
The legislation was not an ideological victory for conservatism, but Reagan planned to use the issue as a springboard for the presidency as evidence of his success as a conservative reformer.[97] While the welfare rolls
decreased in California, it was attributable to an economic upturn, as
well as the implementation of a liberal abortion law, which resulted in
poor women having fewer babies.[98] Years later, Beilenson remarked that
he did not think Reagan knew what was in the bill he signed.[99]

As the sensational revelations of the Watergate scandal enveloped
the Nixon presidency, Reagan remained the most dogged defender of
the embattled president of any Republican officeholder in the country.
Although "law and order" was his political mantra, Reagan insisted on
Nixon's innocence until the bitter end, castigating the congressional investigations as a "lynching" and a "witch hunt." Reagan also urged the
public to withhold judgment on Vice President Spiro Agnew, who was
separately under investigation for taking bribes. Of Agnew, Reagan said,
"He, like any other citizen of high character, should be considered innocent until proven otherwise."[100] The same week he defended Agnew,
Reagan said that a man accused of killing a police officer, but who was
yet to be tried, deserved the electric chair.[101]

Nixon's eventual resignation dispirited Reagan, and he supported
Nixon's pardon on the grounds that his resignation was "more than ade-
quate for the crime."[102] He considered the new president, Gerald R. Ford,
who'd become vice president upon the resignation of Agnew, a usurper.[103]
His displeasure intensified a few weeks later when Ford selected Nelson
Rockefeller as his vice president, without either considering or consulting Reagan. Ford insulted Reagan further by offering him the position
of secretary of commerce, a cabinet position of minor importance and
prestige.[104]

Ford's ascension to the presidency coincided with Reagan's lame-duck
status as governor. In the fall of 1973, the California electorate's repudiation of Proposition 1, a tax-cutting initiative that Reagan sponsored,
diminished some of his political luster.[105] Reagan had hoped its passage

would be a further vehicle for his national ambitions, but its critics campaigned against it, branding it as inimical to Blacks, the poor, and the elderly.[106] Its defeat marked the first and only time Reagan was defeated in an election in which either he or his pet measure was on the ballot.

The following year, the California electorate punished the Watergate-riddled Republican Party by electing a Democrat to every state constitutional office, except for that of attorney general, earning them a near veto-proof majority in the state assembly and senate. In an ironic twist of fate, Pat Brown's thirty-six-year-old son, Secretary of State Edmund G. "Jerry" Brown Jr., who had called Reagan's Proposition 1 a "hoax," was elected to succeed Reagan as California governor. Despite his recent political setbacks in the final months in Sacramento, Reagan left office with a relatively positive public approval of the job he had done as governor at a time when the Watergate scandal was causing irreparable harm to the Republican brand. A poll conducted by California pollster Mervyn Field showed that Reagan's approval numbers far surpassed those of his predecessor, Pat Brown.[107]

In January 1975, Reagan ended his second term as governor of California as he began his first: preparing a run for the presidency. Despite all of his extreme campaign stances, harsh rhetoric, and crackdown on campus protests, Reagan had governed in a moderate and pragmatic fashion.[108] He presided over an astonishing number of tax increases and, under his stewardship, California government grew. Whereas Pat Brown's final budget had totaled $4.6 billion, just four years later, Reagan's had more than doubled, to $10 billion.[109] Only days after he left office, conservative state senator H. L. Richardson griped, "When you come down to it, we have a hell of a lot more government in California than before Reagan came in."[110] Reagan's most serious problem in stemming the growth of California government was his inability to develop a deep understanding of the complexities of the nature of the system he wanted to overhaul. His critics charged that "he never bothered to try."[111]

For Black Californians, Reagan's pragmatic governance and personal affability could not undo the dog-whistle rhetoric of "law and order" and "welfare queens" or his coziness with former segregationists. Reagan's naive, all-American public veneer masked his relish for telling crude stories and jokes to male legislators in Sacramento, including scatological wisecracks and racial slurs.[112] William Bagley recalled how his fellow legislators in Sacramento used to joke about Reagan's unpopularity with Blacks. Bagley's assembly office even included a large portrait of Reagan with an Afro haircut.[113] To counteract his critics, Reagan replied that he had appointed more Blacks to statewide office than any previous governor. Of Reagan's 3,709 appointments to state jobs, however, the campaign of Jimmy Carter, Reagan's 1980 Democratic opponent, counted only nine who were Black.[114] Furthermore, there were no Blacks among Reagan's six-member state cabinet, and none were even remotely close to his inner circle. Robert Keyes, a Black former professional football player for the Oakland Raiders and San Francisco 49ers, was Reagan's closest Black aide, serving as his liaison to the Black community.[115] Not long after Keyes resigned to become a director for urban affairs at Lockheed Aircraft Corporation, he endorsed Ford for president and severed ties with Reagan, alleging difficulties with Reagan's inner circle.[116] Keyes even accused Reagan of being a racist.[117] A few years later, Keyes was tragically stricken with heart disease and on his deathbed called Reagan to make amends, but Reagan, still embittered over Keyes's endorsement of Ford, refused to take the call.[118]

As the 1976 presidential election loomed, Reagan was still the darling of the Right, and his star had never waned among his hard-core legion of conservative admirers across the country. With his sights riveted on the presidency, he would have the daunting task of toppling an incumbent president from his own party. In plotting his primary challenge, Reagan would run to the right of the conservative Ford on all issues, especially civil rights.

CHAPTER 6

REAGAN'S NEAR MISS IN 1976

Welfare Queens, Jesse Helms, and George Wallace Voters

If there's a Southern strategy, I'm part of it.
—Ronald Reagan at a rally
in Mississippi (November 17, 1973)[1]

Reagan decided to challenge President Ford for the Republican nomination in 1976 partly because he opposed Ford's policy of détente with the Soviet Union, considered Ford too moderate, and thought Ford was a usurper of his rightful legacy. Reagan also harbored an unshakeable conviction that God had chosen him to lead a conservative renewal of America. As an insurgent candidate challenging an incumbent president, and still widely perceived as a Goldwater extremist, Reagan confronted daunting odds. The reigning dean of the national political reporters, James "Scotty" Reston of the *New York Times*, wrote, in September 1975, "The notion that Ronald Reagan can get the Republican nomination from Ford is patently ridiculous unless you suspect the Republicans of suicidal tendencies."[2]

In his effort to woo the working-class whites and Southerners who had backed George Wallace in 1968 and 1972, Reagan would stake out the most conservative stances on hot-button racial issues. In his campaign stump speeches, Reagan popularized the racist trope of "welfare queens," said to be mooching off hard-working white taxpayers. For Jack and Nelle Reagan's son, defeating the Soviets trumped other considerations, and wooing racists like North Carolina senator Jesse Helms, who shared his hostility for détente and the federal government, was a small price to pay. Despite Reagan's loss to Ford for the nomination, his 1976 primary campaign demonstrated how his brand of racial conservatism was ascendant and the Rockefeller, pro–civil rights wing of the Republican Party was in eclipse.

CONSERVATISM AFTER WATERGATE: WAITING FOR REAGAN

After Watergate, the resignation of President Nixon, and the ensuing calamitous mid-term elections of 1974, the conservative moment found itself at a crossroads. Conservatives had been profoundly disillusioned with the Republican Party during the Nixon presidency, and his successor, Gerald Ford, a colorless Washington insider whom they regarded as insufficiently conservative, offered them little solace.[3] Ford's selection of conservative bête noire Nelson Rockefeller as his vice president sealed their disappointment. A number of conservative activists, including *National Review* publisher William Rusher, dreamed of creating a new, unabashedly conservative party, headed by Reagan, in alliance with George Wallace and his constituency of disaffected whites.[4] At first glance, Reagan's sanguinity appeared to be the antithesis of Wallace's rage, but Reagan rivaled Wallace in exploiting America's fears. George Wallace's wife, Cornelia, was not the only one to note how her husband and Reagan were "in the same boat."[5] Reagan considered the idea, but having already left one party, he decided to remain a Republican. A few weeks after he left Sacramento, Reagan spoke at the Conservative Political Action Conference, where he exhorted the Republican Party to not raise "a banner of pale pastels, but bold colors which make it unmistakably clear where we stand on all the issues troubling the people."[6]

However, Reagan's metaphor of "bold colors" seemingly left no room for Black outreach. In a speech to the Republican leadership conference, he suggested that broadening the Republican base to reach out to Blacks and other groups would be akin to abandoning the party's bedrock conservative principles.[7]

In anticipation of his presidential primary run in 1976, Reagan meticulously tended his Southern flank. As early as November 1973, Reagan had ventured to Jackson, Mississippi, in an attempt to fill the political vacuum left in the wake of Vice President Spiro Agnew's resignation. Appearing before an overflow crowd at a Mississippi Republican Party fundraising dinner, Reagan was introduced as being better understood and respected in Mississippi than anywhere else in the country. Reagan did not disappoint the adoring crowd, proudly proclaiming, "If there's a Southern strategy, I'm part of it." Mississippi GOP State committeeman Victor Mayer remarked, "I haven't applauded so much since a Goldwater rally."[8]

In contemplating an insurgent campaign against a sitting president, Reagan had few Republican officeholders willing to support his long-shot bid. One was his close political ally and campaign chair Senator Paul Laxalt, from the neighboring state of Nevada. The other was Senator Jesse Helms, the conservative firebrand from North Carolina, who would become an indispensable ally. Elected in 1972, Helms traveled to Reagan's home in August 1973 to pledge his support for Reagan's future presidential candidacy.[9] A conservative warrior like Reagan, Helms was also a committed segregationist. In the early 1960s, as an usher and deacon at the First Baptist Church in Raleigh, he had refused to seat Blacks and had even threatened to leave the congregation if it decided to integrate. Helms had first gained infamy while working as a political advisor for the segregationist Willis Smith in a bitter 1950 senatorial campaign against liberal Democratic senator Frank Porter Graham. Helms had created handbills for the campaign with the headlines "White People—Wake Up Before It's Too Late" and "Do You Want Negroes Working beside You, Your Wife and Daughters in Your Mills and Factories?"[10] Helms's diatribes against the civil rights movement were the defining issue in his rise to notoriety as a television personality in Eastern North Carolina in the 1960s. The *Charlotte-Observer* called him "the rear-guard action against racial equality."[11]

On July 25, 1975, Helms enlisted Reagan to speak at a fundraiser at the Kerr Scott Pavilion in Raleigh, North Carolina, in an effort to retire Helms's 1972 campaign debt. Before an enthusiastic crowd of over two thousand supporters, Reagan described how the North Carolina senator reminded him of the Confederate general Stonewall Jackson, who, like Helms, stood "like a stone wall in the Senate for the things he believes are best for North Carolina and the entire country." Helms supporters were angry over President Ford's recent decision to extend the Voting Rights Act for seven years, and so were heartened to hear Reagan dismiss Congress' recent extension of the Voting Rights Act as nothing more than "pure demagoguery."[12]

By the mid-1970s, the dwindling number of Black Republicans supported Ford over Reagan, but with some ambivalence. They appreciated
that Ford had joined the majority of his fellow northern Republicans in
voting for the Civil Rights Act of 1964 and Voting Rights Act of 1965,
as well as his last-minute support for the latter's extension in 1975. But,
in 1973, during his confirmation as vice president, Ford's embrace of
"law and order" rhetoric and his support for efforts to impeach Supreme
Court justice William O. Douglas, a man revered for his expansive views
of civil rights and liberties, had left him with the support of just one
member of the Congressional Black Caucus.[13] And, once president,
Ford's harsh rhetoric on the issue of busing and his unwillingness to rebuke an angry army of white Bostonians protesting busing led NAACP
executive director Roy Wilkins to rebuke Ford for not supporting desegregation of Boston's schools.[14] But Black Republican voters had become
a marginal force in Republican politics—far outmatched by a powerful
bloc of conservative white voters in the South, many of them former
Democrats, like Jesse Helms, who had become Republicans after LBJ
signed the Civil Rights and Voting Rights Acts.

WELFARE CHEATS, LUXURY HOUSING PROJECTS, AND STRAPPING YOUNG BUCKS

A stark feature of Reagan's 1976 primary campaign was his continual
slighting of Black Americans. Take a few examples from the very beginning of his campaign. At the news conference announcing his candidacy on November 18, 1975, Reagan claimed he was unaware of the
sensational revelations that his longtime ally, the late J. Edgar Hoover,
had conducted clandestine harassment actions against Martin Luther
King Jr.[15] The next day, in Charlotte, North Carolina, the state where
the lunch-counter sit-in movement had been inaugurated only fifteen
years earlier, Reagan declared that he "opposed these types of demonstrations," because "there can never be any justification for breaking the
law."[16] Despite the pivotal role the sit-ins played in toppling Jim Crow,
Reagan claimed that these "illegal" actions hindered minority advance-
ment "and probably contributed to the prejudices. Some people were
able to say, see, I told you so."[17]

These remarks flabbergasted a Black reporter, who asked Reagan how
Blacks could otherwise have gained their civil rights in places like North
Carolina. Reagan evaded the question and resorted to his shopworn

anecdotes by responding, "I have often stated publicly that the great tragedy was then that we didn't even know that we had a racial problem. It wasn't even recognized. But our generation, and I take great pride in this, were the ones who recognized and then began doing something about it."[18] Then, for the umpteenth time, Reagan recounted the "Jackie Robinson story" and, not content to stop there, continued with a story about the integration of the military, inspired by the exploits of Dorie Miller, a decorated Black soldier whose heroism was popularized in the 1970 movie *Tora! Tora! Tora!*

> One great story that I think of, the time that reveals a change that was occurring . . . [was] when the Japanese dropped the bombs on Pearl Harbor, there was a Negro sailor whose total duties involved kitchen-type duties—cooking and so forth—who cradled a machine gun in his arms, which is not an easy thing to do, stood on the pier blazing away at Japanese airplanes that were coming and strafing him, and that was all changed. And we went on with those developments.[19]

Of course, the notion that the actions of one Black soldier in firing a machine gun at Japanese airplanes during the attack on Pearl Harbor lit the fuse that integrated the military is preposterous to say the least. In fact, the United States military remained segregated throughout World War II, and it was President Truman's Executive Order in 1948 that paved the way for the eventual integration of the military years later.[20] Reagan's recollection of scenes from various war movies were so vividly etched in his imagination that he seemed to have difficulty differentiating fact from fiction, as when he claimed to have personally witnessed the liberation of Nazi concentration camps despite never having left the United States during World War II.[21]

In January, while campaigning in New Hampshire, Reagan talked about the sinister figure of the "welfare queen," a regular feature of his stump speech. According to *Washington Star* reporter John Fialka, at nearly every campaign stop, Reagan informed his listeners of a massive fraud that "welfare workers" had tried to "hush up":

> There's a woman in Chicago, she has 80 names, 30 addresses, 12 Social Security cards, and she's collecting veterans' benefits on four nonex-

istent deceased husbands. And she's collecting Social Security on her cards. She's got Medicaid, getting food stamps, and she's collecting welfare under each of her names. Her tax-free cash income alone is over $150,000.[22]

Reagan never actually used the words "welfare queen," nor did he refer to the woman as Black—but he didn't have to. The notion of a pandemic of welfare fraud originated in the early 1960s when *Reader's Digest*, one of Reagan's favorite news sources, published a series of exposes about mothers abusing welfare. The term "welfare queen" was coined in the 1970s and tapped into racial stereotypes that African American women were promiscuous, dishonest, and lazy.[23] The demonization of impoverished Black women on public assistance had been a longstanding trope, and Reagan fanned the flames of racial resentment while coming across as a "pleasant man who understands why people are angry."[24] The underlying racial subtext of welfare women feeding off the public trough resonated with an increasingly conservative Republican electorate and played well in fiscally conservative, predominantly white New Hampshire, with voters angry over "welfare chiselers."[25] In addition to stoking racial resentments, Reagan was also seeking to highlight his record reforming California's welfare system and his promise to do the same at the national level.[26] In doing so, Reagan was tapping into a rich vein of anger over welfare. In America's bicentennial year, a Harris poll found that 89 percent of Americans agreed with Reagan that "the criteria for getting on welfare was not tough enough," and 85 percent thought welfare recipients "cheat by getting money they are not entitled to."[27]

Like so many of Reagan's favorite anecdotes, this one contained significant inaccuracies.[28] Chicago authorities identified the woman in question as a forty-seven-year-old Black Chicago woman named Linda Taylor, who had been indicted for using aliases—four not eighty—and was ultimately convicted of using only two of them. The amount of her alleged welfare fraud was not $150,000, as Reagan claimed, but a mere $8,000.[29] Still, Taylor had defrauded the government—and was possibly a murderer.[30] Reagan's penchant for exaggeration helped him create a sense of outrage in his audience and in the process stirred racial resentments for political gain. Reagan also embellished the number of welfare recipients that had been taken off California's welfare rolls during his time as governor. He claimed, "We lopped 400,000 off the welfare rolls," when the actual figure was 232,000.[31] *Washington Post* columnist Jules Witcover noted that Reagan continued to repeat his original claim even after the press debunked it.[32]

Another of Reagan's favorite tales on the campaign trail in New Hampshire was about the Taino Towers, a subsidized housing project in East Harlem whose residents were mainly Black and Puerto Rican. Reagan skillfully prefaced his remarks by praising his largely white New Hampshire audience as "hard-working people" who paid their bills in a timely fashion and "put up with high taxes." Then he contrasted their lives with the slum dwellers in the Taino Towers, who lived in lavish apartments "with 11-foot ceilings, with a 2-foot balcony, a swimming pool and gymnasium, laundry room and play room, and the rent begins at $113.20 per month and that includes utilities." In addition, they enjoyed "a doorman and indoor parking with twenty-four-hour security."[33] Once again, Reagan had distorted the details to maximize the outrage of his audience. John Fialka interviewed Robert Nichol, the project coordinator for the Towers, who told him that only 92 of 656 units had high ceilings, and those units were six-bedroom units reserved for large families. And, depending on their income levels, residents paid from $300 to $450 per month. Finally, the residents of the Towers shared the pool, gymnasium, and other amenities with the neighboring community of two hundred thousand people, who lived near the project.[34]

Later, as Reagan campaigned in the northern counties of Florida along the borders of Georgia and Alabama, Jon Nordheimer of the *New York Times* observed that he "hammered away at the welfare and law-and-order . . . issues long attractive to Southern conservatives."[35] Campaigning at an overflow rally in Fort Lauderdale in early February of 1976, Reagan took on food-stamp recipients. He told rally goers: "Working people were outraged when they waited in lines at grocery store check-out counters while a 'strapping young buck' ahead of them purchased T-bone steaks with food stamps." He had used this grocery-line anecdote in New Hampshire, but this was the first time that he had used the term "young buck," which, as Nordheimer pointed out, "generally denotes a black man." The epithet "buck" had a long history of being used to refer to a dangerous young Black man who lusts after white women. In response to criticism over Reagan's use of the term, his Florida campaign manager, L. E. Thomas, a Chevrolet dealer from Panama, denied that Reagan's references were racist, but then he went on to incredibly add that Black people "would rather be promised a ham and get a loaf of bread than the promised two loaves and get it. It's just the way they think."

Reagan's narrow loss in the February 24 New Hampshire primary was followed by losses in Massachusetts, Vermont, Florida, and his birth state of Illinois, deflating his supporters, rattling his campaign, and raising grave concerns about how long he could sustain his challenge against a sitting president.[36] With his campaign running out of money, spokesman Lyn Nofziger counseled journalists to "wait till North Carolina" before writing Reagan's epitaph.[37]

JESSE HELMS AND A SOUTHERN REJUVENATION

Behind the scenes, Jesse Helms and his close aide and long-time political alter ego, Thomas F. Ellis, had seized control of Reagan's North Carolina campaign from the national campaign staff. Ellis and Helms were steeped in racial demagoguery. They had established the Congressional Club of North Carolina, which pioneered the practice of sending out direct-mail fundraising appeals. One of their letters warned voters that militant Blacks and homosexuals were about to take over the country (Helms had long referred to civil rights workers as "sex perverts").[38] As a young lawyer, Ellis had been a staff attorney for a commission formed to expedite North Carolina's attempt to circumvent the *Brown v. Board of Education* ruling, and he had also served as a director of the controversial Pioneer Fund, an organization that funded dubious research on the relationship between race and intelligence.[39] In November 1975, Reagan's campaign named Helms the North Carolina campaign chair, with Ellis as the state coordinator in charge of day-to-day operations.[40]

Helms was determined to resuscitate Reagan's flagging presidential bid. He and Ellis viewed Reagan's early campaign miscues with consternation and pressed for Reagan's national political team to conduct a more ideological campaign.[41] In the final weeks of the Florida primary, Reagan gained traction when he unveiled hard-hitting critiques against the Ford administration's supposed "give away" of the Panama Canal to the leftist regime of Panama. The previously obscure issue of the canal roused conservatives dispirited by America's recent humiliating departure from Vietnam.[42] With Helms and Ellis's encouragement, Reagan continued this line of attack about the canal in North Carolina. Abandoning his Senate duties, Helms campaigned alongside Reagan in the conservative eastern part of the state, where many Republican voters had followed Reagan's and Helms's exodus from the Democratic Party out of dissatisfaction with the Democrats' policies on civil rights. Many of them had been former Dixiecrats and ardent champions of George Wallace.

Helms and Ellis resorted to their tactic of using race as a wedge issue. In the final days of the primary, Ellis circulated a campaign flyer with a quotation from a *Raleigh Times* article repeating a rumor that President Ford wanted Senator Edward M. Brooke, who was Black, to be his running mate.[43] The flyer also contained a quotation from Senator Brooke saying that busing was "constitutional" and "should be used."[44] The attempt to link Ford with Brooke was political dynamite in much of North Carolina in the mid-1970s, especially among Republican primary voters. The national Reagan campaign opposed this overtly racist ploy and ordered Ellis to destroy the fliers. He complied, at least partially. Less than a week before the North Carolina primary, a *Raleigh News and Observer* reporter found some of them at a Reagan campaign office in downtown Raleigh and notified the press.[45] Although Reagan denounced both Ellis and the fliers, and denied that he was trying to inject race into the campaign, Ellis was not reprimanded; he retained control over Reagan's North Carolina campaign and later traveled with Reagan to Texas.[46]

The contretemps surrounding the fliers ultimately redounded to Reagan's benefit. His emphatic denunciation of the clipping ensured that the national press would cover the story, allowing Reagan an opportunity to condemn racism on the national stage.[47] When Reagan's hagiographers have tackled the issue, they omit Reagan's history of association with such suspect characters as Helms and Ellis and point instead to Reagan's condemnation of the fliers as proof that he was not himself a racist.[48] As historian Rick Perlstein insightfully put it, "Reagan got to have it both ways on that one, loudly denouncing it to the press while benefitting from the race-baiting too."[49]

On March 23, 1976, Reagan surprised even himself with a shocking come-from-behind victory in North Carolina.[50] Journalist Lou Cannon called it the "turning point" in Reagan's pursuit of the presidency and ascribed Reagan's slim twelve-thousand-vote margin of victory to the efforts of Helms and his vaunted political machine.[51] Helms's hometown newspaper, the *Raleigh Times*, declared it a "Helms-Reagan victory" and attributed Reagan's "new life" to the senator's active campaigning.[52] Reagan's North Carolina victory over Ford marked the first time since 1952, when Senator Estes Kefauver of Tennessee defeated President Truman, that an incumbent president was defeated by a challenger in a primary election. The *New York Times* columnist William Safire called it a "whole new ball game," noting the "electric shock that crackled through Texas the following day."[53] Reagan's comeback demonstrated his surging appeal in the South, which was the site of an upcoming series of primaries in Texas, Georgia, and Alabama. Conservative journalist John Chamberlain wrote that North Carolina proved Reagan "has the Southern strategy working for him."[54]

REAGAN'S 1976 SOUTHERN STRATEGY AND GEORGE WALLACE VOTERS

Reagan's surprising North Carolina triumph reinvigorated his insurgent campaign, however, it was still so strapped for money that the campaign had to relinquish its charter plane and fly commercial.[55] The campaign also made the strategic decision to bypass the New York and Pennsylvania primaries on April 2 and instead follow Goldwater's mantra of "hunting where the ducks are," in Dixie. They planned to focus on the May 1 Texas primary, where citizens could vote in either party's primary. This afforded Reagan the opportunity to court the sizable contingent of George Wallace voters. The former segregationist, who had been seriously wounded by an assassin's bullet in 1972, was fading in his final attempt to win the Democratic nomination. On May 4, Alabama and Georgia would hold their primaries, both of which had cross-over voting.[56]

By mid-April, media coverage of the Texas primary campaign included stories on the large number of Wallace supporters attending Reagan's campaign events in large and small towns throughout Texas. Syndicated columnists Rowland Evans and Robert Novak reported that a Reagan rally in downtown Fort Worth lacked the usual well-heeled glamor of a Texan Republican event and resembled more of a Wallace crowd, with "women in house dresses, sport-shirted men, and lots of small American flags." In pursuit of Wallace voters, Reagan introduced a new line of attack in his Texas stump speech, accusing Ford of posturing as a fiscal conservative while favoring "liberalized welfare payments."[57] Texas conservatives were livid over a recent decision by a Federal District

Court judge ordering more than twenty thousand Dallas students to be bused in compliance with a 1971 school desegregation plan.[58] Reagan, in turn, called for a constitutional amendment to outlaw busing.[59]

The Reagan campaign made a concerted effort to court Wallace voters. Both Helms and Ellis came to Texas to assist Reagan, and they brought along Arthur Finkelstein, a bright, young New York political consultant who had helped with Reagan's victory in North Carolina.[60] With an eye on targeting conservative voters, Finkelstein acquired a mailing list of Texans who opposed abortion rights. On the list he found the name of Rolly Millirons, a North Texas Democrat who had served as George Wallace's Fort Worth campaign manager in 1968 but was planning to cross over and vote for Reagan.[61] Finkelstein made a radio and television advertisement featuring Millirons, which the Reagan campaign broadcast throughout Texas. Millirons told his fellow Texans:

> I've been a Democrat all my life. A Conservative Democrat. As much as I hate to admit it, George Wallace can't be nominated. Ronald Reagan can. He's right on the issues. So for the first time in my life, I'm gonna vote in the Republican primary. I'm gonna vote for Ronald Reagan.[62]

Just two days before the May 1 Texas primary, Reagan spoke against the backdrop of an American flag near Wallace's own backyard, in Huntsville, Alabama, lambasting the federal government's practice of suing all-white private schools that received federal funds in an effort to force them to integrate.[63] Reagan also revived the issue of Ford's signing the July 1975 extension of the Voting Rights Act, with its sanctions against Texas and other Southern states. Reagan accused the president of "leading a new wave of carpetbaggers to look over the shoulder of your local officials, just as Reconstruction did in 1865."[64] Dredging up this old caricature of Reconstruction was part of Reagan's drive to appeal to the prejudices of Wallace voters, who were pivotal to the outcome of the Texas primary

On May 1, 1976, Reagan scored a landslide victory in the Lone Star State that stunned the Ford campaign. It was the largest primary defeat ever suffered by an incumbent president. Reagan's landslide was largely attributable to the massive Democratic crossover vote. Republican turnout in towns such as El Paso had virtually doubled over that of the previous presidential primary, indicating that thousands of new voters who had never been involved in Republican politics had voted for Reagan.[65]

The "May Day Massacre" of Ford in Texas occurred just three days prior to the Georgia, Alabama, and Indiana primaries, all of which also allowed crossover voting.[66] Local Georgia election officials reported that they were being inundated with calls from Wallace supporters who intended to vote for Reagan because they agreed with his policies and Wallace not having a chance at the nomination.[67] In Georgia, Reagan won in a lopsided victory, sweeping all forty-eight delegates and receiving 68 percent of the vote. According to the *Atlanta Constitution*, Wallace himself asked for a Republican ballot in Alabama and voted for Reagan.[68] The results in Alabama were virtually identical, with Reagan winning all of the delegates and garnering 71 percent of the vote.[69] In the most surprising event of the evening, Reagan stunned Ford in Indiana.[70]

The next battleground was Ford's home state of Michigan, where a defeat would strike a devastating blow to his chances to win the nomination.[71] What particularly alarmed the Ford camp was the prospect of the 809,230 Michigan voters who gave George Wallace an overwhelming victory in the 1972 Democratic primary crossing over to vote for Reagan.[72] In the nervous days before the Michigan primary, the president's campaign was stung by the news that scores of Wallace voters had decided to cast their vote for Reagan.[73] Since 1972, the *New York Times* had been following the political evolution of Dewey Burton, a young blue-collar autoworker at the Wixom Ford plant, just outside Detroit. Burton epitomized the white working class's growing political disaffection with the liberal wing of the Democratic Party. In 1972, Burton voted for Wallace because of his strident opposition to busing. In 1976, when the *New York Times* visited Burton in the days before the Michigan primary, he announced that he would become a "primary jumper" and cross over to vote for Reagan. Burton explained that Reagan displayed the "qualities of independence and freshness that Wallace showed four years ago, but without the shadow of racism behind it."[74] In response to the *Times* article, the Reagan campaign budgeted approximately $80,000 for television ads in an attempt to woo Wallace voters in the president's backyard.[75]

In the end, Ford's home advantage propelled him to a victory over Reagan.[76] While thousands of Wallace voters crossed over to vote for

Reagan, thousands more Michigan Republicans remained loyal to their fellow Michigander.[77] The embattled incumbent had dodged a major bullet, and Ford's resounding win in Michigan reinvigorated his campaign and provided a buffer for his certain upcoming defeats in the South.[78]

REAGAN'S RHODESIA FLAP

Only a few days before the Texas primary, Secretary of State Henry Kissinger stepped off his jet in the Kenyan capital of Nairobi and declared, "Time is running out for Rhodesia's white rulers," and "The future of Africa must be shaped by Africans." Days later, Kissinger delivered a major speech in Lusaka, Zambia, emphasizing the US's commitment to African majority rule.[79] Much to the dismay of African Americans who had supported African nations seeking self-rule, Reagan criticized these diplomatic efforts to facilitate the prompt transfer of power from Rhodesia's 270,000 whites to its six million Blacks. He and the conservative intellectuals who had coalesced around the *National Review* had long perceived the African decolonization movement in the same vein as the civil rights movement—as a threat to Western civilization and a ruse for Soviet penetration of the African continent.[80]

Amid Kissinger's African diplomacy, Reagan warned the secretary of state to avoid "impulsive reactions" that could incite violence in Rhodesia. He also expressed concern for the need to preserve the rights of the white minority.[81] Reagan's reluctance to criticize the white-minority government in Rhodesia was in line with groups, such as the American White Citizens' Council, which believed Rhodesia was one of the last bulwarks of white civilization against Communism.[82] The timing of Kissinger's trip with the slew of upcoming Southern primaries alarmed some of Ford's political advisors. A top strategist told *Newsweek*, "Sending Kissinger to Africa to be the black man's brother before three Southern primaries was insane."[83]

On June 2, just six days before the crucial California, New Jersey, and Ohio primaries, Reagan delivered an unscripted remark before the Sacramento Press Club that caused an uproar. If elected president, he said, he pledged to send "a token force"—or even a larger US force if necessary—to prevent a civil war in Rhodesia.[84] When pressed for specifics in a follow-up question, Reagan said sending ground troops to Rhodesia would be worth it, in the interests of peace and avoiding bloodshed and falsely asserted that the sole dispute between the white minority regime and the Black majority in the capital was the timetable for achieving majority rule.[85]

With these ill-considered comments, Reagan became mired in political quicksand. They rekindled fears that he was a warmonger determined to use force to preserve the perpetuation of white supremacist rule in Rhodesia.[86] If Kissinger's support for Black Rhodesian self-determination had bedeviled the Ford campaign in Texas and the Deep South, now President Ford sprang into action to exploit Reagan's faux pas, calling the prospect of an American president sending troops to Southern Africa "irresponsible."[87] Campaigning in San Francisco, an angry Reagan accused the media of distorting his comments to sell newspapers, but at a $250 per plate fundraiser at the posh Mark Hopkins Hotel, he acknowledged his mistake, but his attempt to clarify his comments was unconvincing.[88] The *New York Times* took exception to Reagan's remarks, pointing out that white ruler Ian Smith had vowed whites will "not in a thousand years" relinquish power to a Black majority government in Rhodesia.[89]

For Robert Keyes, who had been Reagan's highest-ranking Black aide as governor, the Rhodesia flap was the last straw. Keyes called a press conference at the Los Angeles Hilton to announce his support for Ford. To add insult to injury, Keyes charged that Reagan had mistreated him and other minority members of his staff. Kenneth Reich of the *Los Angeles Times* reported that Reagan's California campaign director, Lyn Nofziger, had showed up at the press conference to "keep Keyes honest," but an unruffled Keyes shot back, "I don't like bigots, either."[90]

In a tight race, Reagan's comments reinforced concerns that he was reckless and dangerous.[91] Although the Rhodesian flap failed to prevent Reagan's nearly 2 to 1 victory in his native California, it knocked Reagan off of his stride in Ohio and New Jersey, where Ford scored large victories that blunted Reagan's California delegate sweep.[92] African Americans seethed that Reagan's remarks conveyed the impression that he was willing to go to war in furtherance of the continuation of "white rule in the mineral rich African nation."[93] The *Pittsburgh Courier*, for example, a Black newspaper, accused Reagan of "intruding into an area where he has as much comprehension as a retarded eighth grade school boy." The *Courier* further charged that self-rule for Black Rhodesians was at "variance with the former California governor's racist concept of supremacy."[94]

BLACKS, REAGAN, THE KANSAS CITY CONVENTION, AND BEYOND

With the end of the primary season, virtually all polling showed President Ford with a razor-thin lead over Reagan in the race for delegates, but short of the requisite 1,130 for a first-ballot victory at the Kansas City convention in August. In the interim, Reagan and Ford engaged in a grueling exercise of guerrilla warfare for the approximately 150 remaining uncommitted delegates.[95] The inconclusive primary contest for the Republican nomination created the specter of a brokered convention. As the incumbent, Ford had the advantage of using the prestige of his office to woo the crucial handful of uncommitted delegates.

The more typically fractious Democratic Party had settled on the former one-term governor of Georgia, Jimmy Carter, as their standard-bearer. A Southern racial progressive, Carter embodied the ethos of the New South that sought to transcend segregation, and his Southern heritage threatened to curtail the inroads Republicans had made in the South since Goldwater.[96] The Reverend Martin Luther King Sr. and US representative Andrew Young were early supporters who helped their fellow Georgian muster support among Blacks throughout the country.[97] At the Democratic convention in Madison Square Garden, Blacks were especially exhilarated by the rousing keynote address delivered by Black congresswoman Barbara Jordan of Texas—the first ever by a Black politician.[98] Carter further cemented Black support by selecting liberal senator Walter Mondale, a disciple of Hubert Humphrey, as his running mate.[99] After Martin Luther King Sr. punctuated the "Happy Garden Party" with a Baptist benediction, the festive Democrats left New York jubilant from polls showing that Carter enjoyed a 2 to 1 lead over both Ford and Reagan.[100]

Conversely, Blacks continued to view the deadlocked Republican race through a dour prism. They were pained at the party's indifference or, worse, its hostility to their concerns. On the eve of the convention, the *Pittsburgh Courier* summed up the community's somber mood:

> We feel that President Ford for all of his awkwardness and despite all of his "irrational" vetoes is more "electable" than Ronald Reagan. Indeed, one has to take a second look at any citizen who admires either one of them, but the Reagan partisans are out of this world.

From the speeches of Reagan, it appears he would carry America back to the 19th century. His conservatism is so deep that he would make Herbert Hoover look like a left-winger.[101]

In an unprecedented and audacious gambit to divert attention from Reagan's slim deficit in delegates, Reagan's national campaign manager, John Sears, convinced Reagan to select the liberal Republican senator Richard Schweiker of Pennsylvania to be his vice presidential running mate. Sears hoped that Pennsylvanian could make inroads with the more moderate delegations of New Jersey and Pennsylvania. After the dust settled, however, the maneuver backfired. The selection failed to help Reagan with the moderates, and it infuriated Reagan's conservative Southern base; even Jesse Helms was on the brink of mutiny.[102] Reagan and Schweiker personally lobbied the handful of wavering Black delegates in the days leading up to the Kansas City convention, but Schweiker's admirable civil rights record could not make them forget Reagan's own dismal record.[103] Schweiker's efforts to assure the Black delegates that Blacks "would have a very important role to play" in a Reagan administration proved unconvincing.[104] Even Reagan's last-ditch pledge to enforce, by the "point of a bayonet," the civil rights laws he initially opposed failed to move any of the delegates.[105] The prospect of Black Republicans selling Reagan to Black America elicited howls of laughter from one Black delegate, who mused to Vernon Jarrett of the *Chicago Tribune*, "Sell Reagan to other black folk? Hell man, I haven't been able to sell him to me yet."[106]

As the thousands of delegates, media, political operatives, and others streamed into Kansas City's new glinting Kemper Arena, a palpable uncertainty pervaded the proceedings. The outcome of the race was unknown, but the "whiteness" of the Republican Party was clear. *Washington Post* reporter Jules Witcover remarked that the Republican delegates were from the mostly middle-aged Kiwanis and country club demographic, and 97 percent of them were white.[107] Witcover jested: "They are so white that the occasional black face is enough to turn heads, except that the singular black can be counted on to be in proper Republican uniform, as if he too is bucking to get into the club."[108]

With tempers flaring in the Kemper Arena, Ford prevailed by the painfully close margin of 1,187 to 1,070. Reagan's tearful remarks on the final evening of the convention electrified the delegates and made Ford's acceptance speech look weak by comparison, leading many Ford supporters to wonder if they had nominated the wrong candidate. After the Kansas City convention, Reagan returned with Nancy to their recently purchased ranch perched atop the Santa Ynez Mountains, near Santa Barbara, California.

In the long run, Reagan had won by losing to Ford in the 1976 primary. His moving concession speech and overall comportment throughout the marathon primary campaign dispelled Reagan's reputation as an extremist. His ideological fervor of the mid-1960s had been supplanted by an older, more genial and familiar façade. Had Reagan won the Republican nomination, it would have been an uphill battle to defeat the scandal-free, idealistic Carter in the shadow of Watergate. But, having come so tantalizingly close to the prize he had coveted for nearly a decade, Reagan was not yet ready to abandon his dreams of the presidency. Having established himself as the most popular conservative in the country, his "near miss" would become a "triumphant defeat."[109]

CHAPTER 7

LET'S MAKE AMERICA GREAT AGAIN

Reagan's 1980 Triumph

I'm scared to death of Ronald Reagan.
—Martin Luther King Sr. (March 1980)[1]

Oh Ronnie, I wish you could be here to see all these beautiful white people . . . black and white people I mean.
—Nancy Reagan (March 1980)[2]

Reagan's deepest appeal is to those who cheered George Wallace on but who felt a bit shabby and soiled after he worked them over, massaged their hate glands, made them queasy with acrid emotions sweated out of them. Reagan croons, in love accents, his permission to indulge a fictional hatred of poor people and blacks. Nothing personal about it. It is really an act of patriotism not to let the hardworking middle class be dragged down to their level.
—Gary Wills (August 1980)[3]

After his narrow defeat of President Ford in the 1976 general election, Jimmy Carter became the first president elected from the Deep South since 1848.[4] He swept every state in the Old Confederacy except for Virginia. In response to Reagan's primary challenge, Ford's rightward lurch factored into his receiving a paltry 6 percent of the Black vote.[5] Carter's winning of the Black vote made the difference in the highly contested battleground states of Ohio, Pennsylvania, and Texas, leading many political experts to attribute Ford's defeat to his lack of outreach to Black voters.[6]

Reagan meanwhile recovered from the grueling primary challenge and returned to private life, basking in his status as the titular leader of the conservative movement. After casting his vote near his Pacific Palisades residence, Reagan refused to rule out another run for the presidency. He believed Carter won so decisively in the South because "blood was thicker than philosophy,"[7] and he was convinced that Carter's liberalism would eventually alienate his Southern supporters. Most pundits, however, dismissed Reagan as too old for another run—he would turn sixty-nine in 1980. Murray Kempton typified this conventional wisdom when he called Reagan "one of the great candidates in our memory, perhaps the greatest, who never got his chance."[8]

But Reagan always had exquisite political timing, and his "near miss" in 1976 burnished his national reputation. In the event the inexperienced Carter faltered, Reagan would become the president in waiting, so, after Carter's election, he immediately took steps to stay in the public eye, writing newspaper columns and radio scripts.[9] In addition to earning him a lot of money, this work also led to much speculation that he was laying the groundwork for another presidential run.[10] An August 1977 Gallup poll showed that Reagan was known by nine out of ten Americans and that, among Republicans, he was the top choice as their next nominee for president.[11] It came as no surprise when Reagan declared his candidacy for the 1980 Republican presidential nomination.

WRESTING WHITE EVANGELICALS AWAY FROM CARTER

Republicans' dread of Carter maintaining his grip on the South was allayed by the steady drumbeat of bad economic news and questions about Carter's leadership. Elected as an outsider who had vowed to purge Washington, DC, of the dishonesty and corruption that had led to the traumas of the Vietnam War and Watergate, Carter had crisscrossed the country for over two years in the run-up to the election asking virtually everybody he encountered to vote for him. Yet, his unwillingness to display the same solicitousness to powerful members of Congress poisoned his relationship with congressional Democrats and other Washington insiders.[12] Carter's first year "ended with an awkward loss of elan and momentum," wrote *New York Times* Washington bureau chief Hedrick Smith.[13] His failure to project an aura of leadership and grapple with the panoply of economic and foreign policy setbacks of the late 1970s made the American public more susceptible to Reagan's patriotic nostrums of national strength and renewal.[14]

Carter's Evangelicalism had been a major ingredient of his success with white Southerners, who had been trending Republican for years. Carter's dramatic political rise was an important reason for *Newsweek* declaring 1976 to be the "Year of the Evangelical."[15] By 1978, however, Carter's IRS administrator decided to deny tax-exempt status to private, segregated Christian academies that had burgeoned in the South over the past generation in order to circumvent the *Brown v. Board of Education* decision. This eroded his support among his fellow Southern Evangelicals.[16] By the eve of Reagan's entry into the 1980 presidential contest, white fury over the new IRS guidelines galvanized Southern Christian Evangelicals into a potent conservative political force.[17] This racially charged issue would be pivotal in laying the foundation for a mass exodus of Southern Evangelical whites into Reagan's conservative coalition.[18] Carter's mounting political difficulties among white Southerners encouraged conservative Republicans to double down on the Southern strategy and to reject the incoming Republican National Committee chair William Brock's plan for Black outreach.[19]

Before the federal mandates to desegregate public schools in the 1950s, all-white private religious schools in the South were scarce. By the late 1960s, however, approximately four hundred thousand children were attending these private religious schools in eleven Southern states. African Americans and their liberal allies argued that white flight from public schools "would perpetuate school segregation, and impede public education reform in many rural, Southern districts."[20] In 1970, liberal senator Walter Mondale, Reagan's future political foe, called the growth of these segregated academies "the biggest change taking place in American education today."[21] After Black parents in Mississippi filed suit in May 1969 calling on the Nixon administration to revoke the federal tax exemptions that the IRS granted to segregated religious schools, a federal district court ordered the IRS to halt the practice unless it found that the schools also admitted Black children. Because the decision gave the IRS wide latitude in implementing the policy, it was at best a partial victory for the plaintiffs.[22] The issue continued to fester after the Nixon administration filed a brief calling for the IRS to continue the policy of exempting segregated religious schools. In response, the *New York Times* accused the administration of allying with white supremacists.[23] In January 1976, the IRS revoked the tax-exempt status of the Christian Bob

Jones University in Greenville, South Carolina, over its prohibition on interracial dating.[24] That case would wend its way through the courts for years and would reverberate politically along the way.

In 1978, the second year of the Carter administration, IRS commissioner Jerome Kurtz announced new regulations requiring any private school formed after a desegregation ruling to prove it was attempting to integrate in order to retain tax-exempt status. This was a blockbuster modification of existing policy that shifted the burden of proof to the private academies as a prerequisite for receiving tax exemptions.[25] These new guidelines provoked outrage from defenders of the schools. In response, Paul Weyrich, a young right-wing activist and an anti–Vatican II Catholic, along with his friend Robert Billings, founded a group called Christian School Action to fight the IRS proposals. Within a few weeks of the IRS's change of policy, it had received over 120,000 letters protesting the new regulations, the most it had ever received on any other proposal; an additional 400,000 letters of protest were sent to members of Congress.[26] Commissioner Kurtz received so many alarming personal threats that the Secret Service provided protection for him and his wife.[27] Later, Weyrich explained that "what galvanized the Christian community was not abortion, school prayer or the ERA. . . . What changed their minds was Jimmy Carter's intervention against the Christian schools, trying to deny them tax-exempt status on the basis of so-called de facto segregation."[28] Billings also declared, "Jerome Kurtz has done more to bring Christians together than any man since the Apostle Paul."[29]

The turmoil over the new guidelines prompted the IRS, in December 1978, to hold four days of combative hearings in Washington, DC.[30] While Representative Barry Goldwater Jr. called the IRS proposal an "outrage," and Republican senator Orrin Hatch blasted it as "repulsive," Clarence Mitchell, chair of the Leadership Conference on Civil Rights, testified at the hearings that the controversy was the newest chapter in the long history of opposition to *Brown v. Board of Education*.[31] "Every school that's started to evade desegregation has called itself Christian," he said. "That's not my idea of being Christian."[32] The fact that so many of the church school organizers who testified against the proposed regulations were from the South made it difficult to distinguish between Evangelical conservatives and the Southern segregationists.[33]

Unsurprisingly, the clamor over the IRS regulations captured Reagan's attention. Weeks before the congressional hearings, Reagan addressed the issue in one of his nationally syndicated radio spots, chastising the IRS for threatening religious freedom. He continued with the dubious assertion that "virtually all schools [whose tax-exempt status was being revoked] are presently desegregated."[34] While there was no evidence that Carter and his political aides were involved with drafting the new IRS regulations, Christian Evangelicals blamed Carter, deemed him a traitor to his faith, and indicated they would throw their support to Reagan, a divorced Hollywood actor who rarely attended church. In addition to the IRS regulations, Evangelicals seethed over Carter's support of the Equal Rights Amendment, abortion rights, and deemed him as a captive of the godless, liberal wing of the Democratic Party.

Affirmative action became another hot-button racial issue during the Carter presidency, and the subject furnished Reagan and other conservatives with yet another opportunity to make further inroads with angry disaffected whites, especially in an era of economic stagnation, when blue-collar jobs were becoming scarce. It enabled Reagan and conservatives to shroud themselves in an ideology of color-blind conservatism, perversely claim that white men were now the true victims of racial discrimination, and stigmatized affirmative action programs as racial "quotas." As early as 1977, a Gallup poll found only 11 percent of Americans condoned giving preferential treatment to Black Americans in employment and higher education.[35]

By his equivocations on affirmation action, Carter straddled the issue, hoping in vain that it would go away. On October 12, 1977, only nine months into his term, oral arguments were heard in the case of *The Regents of the University of California v. Allan Bakke*, arguably one of the most scrutinized and debated cases ever to wend its way up to the US Supreme Court. At issue was the constitutionality of the affirmative action program of the University of California at Davis's medical school, a policy designed to set aside sixteen places for members of "educationally and economically disadvantaged" minorities. In October 1976, the California Supreme Court had ruled that the policy violated the constitutional rights of Allen Bakke, a thirty-two-year-old white engineer applying for admission.[36]

On June 28, 1978, the court handed down a confusing, Solomonic ruling. It upheld the California Supreme Court's decision to admit Bakke to the Davis medical school but invalidated the school's special admissions program on the grounds that it was an unconstitutional quota. By the same token, it upheld affirmative action programs and allowed the race or ethnic background of a candidate to be taken into consideration. In the most memorable line of the opinion, Justice Harry Blackmun justified the need for affirmative action's preservation: "To get beyond racism, we must first take account of race. And in order to treat some persons equally, we must treat them differently."[37]

Bakke caused problems for Carter across the political spectrum. For his supporters, the case exposed his administration's internecine bickering and irresolution. Civil rights leaders, so crucial to Carter's electoral coalition, viewed the decision and Carter's vacillation about it with disdain. Among white voters, the perception that Carter embraced quotas alienated many working-class people who were grappling with deindustrialization and escalating unemployment. The contentious issue of affirmative action exacerbated the fissures within the decaying New Deal coalition between Blacks on the one hand who supported it and, on the other hand, many prominent Jews and working-class whites who opposed affirmative action, furnishing Reagan and conservatives an auspicious opportunity to reframe the civil rights issue around the supposed scourge of reverse discrimination.

REAGAN AND THE 1980 CAMPAIGN: EVANGELICALS AND STATES' RIGHTS

Though some voters had concerns about Reagan's age, his tendency to give simplistic solutions to complex issues struck a responsive chord with Americans frustrated with Carter's opaqueness and incompetence.[38] In the fall of 1978, Reagan was a ubiquitous presence campaigning on behalf of Republican congressional candidates and electrified packed halls with his charisma.[39] By the middle of 1979, Reagan had emerged as the front-runner for the 1980 Republican nomination. He spent that year building a formidable political organization that far surpassed those of his Republican rivals and, on November 13, 1979, the sixty-eight-year-old announced his campaign for the presidency in a nationally televised address. In it, he vowed to restore America's confidence and greatness.[40] Reagan's optimism appeared to be the perfect antidote to the economic crisis of stagflation, the mystifying combination of high unemployment and high inflation, as well as to a series of foreign policy setbacks and the aura of "malaise" that bedeviled the nation during the Carter administration.

In the weeks after Reagan's announcement, racial issues, like all other domestic matters, were subsumed by the explosive story of the fifty-two American diplomats who were taken hostage by the Iranian revolutionary government in Tehran. In the short term, the crisis benefited Carter because it spawned an upsurge of patriotism that severely wounded Senator Edward Kennedy's insurgent challenge from the left.[41] But over the course of the protracted crisis—which lasted 444 days—the public grew frustrated with Carter's inability to secure the release of the hostages. Reagan's criticisms of Democrats' flaccid and spineless approach to foreign policy seemed validated when the Soviet Union surprised American intelligence by launching an invasion of Afghanistan. A befuddled Carter responded with a grain embargo and cancelled American participation in the upcoming 1980 Summer Olympic games in Moscow. To make matters worse, the intractable problem of stagflation and crushingly high interest rates ground the economy to a standstill. Reagan's certitude and relentless optimism seemed the palliative for the gloomy malaise that came to characterize the Carter years.

With the spotlight on the domestic and foreign policy challenges of the late 1970s, the growing clout of Evangelicals remained off stage. But during the 1980 election cycle, the unprecedented political mobilization of Christian Evangelicals on behalf of Reagan would emerge as the most newsworthy political development. In 1979 Jerry Falwell, a fundamentalist Baptist minister from Lynchburg, Virginia, who had gained a large following with his *Old-Time Gospel Hour* television program, formed the Moral Majority. His goal was to rally Evangelicals behind political candidates who espoused a "pro-life, pro-moral, and pro-America" agenda.[42] Despite Falwell's opposition to abortion, secularization, and feminism, it was the racially charged issue of the IRS eliminating tax exemptions for private segregated Christian academies that had initially spurred his political activity. Race, more than any other issue, including abortion, spurred the rise of the Religious Right in the 1970s.[43] Although Falwell was not the only Evangelical Christian minister spearheading a grassroots political army of disaffected

Evangelicals, his Moral Majority would become the most important to Reagan's political success in 1980.

Like Jesse Helms, Falwell was another unabashed racist. His segregationist bona fides surfaced as early as 1958, when the twenty-four-year-old minister told his all-white congregation that the Bible condoned segregation and blasted *Brown v. Board of Education*:

> If Chief Justice Warren and his associates had known God's word and had desired to do the Lord's will, I am confident that the 1954 decision would not have been made. . . . The facilities should be separate. When God has drawn a line of distinction, we should not attempt to cross that line. . . . The true Negro does not want integration. . . . He realizes his potential is far better among his own race.

Falwell warned that integration "will destroy our race eventually."[44] Years later, he gained notoriety with a sermon he gave during the height of the Selma crisis, on March 21, 1965, titled "Ministers and Marches." In the sermon, Falwell attacked Martin Luther King Jr. and other Christian ministers for their civil rights activism: "Does the church have any command from God," he queried, "to involve itself in marches . . . such as many ministers and church leaders are so doing today?" Falwell answered his own question in the negative: "Christians should be concerned with fixing churches and not social justice, which should be left to the politicians." He also blamed Communism: "It is obvious that the communists, as they do in all parts of the world, are taking advantage of a tense situation in our land and are exploiting every incident to bring about violence and bloodshed."[45]

The civil rights movement that shook Falwell's hometown of Lynchburg had hardened his resolve to defend the racial status quo. In 1966, as Lynchburg braced for court-ordered desegregation of the local schools, Falwell announced the formation of his Lynchburg Christian Academy, a private segregated academy. Falwell also invited the segregationist governors George Wallace and Lester Maddox, of Georgia, as guests on his *Old-Time Gospel Hour*. Maddox had gained his racist reputation for refusing to serve three Black students at his restaurant and adopted the pickaxe as his symbol of defiance. With a less coarse manner but still racist, Falwell had also recently come to prominence for violating the newly enacted Civil Rights Act, and he defiantly refused to desegregate his Thomas Road congregation.[46]

Falwell had lacerated Martin Luther King Jr. for venturing into politics, but by 1979, Falwell, whose ministry was raking in an average of $4.6 million per month, was spending the bulk of his time traveling across the country in his own private jet and setting up Moral Majority chapters across the nation in hopes of galvanizing Evangelicals to oust Carter from the White House.[47] Although Falwell downplayed his racial views as his reason for entering politics, he founded the Moral Majority just after the IRS's revocation of the tax-exempt status of private segregated Christian academies.[48] He ascribed his entry into politics to the cultural and social changes that were sweeping through American society. Falwell moaned, "In some states it's easier to open a massage parlor than to open a Christian school."[49] After having mercilessly attacked King for becoming a political minister, Falwell became one of the most prominent political ministers of the 1980s. Whereas King's commitment to ending segregation rights was the cause of his life, Falwell's midlife entry into the political fray was motivated in large part by opposition to the desegregation King championed.

Reagan's political advisors took notice of the growing political import of white Southern Evangelicals. Lyn Nofziger recalled that the Evangelical Christians were "a natural constituency" because they shared many of Reagan's political views.[50] One of their many obvious commonalities was hostility to civil rights activism. In anticipation of the crucial March 8, 1980, South Carolina primary, Reagan agreed to make a campaign appearance at Bob Jones University in Greenville, South Carolina, a citadel of white supremacy.

Bob Jones Sr. had founded the university in 1926, the year after the Scopes Trial, as a refuge for Evangelicals from the rising tide of secularism. Like Falwell, Jones was also an unrepentant racist. As late as 1960, he wrote that Blacks should be grateful to whites for enslaving their ancestors because otherwise "they might still be over there in the jungles of Africa, unconverted." Like many segregationists, Jones believed that integrationists were usurping God's authority by removing the boundaries between the races.[51] In 1975 the federal government forced the university to admit Black students, but the university imposed stringent rules barring interracial dating. This prompted the Ford administration to revoke Bob Jones's tax-exempt status retroactive to 1970 and ordered the university to pay $490,000 in back taxes. By the time Reagan spoke at Bob Jones University, on January 31, 1980, the IRS decision was still on appeal.

None of this kept Reagan from delivering a rousing speech before an enthusiastic crowd of over six thousand students and faculty. Referring to the fundamentalist college as a "great university," Reagan assailed the new IRS guidelines "as an example of government bureaucrats establishing racial quotas."[52] According to *New York Times* reporter Robert Lindsay, Reagan "received one of his warmest receptions of his third presidential campaign" with three standing ovations and fourteen interruptions for applause.[53]

Reagan's appearance at Bob Jones University coincided with a particularly wrenching period in his third campaign for the presidency. His campaign team was shaken by bitter infighting among his top political operatives, leading Reagan to fire his campaign manager, John Sears.[54] Reagan's surprising second place finish behind George H. W. Bush in the January 21 Iowa caucus elicited concerns that Reagan was running a risky strategy of ignoring his rivals, a strategy exemplified by Reagan's refusal to debate his foes in Iowa.[55] Ever since the March 1966 incident at the National Negro Republican Assembly in Santa Monica, Reagan had refused to debate any of his political opponents. After his defeat in the Iowa caucus, he reversed course, and his noteworthy debate appearance in Nashua, New Hampshire, fueled his win in the pivotal 1980 New Hampshire Republican primary.[56] With the change of personnel, which included the return of longtime and trusted California aides Ed Meese, Lyn Nofziger, and Michael Deaver, Reagan regained his verve on the campaign trail.[57] By March, Reagan was poised to seize the Republican nomination.

By late spring 1980, the inability of Carter to free the hostages in Iran, along with deepening economic woes, caused his lead over Reagan to evaporate. On April 24, an ill-fated military operation to rescue the hostages ended in failure and the death of eight soldiers. Two months later, a New York Times/CBS poll revealed that only 20 percent of Americans approved of Carter's conduct of foreign policy.[58] To add to Carter's mounting woes, the most moderate of the Republican presidential nominees, Republican congressman John Anderson of Illinois, who was drawing an enthusiastic following among college students, decided to mount a run as an independent candidate to possibly siphon off liberals and independents from Carter.

With Carter's standing among the American people plummeting, Republicans headed to the economically ravaged city of Detroit in July to nominate Reagan. Of the 1,994 Republican delegates, only 56, or 2.8 percent were Black, representing a decline from 3.4 percent in 1976. The Black-owned *Michigan Chronicle* ran the headline "G.O.P. Meet: No Blacks Wanted?"[59] The decision to hold the convention in Detroit, which was 56 percent Black, had sparked much controversy within the party. Many high-ranking Republicans, including Reagan, had complained that the city was depressing and preferred to hold the convention in the booming Sunbelt city of Dallas.[60] Most of the delegates were staying at the newly constructed Renaissance Center, a gigantic hotel complex separated from the rest of the city by a thirty-foot concrete wall. From the top of the hotel, journalist Teddy White observed, "One could not see the dingy city of those who still lived, hoped, and wanted jobs in Detroit."[61] Many Black businessmen groused that the delegates seemed nervous about patronizing local establishments.[62]

The Republican platform reflected the growing clout of the racially conservative Southern wing of the party. With Reagan's approval, they inserted a plank pledging to "halt the unconstitutional regulatory vendetta launched by Mr. Carter's IRS against the independent Christian schools" and endorsed a constitutional amendment to outlaw busing.[63] The platform also pledged that a Reagan administration would appoint very conservative judges who would reverse the expansive civil rights jurisprudence of the Warren court. In fact, the racially regressive thrust of the Republican platform was so pleasing to the Ku Klux Klan that it released a statement in praise, saying, "It reads as if it were written by a Klansman."[64]

On the evening of July 17, 1980, Reagan accepted the Republican nomination and fulfilled a long-held dream of the party's right wing. In a well-crafted speech, he pledged a renewed prosperity and a return to "old-fashioned American values."[65] Reagan's primetime speech promised to restore America's greatness, and it electrified the delegates hungry to reclaim the presidency.[66] In an attempt at Black outreach, Reagan stressed his "concern for the poor and disadvantaged."[67] Following Reagan's speech, DC delegate Melvin Burton exemplified Blacks' manifest concerns over Reagan: "It will take more than one short speech to mend the wounds."[68]

Following his commanding performance at the Republican National Convention, Reagan departed Detroit in an enviable political position, with a sizable lead over Carter in the polls.[69] Reagan's solicitous words at his convention failed to appease Blacks. Just a few weeks before the convention, Reagan had declined the NAACP's invitation to address their annual convention held in Miami Beach. A campaign official cited "shoddy mail-handling for the delay" that caused them to overlook a planned vacation to Mexico for the nominee. The next day, the Reagan campaign abruptly announced the vacation to Mexico was now a working "retreat."[70] NAACP executive director Benjamin Hooks criticized Reagan's snub, accusing him of writing off the Black vote by passing up the group's convention for a "week of play and recreation."[71] By early August, Reagan's cool relationship with Blacks was one of the few blemishes in his otherwise promising campaign to topple the embattled Carter.

THE GENERAL ELECTION CAMPAIGN: NESHOBA COUNTY, STATES' RIGHTS, AND THE BACKLASH

In hopes of countering the negative press surrounding his recent snubbing of the NAACP, Reagan agreed to speak at the National Urban League's annual convention, scheduled for August 5, in New York City. While there, he also planned to visit the organization's president and renowned civil rights leader, Vernon Jordan, who was recovering in a New York hospital from grievous wounds he had sustained from a sniper attack by a white supremacist in Fort Wayne, Indiana, in May. If these overtures were meant to moderate his image, they were dampened when Reagan chose to speak at the Neshoba County Fair, in Philadelphia, Mississippi, only miles away from the site of the murder of three civil rights workers in 1964. Carter had eked out a razor-thin victory over Ford in the Magnolia State in 1976, and Trent Lott, a young, ambitious Republican congressman from Mississippi, and Charles Pickering, co-chair of Reagan's Mississippi campaign, thought that Reagan's appearance at the fair, a premier showcase for politicians, could push Mississippi into Reagan's column "by reaching out to George Wallace inclined voters."[72]

Since the end of the nineteenth century, the Neshoba County Fair had been an annual event where Mississippi politicians launched their political campaigns. That made it the site of many racist diatribes from white supremacist politicians such as Senators Theodore G. Bilbo and James Eastland, and former governor Ross Barnett. At that site, many Mississippi politicians had called for "states' rights," the long-standing political euphemism for preventing the federal government from interfering with the racial customs of the South.

The symbolism of Reagan making his first campaign appearance in Philadelphia, Mississippi, just two weeks after accepting the Republican nomination, rattled Reagan's pollster, Richard Wirthlin. He worried that the trip would corroborate the accusations that Reagan was grossly insensitive to the concerns of African Americans—he had already received the Klan's endorsement.[73] In an emotional meeting in Reagan's bedroom, Wirthlin beseeched the candidate to cancel the appearance. Once again, Reagan lost his temper when confronted with the insinuation that he was racist or supported racist policies. He became so annoyed at his pollster that he "reddened and hurled his briefing papers" at him.[74]

On August 3, 1980, Reagan boarded his newly chartered United jetliner at Los Angeles International Airport, accompanied by Louisiana's newly elected Republican governor, David C. Treen, a former chair of Louisiana's States' Rights Party, known as the Dixiecrats.[75] Reagan was the first presidential nominee of a major political party to attend the fair since the event started in 1889, and that fact was not lost on the twenty thousand white people gathered there, many proudly waving Confederate flags and chanting, "We want Reagan! We want Reagan!"[76] In his speech, Reagan declared, "I believe in states' rights." He vowed, if elected to the presidency, to "restore to states and local governments the power that properly belongs to them." For decades, Reagan had spoken of the need to curtail the power of the federal government in favor of more local control, but this was the first time he ever used the loaded term "states' rights."[77]

Then and now, Reagan's resounding endorsement of states' rights at the fair has been the subject of much controversy. Although states' rights were not the centerpiece of Reagan's speech, and he had long called for a rollback of federal power, anyone fluent in American history knew that the term was linked to the South's defense of slavery and to segregationists' calls for "massive resistance" after *Brown v. Board of Education.* Even worse, Reagan never acknowledged in his speech the murders of the three civil rights workers, and it is not possible that Reagan and his campaign staff were unaware of the proximity of the site of the murders to the fair.

As a chief lieutenant to Martin Luther King Jr., Andrew Young had been a firsthand witness to the terror of racist violence in Neshoba County. He recalled King standing at the steps of the Neshoba County Courthouse in the summer of 1966 describing how the murderers of the three civil rights workers were "no doubt within the range of my voice," and he remembered a voice from the white mob guarding the courthouse door yelling, "Ya damn right. We're here right behind you."[78] This memory haunted Young, and days after Reagan's speech at the fair, a distraught Young called out the codes implicit in the term "states' rights" in an op-ed in the *Washington Post*:

> What "states' rights" would candidate Reagan revive? Is Reagan saying he intends to do everything he can to turn the clock back to the Mississippi justice of 1964? Do the powers of state and local governments include the right to end the voting rights of black citizens? Would Reagan dare to commission, directly or indirectly, the Sheriff Raineys and the vigilantes to ride once again, poisoning the political process with hatred and violence?[79]

Reagan's campaign indignantly denied any malign intent, but the message was clear. Above all, Reagan's states' rights speech highlighted conservatives' quest dating back to the early years of *National Review* to make the Southern Republican party a respectable, modern version of an all-white party.

After the speech, Reagan flew to New York City and visited Vernon Jordan in the hospital.[80] The next day, Reagan addressed the National Urban League convention, where he accused the Democrats of failing to deliver on their promises to Black America.[81] Stressing his plan to bring jobs to the nation, Reagan's tepid reception by the Urban League markedly contrasted with the ecstatic reception he received two days earlier in Mississippi.[82] Within hours of his Urban League speech, Reagan visited the South Bronx and stood in the same garbage-strewn lot on Charlotte Street where Jimmy Carter had promised a new federally sponsored job-training center on October 5, 1977.[83] His attempt to highlight Carter's failure to keep his promises of redeveloping the blighted ghetto received a hostile reception from a group of approximately fifty Black bystanders. The throng jeered, "Talk to the people and not the press," which prompted Reagan to walk toward the crowd, but the taunts only increased.[84]After shouts of "What are you going to do for blacks?" cascaded from all sides, Reagan retorted, "I can't do a damn thing for you if I don't get elected."[85] As Reagan left the scene, a few demonstrators chanted, "We want Kennedy."[86] When a reporter asked Reagan if he would make similar visits in the future, Reagan said, "Of course," but then he turned the knife: "I'd like to visit someplace where they are doing something for themselves."[87] Despite these perfunctory attempts at outreach to Black Americans, Reagan's awkward attempts could not expunge his abysmal record on civil rights. More than anything else, they were meant to mitigate the white electorate's concern that Reagan was a racist.

In the second week of August, Reagan ceded the spotlight to the Democrats, who gathered for the nominating convention in the sweltering mid-summer humidity of New York City. Carter withstood Kennedy's primary challenge, but the liberal lion stayed in the race until the end. Accordingly, an air of defeatism lingered about Madison Square Garden. The most recent Gallup poll revealed that Carter's approval stood at a woeful 21 percent, with 77 percent disapproving. Reagan's Southern outreach was reaping dividends, as an ABC-Harris poll showed Reagan led Carter by twenty points in the president's native South.[88]

With the Iranian hostages and the anemic economy as the dominant concerns of the American public, Carter began the uphill reelection campaign with a strong appeal to Black voters anxious over the possibility of a Reagan presidency.[89] The day after his rather somber acceptance speech, the historically literate Carter told a group of Black delegates that the upcoming campaign provided the starkest ideological clash on racial matters since Goldwater's challenge to President Lyndon B. Johnson in 1964. Reminding them of Reagan's visit to Mississippi, Carter warned, "When [Reagan] says anything about states' rights, I don't want any of you to forget that that's a code word [for] discrimination." Continuing his remarks to Black delegates, Carter said, "One of the things that bothers me is the attempted resurrection of the Ku Klux Klan, but we're going to put them back in their grave and keep them there." Carter's comments evoked an emotional response from the delegates, who frequently interrupted him with cheers and chanted, "We want Jimmy! We want Jimmy!"[90]

On Labor Day, Reagan made a critical gaffe that afforded Carter his long-awaited opportunity to inject race into the campaign. In response to a heckler wearing a Jimmy Carter mask at the Michigan State Fair, Reagan shouted back, "I'm happy to be here while [Carter]," who was campaigning in Tuscumbia, Alabama, "is opening his campaign down there in the city that gave birth to the Ku Klux Klan." Reagan's quip elicited "audible" groans from the audience.[91] News of the blunder reached President Carter, campaigning in Tuscumbia, which, though it had been a Klan stronghold, was not the birthplace of the original Klan. Carter blasted Reagan's remarks as "uncalled for, inaccurate, and . . . something that all Southerners resent."[92] The Grand Wizard of the Knights of the Ku Klux Klan kept the matter alive by declaring his support once again for Reagan as "the best of the three" main candidates.[93]

Reagan's blunder was matched by a toughening of Carter's campaign rhetoric and a frenzied effort to capitalize on Reagan's many stumbles, especially those around race.[94] On September 16, a combative Carter returned to Georgia, where he spoke before a crowd of 350 civil rights leaders at Martin Luther King Jr.'s Ebenezer Baptist Church, perhaps the most illustrious civil rights pulpit in the nation. After stepping up to the lectern, Carter attacked Reagan for resorting to racist tactics: "You've seen in this campaign the stirrings of hate and the rebirth of code words like 'states' rights' in a speech in Mississippi and in a campaign reference to the Ku Klux Klan relating to the South." He continued: "This is a message that creates a cloud on the political horizon. Hatred has no place in this country." Carter warned if Reagan should prevail, "you're not going to get your telephone call answered at the White House."[95]

Carter's attempt to highlight the racist tenor of Reagan's Mississippi speech failed to gain traction. Most Americans did not believe the genial former actor and governor of California to be racist. Instead of Reagan's Neshoba speech or Klan endorsement, the narrative shifted to Carter's "meanness" and desperation to divert attention from the ongoing saga of the hostages and the sputtering economy.[96] The *Washington Post* editorialized that Carter's attack on Reagan highlighted the president's tendency to convey a "mean and frantic nature," and the paper denied that Reagan was a "racist" or "hater."[97]

In a news conference two days after the Atlanta speech, an emotional and defensive Carter bristled over the charge that he was running a "mean campaign" and disavowed having suggested that Reagan was "a racist in any degree."[98] But Carter insisted that Reagan had "injected code words in the campaign," not he. In a particularly tense exchange, Lisa Myers, a reporter for the *Washington Star*, pointed out that it was Patricia Harris, Carter's Black housing and urban development secretary, who first injected the Klan into the presidential race. An exasperated Carter replied, "I'm not blaming Governor Reagan. . . . The press seems to be obsessed with the issue." The perverse dynamic of Carter having to exonerate Reagan for his Mississippi states' rights speech unsettled his aides. Realizing that Carter's attacks had failed, Carter conceded that if he had a second chance, he "would do it differently."[99] Reagan, whose Neshoba County speech was intended to rile up George Wallace–inclined voters, blasted Carter's Ebenezer speech as "shameful," because "we ought to be pulling the country together."[100]

After weeks of protracted negotiations, the parties agreed to hold only one presidential debate, in Cleveland, Ohio, on October 28, the Tuesday before the election.[101] The economy and foreign policy dominated the ninety-minute televised debate. The stakes could not have been higher: "It has become the world heavyweight championship and the Super Bowl combined," wrote columnist Elizabeth Drew.[102] As the debate turned to domestic concerns, Reagan fielded a question from Black journalist William Hilliard, managing editor of the *Portland Oregonian*, on the state of race relations in the US. He gave a familiar answer: "I am an eternal optimist, and I believe this nation has made great progress from the days when I was young and when this country didn't even know it had a racial problem." Sensing an opportunity, President Carter, a white Southerner who grew up with Jim Crow but became a civil rights supporter, pounced, "I noticed that Governor Reagan said that when he was a young man there was no knowledge of a racial problem in this country. Those who suffered from discrimination because of race and sex certainly knew we had a racial problem. We have gone a long way toward correcting these problems, but we still have a long way to go."[103]

This evocative exchange on race, however, was lost amid the chatter about Reagan's commanding performance. An ABC instant poll showed that voters thought Reagan had won the debate by a 2 to 1 margin. With his folksy "there you go again" quips, Reagan exuded a reassuring fatherly image to the American people.[104] By contrast, a tense and tired Carter displayed a mastery of the issues but was more aggressive, even belligerent. In his closing remarks, Reagan memorably asked the viewing public: "Are you better off than you were four years ago?" With only one week to go before the election, the debate gave Reagan added momentum.[105]

After the debate, a *New York Amsterdam News* poll showed that 80 percent of Black Americans thought Carter had won the debate.[106] Watching in Chicago, Illinois state senator Harold Washington, who would later become Chicago's first Black mayor, erupted in laughter after hearing Reagan speak of a time when the country didn't know it had a race problem: "How could he have been raised in America and not know about racial discrimination?"[107]

On November 4, 1980, Reagan scored a landslide victory, winning 50.9 percent of the popular vote to Carter's 41.2 percent, with independent candidate John B. Anderson a distant 6.6 percent. Apart from Carter's triumph in his native Georgia, Reagan swept the South, winning 61 percent of white Southerners. Evangelicals' success in mobilizing a grassroots army of Christian voters expedited Reagan's Southern stampede. Reagan's success extended to down-ballot races throughout the country. On his coattails, Republicans took over the Senate for the first time since 1954. A number of stalwart civil rights supporters, including George McGovern, Frank Church, Birch Bayh, Gaylord Nelson, Warren Magnuson, and John Culver, were among the Democratic casualties. The Republican majority presented Reagan with the opportunity to pack the federal courts with conservative judges who were determined to reduce the judiciary's role in civil rights and civil liberties enforcement.

The 1980 election struck African Americans across the country like a thunderclap. Julius Nicholas penned an editorial in the *Philadelphia Tribune* likening his fears of a Reagan presidency to "a Jew on the eve of Adolph Hitler's chancellorship." Walking through the ghetto of Chester, Pennsylvania, Nicholas observed, "News of President-elect Ronald Reagan's victory spread like a deadly poisonous gas, crippling everything in sight. The poor and oppressed minorities in the city were left reeling by the paw of the beast."[108] At a November 22 news conference in New York, NAACP executive director Benjamin Hooks expressed concern at the fearful mood that had pervaded Black communities, and he noted the number of Black people "who are buying pistols and ammunition and rifles and who are preparing for overt violence."[109] Their fear was that Reagan's victory would result in the rollback of the hard-fought civil rights gains of the 1960s.[110] Hooks urged Reagan to hold a television address on all three networks to quell the "hysterical fear" gripping Blacks.[110] Reagan agreed instead to convene, along with Vice President-elect George H. W. Bush, an hour-long meeting on December 11 with a number of prominent civil rights leaders. The parties had an "open dialogue" but could not resolve their profound disagreements over Reagan's support of tax credits for private schools, a lower minimum wage, and his opposition to busing and the expansion of the Voting Rights Act to all fifty states.[112] After the meeting, Joseph E. Lowery, head of the SCLC and a former associate of Martin Luther King Jr.'s, concluded, "I don't think there's any question that we are in for difficult times."[113]

Reagan and his aides dismissed the concerns of the civil rights leadership. In order to cloak their racially regressive policies under the shroud of color-blindness, they had been actively cultivating a network of Black conservatives to implement their agenda of "color-blind conservatism." On December 14, 1980, this new generation of Black conservatives assembled at the elegant Fairmount Hotel in San Francisco for a two-day conference on "black alternatives."[114] Ed Meese, Reagan's close aide and chief advisor on civil rights, attended the conference and listened to speech after speech denouncing affirmative action, rent control, the minimum wage, and busing and advocating for "self-reliance." Clarence Thomas, then a young aide to Senator John Danforth of Missouri, teemed with "barely controlled exhilaration" at the prospect of speaking before Blacks who might "agree with him for a change." These conservative Blacks were promised jobs in the Reagan administration, where they would become the vanguard of the civil rights counterrevolution and would help to blunt charges that the administration's policies were racist.

Black conservatives such as Thomas would amass power in the Reagan administration, but most Blacks agreed with Vernon Jordan's proclamation that 1980 was a year of "storm warnings" for Black Americans and a "continued erosion in the black condition." Jordan believed that racial tensions had increased "alarmingly," and as the economy continued to sputter, Blacks bore the brunt of it.[115]

On January 20, 1981, Ronald Reagan, a few weeks shy of his seven-tieth birthday, took the oath of office. Within minutes of being sworn in, reports arrived that a deal had been reached to release the American hostages in Iran. Amid the euphoria, some commenters spoke of how Reagan's ascension to power augured a new period of patriotic optimism. On the other hand, many liberals and Blacks were struck by the paucity of people of color at the most lavish, opulent, and costly inauguration ever held in the nation's capital, provoking Barry Goldwater to moan about its "ostentatiousness," particularly "at a time when most people in this country just can't hack it."[116] In addition to Reagan's racist policies and rhetoric, the sumptuous inaugural balls, and calls to return Amer-ica to a fictional golden past nauseated many progressives and people of color.[117] In view of Reagan's political history and policy proposals, they perceived the new president's right-wing policies as synonymous with racism. White Mississippi journalist Hodding Carter III encapsulated it best when he wrote: "It's a new America, Ronald Reagan's America, . . . it smells a lot like the old Mississippi."[118]

PART III

PRESIDENT REAGAN

Rolling Back the
Civil Rights Revolution
1981–1989

CHAPTER 8

LAUNCHING A COUNTERREVOLUTION IN CIVIL RIGHTS

Black people in this country believe, whether he denies the allegation or not, that he is a racist.
—Representative Mickey Leland, chair of the Black Caucus of the Democratic National Committee (September 1982)[1]

Under Mr. Reynolds . . . the civil rights division has changed sides. It no longer is an advocate for blacks or minorities. . . . Rights for Americans seems to him . . . to mean rights for white males.
—Former attorney general Nicholas Katzenbach (1988)[2]

R onald Reagan assumed the presidency in January 1981 amid the worst economic downturn since the Great Depression and an alarming spike in Cold War tensions. From the outset of his presidency, his preternatural optimism and inimitable grace and humor in the wake of an assassination attempt in March 1981 endeared him to millions of Americans searching for heroes after a string of national traumas: political assassinations, the Vietnam War, Watergate, the Iran hostage crisis, and more. Black Americans, however, recoiled at the Reagan administration's ideological opposition to the civil rights reforms of the past two decades. While Reagan's tributes to "old-fashioned" and "small-town" American values provoked a wave of patriotism and nostalgia among whites for a bygone era, Blacks scoffed at Reagan's mythical vision of America, which, they felt, relegated them to second-class citizenship. By the middle of 1981, Blacks and their civil rights allies began mobilizing to thwart Reagan's attempt to roll back the gains of the civil rights revolution.

BLACKS AND THE REAGAN ADMINISTRATION: ON THE OUTSIDE LOOKING IN

Given Reagan's troubling record and rhetoric on civil rights, African Americans were never susceptible to Reagan's beguiling charm that sustained him through a series of scandals that would have toppled other presidents. Reagan harbored the myopic view that with the passage of the landmark civil rights legislation of the 1960s, which he, of course, had opposed, America was now "a color-blind" society whose doors were open to African Americans as long as they took "the initiative to walk on through."[3] Reagan's preposterous notion that America had ever transcended racism remains a staple of the conservative zeitgeist. Most dramatically, Reagan's most memorable line from his inaugural address, "Government is not the solution to our problem; government is the problem," ignored the fact that it was the intervention of the federal government that abolished slavery, toppled segregation, and had taken steps to redress centuries of institutionalized racism. Of all the predictions made of the incoming Reagan administration, writes historian Kenneth O'Reilly, "the notion of an imminent assault on the civil rights gains of the 1960s was perhaps the most common."[4]

From day one, a chasm opened between the Reagan administration and African Americans. The absence of African Americans at the Reagan White House's first three large social functions sparked talk of a new "social racism," and even "renewed racism."[5] A procession of advisors entered and exited Reagan's White House political turnstile, but it was First Lady Nancy Reagan who wielded the greatest influence on her husband. Longtime aides trembled in her presence, and as Reagan's chief of staff, Don Regan, would learn, crossing Nancy would result in being fired.

With respect to racial matters, Loyal Davis's stepdaughter displayed little compassion for the underprivileged or for Blacks. On the contrary, Nancy Reagan was an avid cultivator of the wealthy and powerful. In spite of her many intimate friendships with gays in the fashion and entertainment world, she dissuaded the president from speaking out on the AIDS crisis in the 1980s because many of his staunchest Evangelical supporters dismissed it as a "gay" disease. She even turned down a desperate plea from her close friend Rock Hudson to use her clout to get him admitted to a French hospital as the dying actor sought treatment for AIDS in Paris.[6] Early on, the press dubbed her "Queen Nancy" for her lavish spending on refurbishing the White House and for her expensive jewelry and wardrobe.

Reagan's cabinet choices were virtually all wealthy white males. His attorney general nominee, William French Smith, a wealthy Los Angeles corporate attorney who was also Reagan's personal attorney and Kitchen Cabinet member, had no background or interest in civil rights. As a member of the University of California Board of Regents, Smith had voted to fire Angela Davis, and he opposed the push for the university to divest its holdings in companies doing business with the racist South African government.[7] Most ominously, Reagan chose William Bradford Reynolds, another corporate lawyer and a scion of the DuPont family, to head the Civil Rights Division (CRD) of the Department of Justice.[8] A staunch conservative, Reynolds would emerge as the chief spokesman against racial preferences in hiring and college admissions, which he insisted foisted on America "a kind of racial spoils system" favoring Blacks and other historically disadvantaged minorities against whites.[9] In the early months of his tenure, Reynolds's feverish assaults on affirmative action and efforts to recast civil rights led to a series of resignations among seasoned veteran attorneys in the CRD division.[10] Under Reynolds, the CRD emerged as the fulcrum for the Reagan administration's civil rights counterrevolution.

Except for the appointment of Samuel R. Pierce to head the Department of Housing and Urban Development (HUD), Reagan did not appoint any African Americans to his administration's top one hundred jobs, and there were only nineteen in the most significant four hundred jobs.[11] Pierce's selection provided no solace to the civil rights community; he was a conservative attorney who sat on the board of giant corporations.[12] William Sullivan, a senior official at the FBI in the 1960s, had reportedly once proposed to J. Edgar Hoover that Pierce replace Martin Luther King Jr. as the leader of the civil rights movement. This allegation was one of the many reasons African Americans disparaged Pierce as Reagan's "Uncle Tom."[13] At a June 1981 White House reception for municipal leaders, Reagan mistook Pierce for someone else, greeting him as "Mr. Mayor." His low profile within the administration earned him the moniker "Silent Sam." Still, Pierce was the only cabinet member to serve throughout Reagan's two terms, even if his stewardship of HUD was marred by financial improprieties and allegations of rampant corruption involving the theft of millions of dollars.[14] During congressional investigations of his HUD stewardship, Pierce earned the ignominy of becoming the first cabinet member to invoke the Fifth Amendment at a congressional hearing since Albert Fall in the Teapot Dome scandal in the 1920s.[15]

Many of Reagan's actions signaled a new, hostile approach to civil rights. He initially tapped M. E. Bradford to chair the prestigious National Endowment for the Humanities. Bradford, best known for his criticisms of Abraham Lincoln as "a dangerous man" comparable to Hitler, represented the nostalgic Confederate remnant in the conservative movement.[16] Bradford's extremism, however, led his advisors to persuade Reagan to name instead William Bennett, who would emerge as a conservative culture warrior as head of the Department of Education and later as drug czar in the George H. W. Bush administration, in charge of the racist War on Drugs. In another move, Reagan announced his decision to abolish the Republican Party's special liaison offices that had been created to reach out to African Americans, Latinos, and other nonwhites.[17] In a meeting with Black lawmakers, he insulted them by resurrected his oft-repeated tale of the "welfare queen."[18] By the summer of 1981, *Newsweek* was characterizing African Americans' "isolation from power" as "more acute now than at any time since the dawn of the New Deal."[19]

REAGANOMICS: ASSAULT ON THE SOCIAL SAFETY NET

In the first year of the Reagan administration, nothing galvanized his critics more than their belief that Reagan's proposed budget cuts unfairly targeted the poor at the expense of the rich. The passage of an economic plan to revive the moribund economy plagued by high interest rates, inflation, and unemployment became Reagan's paramount domestic priority. Reagan assigned the task of formulating the plan to his Office of Management and Budget director, former congressman David Stockman, the youngest Cabinet appointee in 160 years. Like Reagan, the thirty-four-year-old Stockman was a former liberal who had converted to libertarianism and free-market economics.[20] Stockman conflated the civil rights revolution with the Great Society programs, which he sardonically called the "Second American Revolution." Endowed with the missionary zeal of a convert, Stockman regarded Social Security as a "giant Ponzi scheme" and was determined to wage a frontal assault on the welfare state.[21]

With Reagan's blessing, Stockman hatched the most dramatic transformation in US economic policy since the New Deal. Dubbed "Reaganomics" or "supply-side economics," it espoused the untested theory that lower marginal tax rates on wealthy earners combined with a massive increase in the defense budget, would spur economic growth to such an extent that the Treasury's coffer would have surplus revenue. At the same time, it proposed draconian reductions in social spending for programs such as Head Start, the Comprehensive Employment and Training Act (CETA), school lunches, food stamps, and the Legal Service Corporation, all of which benefited poor Americans, many of whom were African Americans.[22] Critics charged that Reagan's economic policies demonized the poor. In 1983, top Reagan aide Ed Meese corroborated these concerns with his controversial claim that the administration "had considerable information that people go to soup kitchens because the food is free and that's easier than paying for it."[23]

On March 10, 1981, Reagan delivered his budget proposal to Congress. It called for slashing the budgets of more than two hundred domestic programs by $48.6 billion, while cutting taxes for the wealthy and dramatically increasing defense spending. Reagan's proposals left intact most of the programs of the New Deal that had originally excluded millions of African Americans, including Social Security, the GI Bill, and the federal minimum wage.[24] Instead, he swung his budget axe at the Great Society programs of the mid-1960s, which had disproportionately benefited the poor, who were still predominantly Black. Critics saw Reaganomics as a "cruel assault on the poor, and tantamount to 1920s trickle-down economics."[25] African American congressman Augustus F. Hawkins accused Reagan of reversing "the role of Robin Hood completely by taking from the poor and giving to the rich."[26]

Reagan's audacious proposals prompted the Congressional Black Caucus (CBC) to unveil an alternative federal budget that would raise $27 billion more in taxes and spend $25 billion more on food stamps, education, and Medicaid. Along with the Democratic Speaker of the House, Tip O'Neill, the CBC emerged as the bulwark against the Reagan administration's assaults on the social safety net. Walter Fauntroy, the CBC head, cited Hubert Humphrey's memorable quote: "The moral test of government is how it treats those who are in the dawn of life, the children; those who are in the twilight of life, the aged; and those who are in the shadows of life, the sick, the needy and the handicapped." Fauntroy concluded, "By that standard, the Reagan budget proposal fails the moral test of government."[27]

In the midst of the contentious debates over Reagan's budget, John Hinckley Jr., a deranged young man yearning to impress the actress Jodie Foster, attempted to kill the president. He fired six bullets, one of which struck Reagan and lodged in his left lung, an inch from his heart. He lost over half of his blood volume, and unbeknownst to the American public, the seventy-year-old-Reagan had been very close to death in the emergency room. The surgery to remove the bullet was successful, and Reagan became the first president to survive after being wounded in an assassination attempt. His grace and courage in the face of the attempted assassination precipitated an outburst of patriotic fervor unseen since the early 1960s. To some, his resilient spirit symbolized a renewed American vitality and rekindled the public's esteem for the presidency. It also gave his conservative economic program a boost. The assassin was a young white man, from a wealthy, conservative family. Nevertheless, the *Pittsburgh Courier* anxiously mused, "How will Reagan's wounds be used against Blacks' interests?" [28] One Black pundit worried that the opposition to Reagan's budget that had been growing before the assassination was beginning to evaporate.[29]

On Tuesday evening, April 28, 1981, only thirty days after the near-fatal assassination attempt, a wan yet beaming Reagan entered the House of Representatives to a thunderous three-minute applause from members of both Houses of Congress. In a wavering voice that demonstrated the residual effects of his serious chest wound, Reagan seized the potential of the moment for some political theater.[30] In perhaps the most dramatic presidential appearance before Congress since Franklin Roosevelt returned from the Yalta Conference at the end of World War II, Reagan stirred the millions of Americans watching television in an address about the budget. In the wake of his assassination attempt, Reagan had reached unprecedented levels in popularity—public opinion polls revealed that only 18 percent of the American public disapproved of his performance as president.[31] Speaking to reporters on the morning of the speech, Speaker O'Neill conceded Reagan's political invincibility: "Because of the attempted assassination, the president has become a hero in the eyes of the country," he said. "We can't argue with a man as popular as that."[32]

For the next six years, O'Neill, the white-haired, corpulent, cigar-chomping Boston pol, would become Reagan's foil and sparring partner. The embodiment of old-style New Deal liberalism, O'Neill was in a season of political purgatory outmatched by the glamorous Reagan. In the 1980 campaign, the Republicans had run a series of highly effective political commercials caricaturing the Speaker as the symbol of the old, corrupt political system. Like Reagan's other Democratic foes, O'Neill had a stellar record on civil rights. As a thirty-two-year-old member of the Massachusetts state legislature, he sponsored Massachusetts' historic fair employment act prohibiting racial discrimination among state government employees. Later, as Speaker of the Massachusetts House, he shepherded a bill extending that law to employees of public-financed higher education.[33] For Tip O'Neill, civil rights was always a matter of conscience, and not political expediency, since African Americans constituted only 2.3 percent of his constituency.[34] As a congressman, he worked tirelessly for the passage of the Fair Housing Act of 1968. In perhaps his most courageous moment, he braved the sneers and howls of many of his Irish and Italian American working-class Cambridge constituents to support busing during the racial upheaval that swept Boston in the 1970s.

Along with Speaker O'Neill, the CBC and their liberal allies would be the redoubt against Reagan's onslaught of programs targeted at helping African Americans and the poor. On May 7, 1981, the day that 270 congressmen voted in favor of Reagan's budget, African American journalist Carl Rowan addressed the Pittsburgh Branch of the NAACP and called it a "day of lunacy."[35] Such searing criticism prompted White House aide Stephanie Lee-Miller to circulate a memo urging cabinet members to increase their exposure with the African American community.[36] A few days later, Reagan decided to address the forthcoming annual convention of the NAACP in Denver on June 29, 1981, a reversal of his snubbing of the venerable civil rights organization the previous year.[37]

As he was about to give his first major speech to an African American audience as president, NAACP chair Margaret Bush Wilson stood before the crowd of five thousand and indicted Reagan's budget for reviving "war, pestilence, famine, and death." She went on to needle him for refusing to address the convention the previous year and said, "The NAACP does not necessarily subscribe to the views which are about to be expressed." The understated remark drew chortles from the audience, Reagan reddened, and Nancy Reagan, separated from her husband by Benjamin Hooks and his wife, seethed with rage.[38]

Facing one of the coolest receptions in his public life, Reagan delivered an earnest but sharp address condemning bigotry and violence and advocating his belief in "equal treatment for all citizens," not just those who voted for him. Pivoting to the economy, Reagan defended his economic proposals and accused his critics of "demagoguery." In his most controversial statement, he reiterated his patronizing view that government programs had created "a new kind of bondage for blacks."[39] He refused to say whether he would keep the key provision of the Voting Rights Act of 1965, a preclearance that imposed special restrictions on Southern states and a few counties in the North that had historically discriminated against Blacks, which was set to expire the following year.[40] Notwithstanding Reagan's pluck in facing such an unsupportive audience, NAACP leader Benjamin Hooks insisted afterward that Reagan's twenty-minute speech did not mean "we of the NAACP have been persuaded to his point of view." On the contrary, Reagan's budget, Hooks said, was bound "to inflict additional hardships on the poor, of which blacks and minorities are a disproportionate share." Throughout the duration of the convention, NAACP members expressed their displeasure over Reagan and his economic agenda. Coretta Scott King described Reagan's budget cuts as a "shameful assault on the children of America."[41] The *New York Times* observed more eloquence than commitment in the president's speech and said the social programs Reagan threatened to cut were not a new kind of bondage for Blacks but, for the time being, "their only hope."[42]

The cavalcade of criticism, however, could not stop Reagan's economic plan from steamrolling through Congress. In early August, from his mountaintop ranch perched high above Santa Barbara, Reagan signed the Omnibus Budget Reconciliation Act of 1981 and, a few days later, the Economic Recovery Tax Act. Signed with much fanfare, OBRA and ERTA were the twin pillars of Reaganomics, representing a rupture from a generation of economic orthodoxy. To begin with, OBRA constituted the largest retrenchment in nonmilitary spending in American history—$35.2 billion in cuts to discretionary programs created during the Great Society aimed at helping the poor. Among the substantial reductions were food-stamp funding, school-lunch programs, job corps, and public housing support. The CETA apprenticeship program lost all of its funding. Among the other casualties of OBRA was the Community Action Agency, originally known as the Office of Economic Opportunity, which was a cornerstone of the Great Society.[43]

The juxtaposition of the budget cuts with the passage of ERTA—the largest tax cut in American history—reinforced outrage that Reagan's proposals amounted to class warfare against the most vulnerable. It reduced the marginal income tax rate by 23 percent over three years, with the highest rate dropping from 70 percent to 50 percent. By the end of his two terms, it would go down to 28 percent. Reagan's 1981 tax cuts showered $164 billion on the private sector and led to massive budget deficits. The *Los Angeles Sentinel* blasted Reagan as "the least popular President among blacks since Herbert Hoover."[44] Combined with the former SAG president's firing of over eleven thousand striking air-traffic controllers who had refused his order to return to work, which led to the Federal Labor Relations Authority decertifying the Professional Air Traffic Controllers Organization (PATCO), Reagan's assault on labor, a central pillar of the New Deal order, was off to a bracing start.

The slashing of billions of dollars from social programs in the midst of a worsening recession led thousands of African Americans and poor whites to flock to soup kitchens across the country in search of a hot meal.[45] The *New York Times* observed in Reagan's first year, "Much of the progress that had been made against poverty in the 1960s and 1970s had been wiped out."[46] Tip O'Neill recalled the "most depressing thing of all was the hatred of the poor that developed all across America."[47] An epidemic of "homelessness," unseen since the Great Depression, began dotting the American landscape. Anger over Reagan's budget and the firing of the PATCO workers precipitated the largest, most spontaneous outpouring of protest since the Vietnam War. On September 19, 1981, the AFL-CIO sponsored a nationwide rally, which received strong endorsement and support from civil rights organizations, drawing over 260,000 protestors to Washington, DC, alone. Invoking the memory of her husband, Coretta Scott King called the march a continuation of the 1963 March on Washington so that "with one voice we can protest the wholesale selfishness" that Reagan's leadership had fomented around the nation.[48]

AN ATTEMPT TO CRIPPLE THE VOTING RIGHTS ACT

With the Voting Rights Act (VRA) set to expire on August 6, 1982, other than his slashing of social programs for the poor, nothing loomed larger to the civil rights community at the outset of the Reagan administration than its future.[49] Of its import, Coretta Scott King remarked, "Securing the right to vote was a blood covenant, a right won and sealed by the deaths of men and women, whites and blacks, whose blood spilled on the Alabama soil."[50] At its January 7, 1981, meeting, the Leadership Conference on Civil Rights (LCCR), an umbrella group comprising more than 150 civil rights organizations, decided to make the extension of the VRA its top priority for the upcoming Ninety-Seventh Congress.[51] Known as the "crown jewel of the civil rights movement," the VRA's revolutionary impact was clear. In 1969, African American voters in Mississippi had increased from a mere 6.4 percent in 1964 to 67 percent just five years later.[52] With relative ease, Congress had extended the VRA's special provisions for five years in 1970, and again for seven years in 1975. While courting Southern voters in 1975, Reagan excoriated the extension as "pure, cheap, demagoguery," and his landslide victory in 1980 stoked fears he was intent on crippling it.[53]

The heart of the VRA was Section 5, also known as "preclearance," which required nine Southern states and some northern jurisdictions that had historically discriminated against African Americans to seek approval from a federal court or the Department of Justice in order to enact any changes to voting regulations. From the VRA's inception, its conservative opponents had chafed over "preclearance" as punitive and discriminatory against the South. Strom Thurmond, now head of the powerful Senate Judiciary Committee, argued that Section 5's success had proven it had outlived its usefulness, and he urged it be extended to all fifty states, a tactic that would dilute its potency. Furthermore, Thurmond and other Southern senators said preclearance jurisdictions should be able to "bail out" upon a showing of "good faith."[54] Concerns for the future of the VRA were heightened after, in his confirmation hearings, attorney general nominee William French Smith raised doubts about the "efficacy of certain procedures."[55] In response, the LCCR and other civil rights organizations began mounting a concerted grassroots effort to pressure Congress to secure the VRA because they deemed it as "the lifeblood of Black political progress."[56]

The battle over the VRA centered on the controversial 1980 Supreme Court case *Mobile v. Bolden*, in which the court ruled, in a 5–4 decision, that under Section 2 of the VRA, plaintiffs had the burden of proving "intentional" discrimination.[57] Proving discriminatory *intent* as opposed to discriminatory *effects* was a stringent, often impossible burden that would substantially impair the enforcement of the VRA. Civil rights lawyers argued that unless *Bolden* was repealed, the result would lead to at-large elections, which are often discriminatory because in racially polarizing communities, at-large elections were often used to prevent Black voters from electing the candidates of their choice. They further alleged that retaining the *Bolden* intent standard would lead to racial gerrymandering and even changes in polling places that would cripple the VRA. With the act set to expire and passions running high, the VRA became the opening wedge in a series of titanic civil rights struggles in the Reagan era. The battle over the VRA's extension pitted the energized civil rights lobby against an emboldened clique of ideologues in the Reagan Justice Department who sought to circumscribe major provisions of the VRA under the guise of "color blindness" and "local control," the latter another code phrase for "states' rights."

On April 7, 1981, Republican senator Charles "Mac" Mathias of Maryland, one of the last of the liberal Republicans, and Democratic senator Edward Kennedy introduced a bipartisan bill that was sponsored in identical form in the House. It kept preclearance intact and overruled *Bolden*'s intent test requiring plaintiffs proving that the laws are "enforced in a fashion that results in a denial or abridgement of voting rights."[58] With the prodding of the LCCR, which feared that Thurmond and arch-conservative senator Orrin Hatch would bury the bill in the Senate, the Democratic-controlled House of Representatives would take the lead in moving the bill through committee, shepherded by Representative Don Edwards.[59] A civil rights champion who had drafted every civil rights bill in the House, Edwards had braved the heckling of angry white mobs while attempting to register Mississippi Blacks to vote in 1964.[60] On May 6, Edwards's judiciary subcommittee commenced hearings in the House.[61] Republican representative Henry Hyde, the ranking minority member on the subcommittee, insisted that the VRA stigmatized the Southern states as racist and proposed "junking" the preclearance provisions on the grounds that states of the Old Confederacy "have been in the penalty box for nearly 17 years and have improved their record."[62] On June 5, the subcommittee traveled to Austin, Texas, and then a week later to Montgomery, Alabama, where over eighteen days they heard compelling testimony from over two hundred individuals about the systematic and continuing voter discrimination against African Americans and Latinos. For the first time since the VRA passed, in 1965, no representatives from either the White House or the Justice Department appeared before the subcommittee to express their views.

The prospects for passage of the House bill appeared assured after Representative Hyde underwent a conversion upon hearing the testimony from African Americans in rural Alabama that described continued intimidation and harassment when they attempted to vote. Hyde even sent a note to Reagan suggesting that he broaden his constituency by endorsing the VRA.[63] On July 31, the House Judiciary Committee passed a bipartisan bill overruling *Bolden* and extending the preclearance provisions for another ten years by a vote of 23–1. The bill would await a vote before the entire House after legislators returned from the summer recess.[64]

The Senate waited to act until after Attorney General Smith submitted his confidential memo to Reagan on the VRA in October. Following Assistant Attorney General Reynolds's recommendations, Smith urged the retention of the more onerous standard of proof set out in *Bolden*.[65] On October 2, the same day that Attorney General Smith's confidential memo landed on Reagan's desk, debate over the VRA commenced on the House floor. The vast majority of the House, including Republicans, broke with the administration, as they acknowledged the sensitive nature of the issue that was so much "more of a concern to blacks than it is to whites."[66] By a vote of 389 to 24, the House overwhelmingly approved the bill.[67] Reporting for the *New York Times*, Steven Roberts noted that the lopsided vote obscured "the regional antagonisms that smoldered beneath the surface."[68]

With the House bill now passed to Strom Thurmond's Senate Judiciary Committee, the White House's dithering enabled the civil rights lobby to get a head start in mounting the most extensive lobbying on a bill since the 1960s.[69] Behind the scenes, an internecine battle over the VRA brewed between the hard-liners in the Justice Department and the political branch of the White House. Reynolds and other ideologues in the Justice Department urged retaining the *Bolden* "intent" standard on the specious grounds that the "effects" test would make proof of voting discrimination so easy that it would lead to "quotas" and proportional representation based on race. Reagan's political advisors disagreed and persuaded him not to oppose the House bill because it would confirm the charges that he was insensitive to Blacks. Reagan instructed them to arrange a press conference where he could express his support for the bill.[70] But there was one major hitch: nobody informed the attorney general of the president's decision.

As soon as Reynolds got wind of Reagan's decision, he told the attorney general of the need to reverse course. Smith, Reagan's former personal lawyer and a Kitchen Cabinet member, immediately stormed to the White House and demanded the president weaken Section 2 of the VRA with amendments. Smith told his former client that the bill would produce quotas in voting and reminded Reagan that he'd campaigned against quotas. The passionate exhortations of his usually even-tempered attorney general and longtime personal attorney persuaded Reagan to change his mind, and he canceled the scheduled press conference.[71] An unidentified White House advisor noted, "This is the first time I've seen the President change his mind after having made a decision."[72] Instead, Reagan released a seven-paragraph statement, his first official statement on the Voting Rights Act. It criticized the House bill for imposing "overly rigid standards" for the Southern states and faulted the "intent" standard because it would be too easy for voters to prove discrimination.[73]

Reagan's decision sparked a fusillade of pent-up anger from his opponents. Civil rights groups charged that Reagan's proposals would "render the Act meaningless."[74] The *Washington Post* called it virtually impossible to prevail in voting discrimination cases under the "intent" standard.[75] Reagan's decision to side with Reynolds over his more pragmatic political aides signified the ascent of "color-blind conservatism." The eminent sociologist Nathan Glazer, an outspoken critic of many of the Great Society Programs of the mid-1960s, nevertheless conceded, "There were two elements in the Republican appeal to color blindness: one was the appeal to the South: the other was the appeal to racism, no question about it."[76]

In due course, the pragmatism of the moderates in the White House would be outmatched by the ideological fervor of Reynolds and his lieutenants determined to reconstruct the CRD of the Justice Department. The hard-liners in the Justice Department were fortified by the recent arrival of a brilliant twenty-six-year-old Harvard Law School graduate named John Glover Roberts, who had just completed a Supreme Court clerkship for conservative justice William H. Rehnquist. The Voting Rights Act became young Roberts's largest portfolio. According to Ari Berman, opposition to the "effects" test became an obsession for Roberts.[77]

In preparation for Senate hearings on the bill, Roberts drafted a flurry of memos to Attorney General Smith denouncing the "effects" test as another attempt at affirmative action because, he alleged, it would lead to quotas in voting. Veteran civil rights lawyers asserted that Reynolds and Roberts were insensitive to the historical scourge of institutionalized racism. They debunked Roberts's assertion that Section 2 would lead to quotas and proportional representation as a patently absurd "scare tactic."[78] After all, quotas in voting had never been imposed, and Blacks' voting power was still diluted by at-large elections. Armand Derfner, an eminent civil rights attorney who began his career defending voting rights activists in the South, noted that in the "seven southern states initially covered by the act, blacks made up 25 percent of the electorate, but held only about 5 percent of the seats."[79]

The beginning of Senate hearings on the VRA in late January coincided with a spate of articles commemorating the first anniversary of Reagan's inauguration. The American Civil Liberties Union (ACLU) warned: "Nineteen eighty-one was a bad year for civil liberties," and "1982 could be worse."[80] Armed with John Roberts's memoranda, Reagan's Justice Department would try to make up for their dilatory entry into the VRA debate with an ideological fervor unseen in voting rights cases. Attorney General Smith testified on the opening day with a withering attack on the "effects" test, making the far-fetched assertion that "it could destroy the American political structure." Smith claimed, "Quotas would be the end result. . . . The only ultimate logical result would be proportional representation. I don't see how anyone could seriously advocate that."[81]

When Senator Edward Kennedy said the Reagan administration's position on VRA had caused a "crisis of confidence among blacks and other minorities," Smith replied with the familiar defense that the president "does not have a discriminatory bone in his body." Smith's remarks elicited howls of laughter in the packed hearing room, until Committee chair Orrin Hatch silenced the raucous outburst with his gavel.[82]

The civil rights lobby threw itself behind the House bill's rigorous enforcement mechanisms. They saw the administration's focus on the inflammatory concept of "racial quotas" as a diversionary tactic. After all, the plain words of the House statute stipulated that "the mere fact that a minority group was not elected in numbers equal to the group's proportion of the population was not tantamount to a voting rights violation."[83] The *New York Times* editorialized that quotas had never been imposed in any case, from 1965 to 1980, "when the law favored civil rights lawyers, without substantial evidence that minorities were excluded from politics." The *Washington Post* called talk of quotas a "scare tactic."[84] Passions were so high that the leadership of the Southern Christian Leadership Conference and the National Coalition to Save the Voting Rights Act embarked on a 160-mile journey beginning in Carrollton, Alabama, on February 6, 1982, through Selma and ending in Montgomery. The longest march in civil rights history, it sought to evoke the spirit of the iconic 1965 Selma-to-Montgomery march.[85]

On March 24, the Reagan administration scored a triumph when Hatch's Senate Subcommittee on the Constitution, by a 3–2 party-line vote, passed a ten-year extension of the Voting Rights Act but retained the cumbersome *Bolden* "intent" standard.[86] Despite the subcommittee's approval, the fervor of the Justice Department's opposition persuaded a number of Republican senators on the Judiciary Committee to oppose the bill. With the full Senate Judiciary Committee deadlocked along party lines, Democrats feared that the bill would die there.

Within the Republican Senate caucus, a rift surfaced between the vestiges of the old, moderate Rockefeller wing (which had always been stronger in the Senate than in the House) and the ascendant hard-core conservatives, who favored a more homogenous party. The public schism was becoming worrisome to Republicans. After weeks of internal bickering, Senator Robert Dole, a former Republican vice presidential nominee who still dreamed of the presidency, stepped in to broker a compromise. Although a supporter of the Civil Rights Act of 1964 and the Voting Rights Act of 1965, Dole also had strong ties with the conservative wing of the party. He fretted that the hard-liners' opposition to the VRA would tar the entire Republican Party with a racist brush: "I don't think we throw in the towel and say well, only eight percent [of them] vote for us."[87] He offered a compromise stipulating the "effects" test be determined by the "totality of circumstances." In an effort to ease conservatives' hysteria over racial quotas, Dole added the following clause: "Nothing in this section establishes a right to have members of a protected class elected in numbers equal to their proportion in the population." Furthermore, Dole's proposed compromise capped the preclearance requirement at twenty-five years. Dole's compromise was a stroke of legislative dexterity, and the Judiciary Committee approved it by a vote of 14–4. After clearing the committee, the matter went to the full Senate for consideration.[88]

Throughout the ordeal over the VRA extension, Reagan, as usual, stood apart from the gritty political details. On May 3, 1982, Reagan heeded the recommendation of his White House political advisors, who noted that his opposition to Dole's compromise was fruitless because it had the support of virtually all members of the Judiciary Committee, and Reagan's opposition would reinforce the perception that he was hostile to Blacks.[89] Nonetheless, Reagan's political ally Jesse Helms vowed to filibuster the bill "until the cows come home."[90] After Helms inveighed against the bill for five days, the Senate voted 86–8 to invoke cloture and then passed the Dole compromise by a vote of 85–8. Then, on June 29, 1982, standing in the Rose Garden before the nation's leading civil rights leaders, Reagan signed into law a twenty-five-year extension of the Voting Rights Act. He called the right to vote "the crown jewel of American liberties, and we will not see its luster diminished." In stark contrast with LBJ, who spoke with great eloquence for over twenty minutes and handed out fifty pens, Reagan devoted a mere four minutes to his speech, and handed out only one pen.[91]

Reagan's last-ditch support for the extension of the Voting Rights Act failed to appease African Americans. Immediately after Reagan signed the bill, the NAACP's Benjamin Hooks congratulated the president for "belatedly" coming along to support the act but asserted that African Americans had "no confidence that the Justice Department will support the law."[92] Hooks's concerns were well founded. Reagan's grudging support was merely a matter of political expediency—he lacked the votes to stop the bill. In a widely reported speech before the American Bar Association a few months later, Reagan infuriated critics when he took credit for the bill, which he and his Justice Department had vigorously opposed.[93]

Behind the scenes, William Bradford Reynolds was furious over the compromise. Along with John Roberts, the combative head of the CRD braced for a long generational battle to reshape civil rights policy in a more conservative direction. To this end, Reynolds inaugurated a new system of centralized control over the CRD that enabled him to closely monitor the work of the idealistic career lawyers resolved to vigorously enforcing civil rights laws. Many dedicated career lawyers who had joined the CRD over their mission to vigorously enforce civil rights resigned in disgust.[94] One of the veteran attorneys who quit accused Reynolds of "emasculating the civil rights laws as we know them."[95] With respect to voting rights, the CRD's objections to proposed electoral changes under the jurisdictions covered by preclearance plummeted to historic lows during Reynolds's tenure.[96] Civil rights groups accused the Justice Department of undermining the tougher changes in the preclearance standard.[97] A few years later, Reagan's Justice Department tried to renege on the compromise, filing a brief attacking the use of the "totality of circumstances" test in a high-profile North Carolina case. During the Reagan years, private lawyers filed ten times as many voting rights cases as the Justice Department. Opponents of the VRA would continue their long campaign to dilute its effects culminating in the nomination of John Roberts to be the Supreme Court's seventeenth chief justice, in 2005. In 2013 Roberts would author the *Shelby v. Holder* decision, which overruled preclearance and drove a stake through the heart of the VRA.

THE BOB JONES FIASCO

At the same time the Justice Department was seeking to cripple the VRA, Reagan became enmeshed in more controversy surrounding Bob Jones University. In a shocking move, the Treasury and Justice Departments announced on January 8, 1982, that they were no longer denying tax exemptions to private schools that discriminated against African Americans in admissions or prohibited interracial dating.[98] The reason for the switch was political. For the past few months, Senator Strom Thurmond, a trustee of the university, and Mississippi representative Trent Lott had pressed for a change in policy. The decision epitomized the administration's willingness to meet the demands of Evangelicals, who had proved vital to his 1980 win.[99] Though Reagan campaigned at Bob Jones University and had recently given his support to a memo written by Lott requesting that the president reverse the IRS position, Reagan later said that he did not realize the tax exemptions were a civil rights issue, nor did he realize that Bob Jones University and other private Christian academies practiced segregation.[100] In the minds of millions of Americans, no other incident in Reagan's first year cast more doubt on Reagan's credibility on civil rights as the fiasco over tax exemptions for segregated schools.[101]

Critics excoriated the sharp reversal of policy as "appalling," "criminal," "saddening," "outrageous," and "providing aid and comfort to racists in our midst."[102] Tom Wicker of the *New York Times* pondered, "If this isn't actively promoting racial discrimination, what is? And it's out of the taxpayers' pockets at that."[103] Over a hundred career lawyers in the Justice Department, already irate over the department's handling of the VRA extension, signed a letter of protest to William Bradford Reynolds. Over twenty of them resigned in protest.[104] Robert Plotkin, the former chief of the CRD's special litigation section, lamented, "I'd say they're emasculating the civil rights laws as we know them. It's a variant of their economic beliefs—that people be free to do what they want, that the cream will rise to the top and the rest will fall."[105]

In order to underscore the severity of the matter, Michael Deaver, Reagan's trusted aide, arranged for Reagan to meet with Thaddeus Garrett and Melvin Bradley, two lower-ranking African American administration officials. Garrett, an ordained minister, explained to a stunned Reagan the racist implications of the policy.[106] He told Reagan about a sermon he had heard in church over the past weekend inspired by the president's Bob Jones decision. The preacher had recounted a parable of a woman saving the life of a wounded snake and being bitten in return by the ungrateful reptile. "Reagan is the snake!" the preacher exclaimed. The congregation had erupted in reply: "Amen."[107]

Stung by the torrent of outrage, Reagan reversed course in an attempt to mitigate the political damage. On January 12, 1982, he announced that he was submitting legislation to Congress prohibiting tax exemptions for organizations that discriminate but maintained he would not reverse his decision on Bob Jones University until Congress voted on his proposal. To this contradictory pronouncement, Reagan added that he was "personally opposed to racial discrimination in any form. I would not knowingly contribute to any organization that supports racial discrimination."[108]

Not surprisingly, Reagan's retreat failed to allay critics who noted there had been no plan to introduce this legislation prior to the public relations disaster. In the interim, the White House forwarded the legislation to the House Ways and Means Committee for hearings set to begin February 4, 1982, but prospects for congressional action on this hastily drawn piece of legislation were dim.[109] Reagan's contrition and efforts to defuse the matter failed miserably, and it would be one of the lowest moments of his first term. An ABC poll conducted between January 22 and January 30 revealed that only 18 percent approved of Reagan's handling of the issue, compared with 78 percent who disapproved.[110] Lou Cannon observed that the Bob Jones controversy was the prime illustration of Reagan's being "so cut off from the counsel of black Americans that he sometimes did not realize that he was offending them."[111]

Meanwhile, on February 19, 1982, a panel on the US Court of Appeals for the DC Circuit ruled that no changes could be made on the issue of Bob Jones University's tax-exemption until the US Supreme Court ruled on the matter, which was pending before it.[112]

In the run-up to the midterm elections, the Bob Jones case continued to cast a pall over the Reagan administration. On October 12, 1982, William Bradford Reynolds joined attorneys for Bob Jones University in arguing that Congress had never authorized the IRS to deny tax-exempt status for schools that practice racial discrimination.[113] Seven months later, the Supreme Court decided against Reagan's Department of Justice, ruling by a vote of 8 to 1 that "the national interest in eradicating racial discrimination substantially outweighed whatever denial of benefits to petitioners' exercise of the religious beliefs."[114] Justice William Rehnquist, John Roberts's mentor, issued the lone dissent.

In one of his administration's biggest defeats in the Supreme Court, Reagan's only comment was "We will obey the law." Civil rights advocates greeted the decision with relief, but they continued to call out the ideologues in the Justice Department for pressing the administration to give Bob Jones tax-exempt status in the first place. The *New York Times* succinctly editorialized: "President Reagan and the lawyers he put in charge of protecting civil rights should be ashamed."[115] A top Reagan advisor admitted, "It nearly caused me heart arrest."[116]

Other matters on the civil rights front continued to hound Reagan. His nomination of William M. Bell, a conservative African American businessman, to head the Equal Employment Opportunity Commission (EEOC) drew derision from across the political spectrum. Bell had no law degree, nor did he have any experience in civil rights matters. Connecticut's Republican senator Lowell Weicker barked: "Whoever came up with that nomination should be shot."[117] The clamor against Bell was so intense that the administration withdrew his nomination, leaving the agency's three thousand employees without a leader for months. It was one of the first times that African Americans opposed the nomination of a fellow African American to a post of such significance.[118] Reagan eventually chose another African American conservative for the job, one who had also spoken out against racial preferences—future Supreme Court justice Clarence Thomas.

News that the EEOC had cut by half the number of discrimination suits brought against employers testified to the administration's laxity in enforcing employment discrimination.[119] Privately, the administration had proposed closing EEOC field offices throughout the country, stoking fears that they intended to dismantle the entire federal enforcement apparatus.[120]

As the midterm elections loomed, Republicans feared that Reagan's racial record would repel white moderates, particularly educated women.[121] "What the administration is trying to do," moaned Althea Simmons, the Washington, DC, director of the NAACP, "is not just put the issue of civil rights on the backburner, but take it off the stove completely."[122] An NBC poll taken in January 1982 revealed that only 7 percent of African Americans approved of Reagan's handling of civil rights issues, and a New York Times/CBS poll found that 0 percent of them thought he cared about their problems.[123] On Election Day, spurred on by heavy African American turnout, the electorate delivered a rebuke to the Republican Party, resulting in the loss of twenty-six seats in the House of Representatives.[124]

Haley Barbour, a young, ambitious Republican from Mississippi, was defeated in his senatorial bid against the incumbent, eighty-one-year-old

John Stennis. In a postmortem memorandum to Chief of Staff James Baker, Barbour attributed his loss to the "fear and loathing" the Reagan administration evoked in "black voters across the nation." Barbour bewailed that Stennis, a former segregationist, and an author of the Southern Manifesto, received over 90 percent of the African American vote, leading Barbour to conclude that Blacks "just hated Reagan worse than they hated Stennis." Looking forward to Reagan's reelection campaign in 1984, Barbour urged the administration take constructive steps to minimize African American animosity toward Reagan.[125] Barbour's pleas would have to overcome the partisans, led by William Bradford Reynolds, in the Justice Department, whose uncompromising, legalistic attitudes on the VRA and Bob Jones University were just getting started in their generational battle to implement "color-blind conservatism."[126]

Reagan proved even less sympathetic to African Americans in his first two years than his campaign rhetoric had suggested he would be. In November 1981, historian Eric Foner noted that if the civil rights triumphs of the 1960s represented a Second Reconstruction, perhaps the Reagan administration's abandonment of its responsibilities to address problems of racial injustice meant the nation was entering the Second Redemption, like the white supremacist redeemers who overthrew the first Reconstruction in the 1870s.[127]

As the Ninety-Eighth Congress was about to convene, at the beginning of 1983, the stage was set for fierce struggles between the Justice Department and the LCCR over the administration's quest to recast civil rights in a more conservative direction. The VRA extension was merely the opening gambit in a protracted struggle. In the coming year, the battleground would shift to a bruising battle over the fate of the bipartisan Civil Rights Commission. Unlike the battle over the VRA, this time Reagan's administration would succeed in its objectives.

CHAPTER 9

CONTROLLING THE CIVIL RIGHTS COMMISSION AND IGNITING OLD CONSERVATIVE BATTLES

The 1984 Republican platform, all the ideas we supported there—from tax policy, to foreign policy; from individual rights to neighborhood security— are things that Jefferson Davis and his people believed in.

—Mississippi congressman Trent Lott (1984)[1]

We do not admire their President. We know why the White House is white.

—Poet and novelist Alice Walker (1984)[2]

The 1982 midterm elections provided a temporary reprieve for African Americans reeling from the tremors of Reagan's first two years, but the battle was just beginning. For the next two years, civil rights organizations and the Reagan administration continued to spar over Justice Department efforts to recast civil rights in a more conservative direction under the mantle of "color-blind conservatism." Ed Meese and William Bradford Reynolds led Reagan's effort to dismantle affirmative action, undermine the independence of the bipartisan Civil Rights Commission (CRC), and nominate young, conservative federal judges determined to overturn the landmark precedents of the Warren Court, which had extended the blessings of liberties to Blacks, women, and others.[3] For Blacks, perhaps the most frustrating consequence of the Reagan administration's civil rights policies was that it forced the nation to refight the battles of the 1960s and 1970s and diverted precious energy from the unfinished business of the civil rights revolution: the battle for economic justice.

AFFIRMATIVE ACTION

After the *Bakke* decision, affirmative action became settled law. At the same time, it polarized the nation along racial and ideological lines. From the beginning of Reagan's presidency, assaults on affirmative action as "reverse discrimination" became the cornerstone of the administration's civil rights policy. Instead of fighting on behalf of the historical victims of discrimination, the administration privileged the rights of white men and branded affirmative action, "reverse discrimination." Like his attacks on the Rumford Fair Housing Act, Reagan's stance on affirmative action was politically effective and resonated with the white, working-class "Reagan Democrats."[4] In his first news conference, Reagan came out swinging: "There will be no retreat" on affirmative action, which he likened to "quotas."[5]

Supporters of affirmative action recoiled over how Reagan, who had staunchly opposed every significant piece of civil rights legislation of the past twenty years, now argued that the triumph of the civil rights revolution had ended all vestiges of racial discrimination in housing, education, voting, and employment. They scoffed at the premise that America had erased centuries of physical, legal, spiritual, and political oppression in less than two decades and rebranded "color-blind conservatism" as "laissez-faire racism." To proclaim the dawn of a new race-neutral idyll in America, Reagan had to wish away the lingering and often devastating effects of centuries of structural racism. Proponents of affirmative action, on the other hand, argued that it was necessary to expedite the creation of a color-blind society, which had not come to fruition.[6] Furthermore, as historian Ira Katznelson demonstrated, the federal programs of the 1930s and 1940s, such as Social Security, unemployment insurance, and the GI Bill, excluded African Americans. Because these programs were so instrumental in creating the white middle class, they constituted an "affirmative action for whites."[7]

William Bradford Reynolds was the animating figure behind the Reagan administration's assault on affirmative action. In his first appearance before a congressional subcommittee, on September 23, 1981, Reynolds reversed longstanding policy in testifying that the administration "no longer will insist upon or in any respect support the use of quotas or any numerical or statistical formulae designed to provide non-victims of discrimination preferential treatment based on race, sex, national origin, or religion."[8] The chair of the subcommittee, veteran African American congressman Augustus Hawkins, expressed alarm and dismay over what he termed the Reagan administration's "callous, insensitive and misguided abandonment of traditional remedies for employment discrimination," calling it "patently idiotic."[9] Behind the scenes, Reynolds and his allies in the Justice Department searched for test cases they hoped would result in the Supreme Court overturning the *Bakke* decision. Richard Seymour, an attorney for the Lawyers' Committee for Civil Rights Under Law, accused Reynolds of having "a private philosophical hang-up that is impeding his ability to uphold the law on civil rights" and suggested that Reynolds "shouldn't be in that job."[10]

Not all of the usual Republican constituencies yearned to end affirmative action. Powerful business organizations like the US Chamber of Commerce, the National Association of Manufacturers, and the Business Roundtable opposed an abrupt end to affirmative action policies. They favored easing some of the regulatory burdens and excess paperwork associated with affirmative action but did not want to unsettle what had become an established part of business practices.[11] Other administration officials urged caution. Eventually, rifts emerged between the ideologues in the Department of Justice and the more pragmatic officials in the Departments of Labor and Commerce. At a meeting with the US Chamber of Commerce, Secretary of Labor Ray Donovan stated his belief and intention to comply with existing law.[12]

As usual, Reagan's focus on the big items of tax cuts and the defense buildup against the Soviets caused his usual detachment from the basic details of the administration's policy on affirmative action. At a news conference on December 17, 1981, Reagan seemed not to be on the same page with his Justice Department. He acknowledged that he was not familiar with the recent Supreme Court decision in *United Steelworkers of America v. Weber*. *Weber* upheld private employers' use of voluntary affirmative action plans to eliminate "manifest racial imbalance." Reagan added that he could not "find fault with" programs that expand opportunities for minorities.[13] White House aides quickly issued a statement clarifying that the president opposed *Weber* because it sanctioned racial quotas and agreed with Reynolds that it should be overturned.[14]

Throughout Reagan's first term, the battle to end affirmative action was undermined by the president's overall fixation on selling his economic plan, resulting in incoherent policy. The administration's awkward attempts to scuttle affirmative action were further complicated by sharp differences between the ideologues in the Justice Department on the one hand, who viewed affirmative action as the quintessence of "big government," and the more pragmatic officials on the other, who had adjusted to affirmative action and realized its benefits in creating a more diverse society.[15] Though unable to end affirmative action, the administration slashed the budgets for enforcement for the Equal Employment Opportunity Commission.[16] Reagan's head of the EEOC, Clarence Thomas, a conservative African American and the future Supreme Court justice, opposed goals and timetables, and enforcement of complaints plummeted precipitously. In the meantime, opponents of affirmative action hoped that a decisive reelection victory or a change in the composition of the Supreme Court would be the end of it.

TURNING THE CIVIL RIGHTS COMMISSION INSIDE OUT

The Reagan administration's frustration over the difficulty of ending affirmative action and vitiating the Voting Rights Act prompted it to target the bipartisan Civil Rights Commission. The CRC arose from the Civil Rights Act of 1957, which provided for the creation of an independent, bipartisan agency composed of six part-time members. The act granted the CRC subpoena power to hold hearings and investigate charges of discrimination. After the passage of the VRA, in 1965, the CRC shifted from monitoring voting to monitoring compliance with civil rights laws, as well as broadening its focus to employment, housing, and education discrimination. In the words of Father Theodore Hesburgh, an original commission appointee who served through 1972, the CRC was the national "conscience in the matter of civil rights."[17]

From its founding, the CRC had frequently leveled criticisms at presidential administrations. In November 1972, Nixon fired Hesburgh after he chastised his administration for failing to provide moral leadership on civil rights issues. In particular, Hesburgh had repeatedly sparred with Nixon over Nixon's attacks on busing, which Hesburgh called "the most phony issue in the country."[18] Until Reagan's presidency, Hesburgh was the only CRC member to be fired, and the CRC had remained generally immune from political controversy.

Reagan's desire to stamp his ideological imprint on the CRC began in earnest during his early weeks in office. In January 1981 the CRC released a draft report wholeheartedly endorsing affirmative action as a mechanism for dismantling discrimination, which "was far more pervasive, entrenched, and varied than its critics would assume."[19] The report angered the Reagan administration, and to make matters worse, the CRC issued another report, in September of that year, which highlighted widespread police practices that violated the civil rights of African Americans. This finding particularly outraged the hardcore "law and order" sensibilities of Reagan aide and former prosecutor Ed Meese, who would become the CRC's chief antagonist within the White House.[20] Over time, the constant drumbeat of criticism from the CRC over the administration's policy positions got under Reagan's tough political hide and aroused his prickliness over any insinuation that he was bigoted.

Reagan triggered the opening salvo in his war against the CRC on November 16, 1981, when he abruptly fired its venerable chair, Arthur S. Flemming, a seventy-five-year-old Eisenhower Republican. Reagan also fired Stephen Horn, who, as a legislative aide to Senator Thomas Kuchel, had been closely involved in the passage of the Civil Rights Act of 1964 and the Voting Rights Act of 1965.[21] In May, Flemming wrote perfunctory letters to both Reagan and the attorney general explaining the mission of the commission, delineating its activities, and requesting a meeting in order to "discuss the current state of civil rights in our country." Both of them ignored the invitation.[22] Had Reagan met with the CRC, he might have realized that it planned its reports a few years in advance, and the reports would have been the same for Carter had he been reelected. Instead, Reagan believed the liberal holdovers on the CRC had a "vendetta" against him. Reagan came to the realization that "without new panel members, he would just get hit on the head for another year."[23]

Immediately after his ouster, the usually low-profile Flemming held a news conference where he lamented, "The cumulative impact of civil rights decisions made by the Administration is very disturbing." He also warned that the Reagan administration was drifting back to a philosophy of "separate but equal" in school desegregation cases.[24] Flemming was so concerned over the regressive actions taken by the Reagan administration that he announced the formation of a bipartisan group of sixteen former federal officials to monitor the federal government's enforcement of laws barring discrimination.[25]

As Horn's replacement, Reagan named Mary Louise Smith, who had become the first woman to head the Republican National Committee. A moderate and social liberal best known for her support of women's rights, Smith was a conventional, noncontroversial choice. Of greater significance, to replace Flemming as the new chair of the CRC, Reagan nominated Clarence M. Pendleton, an African American political supporter and protégé of Ed Meese. Referred to as "Penny," Pendleton was a political cipher with no credibility in the civil rights community.[26] His nomination drew ridicule from people familiar with Pendleton's stormy tenure as head of the San Diego Urban League, where he was plagued by allegations of financial improprieties. Pendleton was eventually confirmed in March 1982, but controversy over his financial peccadillos delayed his confirmation for months, and he was ordered to reimburse the Urban League nearly $10,000, which he had taken as vacation pay the day he resigned.[27] Pendleton emerged as a cheerleader for the administration's policies. CRC member Mary Frances Berry recalled how other commission members, including Mary Louise Smith, became "disgusted with Pendleton's disregard for the commission's independence and his boorish public behavior."[28]

While the Senate was deliberating the Pendleton and Smith nominations, Reagan provoked even more criticism by nominating B. Sam Hart of Philadelphia, an African American Evangelical who was supported by Strom Thurmond and had ties with Jerry Falwell's Moral Majority.[29] Aside from Hart's right-wing views, much of the uproar about his nomination stemmed from the fact that Hart was intended to replace Jill Ruckelshaus, a Republican known for her stalwart support of the ERA, women's rights, and civil rights.[30] For civil rights activists, Reagan's announcement of Hart, an obscure Philadelphia radio evangelist, confirmed Reagan's utter disregard for the integrity, independence, and effectiveness of the CRC. The influential Leadership Conference on Civil Rights (LCCR) opposed Hart and said his nomination was an "insult to everyone who shares the nation's irrevocable commitment to equality of opportunity."[31]

Days after the announcement, it was revealed that Hart owed $4,400 in back taxes, had defaulted on a $100,000 Small Business Administration loan, and had never even registered to vote. Hart also reportedly described homosexuality as a chosen lifestyle and condemned homosexuals as a "sorry, despicable, abominable lot—an abomination to both God and mankind."[32] The *New York Times* editorialized that Reagan's pattern of appointing patently unqualified individuals to key civil rights posts revealed his intent to deprive victims of discrimination a voice.[33] These revelations aroused such widespread criticism that Reagan had no alternative but to withdraw Hart's nomination. For the time being, Ruckelshaus retained her job.[34]

Reagan, Meese, and the ideologues in the Justice Department were undeterred in their determination to disempower the CRC. Only two months after the Hart fiasco, Reagan nominated three obscure academics—Robert A. Destro, Constantine M. Dombalis, and Dr. Guadalupe Quintanilla—to replace Mary Frances Berry, Blandina Cardenas Ramirez, and Rabbi Murray Saltzman, all of whom were dedicated to the CRC's historic mission of being the nation's conscience on civil rights.[35] Reagan was attempting to fire Berry, Cardenas Ramirez, and Saltzman because he disagreed with their policy recommendations on busing, affirmative action, voting rights, and civil rights enforcement.

By now, Reagan's objective of "packing" the CRC was obvious. One of Reagan's nominees, Destro, a former director of the Milwaukee Catholic League and an ardent foe of abortion rights, had called for the abolition of the CRC on the grounds that it was "a government lobby for special interest groups," and he took it to task for its inattention to religious and white ethnic discrimination.[36] The NAACP charged that none of the three nominees had the broad experience or the "informed understanding required to effectively discharge their duties as commissioners."[37] The three nominees made it out of the Senate Judiciary Committee in October, but even the Republican-controlled Senate would not grant a vote to confirm them. As the Ninety-Seventh Congress adjourned, the nominations were buried in the Senate Judiciary Committee, but fears for the future of the CRC as an independent body persisted.[38]

These fears were well-founded. By the beginning of 1983, the conflict between the White House and the CRC entered a more antagonistic phase. Over Pendleton's objections, the CRC adopted a more defiant tone in its reports attacking the administration's stand on two affirmative action cases and rebuking the Justice Department for its lax enforcement of desegregation mandates.[39] After the administration failed to comply with the CRC's subpoena for data on the percentage of minority appointments to the administration, the conflict escalated.[40] With the CRC up for renewal on September 30, the administration took the offensive.[41] On April 6, 1983, the administration proposed legislation extending the life of the commission for twenty years but also granting the president the power to appoint the commissioners to fixed terms and to remove them with cause. The administration also planned to replace all four remaining incumbents with new nominees, made as recess appointments.[42] One of the incumbents, Rabbi Murray Saltzman, penned an op-ed in the *Los Angeles Times* charging that the proposed legislation would make the CRC "a watchdog without a bark" and stifle its moral authority.[43]

Then, on May 25, 1983, Reagan announced his intention to replace the three commissioners he had previously tried to remove and named as their replacements Destro (again), John L. Bunzel, and Morris B. Abram. The civil rights community fiercely opposed Reagan's wholesale replacement of the incumbent commissioners, and legal experts questioned whether Reagan had the legal authority to dismiss the members. Mary Frances Berry, the most outspoken commissioner, said she was contemplating filing a lawsuit to preserve the commission's independence. Representative Parren J. Mitchell, a former member of the Congressional Black Caucus, accused Reagan of "attempting the political rape" of the CRC.[44] In response, the administration and its allies attacked Berry as a "communist sympathizer."[45] Berry, Cardenas Ramirez, and Rabbi Saltzman remained commissioners pending Senate approval of their replacements.

Tensions flared in July 1983 as the hearings began in the Senate on whether to confirm Reagan's three nominees. From the beginning of the proceedings, the ranking Democrat on the Judiciary Committee, Senator Joseph Biden, announced he would oppose the three nominees because he wanted to protest the "horrible signal" the administration was sending in trying to undermine the independence of the commission.[46] During the hearings, Republican senator Charles "Mac" Mathias of Maryland accused Reagan of firing the members because they have "repeatedly criticized his civil rights policies," and he charged the president with "trying to exercise his raw, naked legal power in a way that will diminish" the commission's independence.[47] Meanwhile, on August 4, 1983, the Democratic-controlled House of Representatives approved a bill by a lopsided margin, 286–128, that extended the life of the commission for five years and stipulated the removal of commissioners only for neglect of duty or malfeasance.[48]

After the Senate reconvened in late September, Reagan's nominations appeared to be in serious jeopardy. Moderate Republican senator Arlen Specter and Senator Mathias floated a compromise bill to preserve the CRC's role as an independent body, but the administration refused to consider any compromise that did not include the ouster of commissioners Berry, Cardenas Ramirez, and Saltzman.[49] The commission's statutory authorization expired on September 30, 1983, without the parties able to resolve the deadlock, but the enabling law prescribed a sixty-day "wind-down period."[50] During that period, Republican senators Specter and Dole and Democrat Biden attempted to broker a compromise with the White House. The issue of whether the three ousted commissioners would remain was the sticking point.[51]

On October 25, during the whirlwind of news over the surprise US invasion of the tiny Caribbean island of Grenada and the disturbing reports of the deaths of 241 US servicemen in a suicide bombing at a Marine barracks in Beirut, Reagan announced he was firing the three holdover commissioners. As for Mary Frances Berry, Reagan told her that she "served at his pleasure but was not giving him very much pleasure."[52] Reagan's decision sparked outrage from both sides of the aisle. Republican senator Mathias chided Reagan's "callous insensitivity to bipartisan efforts in the House and Senate to resolve the controversy."[53] Lawyers for the NAACP Legal Defense and Education Fund disputed Reagan's claim that he had the authority to fire the commissioners. Upon hearing word of their terminations, Berry and Cardenas Ramirez convened a press conference announcing that they were filing suit against Reagan to seek an injunction prohibiting the president from interfering with the independence of the commission.[54] On November 14, Judge Norma Holloway Johnson of the US District Court in Washington, DC, granted a preliminary injunction barring the dismissal of the commissioners. At the end of her opinion, the judge noted the "public interest" in granting the injunction because of the vital work of the commission in promoting the "advance of civil rights in this country."[55]

Prior to Judge Johnson's ruling, a compromise bill in the Senate had been crystallizing. Senate Majority Leader Howard Baker, along with

Senators Dole, Biden, and Specter, and Ralph Neas of the LCCR, had reportedly reached a long-distance telephone agreement with Meese, the White House's point man in the negotiations, who was attending a summit with the president in Tokyo. The oral agreement stipulated that the CRC would be reconstituted as a hybrid agency composed of eight members serving six-year staggered terms; four members would be appointed by the president, and four members would be appointed by Congress— two commission members would be named by the Speaker of the House, and two by the president pro tempore of the Senate. Additionally, no more than four commissioners could come from one political party, and none of the new appointees would be subject to Senate confirmation.[56]

With this oral understanding between Meese and the congressional leaders, the Senate voted 78–5 to approve the compromise bill, which the House was certain to approve before the commission expired.[57] Realizing he had no alternative, Reagan signed the bill reconstituting the CRC on November 30, 1983. Despite the hoopla surrounding the compromise, Reagan expressed "reservations" about its erosion of presidential power to remove commissioners. He also indirectly criticized the CRC saying, "All seem to agree that the commission's best and most productive days were its earlier ones."[58]

A few days before the president signed the bill, rumors circulated that he and Meese were going to renege on the oral agreement Meese had hammered out over the phone with the senators. The first indication was his refusal to reappoint Mary Louise Smith because of her opposition to administration positions. The rumors proved to be true when Reagan announced he was replacing Smith and Jill Ruckelshaus with Esther Gonzalez-Arroyo Buckley, an unknown high school science teacher from Laredo, Texas, whose only qualifications were that she had worked on Reagan's Texas campaigns. The additional appointment of Francis Guess, a relatively unknown Tennessee labor commissioner, touched off further recriminations that Meese had broken his oral agreement.[59] Smith expressed her profound disappointment in her party, which she said "was born in the struggle against slavery."[60] Afterward, CCR's staff director, Ralph Neas, who played a key role in negotiating the compromise, asserted that the failure to reappoint Smith was "entirely inconsistent with the agreements we worked out." Senator Biden expressed "shock" that after six months of negotiation the White House would violate its "commitment" to reappoint Smith. He said the move "calls into question the ability of Republicans and Democrats alike to negotiate with anyone who purports to speak for the White House."[61] Angry civil rights leaders accused the White House and Republican congressional leaders of "double-crossing" them by failing to reappoint Smith and Ruckelshaus.[62] In response, congressional Republicans and Edwin Meese flatly denied that a deal had been agreed to.[63] However, after Pendleton griped to Reagan at a November 15, 1983, meeting regarding what Reagan termed "Congress's so-called compromise to keep me from making new appointments," the president boasted, "The boys are playing games, but I think I can snooker them."[64] Not long after the charges that Meese reneged on the agreement, Reagan nominated him to be the next attorney general.

As a result of Reagan and Meese's chicanery, the administration now had a CRC with a majority of members reflecting their views. An angry Ralph Neas charged, "The White House has accomplished the goal it has been seeking for six months—to pack the commission."[65] In addition, the appointment of the outspoken conservative Linda Chavez as staff director increased the administration's power over the CRC. Chavez assumed a more aggressive role than previous staff directors had and signaled her intention to emphasize the adverse effects of affirmative action, racial quotas, and bilingual education.[66] On January 8, 1984, Chavez declared, "African American problems were no longer civil rights problems and neither the commission nor the government would solve them." In an unprecedented move, Chavez also said she planned to cancel a release of a CRC study that showed that African Americans in "Alabama earned less, were less well educated, and had poorer housing than whites," because, she said, that was not proof of discrimination.[67]

It took only a few weeks for the newly reconstituted CRC to become an arm of the administration. On January 17, 1984, after an "impassioned debate," the CRC reversed policy and denounced the use of numerical quotas for the promotion of Blacks. Mary Frances Berry and Blandina Cardenas Ramirez subsequently blasted the CRC for changing policy without conducting a hearing.[68] The mission of the CRC had been inverted.

When the reconstituted CRC convened for its first meeting in January 1984 at a luxurious resort in the affluent suburb of Hunt Valley,

Maryland, the new eight-member commission displayed a solid five-vote majority echoing the Reagan line. Neas once again excoriated the new commission as "a panel that only Ed Meese could love."[69] Under the leadership of Pendleton and Chavez, the CRC discarded its traditional procedures and fact-finding activities and conducted its investigations in line with the Reagan White House's goals of civil rights retrenchment.[70] Instead of monitoring the administration, Clarence Pendleton said, "we are part of the administration."[71]

The administration's assault on the integrity of the CRC succeeded in undermining its integrity and independence. Mary Frances Berry grieved that the CRC was no longer the nation's conscience on civil rights and despaired for women and minorities in this country.[72] A few years later, Pendleton suggested in an interview that there will no longer be a need for the CRC by 1989 because "all the [civil rights] laws are on the books," and there is "nothing else to study."[73] John Shattuck, executive director of the ACLU, declared, "[Reagan's] use of raw executive power to pack the commission symbolizes an administration willing to bend the law at every opportunity to reverse a quarter century of bipartisan progress" on civil rights.[74] The CRC survived, but during the 1980s, its staff dropped from three hundred to seventy-seven, and its budget was sliced from $11.6 million to $7 million. Since the Reagan administration's taming of the CRC, it has never regained its independence and became "a ghostly imitation of what it once was."[75]

Reagan's assault on the CRC coincided with the twentieth anniversary of the March on Washington. On a suffocatingly humid day, an estimated crowd of 250,000 people, about the same as the 1963 march, came together on the National Mall calling for "jobs, peace, and freedom," in hopes of resurrecting Martin Luther King Jr.'s original call to conscience. A succession of notable speakers clamored for the creation of a grassroots coalition to defeat Reagan. Coretta Scott King lambasted the Reagan administration for being "out of touch with all but an elite group of Americans, an administration which has continually attempted and often succeeded in turning back the clock on the advances of the last 20 years."[76] Spontaneous shouts of "Run, Jesse, run! Run, Jesse, run!" erupted as the Reverend Jesse Jackson was introduced and approached the podium.[77] Reagan was at his ranch in California, but, according to Atlanta mayor Andrew Young, anger at the president's policies "was the organizing factor that pulled the coalition together." Appearing on the CBS program *Face the Nation* the following morning, Young wistfully spoke of a coalition of environmentalists, women's rights advocates, and Blacks that he hoped would emerge to defeat Reagan the following year.[78]

THE MLK HOLIDAY: WE WILL KNOW IN ABOUT THIRTY-FIVE YEARS, WON'T WE?

The upsurge of African American protest around the twentieth anniversary of the March on Washington dovetailed with the culmination of efforts to make King's birthday a national holiday. Unlike the contentious debates over the CRC, African Americans and their liberal allies here scored a decisive triumph in the face of the Reagan administration's opposition.

Efforts to declare a King holiday had begun only a few days after King's assassination, when Michigan congressman John Conyers, a cofounder of the Congressional Black Caucus, proposed such a bill, but it wasn't until 1979 that the campaign gained steam when President Carter and his rival, Senator Edward Kennedy, were both vying for the African American vote in anticipation of the 1980 Democratic presidential primary. In March and again in June of that year, Congress reconsidered a bill, but House Republicans and conservative Southern Democrats put up fierce opposition.[79] Strom Thurmond and Democratic representative Larry McDonald, the second president of the John Birch Society, even dredged up the old allegations that King was a Communist dupe. Representative McDonald said that honoring Dr. King with a holiday would put the United States "on the side of the reds."[80] The bill fell short in the House by just five votes.[81]

Thanks to the unstinting efforts of Representative Conyers, the movement to declare a King holiday continued to gain momentum. In 1982, thousands of ordinary citizens inundated Reagan with letters in support of the King holiday. By then, Reagan had started to pay tribute to King, quoting from his iconic "I Have a Dream" speech and occasionally citing decontextualized snippets of other speeches that obscured King's more radical aims, especially King's commitment to combatting economic injustice and ending the Vietnam War.[82] Reagan attempted to domesticate King in order to make him a poster child for Reagan's brand of "conservative color-blindness."[83] With respect to the King holiday, Reagan claimed publicly that it was "too expensive."[84] In private, he thought King unworthy of a holiday.[85]

The Democratic-controlled Post Office Committee and Civil Service subcommittee convened hearings on Conyers's bill for a King holiday on February 23, 1982. As before, Representative McDonald led the opposition. He suggested that the FBI tapes on King, which in 1977 had been sealed for a period of forty years, should be made public, "lest there be any embarrassment," and the hearings collapsed in mutual recrimination.[86] At the hearings, King's widow angrily denounced the "traveling right-wing circus" that specialized in "character assassination and infantile name-calling."[87] The House did not take up the matter again until the following year.

Emboldened by the electorates' rebuke of Reagan in the 1982 midterm elections, Representative Conyers and his colleagues in the CBC resumed their efforts. They assembled 176 House cosponsors for a new King holiday bill, including ten Republicans. At a question-and-answer session on January 21, 1983, Reagan said he "could see making [King's birthday] a day to remember" but would oppose making it a national holiday "in the sense of business closing down and government closing down, everyone not working."[88] Nonetheless, sensing the growing political momentum for a holiday, the White House designated Mel Bradley to investigate options to the proposal, such as a day of recognition without shutting down the country.[89]

The White House's equivocations stood in vivid contrast to the CBC's zeal in fulfilling their fifteen-year crusade to make King's birthday a national holiday. On June 7, 1983, House Speaker Tip O'Neill, singer Stevie Wonder, and Coretta Scott King headed an all-star lineup of witnesses appearing before the House Post Office and Civil Service subcommittee urging the House to act. Speaker O'Neill lauded King as "America's Gandhi" who deserved a holiday because "he taught us, all of us, how to change our society for the better, and how to do it peacefully."[90] He repudiated an alternative proposal offered by Representative William Dannemeyer to make the third Sunday a day of prayer and remembrance, and not a national holiday, because the holiday would cost taxpayers $225 million a year in lost productivity. "There are so many Sunday remembrances," O'Neill said. "It's Cap Day in Boston for the Red

Sox."[91] The House finally voted on August 2, 1983, to make King's birthday a national holiday with a 338–90 majority.[92]

In the Republican-controlled Senate, the bill's prospects appeared bleak because its fate rested in the Senate Judiciary Committee, chaired by Strom Thurmond. Jesse Helms, Reagan's old ally, lurked as another determined foe and pledged another filibuster. White House aides still insisted that there was no legal or economic justification for another holiday.[93] Even if the bill passed the Senate, Reagan was still on record opposing it. In a morning briefing on August 4, Reagan reiterated his opposition to the holiday on the grounds that it was too costly.

A few days later, however, under prodding from Senate Majority Leader Howard Baker, Reagan told his aides he was "inclined" to reverse course but still had not made a final decision.[94]

As Congress reconvened in September after its summer recess, tensions remained high in anticipation of a combative debate in the Republican-controlled Senate. Just days before the Senate hearings, the influential Conservative Caucus, with close ties to Reagan, called for a delay in a King holiday of at least forty-four years, when the results of the FBI's investigations of King would be unsealed.[95] Senator Helms, the savior of Reagan's political career in 1976, became the bill's chief antagonist. In the process, he resurrected the old smears of King's alleged Communist affinities, which Reagan had long embraced.[96] In hopes of softening his party's image for a future presidential run, Senator Dole stepped up to assume the role of floor manager of the debate.

Debate on the bill commenced in the Senate on October 3 and immediately turned acrimonious. Helms took little time in launching a filibuster. He placed a thirty-nine-page report into the Congressional Record reciting the stale accusations of King's subversive activities, charging King with exhibiting an "action-oriented Marxism" that was "not compatible with the concepts of this country."[97] Helms's slurs provoked an angry retort from Senator Edward Kennedy, who accused Helms of using "red smear" tactics to defeat the legislation and making completely inaccurate and false claims, which "do not reflect credit on this body," and adding that they "should be shunned by the American people, including the citizens of [Helms's] own state."[98] Under prodding from Majority Leader Baker, Helms abruptly dropped the filibuster and agreed to a final vote in two weeks in exchange for allowing the consideration of specific amendments subject to time limitations.[99]

Despite Helms's antics, momentum for the bill had been increasing. By late September, the bill's passage became inevitable. Accordingly, Reagan grudgingly announced that he would sign the bill. Helms, however, remained defiant and joined the Conservative Caucus's lawsuit to unseal the FBI's voluminous surveillance tapes on King. Helms's rationale was to smear King's reputation by exposing salacious details of his sex life in order to continue the late J. Edgar Hoover's crusade to destroy King's name at any cost.[100] On October 18, US District Court judge John Lewis Smith Jr. denied Helms's motion to release the documents. The Senate then rebuffed Helms's efforts to delay the bill by a vote of 71–12, paving the way for the vote on the holiday.[101]

A few hours after the District Court's ruling, the Senate reconvened for a vote before the full floor. The final debates before the vote unleashed bitter outbursts. Helms was not giving up. The North Carolina firebrand tried to add amendments to send the matter back to the Judiciary Committee. When that didn't work, he distributed a ream of declassified FBI reports on King, reigniting an acrimonious feud with Senator Kennedy, one of the main sponsors of the bill, which became heated after Helms said that Kennedy's brothers John and Robert had cautioned King against associating with suspected Communists in the 1960s.[102]

The Helms-Kennedy tiff was one of the most emotionally laden Senate confrontations since the civil rights debates of the mid-1960s. Later on, an enraged Senator Daniel Patrick Moynihan of New York took to the floor of the Senate and stomped on the FBI documents, calling them a "packet of filth."[103] The normally soft-spoken and measured Senator Bill Bradley of New Jersey provoked audible gasps from the gallery when he said it was impossible for him to give Helms "due respect as a colleague." Bradley went on, "They are playing up to Old Jim Crow and all of us know it. The holiday is their cutting issue."[104]

The following afternoon, October 19, 1983, in a moment of high drama with Coretta Scott King peering down from the dignitaries' gallery, the Senate voted 78–22 to create a federal holiday to honor Martin Luther King Jr. Of the twenty-two senators who voted against the bill, eighteen of them were Republicans, including Reagan's longtime ally

Barry Goldwater.[105] Senators Charles Grassley of Iowa and Orrin Hatch of Utah, both of whom would serve on the Senate Judiciary well into the second decade of the next century, also voted against the holiday.[106]

In a press conference shortly after the vote, his first in nearly three months, Reagan punctured the jubilant mood. Though he reluctantly promised to sign the bill, he said he "would have preferred [a non-holiday in King's honor], but since they seem bent on making it a national holiday," the president said, "I believe the symbolism of that day is important enough that I will sign that legislation when it reaches my desk."[107] When ABC reporter Sam Donaldson pressed Reagan on Senator Helms's assertions of King's Communist ties, Reagan dropped the following bombshell: "We'll know in about thirty-five years, won't we?"[108] These remarks provoked anger from people throughout the world. The *New York Times* said Reagan's "graceless remarks" dignified "the shameless snooping of Dr. King's enemies" and demonstrated "why he fails to impress so many Americans as the symbolic leader of all the people."[109] *New York Times* columnist Anthony Lewis called Reagan's "flippant tone, a moment of chilling self-revelation" that demonstrated his utter "insensitivity to the issues Dr. King raised and the human feelings involved." Lewis continued: "Under the geniality, we saw a void."[110]

Reagan's remarks also dismayed his political aides. His provocative jokes during press conference rehearsals drew laughter from his advisors, but White House communications director David Gergen assumed the president would "never say that at a press conference." A few years later, Gergen recalled, "I almost lost my dinner over that."[111] Days later, former New Hampshire governor Meldrim Thomson Jr., a conservative Republican and member of the John Birch Society, released an exchange of letters with Reagan in which Thomson had called King "immoral." In response, Reagan, the actor turned politician, ironically moaned that the public's perception of King "is based on an image, not reality. Indeed, to them, the perception is reality."[112] In order to quell the uproar, just before he left for a golfing weekend at the all-white Augusta National Golf Club, Reagan called Mrs. King to apologize for his comments.[113] Landing at the golf club, Reagan said Mrs. King accepted his apology and told him that "we all make mistakes and that I attributed it to human error."[114]

On November 2, 1983, in a celebratory ceremony at the Rose Garden, flanked by Vice President Bush, King's family, and other civil rights luminaries, Reagan officially signed the King holiday into law. Reagan's gracious words praising King for "stirring the nation to the very depths of our soul" could not dispel the ill will conveyed in his comments about King.[115] CBC member Charles B. Rangel observed, "The President was eloquent. If we could only get his policies to catch up with his speech, the country would be in great shape."[116] The King holiday was a landmark in America's racial history, but like the fight over the VRA extension the previous year, it occurred in spite of Reagan's opposition. As with the VRA, Reagan signed the King holiday bill only after its passage became inevitable.

REAGAN'S 1984 REELECTION CAMPAIGN: MIDNIGHT IN AMERICA FOR BLACK AMERICA

Inspired by Harold Washington's stunning election as Chicago's first Black mayor in April 1983, Rev. Jesse Jackson formally announced his candidacy for the Democratic nomination for the presidency. Declaring his intention to run the day after Reagan signed the Martin Luther King Jr. holiday into law, Jackson spoke of creating a "rainbow coalition" and denounced Reagan and his record as "anti-black" and "anti–civil rights."[117] Jackson hoped to tap into Black America's fury over Reagan's policies, which led hundreds of thousands of African Americans across the nation to register to vote. Analysts predicted that African American voter registration would increase by two million, with much of the gain concentrated in the South and in other states that Reagan narrowly won in 1980.[118]

In a highly anticipated prime-time speech on January 30, 1984, a date selected by Nancy Reagan's astrologer, Joan Quigley, Reagan announced he was running for reelection. Indications that the economy was finally coming out of the doldrums buoyed his prospects, but African Americans were not benefitting from the recovery. While the overall unemployment rate dropped to 8.3 percent in November, African American unemployment stood at an alarming 17.8 percent, the unemployment rate for Black teenagers had reached 49 percent, and 35.6 percent of African Americans lived below the poverty line.[119] The National Urban League released its annual report in January calling the state of Black America "disastrous" and warned that the poor were being relegated to an "an out-of-sight, out-of-mind" status in American life.[120]

Most political pundits, nonetheless, predicted that the combination of the rebounding economy, the power of incumbency, and Reagan's incomparable political skills made him the prohibitive favorite to win re-election. By June, former vice president Mondale, a longtime civil rights supporter, survived a primary scare from the telegenic and cerebral Colorado senator Gary Hart and had wrapped up the Democratic nomination. The most surprising story of the primary season, however, was the resiliency and dynamism of Jesse Jackson's campaign, which became the vessel for Black grievances against Reagan. While many pundits initially disparaged Jackson as a fringe candidate, he won five primaries and caucuses and finished with 18.2 percent of the primary voters, behind Mondale and Hart.[121] Jackson's glittering, charismatic performance on the campaign trail galvanized African American voters and evoked comparisons to Reagan.[122] Jackson's candidacy increased the pace and intensity of African American voter registration and induced the Republicans to mount their own $10 million voter-registration drive.[123]

Basking in the glow of the economic recovery, Reagan appeared poised to defeat Mondale in a landslide. Despite a disastrous abortive mission in Beirut that cost 265 American lives the previous October, his numerous gaffes and misrepresentations, and "the extraordinary number of his political appointees who were forced to resign because of ethical or legal improprieties," Reagan was famously called by the *New York Times* "the man in the Teflon Suit; nothing sticks to him."[124] Reagan's coronation at the Republican National Convention in Dallas coincided with the Summer Olympic Games in Los Angeles, and party organizers skillfully drew on the games' enthusiastic nationalism.[125] Reagan's now iconic 1984 campaign commercial proclaimed "It's Morning Again in America." That tagline captures Reagan's great skill at tapping into nostalgia for a bygone America that beclouded long-term political problems such as deindustrialization, globalization, and continued racial inequality.

Mondale's stellar record on civil rights notwithstanding, race never surfaced as a central issue in his campaign. At the time, only 6 percent of whites rated civil rights as a top-three issue, compared to 38 percent of Blacks.[126] Unsurprisingly, Reagan's campaign was largely focused on white Americans. In the large crowds Reagan attracted on his campaign stops, *New York Times* reporter Francis X. Clines observed that the faces were "unrelievedly white," with African Americans "the rarest of sights."[127] In an interview with Mike Wallace on CBS' *60 Minutes*, former First Lady Rosalynn Carter observed, "The Reagan administration makes us feel comfortable with our prejudices."[128] Journalist Carl Rowan noted: "When President Reagan asks if Americans are better off than they were four years ago, blacks are one group that can say, resoundingly, No!"[129] In place of the "Morning in America" slogan that appealed to many white Americans, Vernon Jordan of the Urban League saw a "dark midnight in America today."[130]

As expected, on November 6, 1984, Reagan annihilated Mondale to win a second term. His 525–13 victory in the Electoral College was bested only by his idol Franklin D. Roosevelt's in 1936. Reagan's rout occurred in spite of African Americans turning out in record numbers to cast their vote against him.[131] In his victory speech, Reagan broke with tradition by ungraciously refusing to pay the customary tribute to his vanquished foe because he was so incensed by Mondale's closing attacks on his age.[132] To add insult to injury, Jesse Helms prevailed in his reelection battle, the most expensive race in Senate history. Helms's slim margin of victory was largely attributable to Reagan's last-minute television advertisement blitz on Helms's behalf.[133] Reagan's second landslide victory led pundits to proclaim the dawn of a new conservative realignment in American presidential politics.

Reagan's skill in tapping into a renewed patriotism dominated the general election campaign, submerging civil rights.[134] His racial conservatism, nonetheless, contributed to his winning 72 percent of the white Southern vote. Veteran Mississippi political reporter Bill Minor argued that Reagan's overriding strength in the South was attributable to "a great deal of underlying racism, [and] Reagan is a polarizing figure whether he wants to be or not, in a race-conscious state as ours."[135]

Looking forward, African Americans could find some solace in the fact that Reagan received only 9 percent of the Black vote, which meant they had become the "backbone of the Democratic Party."[136] On the whole, however, Reagan's rout of Mondale marked a political nadir for African Americans and their liberal allies. With the administration poised to appoint more conservative judges, they braced for an uphill battle to preserve the civil rights revolution of the 1960s and 1970s.

CHAPTER 10

SOUTH AFRICA

Reagan's Embrace of the Apartheid
Government and the Fight for Sanctions

I think I should say now that he is a racist, pure and simple.
—Archbishop Desmond Tutu (September 1985)[1]

*We find under Reagan a 180-degree shift from "We shall
overcome" to "We shall overturn."*
—Jesse Jackson (June 3, 1985)[2]

W ithin days of Reagan's thumping of Mondale, the issue of Reagan's
appeasement of the racist South African government thrust the issue of apartheid to the forefront of the political debate. Televised clips of
the brutal crackdown against peaceful protestors in South Africa, eerily
reminiscent of the brutality seen in Alabama, Mississippi, and Georgia
in the 1960s, shocked the conscience of the nation. Anger over Reagan's
support of the apartheid regime galvanized African American activists
and their civil rights allies. Just two weeks after the election, a group
of Black civil rights leaders formed the Free South Africa Movement
(FSAM), which sought to impose sanctions on South Africa and end
apartheid.[3] Within days, African American despair over Reagan's landslide victory soon gave way to the greatest wave of political mobilization
since the heyday of the civil rights struggle in the 1960s around the issue
of Reagan's support of South Africa's apartheid regime. In the face of the
Reagan administration's intransigence and demonization of the African
National Congress (ANC) as pro-Soviet puppets, Black activism played
a pivotal role in ending apartheid.

CONSTRUCTIVE ENGAGEMENT AND ITS DISCONTENTS

Since the end of World War II, American civil rights leaders and Black South Africans had forged political, cultural, and emotional bonds in their joint efforts to challenge white supremacy on both sides of the Atlantic.[4] Just days after receiving his Nobel Peace Prize in 1964, Martin Luther King Jr. urged Western governments to withdraw their investments in South Africa. The following year, King went further and denounced South Africa's white rulers as modern-day barbarians who had revived the racial ideology of the Nazis.[5] King's exhortations went unheeded due to American preoccupation with the Vietnam War. Until the mid-1970s, the weak insurgencies against white rule in Rhodesia, Namibia, Angola, and other countries relegated the entire South African region to a Cold War backwater.

The collapse of Portuguese colonial rule in Mozambique and Angola in 1974 thrust sub-Saharan Africa into the vortex of the Cold War. After 36,000 Cuban soldiers poured into Angola, Jimmy Carter grappled with the delicate balancing of Cold War considerations and his espousal of human rights and desire to effectuate a transition to Black majority rule in neighboring Rhodesia and Namibia. While Carter elevated the importance of human rights and criticized the racist apartheid regime in more strident tones than his predecessors, in the end, halting Soviet expansion in South Africa trumped Carter's hatred of racism, and he refused to impose punitive sanctions.[6]

Unlike Carter, Reagan never wrestled with the racist brutality of the South African government. Seeing South Africa as a bulwark against the spread of Soviet influence, Reagan scoffed at Carter's attacks on Pretoria's human rights record. During his 1980 presidential campaign, Reagan had insisted, "South Africans certainly don't need us to tell them how to solve their race problems." Weary of Carter's talk of human rights, the white minority government in Pretoria greeted Reagan's triumph as a victory that they hoped would end their diplomatic isolation.[7] Given Reagan's campaign rhetoric and the conservative movement's affinity for South Africa as a citadel of Western civilization, Pretoria had ample reason for optimism. Unsurprisingly, and to the dismay of African Americans, Reagan immediately reversed Carter's harsh rhetoric against apartheid.

By the 1970s, ending the racist brutality of white supremacy in sub-Saharan Africa emerged as Blacks' paramount foreign policy consideration.[8]

They had been aghast at candidate Reagan's careless talk about invading Rhodesia during the 1976 Republican primary. From the early days of the Reagan administration, the CBC and its allies had seethed over Reagan's conciliatory rhetoric toward South Africa. Reagan's selection of Chester Crocker as assistant secretary of state for African affairs signaled a more amicable policy toward the racist apartheid regime. Crocker, a political science professor at Georgetown University and an expert on African politics, had just published a provocative article in *Foreign Affairs* setting forth a new approach to the apartheid regime, which he called "constructive engagement." Crocker argued that "friendly persuasion" rather than "harsh rhetoric" was the best approach for dealing with South Africa. In support of this strategy, Crocker advanced the dubious proposition that a "window of opportunity" had opened up in South Africa for significant reform under the new nationalist government of Prime Minister P. W. Botha.[9]

In an expansive interview with Walter Cronkite of CBS News on March 3, 1981, Reagan blithely mentioned the "sincere and honest effort" of the South African government to alter its brutal regime. He continued his defense of South Africa with clearly wrong historical claims: "We cannot abandon a country that has stood by us in every war we ever fought—a country that is strategically essential to the free world in its production of minerals we must all have."[10] In fact, Prime Minister P.W. Botha's ruling Nationalist Party had supported the Nazis during World War II, and Botha and his immediate predecessor, John Vorster, had been imprisoned for their membership in the pro-Nazi Ossewabrandwag Party. Reagan's remarks exasperated freedom-loving people throughout the world but were widely hailed in Pretoria as signifying a reversal of American policy of the past decades.[11]

Reagan's indulgent views toward the South African white-minority government appalled African Americans. For their part, Reagan's defenders cite Cold War considerations as the sole reason for Reagan's embrace of the white supremacist government in Pretoria.[12] However, the recent revelations that Reagan referred to Black African diplomats as "monkeys" still "uncomfortable wearing shoes" raises the question of whether Reagan's opposition to Black majority rule in South Africa was motivated solely by Cold War considerations of creating a barricade against Soviet and Cuban penetration of the African subcontinent.

As mentioned previously, William F. Buckley and many contributors to *National Review* had long argued that African decolonization posed a dire threat to Western civilization and, thus, never deviated from their support of the apartheid regime.[13] The conservative intelligentsia mostly embraced scientific racism that derided Black culture as primitive and barbaric. This racist notion of the superiority of white civilization against a Black culture ripe for Communist penetration was the same argument Buckley and others had used to justify their opposition to ending Jim Crow in the American South.[14]

By the spring of 1981, Reagan's conciliatory words toward the South African government were matched by the administration's actions. In late March, UN ambassador Jeane Kirkpatrick met with five senior South African military intelligence officials in contravention of a UN arms embargo prohibiting the US (and other member nations) of having military involvement with South Africa. CBC member William H. Gray III of Pennsylvania called for Kirkpatrick's firing and said that Reagan's friendly posture to South Africa was "a slap in the face to 26 million black Americans."[15] The assassination attempt on Reagan temporarily quelled the uproar, but news of Reagan's invitation to South African foreign minister Roelof Frederik "Pik" Botha to visit the White House rekindled outrage.[16] At the same time, Crocker's April visit to eleven nations in sub-Saharan Africa drew jeers and snubs from the presidents of Angola, Botswana, Mozambique, Tanzania, Zambia, and Zimbabwe for consolidating US relations with South Africa.[17]

Reagan warmly received Foreign Minister Botha at the White House on May 15, 1981, after which Botha held a series of meetings with Secretary of State Alexander Haig. The Haig-Botha summit cemented a new era of friendly relations between the US and South Africa. After he returned home, Botha told his colleagues in the South African government, "I believe that in the entire period since the Second World War, there has never been a US government as well disposed toward us as the present government."[18]

Critics, led by the CBC, flayed the Reagan administration's constructive engagement as a policy of "all carrot and no stick," pointing to the lack of any evidence to support the premise that South Africa was making "a sincere and honest effort" to alter its brutal, racist regime.[19] The recent findings of a Rockefeller Foundation study buttressed their attacks.

Warning that "time is running out" on prospects for averting a racial bloodbath in South Africa, the study's authors counseled broadening the arms embargo against Pretoria, ending all nuclear collaboration, and halting US investment.[20] African American activists condemned constructive engagement as a license for procrastination. Just days before Reagan's reelection, Archbishop Desmond Tutu, a recent recipient of the Nobel Peace Prize, blasted the Reagan administration "for aligning itself with the perpetrators of the most vicious system since Nazism" and assailed constructive engagement for making the apartheid regime "more intransigent."[21]

FIGHTING BACK: THE FREE SOUTH AFRICA MOVEMENT

Widespread discontent over constructive engagement had been growing throughout Reagan's first term, and African American congressman Ronald V. Dellums had introduced a series of unsuccessful bills imposing sanctions on South Africa.[22] But it was anger over Reagan's reelection, the failure of Dellums's sanctions bill, and the uptick of racial violence and suppression in South Africa that ignited the groundswell of grassroots protest.

On November 22, 1984, CRC member Mary Frances Berry; Randall Robinson, the president of TransAfrica, an advocacy group formed to influence American foreign policy on African and Caribbean countries; and Walter E. Fauntroy, the Washington, DC, delegate to Congress, were all arrested inside the South African embassy in Washington. They had staged a sit-in and refused to leave until the South African regime released sixteen Black South African labor leaders who had recently been jailed without charges. Eleanor Holmes Norton, a civil rights leader and former head of the EEOC, went to the embassy and informed reporters who had been told of the sit-in, that the action was in response to the Reagan administration's policies toward South Africa, which, Norton charged, were "not only counterproductive, but dangerous."[23] After spending the night in jail, Berry, Robinson, and Fauntroy convened a press conference on Capitol Hill, where they announced they were launching the Free South Africa Movement (FSAM), aimed at pressuring the Reagan administration to change its policies toward the racist regime of South Africa, which "only gives comfort to an oppressive regime as its policies worsen."[24] Within weeks, the anti-apartheid movement galvanized civil rights leaders and swept through college campuses in a manner reminiscent of the civil rights movement of the early 1960s.[25]

The first wave of demonstrations coincided with the arrival in Washington, DC, of the anti-apartheid activist Archbishop Desmond Tutu, a week before the South African cleric was to receive the Nobel Peace Prize, in Oslo. On December 3, 1984, Tutu met with members of the CBC and received a rare standing ovation from the bipartisan House Foreign Relations Subcommittee on Africa after he launched a scorching attack on constructive engagement for "giving democracy a bad name." He also called Reagan's South African policy "immoral, evil, and anti-Christian" and offered to meet with Reagan before leaving for Oslo.[26]

In hopes of defusing the escalating crisis, Reagan accepted Tutu's invitation—his first with a Black South African opponent of the apartheid regime. The cordial façade of the twenty-five-minute December 7 meeting among Tutu, Reagan, and his aides in the Oval Office could not camouflage the impasse over policy. After one of the tensest meetings of Reagan's presidency, Tutu lambasted constructive engagement as an abject failure and told the president that the Pretoria government had become even more repressive than before Reagan instituted the policy. For his part, Reagan stressed his repugnance to apartheid, yet stubbornly refused to impose sanctions or reverse existing policy.[27] In his diary, the president dismissed Tutu as "naïve" and remarked, "The Bishop seems unaware, even though he himself is Black, that part of the problem is tribal not racial. If apartheid ended now there still would be civil strife between the Black tribes."[28] Reagan's belief that he, who had never travelled to Africa, had a better insight than the native South African Nobel laureate fit his long-standing pattern of white paternalism, and racism, toward Africans.

Opposition to Reagan's South Africa policy became bipartisan. Just days after the president's meeting with Tutu, Republican senator Richard Lugar, incoming chair of the Senate Foreign Relations Committee, appeared on NBC's *Meet the Press* and demanded that Reagan denounce apartheid "much more sharply and more often."[29] In a surprising move, thirty-five of the most conservative House Republicans, led by the ambitious backbencher Newt Gingrich of Georgia, warned that economic sanctions would become necessary if South Africa did not demonstrate a commitment to changing its racial policies.[30] Ever since the November arrests of the Free South Africa Movement organizers, throngs of demonstrators had daily descended on the South African embassy to demonstrate their opposition to apartheid, and thousands were arrested. Outside the capital, grassroots pressure stirred a new student movement across college campuses throughout the nation demanding that universities "divest" from companies that had operations and ties with South Africa. After South African police killed twenty unarmed Blacks marching to a funeral in Uitenhage on March 21, 1985, Reagan blamed the victims, suggesting that the "rioters"—who were, in fact, nonviolent—had precipitated the violence.[31]

In the meantime, the grassroots groundswell against apartheid pressured the House of Representatives to approve a series of economic sanctions against South Africa. In a stunning rebuke to Reagan, on June 5, 1985, six House Republicans joined virtually the entire House Democratic caucus in passing a bill that banned new loans to existing or new businesses in South Africa, halted new loans and computer sales to the South African government, and prohibited the importation of Krugerrands, the South African gold coins. Although the bill did not go as far as Congressman Dellums's proposal for complete disinvestment, it was an unprecedented congressional censure of an American president's foreign policy.[32] Having favored sanctions against Cuba, the Soviet Union, Poland, and most recently Nicaragua, Reagan refused to budge on sanctions against South Africa. Speaking for the administration, Assistant Secretary of State for African Affairs Chester Crocker argued that sanctions were "a show of impotence" that would "erode our influence with those we seek to persuade."[33]

The following month, Reagan sustained another blow when a similar bill sponsored by Republican senator Lugar passed the Senate 80–12.[34] After the South African government imposed a partial state of emergency in late July, public protest in the United States against apartheid grew into the largest demonstration over an international issue since the Vietnam War. The arrests of hundreds of anti-apartheid protestors, including such luminaries as Coretta Scott King; two of Robert F. Kennedy's children; former First Daughter Amy Carter; John Jacob, president of the National Urban League; and twenty-two US congresspeople, kept the issue on the front pages.[35] Still, Reagan clung to his policy and expressed optimism that the South African government would lift the state of emergency and implement reforms.[36] In an interview with an Atlanta radio station in August, Reagan displayed his trademark obliviousness to the plight of South African Blacks when he claimed that his policies were promoting positive reforms. He went so far as to laud the South African government for eliminating the segregation that "we once had in our own country."[37] Of course, Reagan's assertion was patently false. If this was not bad enough, Reagan's constructive engagement policy was dealt another public setback when, in a highly anticipated speech on August 15, 1985, Prime Minster Botha backtracked on a promise to adopt significant reforms. Botha defiantly declared: "I am not prepared to lead South Africans and other minority groups to suicide." Archbishop Tutu described himself as "devastated" by the speech and bleakly predicted that the "chances of peaceful change are virtually nil."[38]

Conceding that he had been careless to suggest that the Pretoria government had eliminated apartheid, Reagan appeared to capitulate. On September 9, 1985, Reagan signed Executive Order 12532, which adopted a few of the sanctions sought by Congress, though Reagan insisted that constructive engagement continue.[39] In any case, experts contended that the executive order would have a negligible effect on the economy of South Africa and on American corporations doing business there. CBC members condemned the order as a duplicitous stunt to forestall congressional action and vowed to get a tougher sanctions bill to the president's desk.[40] Back in South Africa, the usually measured Tutu bitterly criticized Reagan's executive order as a ploy "to save himself from the humiliation of a veto override" and accused Reagan of being "much more interested in helping Republicans to be reelected than in ending bloodshed." Tutu continued: "I think I should say now he is a racist pure and simple."[41]

Instead of quelling the controversy, Reagan's executive order spawned more outrage, militancy, and protest. Throughout the chilly winter of 1986, college students constructed shantytowns on campuses across the country to highlight the squalid living conditions of millions of Black South Africans. The shantytowns became the defining feature of the divestment campaign. In the halls of Congress, the CBC was determined to press for a rigorous bill that would end all US economic support for South Africa. Throughout the protests, Reagan displayed his stubborn certitude. When pressed at an April 9, 1986, news conference as to why he condoned violence for the "freedom fighters" in Nicaragua but condemned "the use of violence for people your State Department claims are freedom fighters inside South Africa," Reagan leapt to the defense of Botha: "I can tell you that he agrees with us and finds the past system repugnant and is trying to get changes as quickly as possible."[42] In response, *New York Times* columnist Anthony Lewis queried whether Reagan would "do nothing but murmur ambivalent regrets" if "1,600 white people had been killed in the past year and a half in South Africa."[43]

In the face of international condemnation, Botha's regime remained unbowed. Citing the US' recent raid on Libya as justification for combatting terrorism, on June 12, 1986, the South African government declared a state of emergency in an effort to crush the rebellion.[44] The resulting deaths of hundreds of Black South Africans made a mockery of Reagan's insistence that there was any semblance of moderation within the apartheid regime. Televised images of the violence and bloody police repression evoked memories of Birmingham and Selma from the 1960s. On June 18, 1986, the House of Representatives approved by a voice vote the far-reaching bill Congressman Dellums had introduced the previous year. The most stringent economic sanctions bill in US history, it called for a complete divestment within 180 days and a trade embargo.[45] Facing fierce pressure from some of his closest Republicans allies in Congress, a recalcitrant Reagan insisted that the Pretoria government was a necessary ally in the fight against Communism.[46] Behind the scenes, debates raged within the administration, as the State Department urged Reagan to take a tougher approach to Pretoria and the more hawkish Cold Warriors, represented by White House communications director Patrick Buchanan and CIA director William Casey, urged Reagan to remain firm.

In a widely anticipated speech on July 22, 1986, delivered from the East Room of the White House, Reagan sided with the hard-liners in characterizing sanctions as "immoral" and "repugnant." He even lavished praise on the South African government for its "dramatic changes" and called the ANC a "terrorist organization" bent on fomenting racial war.[47] In closing, Reagan said the South African government "is under no obligation to negotiate the future of the country with any organization that proclaims a goal of creating a Communist country."[48] The speech elicited widespread condemnation across the political spectrum.[49] Congressional Republicans fretted that Reagan's opposition to sanctions was creating a racist image that would undermine the GOP's appeal to young voters.[50]

Even the *Dallas Morning News*, the most conservative major newspaper in the country, urged the administration to abandon constructive engagement.[51] In South Africa, an irate Tutu roared, "The West can go to hell."[52] In his memoirs, Chester Crocker blamed the speech for the administration's eventual loss on the sanctions. "With this speech," Crocker said, "the 'great communicator' became the greater polarizer."[53]

Only three months prior to the midterm elections, Reagan's strident pro-Pretoria stance alarmed congressional Republicans. Senator Richard Lugar took the initiative and sponsored a Senate sanctions bill to avert further political damage to the Republican brand. On August 15, thirty-seven Republican senators broke with Reagan to join all forty-seven Democrats in voting for Lugar's sanctions bill. Although weaker than the House bill, it included a ban on new US public and private loans and investments in South Africa, as well as a ban on the importation of uranium, coal, textiles, steel, and agricultural products. Sensing a significant political victory, Dellums and his allies in the CBC agreed to the Senate bill, which passed the House on September 12 by a wide margin, 308–77. An unyielding Reagan announced his intention to veto the legislation and proposed a diluted sanctions bill instead.[54]

Fearing the adverse political impact of a successful override of a presidential veto so close to the midterm elections, Republican senators Nancy Kassebaum of Kansas, Lugar, and Dole met privately with Reagan to implore him to reverse course. Reagan's obstinacy frustrated Lugar, who told the press that a veto would jeopardize US relations with Black Africa. "We really need to be on the right side of history in this case," he said.[55] Clinging to the notion that the sanctions bill was tantamount to economic warfare that "would seriously impede the prospects for a peaceful end to apartheid," Reagan vetoed the Comprehensive Anti-Apartheid Act on September 26, 1986.[56] Three days later, the House of Representatives voted 313–83 to override the veto. One of the eight-one House Republican defectors was Representative Lynn M. Martin of Illinois, who represented the congressional district where Reagan was born. Martin said:

Mr. President, in this veto message about South Africa you are wrong. What if you had been refused an education in Tampico because of your color? What if your parents couldn't move to Dixon because of travel passes? What if you could not be president because your supporters were denied the vote?[57]

Despite Reagan's furious efforts to corral Republican votes in the upper chamber to avert a humiliating defeat, the Senate voted 78–21 to override Reagan's veto. An exultant CBC leader Mickey Leland declared: "This is probably the greatest victory we have ever experienced."[58] The override was the first time Congress had overridden a Reagan veto, and it was also the most significant foreign policy setback for a president since Congress overrode Nixon's veto of the War Powers Act, in 1973. Most significantly, it was the first time in US history that African Americans had decisively molded US foreign policy.

Without a doubt, the passion of the Free South Africa Movement cast a spotlight on the imperative of ending apartheid. Congress' override of Reagan's veto was the opening salvo in a concerted global rejection of South Africa's regime. Deprived of financial support, the South African rand plunged precipitously and helped force the government of F. W. de Klerk, who succeeded Botha in 1989, to dismantle apartheid. The following year, less than four years after Congress imposed sanctions on South Africa, de Klerk's government freed ANC activist Nelson Mandela, who had been imprisoned for twenty-seven years. In an interview with *Ebony*, his first with an African American journalist since his release in 1990, Mandela touted the FSAM: "My spirits were lifted. . . . It was an impressive role for Black Americans to choose arrest."[59]

FIGHTING BACK AGAINST THE MEESE AND REYNOLDS NOMINATIONS

Spurred in part by the passions of the FSAM, civil rights organizations were emboldened in their determination to fight the Department of Justice's ongoing efforts to turn back the clock on civil rights enforcement. In January 1984, Reagan, just days before announcing his reelection bid, ignited the passion of the civil rights establishment once again by nominating the controversial archconservative Edwin Meese to replace Attorney General William French Smith. Meese had been Reagan's ideological alter ego since joining Governor Reagan's California staff as a legal affairs advisor after his stint as a deputy district attorney in Alameda County. There, he generated controversy for overseeing the arrests of over eight hundred students at the University of California at Berkeley's Sproul Hall

in 1964 during the Free Speech movement, which earned him the notice of Reagan. During his early career as a district attorney, Meese was
noted by colleagues for his unbridled enthusiasm for the police and the
military. One of his favorite hobbies was collecting miniature "model
squad cars and statuettes of pigs," the favorite epithet for the police in
the 1960s.[60]

In Reagan's first term, Meese emerged as the president's point man
on civil rights issues. As noted, he was the animating force behind re-
instating Bob Jones University's tax exemption and the evisceration of
the CRC. Most troubling for Blacks, Meese engaged in a frontal assault
on decades of established constitutional doctrine. He was a foremost ex-
ponent of the then ascendant doctrine of "originalism," which argued
that judges should adhere to the literal meaning of the Constitution as
set forth by the Founding Fathers. Although Meese was eventually confirmed as attorney general, civil rights activists managed to delay his
confirmation by thirteen months.

At the time of the Meese's nomination, Democrats were still livid
over Meese's "double-crossing" during the negotiations over the CRC,
but the nomination generated protest across the political spectrum. The
conservative *Chicago Tribune* called the selection of an attorney general
with no qualifications other than his "personal and unfailing political
allegiance to President" dangerous and damaging to "the credibility of
federal justice."[61] Meese's hometown paper, the conservative *Oakland
Tribune*, catalogued Meese's ethical lapses and his penchant for outrageous comments, such as when he called the ACLU a "criminals' lobby"
and said that people go to soup kitchens not because they are hungry
but because "the food is free."[62] A spokesman for the CBC said Meese's
position on most matters was "diametrically opposed to the Attorney
General's responsibility to protect the constitutional rights of all Americans, and most particularly women, minorities, and the poor." For the
first time since the Nixon administration, the LCCR announced its opposition to a cabinet nominee.[63]

It was not Meese's rigidly doctrinaire views that held up his nomination for over a year, longer than any other Cabinet member in recent history, but a slew of allegations that Meese had helped arrange positions in
the administration for individuals who had assisted him financially, had
obtained special treatment from government agencies in which he had a

financial interest, and had failed to disclose a $15,000 interest-free loan to his wife from a political appointee. At Meese's request, an independent counsel was appointed in April 1984 to conduct a broad investigation of the charges.[64] Although the independent counsel, former Watergate defense counsel Jacob Stein, concluded in September 1984 that there was "no basis" for prosecution, Stein refrained from commenting on the ethical propriety of Meese's conduct on the grounds that it was beyond his jurisdiction. Common Cause, the nonpartisan watchdog group, issued a report contesting Meese's narrative that the independent counsel's report vindicated Meese. It opposed the nomination on the grounds that Messe had displayed a "lack of ethical sensitivity" and "blindness to abuse of position." Former Watergate special prosecutor Archibald Cox wrote the report and noted that it was the first time in Common Cause's history that it had opposed the confirmation of a cabinet-level appointment. In a similar vein, the LCCR maintained that Meese was morally "unfit" to be the nation's law enforcement officer.[65]

As the hearings on the Meese confirmation were set to resume on January 30, 1985, the Senate Judiciary Committee released documents revealing that lawyers for the Office of Government Ethics had determined that Meese violated several ethical standards involving federal conflict of interest rules.[66] The agency director, political appointee David H. Martin, overruled the lawyers' contentions after Meese's attorneys submitted a rebuttal.[67] Finally, on February 23, 1985, thirteen months after the nomination, the Senate voted 63–31 to confirm Meese, but not before he drew more negative votes than any other attorney general nominee since 1925.[68] Still, Meese faced additional ethics charges that would beset him for the duration of his tenure. Meese's mounting legal problems created such a crisis of confidence in the Justice Department that the head of the Criminal Division of the DOJ, William Weld, and six other officials resigned in protest.[69] In July 1988, Reagan accepted Meese's resignation after an independent counsel charged that he was complicit in the high-profile "Wedtech" scandal, in which he had directed an aide to help an old friend win a $32 million US Army contract.[70]

Meese began his turbulent tenure as attorney general by announcing the promotion of the polarizing William Bradford Reynolds to associate attorney general, where he would be in charge of all non-criminal cases.[71] As it was the third-most-powerful position in the DOJ, the nomination required Senate confirmation. Because Reynolds personified Reagan's advocacy of "color-blind" conservatism, his confirmation hearings became a referendum on Reagan's civil rights policies. Blacks and their civil rights allies criticized Reynolds as a rigid ideologue who had seized every opportunity to weaken US civil rights laws. Under Reynolds's tempestuous leadership as the head of the Civil Rights Division, half the African American attorneys had resigned, and many of the career attorneys were reportedly "bored" or "idle" because Reynolds's political appointees handled all the important cases.

In anticipation of the Senate Judiciary Committee hearings, the LCCR reassembled the coalition that had opposed the administration's attempt to vitiate the Voting Rights Act. The hearings attracted more attention than any previous nomination for an associate attorney general in history. On the first day, Ralph Neas argued that Reynolds's leadership was "disgraceful" in its efforts to "repudiate a bipartisan consensus on civil rights that went back to the 1950s."[72] As expected, Reynolds faced aggressive questioning from senators in both parties. Virtually every civil rights organization testified at the hearings, excoriating Reynolds and his policies as dangerous and reactionary. A particularly poignant point came from the Lawyers' Committee for Civil Rights Under Law, a bipartisan group President Kennedy created in 1963, which was opposing a presidential nomination for the first time. The committee claimed that its concern about Reynolds's nomination went beyond specific policies like busing and affirmative action. Rather, it went to the very essence of the government's role in achieving justice for African Americans and other minorities. The organization alleged that during Reynolds's tenure, the Civil Rights Division of the Justice Department had become an *opponent* of civil rights.[73]

Opposition to Reynolds's nomination centered on his lax enforcement of the Voting Rights Act. On his first day of testimony, Ohio Democratic senator Howard Metzenbaum pointedly questioned Reynolds concerning his role in approving the moving of a polling place in Selma, Alabama, from a predominantly African American neighborhood to a municipal building a few blocks away. According to Metzenbaum, this occurred despite the determination by Justice Department staff attorneys that the move was racially motivated. Reynolds justified overruling the recommendation of DOJ attorneys after he concluded that there was neither a racial purpose nor effect in the decision to move the polling place. For many, Reynolds's explanation defied credulity. In response, Metzenbaum said, "I do not understand. You are intelligent, you appear to be a decent human being and yet you come down in some of these cases on the side of the bigots."[74] Lani Guinier of the NAACP's Legal Defense Fund and Frank Parker of the Lawyers' Committee for Civil Rights Under Law furnished the most incriminating testimony against Reynolds. They set out evidence of how Reynolds had consistently ignored the recommendations of the CRD staff to file suit over discriminatory voting changes, as the Voting Rights Act required. As part of his defense, Reynolds testified that he had met with several attorneys for African American voters in eleven redistricting cases in Mississippi, and they had agreed with his decision not to file lawsuits challenging the racially discriminatory redistricting plans.[75]

This mendacious claim—and others—would eventually doom Reynolds's nomination. Evidence was presented to show that Reynolds's assertions that the lawyers for African Americans had agreed with his decision not to file a lawsuit in a Mississippi Voting Rights case was untrue.[76] Additionally, it was proved that he had met with opponents of a Louisiana congressional redistricting plan despite claiming the contrary in his sworn statement. After a two-week hiatus, the hearings reconvened on June 18, 1985, and Reynolds was given a chance to clarify his statements. Reynolds repeatedly apologized for his faulty recollection, but Republican senator Arlen Specter, a swing vote, disclosed a confidential memorandum that yet again contradicted previous sworn testimony that Reynolds had given back, this time way back on March 1, 1982.

Reynolds's misleading statements gave wavering, moderate Republicans who were troubled by his record, but were reluctant to vote against a sitting Republican president, a clear reason to vote against a nominee's confirmation. Republican senators Specter and Mathias joined the eight Democrats on the Judiciary Committee in voting 10–8 against Reynolds's nomination. Specter accused Reynolds of taking positions "directly at variance with established law and contrary to precedents" on a host of civil rights issues. Mathias chided Reynolds for not supporting the "approach Congress for the past 20 years has taken to the problem of assuring civil rights."[77] Upon hearing the news that Reynolds's nomination had been defeated, delegates at the NAACP convention in Dallas erupted in cheers.[78] A disappointed Reagan emphasized that Reynolds's views reflected his own and said, "The policies he pursues are the policies of this administration and they will remain our policies as long as I am President."[79] In spite of the rebuke, Reynolds remained in his post as the head of the Civil Rights Division, and under Meese's leadership, he became even more powerful and influential within the DOJ. By the end of Reagan's second term, LBJ's attorney general Nicholas Katzenbach, the architect of the 1965 Voting Rights Act, bemoaned, "Under Mr. Reynolds, the civil rights division has changed sides. It no longer is an advocate for blacks and minorities. . . . Rights for Americans seems to him to mean rights for white males."[80]

PRESERVING AFFIRMATIVE ACTION

In the heady aftermath of his reelection, Reagan declared the dismantling of affirmative action a top domestic priority. With support from Meese, Reynolds, and other hard-liners in the Cabinet, administration officials leaked word in August 1985 that Meese had prepared a memo for Reagan's signature that would repeal Executive Order 11246. Signed by Lyndon Johnson in 1965, the order required federal contractors to set numerical goals and timetables to remedy possible job discrimination. It affected fifteen thousand companies employing twenty-three million workers at seventy-three thousand sites. Across the political spectrum, a chorus of voices had hailed Executive Order 11246 as a great triumph, because it opened up unprecedented opportunity for African Americans.[81] However, apostles of "color-blind" conservatism claimed that racial discrimination against African Americans and women had always been overstated. One of Reagan's favorite economists, George Gilder, a proponent of supply-side economics, wrote about the "myths of racial and sexual discrimination" and echoed Reagan's own view: "Discrimination has already been effectively abolished in this country."[82]

The depth of corporate America's opposition to ending affirmative action shocked Reagan and other hard-liners. Uncertainty over its future displeased powerful members of the business community who had invested heavily in the program and had come to appreciate its virtues. "It works," said Jim Conway of the National Association of Manufacturers. "Why change it?"[83] More pragmatic figures within the administration, such as Secretary of Labor William Brock, whose department was entrusted with administering the program, told the NAACP in June 1985, "I think this country is going to have to have some affirmative action in the foreseeable future" because "we as a country have lived for 200 years with a major part of our population in remarkable disadvantage. And it takes some time to recover from that."[84] Unable to come to a decision, Reagan dithered on repealing Executive Order 11246. The possibility of Reagan repealing affirmative action was so politically unpopular in Congress that 69 senators and 180 House members signed letters urging Reagan not to sign the order.[85]

While Reagan vacillated on affirmative action, he made a series of speeches commemorating the first celebration of the Martin Luther King Day holiday. In a radio address to the nation, he called affirmative action an affront to King's version of a "color-blind society," one that, in King's words, judges people "not by the color of their skin but by the content of their character." On the same day, Attorney General Meese declared that the elimination of affirmative action was consistent with the original intent of the civil rights movement, and the administration's approach was "very consistent with what Dr. King had in mind."[86] Once again, civil rights organizations lambasted Reagan and Meese for distorting King's views. King, in fact, had endorsed preferences for African Americans and famously said, "It's a cruel jest to say to a bootless man that he ought to lift himself by his own bootstraps."[87] In a *Los Angeles Times* editorial, NAACP leader Roger Wilkins best expressed the gulf between Reagan and King: "Two American men who lived in the same century could have hardly agreed on less." He went on, "King's profound concern for the poor was matched by Reagan's concern . . . for the wealthy and powerful." What was especially galling to Wilkins was how Reagan was "pretending to adhere to ideals that his policies clearly indicate he opposes."[88]

Under relentless pressure from the civil rights lobby and many leaders in corporate America, Reagan retreated. Instead, the hard-liners in the Justice Department took their campaign against affirmative action to the Supreme Court, where they filed briefs arguing that all programs by governmental contractors that grant preferences to minority-group members who were not "personally victimized by discrimination" are unconstitutional.[89] In two cases handed down in June 1986, the Supreme Court dealt the administration a crushing blow by reaffirming its support for affirmative action. Civil right leaders rejoiced over Justice William

Brennan's reprimand of the administration's "misguided" efforts to end measures that would halt discriminatory practices. After the court's decisions, the Justice Department abandoned all of its legal actions to end affirmative action. When asked about the administration's plans on revising or ending affirmative action, a White House official replied, "It's on the top of nobody's list. There is certainly no need to get into it."[90]

For the time being, supporters of affirmative action breathed a collective sigh of relief. However, the Reagan administration would undermine affirmative action for eight years by starving the agencies charged with its enforcement. In 1986, one economist moaned, "If the tax laws of the United States were enforced as slackly as the antidiscrimination laws currently are, very few people would pay taxes."[91] The battle over affirmative action, much like the fight over the VRA, would be a protracted struggle that forced African Americans to fight old battles.

These contentious battles over sanctions and affirmative action transpired against the backdrop of the crucial 1986 midterm elections. While Reagan retained high approval ratings, there were indications that the seventy-five-year-old president was losing his vigor. Aides grumbled about his lack of energy and short attention span, as well as the increasingly dominant role the First Lady exerted on personnel, policy, and scheduling. Having accomplished revolutionary fiscal changes in his first term, Reagan's domestic agenda was exhausted. Under prodding from his wife, he devoted much of his energy to foreign policy and convened a series of summits with the new Soviet leader Mikhail Gorbachev. His preoccupation with seeking peace with the Soviet Union did not preclude him from aggressively crisscrossing the country stumping for Republican candidates in the final weeks of the midterm campaign. Other Republicans, however, could not replicate Reagan's distinctive appeal. That fall, led by energized Black voters, Democrats flipped eight Senate seats and recaptured control of the upper chamber.[92]

The Democrats' new Senate majority meant they could now put a check on the Reagan administration's efforts to roll back the civil rights gains of the 1960s.

CHAPTER 11

THE BATTLE FOR THE JUDICIARY

When it has counted, Robert Bork has often stood against the aspira-
tion of blacks to achieve their constitutional rights and to remove the
vestiges of racial discrimination.

—William T. Coleman (September 1987)[1]

But the thing is, you don't have many suspects innocent of a crime.
That's contradictory. A person innocent of a crime is not a suspect.

—Attorney General Meese criticizing
Miranda v. Arizona (October 1985)[2]

The Democrats' recapture of the Senate buoyed their chances of curtail-
ing the Reagan administration from packing the federal courts with
conservative jurists bent on turning back the clock on civil rights. Blacks
and their civil rights allies were alarmed at the administration's systematic campaign to overturn landmark decisions that had finally begun
to breathe life and vigor into the constitutional guarantees of freedom
and liberty for all Americans, regardless of race, ethnicity, and gender.
In 1986, Reagan's decision to elevate archconservative associate justice
William H. Rehnquist to be the sixteenth chief justice of the Supreme
Court had sparked a bruising confirmation battle. Though he survived
the nomination process, the ordeal spotlighted Rehnquist's troubling
personal and judicial views on race. The following year, Reagan's nomination of the polarizing Robert Bork to fill another vacancy capped a
bitter constitutional struggle over the philosophical direction of the US
Supreme Court. Led by a broad coalition of civil rights organizations furious over Bork's hostility to governmental action on behalf of Blacks and
other minorities, Bork's nomination was defeated by the largest margin

in US history. The Bork nomination galvanized the country like no other previous Supreme Court nomination and illuminated conservatives' judicial philosophy against the recent extension of constitutional protections for Blacks, women, and other groups who had been neglected and mistreated by society.

WAGING A JUDICIAL COUNTERREVOLUTION IN CIVIL RIGHTS

Reagan's 1980 presidential victory had electrified legal conservatives who had long pined for the opportunity to appoint conservative or what they called "strict constructionist" judges who would overturn *Roe v. Wade* (1973), *Miranda v. Arizona* (1966), *Baker v. Carr* (1966), and other landmark decisions they decried as "judicial tyranny." "Wholesale judicial change" became their rallying cry. Early on, Reagan appointed Ed Meese as chair of the White House–Justice Department Selection Committee to identify and screen prospective judicial nominees. In elevating ideology as the paramount consideration, Meese diminished the importance of local party leaders and the ratings of the American Bar Association's Standing Committee of the Federal Judiciary in selecting federal judges. As a result, Reagan nominated many judges whom the ABA's screening committee deemed minimally competent or unqualified.[3] The Federalist Society, founded in 1982 as a conservative counterweight to the predominantly liberal legal academy, provided the Reagan administration with a pipeline of conservative legal thinkers and jurists to staff legal departments and fill court vacancies.[4]

Meese embraced the newly articulated doctrine of "originalism" or "textualism," which maintained that judges should adhere to the literal meaning of the Constitution based on the original understanding of the Framers. Given slavery's centrality to the Constitution, "original intent" was repellent to African Americans. Associate Justice Thurgood Marshall, the first Black Supreme Court Justice and legendary civil rights attorney who argued the *Brown v. Board of Education* case, countered that the Founders never intended to abolish slavery and pointed to *Dred Scott, Plessy v. Ferguson,* and a slew of other cases to show that originalism was a morally abhorrent judicial philosophy infused with racism.[5] Other critics pointed out the impossibility of ascertaining the intent of the Framers. Liberal justice William Brennan said, "It is little more than arrogance to believe that anybody can gauge accurately the intent of the framers." To highlight the difficulty of divining the intent of the Framers, Brennan observed that the Founding Fathers chose deliberately opaque terms, such as "due process," "equal protection," "probable cause," "unreasonable," and "cruel and unusual," which rendered it impossible to ascertain their intent.[6] Even moderates assailed originalism as a simplistic, stubborn dogma based on a frozen view of the Constitution.

More than any other previous administration, Reagan's Justice Department imposed an ideological litmus test on its judicial nominees.[7] Even though Reagan had appointed hundreds of conservative judges to the federal courts, by the spring of 1986, conservatives were becoming impatient because Reagan had only appointed one Supreme Court justice, Sandra Day O'Connor, whom they considered insufficiently conservative. They were also frustrated by their inability to make significant legislative progress rolling back civil rights. Bruce Fein, who had been one of Meese's subordinates working on judicial selection in the first term, told *Newsweek* in October 1985 that the administration realized Reagan could not implement his civil rights agenda through Congress but "had to do it by changing the jurisprudence."[8]

Controversy erupted in the beginning of 1986 over disturbing reports that Reagan's nominee for a seat on the Federal Court of Appeals, Jefferson Beauregard Sessions III, a thirty-nine-year-old US attorney in Mobile, Alabama, had allegedly made a number of racist statements.[9] In hearings before the Senate Judiciary Committee, Gary Herbert, a colleague of Sessions's at the Alabama Attorney General's Office, provided the committee with a sworn statement that Sessions had referred to a white lawyer who had litigated many civil rights cases in Alabama as "a disgrace to his race," had made numerous disparaging references to the ACLU and the NAACP, had referred to an African American US attorney as a "boy," and had admonished an African American member of his staff to be "careful what he said to white folks." Thomas Figures, an African American who had worked for Sessions as an assistant US attorney, provided sworn testimony corroborating Herbert's claims that Sessions disparaged the NAACP as "un-American" and "subversive." Furthermore, he said Sessions thought the Ku Klux Klan and its "members were OK until he learned that they smoked marijuana."[10] Sessions's nomination was further jeopardized by reports that he had played an instrumental role in relentlessly pursuing a group of voting rights activists, including Albert Turner, an African American who had worked for Martin Luther King Jr. and was beaten in Selma, Alabama, on Bloody Sunday in March 1965 during the height of the campaign for voting rights. Sessions filed a massive and frivolous voter-fraud case against them in counties where African Americans were making substantial inroads. The case was so embarrassingly weak that a jury acquitted the three defendants of thirty-six counts after it had deliberated for just four hours. The trial judge had previously dismissed fifty counts before the case even went to the jury. Members of Sessions's office had also complained that he had refused even to investigate evidence of voting fraud by whites.[11]

In his defense, Sessions acknowledged that he made many of the alleged comments but dismissively attributed them to his "loose tongue."[12] After nearly six weeks of combative deliberations, including three days of hearings in which twenty-one witnesses testified, on June 5, 1986, the Senate Judiciary Committee rejected Sessions's nomination, with Howell Heflin, from Sessions's home state of Alabama, providing the pivotal vote. In a soft voice before a packed hearing, Heflin said with a sigh, "A person should not be confirmed to a lifetime appointment if there are reasonable doubts about his ability to be fair and impartial."[13] Despite Sessions's admittedly racially charged statements, Meese blamed the Senate's rejection not on Sessions's record but on "political and philosophical differences with Reagan administration policies and initiatives." Sessions was the first Reagan nominee to be rejected by the Senate Judiciary Committee and only the second rejected in forty-eight years.[14] Sessions returned to Alabama determined to avenge his defeat, and, in 1996, he was elected to the US Senate. Years later, Sessions earned notoriety as the first senator to endorse Donald Trump, and he went on to serve as Trump's first attorney general. This time, Sessions survived that confirmation on a party-line vote.

CHIEF JUSTICE REHNQUIST: TROUBLING ALLEGATIONS

Only weeks after the Sessions defeat, fate handed the Reagan administration its long-awaited opportunity to fill a Supreme Court vacancy when Chief Justice Warren Burger announced his retirement. With the prodding of Meese, Reagan announced he was elevating Associate Justice William H. Rehnquist, the most conservative member of the Supreme Court, to become the sixteenth chief justice. The lone dissenter in the *Bob Jones* case, Rehnquist was an unreconstructed states' rights conservative deeply distrusted by African Americans and the civil rights community. Although Robert Bork was the hardline conservatives' preferred choice to become the next associate justice, Reagan was more impressed with the gregarious Antonin Scalia, Bork's younger colleague on the prestigious Washington, DC, Court of Appeals. A key figure in the Federalist Society, Scalia was just as conservative as Bork, but would attract less scrutiny than Bork whose provocative law review articles criticizing the Warren Court's ruling had made him anathema to the civil rights community.[15]

The Rehnquist nomination to chief justice galvanized African Americans and the civil rights community.[16] In addition to his troubling interpretation of the Fourteenth and Fifteenth Amendments, a multitude of allegations surrounding Rehnquist's pattern of racial improprieties had dogged his 1971 confirmation hearings. In 1986, these charges received renewed scrutiny and turned the elevation of Rehnquist into a brutal confirmation battle, overshadowing the Scalia nomination. The troubling allegations dated back to Rehnquist's stint as a young law clerk to Supreme Court Justice Robert H. Jackson in the early 1950s when he defended segregation. In a memo to Justice Jackson, Rehnquist wrote, "It's about time the Court faced the fact that the white people in the South don't like the colored people."[17]

Newsweek unearthed more damning evidence of Rehnquist's views on race that threatened to derail his 1971 confirmation. During his clerkship, in 1952 Rehnquist reportedly prepared a short memo urging Justice Jackson not to overrule *Plessy v. Ferguson* on the grounds that the court was "being asked to read its own sociological views into the Constitution." Titled "A Random Thought on the Segregation Cases," Rehnquist wrote, "I realize it is an unpopular and unhumanitarian position, for which I have been excoriated by 'liberal' colleagues, but I think *Plessy v. Ferguson* was right and should be reaffirmed."[18] The embattled nominee, however, had an explanation. He wrote a letter to the Judiciary Committee testifying under oath that the opinions expressed in the memo were not his own but were "prepared by me as a statement of Justice Jackson's tentative views for his own use at conference."[19]

On December 10, 1971, the Senate eventually confirmed Rehnquist 68–26, but his explanation triggered charges that he had perjured himself before the Judiciary Committee. Elsie Douglas, Justice Jackson's long-time secretary, called Rehnquist a liar. She maintained that Rehnquist had "smeared the reputation of a great justice" and disputed the notion that Jackson would have asked a law clerk to prepare his own remarks for such an important case.[20] Years later, in preparation for his biography of Justice Jackson, University of Chicago law professor Dennis J. Hutchison scoured "every box, every detail" of Jackson's papers, and after uncovering no instance in which the justice had asked a law clerk to prepare a memo for conference summarizing his views, concluded that Rehnquist's explanation was "absurd."[21] Moreover, Justice Jackson was a spellbinding orator who mesmerized observers with his opening and closing arguments in the Nuremberg case, and he certainly would not have needed a memorandum from a law clerk at a conference with his Supreme Court brethren in such a historic case as *Brown v. Board of Education*.[22]

Additional charges of racial improprieties had further tarnished Rehnquist's 1971 confirmation. After his clerkship with Justice Jackson ended in 1953, Rehnquist moved to Phoenix and began his legal career in the firm run by Denison Kitchel, a close friend of and campaign manager for Barry Goldwater. Rehnquist developed an affinity for Goldwater's popular Sunbelt brand of libertarian, states' rights conservatism. During this time, as previously noted, both Rehnquist and Robert Bork furnished Goldwater with legal and constitutional arguments against the Civil Rights Act of 1964. A few months earlier, appearing as a private citizen before the Phoenix City Council, Rehnquist was one of only three of thirty-three people to testify against a proposed local accommodations law, reprising the argument that it would deprive owners of businesses the "historic right to choose their own customers." He disavowed his position at his 1971 Senate confirmation hearing and made the revealing concession that he had failed to understand how passionately minorities felt about protecting their rights.[23]

Most dramatically, Rehnquist's role in managing the Maricopa County Republican Party's ballot security efforts, from 1958 through 1964, raised troubling questions about whether Rehnquist had challenged the qualifications of voters in minority Democratic precincts. At Rehnquist's 1971 confirmation hearings, two African American Democratic poll watchers filed sworn affidavits with the Senate Judiciary Committee alleging that in 1964 Rehnquist had been removed from the polling place for physically harassing and intimidating people of color who were standing in long lines waiting to vote.[24] Rehnquist flatly denied these allegations, but African Americans saw in Rehnquist a disturbing pattern of hostility. Clarence Mitchell of the NAACP charged that, with Nixon's nomination of Rehnquist, "the foot of racism is placed in the door of the temple of justice."[25]

Because Rehnquist had served as an associate justice of the Supreme Court since 1972, civil rights organizations and their liberal allies had little hope in blocking Rehnquist's elevation to chief justice in 1986. But their concerns over both his jurisprudence and his troubling views on race caused them to mount the most combative Supreme Court confirmation battle since the ones against Nixon nominees Haynsworth and Carswell in the early 1970s.[26] In preparation for the hearings, the LCCR noted that of the eighty-three non-unanimous civil rights cases during Rehnquist's tenure on the Supreme Court, "he voted on 80 occasions to adopt the interpretation least favorable to civil rights complainants."[27]

The most damning part of the Senate confirmation hearings was testimony from four additional witnesses corroborating the claims that Rehnquist had indeed intimidated African American and Latino voters in Phoenix in the early 1960s.[28] James Brosnahan, the distinguished San Francisco litigator who had been an assistant US attorney in Phoenix from 1961 through 1963, flew to Washington, DC, and testified before the Senate Judiciary Committee. Brosnahan said under oath that, on Election Day 1962, Rehnquist had aggressively challenged the credentials of minority voters without foundation to such an extent that they were discouraged from voting. Brosnahan recounted that he arrived at a predominantly African American and Latino South Phoenix precinct with an FBI agent after his office received numerous complaints that voters standing in long lines were being interrogated about whether or not they were literate. Although Brosnahan did not personally witness Rehnquist challenging anybody, Rehnquist was the only Republican official present, and Brosnahan spoke to a number of witnesses who identified Rehnquist as the culprit. In a dramatic moment, Brosnahan drew cheers from the audience when he chided Senator Orrin Hatch for implying that he would travel all of the way from San Francisco to testify falsely about a sitting Supreme Court justice. Brosnahan's testimony was corroborated by other witnesses, who all testified under oath that they personally witnessed Rehnquist challenging voters by asking them if they were "qualified" and instructing them to leave the polling place if they were not able to read.[29] Although it was then legal in Arizona to challenge voters if officials had a reasonable basis for believing they were illiterate, it was illegal to challenge them so aggressively that it rose to the level of harassment. Although, in 1971, Rehnquist had categorically denied that he had challenged voters, fifteen years later he was more circumspect. This time, he simply said he "didn't recall or believe" he had ever challenged any voter.[30]

These convincing allegations led a group of one hundred prominent law professors to urge an extensive debate on Rehnquist, but Republicans still maintained control of the Senate, and Rehnquist's confirmation was never seriously in doubt.[31] Angered over Rehnquist's "persistent and appalling record against minorities" and his "lack of candor" on a host of topics, Senator Edward Kennedy launched a brief, ill-fated filibuster.[32] On September 17, 1986, Rehnquist was confirmed 65–33, garnering the most negative votes of any successful high-court nominee in the twentieth century. The man known as the "Lone Ranger" for his extreme judicial views was now the leader of the Supreme Court. Minutes after the Senate confirmed Rehnquist, Judge Antonin Scalia, who would prove to be just as conservative as Rehnquist, was confirmed 98–0.[33] With the addition of the energetic fifty-year-old Scalia to the court, civil rights advocates feared another imminent retirement would enable Reagan to further stamp his conservative imprint on the judiciary for decades.

ROBERT BORK AND UNSURPASSED UGLINESS

Civil libertarians' fears were realized June 26, 1987, when Justice Lewis F. Powell Jr., the pivotal swing vote on the court, announced his retirement. Conservatives salivated over the prospect of finally exorcising the ghost of Earl Warren with a third Reagan appointment to the Supreme Court. Both Senate Judiciary chair Joseph Biden and Majority Leader Robert Byrd immediately warned the White House that nominating an ideologue like Robert Bork was certain to create "big problems."[34] Reagan ignored their admonitions and, a few days later, nominated the polarizing Bork.[35] Upon hearing the news, conservative activist Richard Viguerie rejoiced: "Conservatives have waited over thirty years for this day."[36]

The Bork announcement set the stage for one of the most fierce domestic battles of the entire Reagan presidency. In 1973, Bork's firing of Watergate special prosecutor Archibald Cox in the Saturday Night

Massacre after the two highest-ranking members of the Justice Department resigned, rather than follow Nixon's order to fire Cox, created lingering suspicions that Bork had acted improperly. Since the 1960s, Bork had emerged as the foremost proponent of "originalism" and the most vociferous critic of the Warren Court's legacy. And because Bork was slated to replace Justice Powell, the court's swing vote, the Bork nomination riveted the nation like no other Supreme Court confirmation in American history.[37]

In the year since the rancor over Rehnquist, the political landscape had changed dramatically. The Democrats now controlled the Senate, and the continuing fallout over the Iran-Contra Affair had punctured Reagan's political invincibility. Within minutes of the announcement of Bork's nomination, Senator Edward Kennedy stormed to the Senate floor and blasted "Robert Bork's America" as being, among other things, "a land where blacks would sit in segregated lunch counters."[38] The civil rights lobby was aghast over Reagan's nomination of the self-described judicial "revolutionary" who had espoused reactionary views on civil rights. The LCCR geared up for battle and branded Bork "an ultra-conservative" whose confirmation would "jeopardize the civil rights achievements of the past three decades."[39] At the annual NAACP conference, executive director Benjamin Hooks declared, "We will fight it all the way until Hell freezes over and then we'll skate across the ice."[40]

The sixty-year-old Bork had amassed a long paper trail that clearly expressed his antipathy to the past generation of Supreme Court cases that had recognized in the Constitution the fundamental liberties that African Americans considered their birthright. Like Reagan, Buckley, Goldwater, and Rehnquist, young Robert Bork sided with the segregationists in privileging the freedom to discriminate over the civil rights of Blacks. Around the time that Martin Luther King Jr. gave his "I Have a Dream" speech," Bork, then a thirty-six-year-old Yale law professor, penned an editorial for the *New Republic* that argued against the public accommodations section of the Civil Rights Act. The piece would haunt him for decades. Although Bork denounced racial segregation as abhorrent, he insisted that coercing business owners to serve members of minority groups would enact into law "a principle of unsurpassed ugliness."[41] The editors of the *New Republic* disagreed so "emphatically" with Bork's stilted adherence to libertarian principles that they published a rare rejoinder referencing Justice Oliver Wendell Holmes's "preference for appeals to experience rather than logic." They conceded that Bork's principle of liberty and distrust of public authority was often justified, but they argued that his unwavering adherence to libertarian theory went too far: "Government without principle ends in shipwreck; but government according to any single principle, to the exclusion of all other, ends in madness."[42] Johnson attorney general Nicholas Katzenbach, a chief architect of the Voting Rights Act, testified against Bork's nomination for solicitor general in 1971, saying, "It is absolutely inconceivable to me that a man of intelligence and perception and feeling could have opposed that legislation on the grounds that it deprived people of freedom of association."[43]

The "unsurpassed ugliness" remark was bad enough, but Bork denigrated every significant Supreme Court decision extending civil rights protections to African Americans. In a 1971 *Indiana Law Journal* article, he criticized the court's 1948 unanimous *Shelley v. Kraemer* decision, which barred enforcement of racially restrictive real estate covenants on the grounds that covenants were "private" and not covered by the Fourteenth Amendment.[44] In that same article, he referred to the Equal Protection Clause as the "Equal Gratification Clause." With respect to voting rights, Bork issued a blistering attack on the court's 1966 decision in *Katzenbach v. Morgan*, which banned the use of literacy tests for voting. Similarly, he attacked the outcome of *Harper v. Virginia Board of Elections*, which, also in 1966, struck down Virginia's poll tax on equal protection grounds. Similarly, he castigated the landmark redistricting case *Baker v. Carr* (1962), which, in tandem with the Voting Rights Act, led to the greatest change in legislative representation in American history—a decision Chief Justice Warren regarded as the "most vital decision in his career."[45] In *Baker*, Bork suggested that Chief Justice Warren was unable "to muster a single supporting argument."[46] Finally, in 1972, Bork was one of only two law professors who testified in support of the constitutionality of proposed Senate legislation that would have dramatically reduced school desegregation remedies that the Supreme Court had declared constitutional—hundreds of other law professors said the law would be unconstitutional.[47]

In response, Bork's defenders charged that he was a moderate jurist in the tradition of Lewis Powell, one well within the mainstream of the law. Critics charged that Bork was not a moderate-conservative paragon of judicial restraint in the tradition of Felix Frankfurter, John Marshall Harlan, and Powell but rather a right-wing activist bent on overturning established judicial precedent. As recently as January 31, 1987, Bork had told the Federalist Society, "I would think an originalist judge would have no problem whatever in overruling a non-originalist precedent, because that precedent by the very basis of his judicial philosophy has no legitimacy."[48] University of Chicago law professor Philip Kurland described Bork's constitutional jurisprudence as "essentially directed to a diminution of minority and individual rights."[49] In a veiled attack on Bork, Justice William Brennan said "judges who succumb to the temptation to make their decisions solely based on reason run the risk of becoming cut off from the people who must live with their consequences."[50] To illustrate this point, former Texas representative Barbara Jordan attributed her ability to finally win her congressional race to *Baker v. Carr* because, before it, her district had been previously malapportioned. Had Bork's views been adopted, Jordan movingly testified, "I would right now be running my eleventh unsuccessful race for the Texas House of Representatives."[51]

Having declared Bork's nomination to be the most important domestic priority of his remaining sixteen months in office, Reagan assailed Bork's critics for their heated rhetoric and accused Democratic senators of forming a "lynch mob" against his nominee.[52] Most experts agreed with White House officials that Bork's stellar legal credentials as a Yale law professor, solicitor general, and a judge on the DC Circuit Court of Appeals would most likely tilt the scales in favor of his confirmation. A week before the hearings began, however, the unusual amount of dissension among the fifteen members of the American Bar Association's Select Committee on the Federal Judiciary over whether Bork was qualified spelled trouble. While ten of the fifteen determined that Bork was well qualified, four of the members deemed Bork "unqualified" due to concerns over his "comparatively extreme views on constitutional principles, particularly how he would apply equal protection of the laws," and one was not opposed.[53] In addition, the four members of the ABA screening panel expressed concern over Bork's temperament, which included his insensitivity to the rights of women and minority persons or groups.[54] Speaking in Montgomery, Alabama,

Coretta Scott King urged people of all races to urge their senators not to confirm Bork: "We've made too much progress and we've looked to the courts as a last resort. Where do we go if we don't have a court that's going to look at problems and issues in a manner that would protect individuals as well as groups?"[55]

As soon as the Senate Judiciary Committee began its nationally televised proceedings, on September 15, the portly Bork, sporting a Fu Manchu moustache, appeared cavalier, subdued, and arrogant, exhibiting little of the dry humor his supporters hoped would sway undecided senators.[56] At the conclusion of his first day of testimony, the four undecided senators on the committee expressed reservations that Bork would be able to allay their concerns. In an effort to repackage himself as a moderate, Bork disingenuously professed he was not a "liberal or a conservative." Having spent over a decade assailing the liberal rights-based precedents of the Warren Court, Bork now said he would uphold them because they had become part of the country's "settled law." Skeptical opponents such as Senator Patrick Leahy charged him with undergoing "confirmation conversions." Senator Specter asked Bork whether he could align his newfound acceptance of precedent with his philosophy of "originalism."[57]

Except for Bork's views on abortion and the "right to privacy," no other issue loomed larger than civil rights. On the second day of Bork's testimony, Senator Kennedy sharply questioned him on his 1963 *New Republic* article. In response, an unrepentant Bork acknowledged that, at some unspecified time, he had changed his mind. An unimpressed Kennedy chided Bork: "With all of your ability, I just wish you had devoted even a little of your talent to advancing equal rights rather than criticizing so many of the decisions protecting rights and liberties. Lawyers can always make technical points, but justice ought to be fair."[58]

A panel of civil rights luminaries—William T. Coleman, Barbara Jordan, Andrew Young, and Burke Marshall—were the most lethal witnesses during the second week of hearings. They all expressed grave concerns over Bork's extreme views on civil rights. Among them, none shone brighter than the elegant and courtly sixty-seven-year-old Coleman, an African American Republican and the former secretary of transportation under Ford. He was a pillar of the legal establishment, and both Bork's supporters and opponents had lobbied for his endorsement. After some vacillation, Coleman decided that the positions Bork had consistently taken were an affront to those who had fought for and benefited from civil rights. Coleman stated, "[Mr. Bork] has shown himself in his writings, over and over again, to be adamantly opposed to the long and well-established judicial role of protecting individual liberty and the disadvantaged and unpopular minority groups against Government coercion."[59] The eloquent Barbara Jordan said her opposition to Bork stemmed from "living for 51 years as a black American born in the South, who has seen the Supreme Court rescue blacks from oppression."[60] The moving testimony influenced Judiciary Committee members Senator Howell Heflin and other key white Southern conservative Democrats, who did not want to upset their African American voters or refight past battles.[61]

By the end of the second week, conservatives were alarmed, even despondent, over reports that many previously undecided senators had turned against Bork. In response, they hurled an array of outlandish allegations against liberals for defaming Bork and accused the Democratic majority of defiling the confirmation process. Their anger reached a crescendo on October 6, 1987, after the Judiciary Committee voted 9–5 against his appointment, all but guaranteeing that the entire Senate would reject him.[62] Throughout the proceedings, Bork supporters were disappointed that the seventy-six-year-old Reagan was too detached from the controversy.

The Bork hearings had been heated. But Bork's opponents on the Judiciary Committee were courteous and respectful, and they granted the nominee every opportunity to respond to their concerns. Unlike President Barack Obama's 2016 Supreme Court nominee Merrick Garland, whom Republican Majority Leader Mitch McConnell refused to grant a hearing, Bork was granted the courtesy of an up or down vote on the merits.

Although the Bork nomination was the most sensational and polarizing Supreme Court confirmation to date in US history, the Reagan administration bore much of the blame for the failed nomination. They had already politicized the process of appointing federal judges by making ideology the paramount factor in their selection, and they had ignored repeated warnings that nominating the provocative Bork would result in a bruising confirmation battle.[63] But more than anything else, Bork's arrogant demeanor imperiled his prospects. He appeared as a pompous, detached intellectual theorist who yearned to be on the Supreme Court because it was what he called an "intellectual feast."[64]

Like Reagan, Bork was indifferent to the Supreme Court's historic role in making the nation a more tolerable place for African Americans. Andrew Young summed up what the Supreme Court meant for Blacks:

> The Supreme Court has never been just about issues and cases. It really could never be an intellectual feast. It is about people. . . . We see the Supreme Court as the final protector . . . of those rights. And a Supreme Court that is intellectualizing about those rights, or a Supreme Court that does not understand the passion and anguish of people whose rights are being denied is a Supreme Court which really does not live up to what I think the American dream is all about.[65]

On October 23, the Senate voted against Bork's nomination 58–42, the largest margin by which the Senate had ever rejected a Supreme Court nominee. Southern Democrats, worried about alienating their African American constituency, were pivotal to Bork's defeat, affirming the growing clout of African American power nourished by the Voting Rights Act of 1965.

While Bork criticized the Civil Rights Act in his infamous *New Republic* piece as "unsurpassed ugliness" for forcing white Southerners to associate with Blacks, nobody was more familiar with "unsurpassed ugliness" than Justice Thurgood Marshall, who as a lawyer for the NAACP battling Jim Crow in the South had faced countless assassination attempts. By the time of the Bork hearings, Marshall's body was beginning to succumb to a host of infirmities, but the ailing seventy-nine-year-old justice retained his fiery resolve to overcome. In conversations with his close friend, fellow liberal Justice William Brennan, Marshall confided that during the Reagan years, he believed "the court's right-wing majority were guilty of casting votes that were racist."[66] Nothing provoked Marshall's ire more than Meese and Bork's notion of "original intent." Just weeks before Powell's resignation, Marshall delivered a rousing speech before the San Francisco Patent and Trademark Law Association, in Hawaii, entreating Americans to restrain their exuberance in celebrating the Constitution's bicentennial. Marshall dismissed the notion that the meaning of the Constitution "was forever fixed at the Philadelphia Convention in 1787" and reminded his audience that the Constitution was, in fact, "defective from the start, requiring several amendments, a civil war, and momentous social transformation." Since the Constitution wove slavery into the fabric of the nation, Marshall did not believe that the Constitution contained "profound wisdom, foresight, and sense of justice." Marshall further observed that the Founders could not have fathomed that the document they were drafting "would one day be construed by a Supreme Court to which had been appointed a woman and the descendant of African American slaves."[67]

It was no mere coincidence that on the eve of Bork's confirmation hearing Marshall revealed his true feelings about Reagan. In an unprecedented television interview with journalist Carl Rowan, Marshall bluntly said, "Honestly, I think [Reagan] is down with Hoover and that group—Wilson—when we really didn't have a chance."[68] Marshall's remarks upset Reagan, ever sensitive to criticism on his racial policies. On November 17, 1987, Reagan arranged for a private meeting with Marshall at the White House residence, where he related his stock anecdotes about his racially tolerant parents and once again recounted his fictitious campaign to integrate Major League Baseball. Reagan later confided in his diary, "I think I made a friend."[69] While Marshall's blunt public remarks to Rowan breached customary decorum, his stinging words reflected the depth of African American grievances that Reagan's amiable demeanor would never assuage.

Moreover, Marshall's firsthand experience with racial terror as the NAACP's lead attorney in the South led him to take umbrage at Reagan's characterization of the Bork hearings as a "lynch mob." Marshall explained, "A lynch mob takes it upon themselves to do something," and Bork had "every chance to defend himself."[70]

Marshall had been subject to his own grueling five-day Supreme Court confirmation in the summer of 1967. Although Marshall was eventually confirmed, his segregationist opponents on the Judiciary Committee red-baited him and attacked his integrity, fairness, and intelligence. Evoking comparisons to literacy tests, former Dixiecrat Strom Thurmond questioned Marshall on the minutiae of the history of the Civil War amendments and other arcane matters in a stated attempt to show that Marshall was not intellectually capable of being a Supreme Court justice.[71] The most shameful insult was Thurmond's query to Marshall about his views of the recently decided case *Loving v. Virginia*, knowing that Marshall and his second wife, a Filipina, would have been subject to arrest had they lived in Virginia.[72] By any reasonable standard, the Senate Judiciary Committee of the 1980s treated Bork more fairly than had the one of the 1960s with Marshall.

Bork's defeat provided a measure of solace to African Americans and their civil rights allies. The Senate also eventually confirmed another Reagan appointee to the Supreme Court, Federal Appeals court judge Anthony Kennedy, who was conservative but not as rigidly so as Bork. Yet, the denial of Bork a seat on the Supreme Court could not counteract Reagan's appointment of 346 federal judges—including three Supreme Court Justices—only 2 percent of whom were African American.[73] By the end of his presidency, Reagan's conservative appointees were the majority on the powerful Court of Appeals and the Court of Appeals for the Second, Sixth, and Seven Circuits.[74] While Reagan's judicial selections did not completely erode the victories of the civil rights direction, they moved the judiciary in a more racially conservative direction. As for Bork, he became a conservative martyr, and his "originalist" jurisprudence, once derided as a fringe view, became dogma in judicial conservative circles.

Still, civil rights advocates could take pride in their pluck and gritty determination to thwart the administration from further undermining the nation's civil rights laws. Their spirits were also heartened by the possibility of a Democratic victory in 1988 given the American public's palpable sense of fatigue after nearly eight years of the Reagan era and the revelations of the Iran-Contra Affair that nearly destroyed Reagan's presidency.

CHAPTER 12

THE WAR ON DRUGS, WILLIE HORTON, AND THE CRIMINALIZATION OF BLACKNESS

Only our deep moral values and strong institutions can hold back that jungle and restrain the darker impulses of human nature.

—Reagan addressing the International Association of Chiefs of Police (September 1981)[1]

By the time we are finished they're going to wonder whether Willie Horton is Dukakis' running mate.

—George H. W. Bush's campaign manager, Lee Atwater (1988)[2]

The explosive fallout from the Iran-Contra Affair sparked more than a year of investigations and debilitated the final two years of Reagan's domestic agenda. Though he remained personally popular, the president's doddering and evasive responses concerning details of the arms sale to Iran in exchange for the release of hostages and the diversion of funds to the Nicaraguan Contras raised serious concerns about his mental competency. It seemed that Iran-Contra had finally cracked the "Teflon from his presidency."[3] At the height of the scandal, members of Congress bandied about the possibility of impeaching Reagan, only two years after he had won reelection by carrying forty-nine states. Like many second-term presidents with dwindling political capital, Reagan devoted the bulk of his energy to foreign policy. In a number of high-stakes summits, Reagan and his Soviet counterpart, the dynamic young reformer Mikhail Gorbachev, hammered out a series of blockbuster arms-control agreements that salvaged Reagan's presidency.

On the domestic front, Congress' override of Reagan's veto of the Civil Rights Restoration Act of 1987 would be the final battle over civil rights during Reagan's presidency. The last time a president had vetoed a civil rights bill had been Andrew Johnson's veto of the Civil Rights Act of 1866.[4] Although the 1987 legislation failed to generate the heated passions of other hot-button civil rights issues, it was a landmark bill; some considered it the most significant civil rights legislation in twenty years because of its broadening of protections for minorities, women, the elderly, and the disabled.[5]

In brief, the Civil Rights Restoration Act was the culmination of a four-year battle to overturn a controversial 1984 Supreme Court decision, *Grove City College v. Bell*, which severely narrowed the application of civil rights laws. In a 6–3 decision, the court ruled that a small private Christian liberal arts college in Pennsylvania, whose financial links to the federal government were limited to federal grants and loans received by some of its students via the financial aid office, was not subject to key provisions of the federal civil rights acts.[6] The decision conformed to Reagan's broader view that anti-discrimination laws constituted an unwarranted, burdensome intrusion into the private affairs of businesses, universities, and other entities.[7]

The Supreme Court's narrow reading of federal law prohibiting sex discrimination in *Grove City* precipitated a tempest among members of the civil rights lobby, who perceived it as a grave threat to the enforcement of Title IX and Title VII of the Civil Rights Act of 1964. In response, Congress sponsored a bipartisan bill stipulating that civil rights enforcement applied to *all* programs at institutions receiving *any* kind of federal funds. After the Democrats' 1986 takeover of the Senate, the bill finally passed on March 2, 1988, but Reagan vetoed it on the grounds that the bill was a dramatic expansion of the scope of federal power, as well as a threat to religious liberty.[8] Lawmakers on both sides of the aisle protested Reagan's rationale for his veto, and they overrode it. The scale of the rebuke corroborated the view that Reagan was on the wrong side of civil rights history.

WAR ON DRUGS: THE NEW JIM CROW

Reagan's decision to ramp up the War on Drugs led to the passage of a series of hastily drawn, ill-conceived, and draconian laws that disproportionately targeted African Americans and poor people of color. The Reagan administration's action was the catalyst for the current crisis of mass incarceration.[9] Although the United States currently accounts for only 5 percent of the world's population, it has approximately 25 percent of the world's prison population. The racially tinged nature of the War on Drugs was its most salient feature. It was a by-product of the calls for "law and order" that crested with the urban uprisings of the 1960s. Since the Reagan years, the African American prison population has skyrocketed, despite the fact that Blacks were using drugs at a similar rate as whites. Although subsequent administrations continued and expanded the War on Drugs, Reagan accelerated the crisis of mass incarceration by cynically seizing on the hysteria surrounding "crack" cocaine, which pervaded the country in 1986, hoping to score political points in the lead-up to the midterm elections.

The War on Drugs antedated Reagan's presidency, and its racial bias was rooted in the long-standing conflation of criminality with Blackness. The urban disorders that erupted throughout the 1960s gave greater resonance to Reagan's and, earlier, Nixon's racially polarizing rhetoric about getting tough on crime, drugs, and welfare fraud.[10] Black crime furnished conservatives with the ammunition to indirectly assault the civil rights movement when it was too popular to mount a direct attack.[11] Nixon perceived the crime issue as a Black, urban issue. "You have to face the fact that the whole problem is really the blacks," Nixon said to his chief of staff, H. R. Haldeman. "The key is to devise a system that recognizes this while not appearing to."[12]

Nixon was the one who coined the term "War on Drugs." Years later, Nixon aide and Watergate co-conspirator John Ehrlichman confessed that the administration had crafted the War on Drugs as a political bludgeon to criminalize African Americans and the antiwar Left.[13] Notwithstanding Nixon's malign intentions, he relied on experts who approached the spiraling heroin crisis in a sensible, humane fashion, treating addiction as a disease rather than a moral failing, and established a network of methadone clinics. By the late 1970s, the issue of drug abuse had largely receded as a public health problem.

Reagan had long associated drug use with the "mess at Berkeley" and the "loathsome" 1960s counterculture. Having risen to political prominence railing against hippies and having experienced his daughter Patti's rebellious embrace of the drug culture, Reagan brooked no sympathy for drug use. He sprinkled his 1976 and 1980 campaign speeches with tough "law and order" rhetoric on drugs, including his mind-boggling 1980 assertion that marijuana is "probably the most dangerous drug in the United States today."[14] Rather than attacking the "root causes" of drug use and the treatment component of addiction, the incoming Reagan administration vowed to criminalize drug use and focused on marijuana users.[15] In addition to slashing taxes on the wealthy and revamping the Federal Judiciary, Reagan made the war on street crime and drugs the preeminent domestic preoccupation of his administration.

On June 24, 1982, Reagan officially declared a War on Drugs when he signed Executive Order 12368, arguably the most destructive executive order of twentieth-century presidential politics. It centralized control over the anti-drug crusade in the White House. In an ominous statement, Reagan stressed that law enforcement, not treatment, would be the centerpiece of his program. He also announced his choice of zealous anti-marijuana crusader Carlton Turner, a Mississippi native, to head the Drug Abuse Policy Office. Turner later claimed that marijuana use leads to homosexuality and AIDS.[16] In his speech, Reagan invoked war metaphors to distinguish his tough policy from former president Carter's "defeatist" attitude on drugs, and he likened his resolve to combat the scourge of drug use to the obstinacy of the French army at the Battle of Verdun in World War I.[17] Reagan's reference to Verdun was peculiar, given that the battle had resulted in the deaths of nearly a million young men and accomplished nothing. Tragically, the War on Drugs would be a similar exercise in futility.

An early indication of the administration's radical approach was Reagan's suspension of the Posse Comitatus Act of 1878, which prohibited any direct involvement by the US military in law enforcement operations.[18] Virtually overnight, the budgets for federal law enforcement agencies ballooned. In his crusade against drugs, the Reagan administration forged an unprecedented connection between the military and the Department of Justice.[19] In the coming years, the suspension of the Posse Comitatus Act blurred the lines between the police and the military and enabled SWAT teams to unleash militarized raids on historic African American and Latino neighborhoods.[20]

Reagan militarized the War on Drugs even though less than 2 percent of the American public listed drug abuse as the most pressing problem confronting the nation.[21] By Reagan's first term, statistics showed that drug use among the American public was waning.[22] In an effort to provide First Lady Nancy Reagan with an opportunity to revamp her public image, which had been sullied by a series of damning reports about her lavish spending on designer clothes and refurbishing the White House, she became the administration's spokesperson to expose the so-called scourge of the drug epidemic on America's youth. The First Lady launched the "Just Say No" campaign and traveled the country exhorting young people to simply reject the idea of experimenting with drugs. Experts derided Nancy Reagan's ubiquitous "Just Say No" crusade as a simplistic public relations stunt that was particularly objectionable because the administration had slashed federal spending for drug rehabilitation programs by 26 percent.[23]

On October 12, 1984, just weeks prior to his reelection, Reagan signed the Comprehensive Crime Control Act, the first significant reform of the federal criminal code since the early 1900s. Among other things, this far-reaching act implemented the much-maligned Federal Sentencing Guidelines, which ended judicial discretion in sentencing, compelling judges to rigidly impose predetermined sentences.[24] If that was not disturbing enough, the act's civil forfeiture clause authorized local law enforcement agencies to share up to 80 percent of the proceeds of property confiscated from accused drug dealers in joint operations with federal authorities. This forfeiture could occur absent an indictment, trial, or conviction. The upshot was that it encouraged corruption and incentivized police forces to allocate their resources toward drug crimes.[25]

By the mid-1980s, drug hard-liners found an opening in their crusade with the emergence of a terrifying form of cocaine known as "crack," an adulterated form that first appeared in the inner cities and became synonymous with African Americans and crime. With the encouragement of Attorney General Meese, the media published an avalanche of sensational stories about the plague of crack cocaine. On March 17, 1986, *Newsweek* ran a cover story, "Kids and Cocaine: An Epidemic Strikes Middle America," alleging that cocaine was "seeping into the nation's schools," even though only 4 percent of high school students had used cocaine.[26] That issue of *Newsweek* sold 15 percent more copies than the average for 1986. Three months later, *Newsweek* ran another lurid cover story titled "Crack and Crime," declaring that crack was the greatest issue confronting the nation since the Vietnam War.[27] By the end of 1986,

Time and *Newsweek* had each run five cover stories on crack. These articles presented images of Black "crack babies," Black "crack whores," and young Black male "gangbangers," reinforcing racial tropes of African Americans as part of a criminal, dangerous subculture that warranted military measures to keep it in check.[28] A few months later, *Time* anointed crack the issue of the year.[29]

The administration seized on the crack issue to revitalize its domestic agenda, which had stalled after the first term. Attorney General Meese led the charge. At a conference of newspaper editors, he exhorted them to press hard on the cocaine story. Meese even tried to conscript criminal defense attorneys into the battle, and he chillingly remarked that there could be "no bystanders" to the drug war, "not even the lawyers."[30] Meese's Justice Department embarked on a radical course, using its new subpoena powers to force criminal defense attorneys to inform on their own drug clients. The government also initiated a host of unprecedented investigations of criminal defense lawyers, leading to widespread fear and paranoia among the criminal defense bar.[31]

The hysteria surrounding crack cocaine reached epidemic proportions following the death of University of Maryland basketball star Len Bias on June 19, 1986, from an apparent crack overdose just two days after the Boston Celtics had selected him as their number two pick in the NBA draft. It was later determined that Bias had died from snorting powdered cocaine, but because he was African American, the media and the public assumed he had been smoking crack. Nearly two weeks later, a second African American athlete, Don Rogers of the Cleveland Browns, also reportedly succumbed from an overdose of crack cocaine. Later, it turned out that Rogers, like Bias, had died from snorting cocaine.[32]

Bias's tragic death sparked a bipartisan uproar calling for immediate action. House Speaker Tip O'Neill, an ardent fan of his hometown Boston Celtics, was perhaps the most powerful and influential American devastated by the death of Bias. Returning to Washington, DC, from the July 4 recess, O'Neill called an emergency meeting and demanded that Democrats pass anti-drug legislation. "The only thing in Boston people are talking about is Len Bias," O'Neill roared, and "the Republicans beat us to it in 1984, and I don't want it to happen again."[33] Against this frenzied backdrop, lawmakers from across the political spectrum spoke in apocalyptic terms of how drugs posed the greatest threat to national security that America had ever experienced. South Carolina Republican congressman Thomas Hartnett called drugs "a threat worse than any nuclear warfare or any chemical warfare waged on any battlefield."[34] Black leaders also joined the chorus, demanding dramatic action to deal with this so-called emergency.[35] For example, the president of the NAACP chapter in Prince George's County, Maryland, branded crack as "the worst thing to hit us since slavery."[36]

Just weeks before the crucial 1986 midterm elections, Reagan took the unprecedented step of appearing with the First Lady in a joint televised address from their private quarters in the White House, where they called for a national crusade against drug abuse. "There is no moral middle ground," Mrs. Reagan said. "Indifference is not an option." Reagan announced that he would submit a series of proposals to Congress aimed at encouraging "a drug free America."[37]

With the moral panic over crack at full throttle, and the pivotal midterms only weeks away, Democrats and Republicans competed over who could be tougher on crime. As a result, Congress dispensed with regular hearings to propose the most sweeping, far-reaching drug law ever contemplated. Its hasty, expedited passage meant that there had been little research into the legislation's implications. The $1.7 billion bill devoted a mere pittance to drug treatment and education compared with hundreds of millions of dollars for more federal drug prosecutors, jail cells, and financing for the Coast Guard, the Customs Service, and the Drug Enforcement Administration.[38] On October 27, 1986, Reagan signed the Anti-Drug Abuse Act. The conservative *U.S. News and World Report* observed that Reagan was "easily the most prominent beneficiary" of the drug furor, which had pushed a "thicket of thorny problems" for the president into the background.[39]

The elimination of judicial discretion in sentencing and the imposition of mandatory minimum penalties for drug possession and distribution inflicted the most collateral damage on African Americans, Latinos, and the urban poor. Of all the stiff minimum-sentencing provisions contained in the Anti-Drug Abuse Act, the 100-to-1 rule mandating disparate sentencing for crimes involving crack versus powdered cocaine was the most destructive and racially discriminatory one. For example, a person convicted of possessing a single gram of crack received the same sentence as a person convicted of possessing 100 grams of powdered cocaine.[40] The 100-to-1 rule was premised on the irrational, racist fear that crack was more dangerous and addictive than powdered cocaine and the prevailing notion that crack trafficking was inherently more violent than powdered cocaine trafficking. The racial subtext underlying the 100-to-1 rule was clear: African Americans used crack because it was more accessible and cheaper than powdered cocaine. Furthermore, the Reagan administration refused to impose similar penalties for crimes involving crystallized methamphetamine, a drug used more commonly by low-income whites. The law Reagan signed with such haste and fanfare, especially the 100-to-1 rule, guaranteed "apartheid sentencing."[41] The most troubling illustration of the racially disparate impact of the 1986 sentencing guidelines is that while African Americans accounted for only 17 percent of crack users, in 2010 they accounted for 83 percent of those receiving federal sentences for crack cocaine offenses.[42]

Without a doubt, Reagan's War on Drugs turned out to be a war on Black America. The disparity in crack-related sentencing, the mandatory minimum sentences, and the militarization of the police in urban areas led to skyrocketing incarceration rates for nonviolent Black drug users. A 1997 study of drug law enforcement in Massachusetts, for instance, found that African Americans were thirty-nine times more likely to be incarcerated for drug crimes than whites.[43] By the second decade of the twenty-first century, African Americans constituted 53.5 percent of those who entered prisons because of a drug conviction, even though they accounted for only 13 percent of the total US population.[44] As a consequence of the War on Drugs, the United States currently incarcerates a higher percentage of African Americans than South Africa did during the height of apartheid.[45]

Obviously, the Reagan administration is not solely culpable for the racist War on Drugs and its tragic consequences. Reagan signed the 1986 law with overwhelming support from both Democrats and Republicans. It was a consequence of a disparate group of bipartisan actors making a number of ill-conceived decisions over a period of time, extending to the George H. W. Bush, Bill Clinton, and George W. Bush presidencies. However, Reagan bears a large share of the blame for using his unparalleled political popularity to launch a new, catastrophic phase of the War on Drugs. It also provided a purpose for First Lady Nancy Reagan. Like his campaign talk on "law and order" and "welfare queens," it was politically popular and effective, particularly in his second term, when his domestic agenda was exhausted. It also was a consequence of his malign neglect of African American communities. For example, in 1980, the United States expended three times more funds on welfare grants and food stamps than on prisons. By the mid-1990s, those numbers were reversed.[46]

The racial disparities in the American carceral state continue to create endemic problems for African American communities. Conviction for the possession of even small amounts of illegal substances rendered an individual ineligible for public housing and student loans, and criminal records hindered and in many cases precluded employment, leading to a lifetime of exclusion, marginality, and poverty. Hundreds of thousands of people convicted of drug offenses were disenfranchised, leading to the dilution of African American political power. In reckoning Reagan's legacy, the racist War on Drugs continues to cast a pall.

WILLIE HORTON AND THE CRIMINALIZATION OF BLACKNESS

As the 1988 election cycle unfolded, Democrats were brimming with optimism. The ease with which they had retaken control of the Senate in 1986 had surprised political pundits. Unlike the elections of 1980 and 1984, they would not have to face Reagan, whose transcendent connection with the American electorate had crushed Carter and Mondale. In addition to the bombshell disclosure of the Iran-Contra scandal, economic anxiety stemming from the October 1987 stock market crash unsettled Republicans' prospects to succeed Reagan. Reagan's presumed successor, the uncharismatic vice president, George H. W. Bush, had many negatives, compounded by questions of his involvement in the Iran-Contra scandal. Even though the American public cheered the sudden and dramatic relaxation of Cold War tensions, there was a yearning for change reminiscent of the late 1950s, when another popular, avuncular Republican president's second term was drawing to a close.

In this propitious environment, a number of candidates entered the race to vie for the 1988 Democratic nomination. Some of Democrats' early confidence evaporated when the two most imposing liberals, New York governor Mario Cuomo and Senator Edward Kennedy, declined to run. The later withdrawals of early front-runner Senator Gary Hart over a sex scandal and Senate Judiciary Committee chair Joseph Biden over allegations of plagiarism left the field bereft of candidates with national acclaim. Jesse Jackson became the final presidential aspirant to enter the fray on the Democratic side, and none of his six white rivals competing for the nomination connected with African Americans, who had grown disenchanted by the Democratic Party's recent rightward lurch in the hope of wooing back Reagan Democrats.

In a reprise of 1984, Jackson's campaign captivated African Americans, but this time he took substantial steps to broaden his fabled "rainbow coalition." Most significantly, he fashioned a cross-racial populist message by appealing to disaffected white voters reeling from the erosion of the manufacturing base.[47] African Americans still accounted for two-thirds of the 6.6 million votes he received in the 1988 primaries, but he attracted three times as many white voters as he had in 1984.[48] Jackson's surprise victory in the Michigan primary on March 26, 1988, humbled the party's favorite, Massachusetts governor Michael Dukakis. Veteran Democratic political strategist Ann Lewis, hired by Jackson, summed it up best: "'84 was a crusade. This is a real campaign."[49] But because of Jackson's presence in the crowded Democratic field, racial issues receded into the background as the other candidates conceded the Black vote to Jackson.[50]

Jackson's status as a front-runner was short-lived after white voters coalesced around Dukakis, an uncharismatic albeit palatable candidate who stressed his competent economic stewardship of Massachusetts, dubbed the "Massachusetts Miracle." By June, Dukakis had outlasted his foes and wrapped up the nomination. Civil rights had never been a focal point of his political career, as it had been for past and future Democratic nominees. As a result, African Americans were never drawn to the bland Massachusetts technocrat.

Blacks' tepid views of Dukakis notwithstanding, they much preferred him to Vice President Bush, the eventual Republican nominee. Scion of a wealthy Connecticut family associated with the moderate wing of the Republican Party, Bush had moved to Texas and positioned himself as a Goldwater conservative. He was not exempt from racial demagoguery; in opposing the Civil Rights Act of 1964, he had told Texas voters: "Congress passed the new civil rights act to protect fourteen percent of the people," but he was equally concerned about the "other 86 percent."[51] Four years later, Bush reverted to his roots as a Rockefeller Republican

and flouted the wishes of his constituents by supporting the Fair Housing Act as a Texas congressman in 1968. By 1988, however, Bush had
been Reagan's loyal vice president for eight years and had been in lock-
step with the administration's overall approach to civil rights, including
its opposition to sanctions against South Africa. As the general election
campaign approached, Bush was dogged by the perception that he was
a sycophant and a political chameleon devoid of core beliefs, sentiments
that were reinforced when *Newsweek* ran a cover story in October 1987
deriding Bush as a "wimp."[52] By the time of the Republican National
Convention in August, Dukakis held a twenty-point lead in the polls,
and the fact that a sitting vice president had not won a presidential election since Martin Van Buren in 1836 cast an ominous cloud on Bush's
electoral prospects.

The only consolation in this gloomy prognosis for Bush was that the
American electorate had an unsettled view of Dukakis, a recent entry
to national politics. In May, the Bush campaign convened a focus group
of white Reagan Democrats in Paramus, New Jersey, who were leaning
toward Dukakis. After being informed of Dukakis's stand on a host of
racially charged issues, particularly his opposition to the death penalty,
members of the focus group swung back to Bush. Bush's campaign manager, Lee Atwater, and his chief media guru, Roger Ailes, an architect of
Nixon's 1968 "law and order" campaign, were struck by how these voters
cringed when they heard that William J. "Willie" Horton, a convicted
Black murderer serving a life sentence, had raped a white woman and
stabbed her husband in Maryland while on a furlough from a Massachusetts prison—part of a program approved by Dukakis.[53] Given the
forbidding political environment, Bush decided that his only chance was
to eviscerate the relatively unknown Dukakis as a Massachusetts liberal
out of step with the mainstream by using Willie Horton to paint Dukakis
as the coddler of a Black rapist.

Atwater was a seasoned Southern political operative schooled in
South Carolina senator Strom Thurmond's nasty brand of racial politics.
He considered Nixon's 1968 Southern strategy "a model campaign . . . a
blueprint for everything I've done in the South since then." Atwater was
only in his thirties, but he had already earned a reputation as the most
ruthless practitioner of negative campaigning.[54] In 1981, while working

in the Reagan White House, Atwater explained how Reagan and the Republicans had succeeded in winning the votes of racists without appearing to be racist:

> You start out by saying, "Nigger, nigger, nigger." By 1968, you can't say "nigger"—that hurts you, backfires. So you say stuff like uh, forced busing, states' rights and all of that stuff, and you're getting so abstract. Now, you're talking about cutting taxes, and all of those things you are talking about are totally economic things and a byproduct of [that] is blacks get hurt worse than whites. . . . We want to cut this, is much more abstract than even the busing thing, uh, and a hell of a lot more abstract than "Nigger, nigger."[55]

The racially explosive Willie Horton issue had first emerged as part of the Bush team's standard opposition research on Dukakis. In an April primary debate, Democratic senator Albert Gore referenced a Massachusetts program—inaugurated by Dukakis's Republican predecessor Francis Sargent in 1972 and continued by Dukakis—that allowed weekend furloughs to state prison inmates.[56] Gore did not press the matter too much, but it sparked the interest of James Pinkerton, the research director for Bush's campaign. After further examination, Pinkerton unearthed political dynamite: Horton had been granted nine previous furloughs without incident, but he never returned from his tenth furlough, in April 1986. In April 1987, Horton raped a white woman, assaulted her fiancé, and stole the man's car; he was eventually captured by police. Upon seeing a photograph of Horton, a Black man with a menacing demeanor, Atwater gloated, "By the time we're finished, they're going to wonder whether Willie Horton is Dukakis' running mate."[57] When news surfaced that Jesse Jackson was visiting Dukakis's home, Atwater publicly speculated: "So anyway, maybe he will put this Willie Horton on the ticket after all is said and done."[58] Bush's political team salivated over the specter of linking Dukakis to Horton. Roger Ailes breezily told *Time* reporter Richard Stengel, "The only question is whether we depict Willie Horton with a knife in his hand or without it."[59]

In a relatively quiescent year that lacked the charismatic Reagan as the Republican standard-bearer, the Bush campaign latched on to Willie

Horton as the centerpiece of its efforts to destroy Dukakis. Not mentioned was the fact that a number of white prisoners in Massachusetts
had committed crimes while on furlough. Furloughs were not unique
to Massachusetts—nearly every state had some kind of furlough program, and thirty-three states allowed furloughs for murderers serving
life terms with the possibility of parole.[60] While Reagan was the governor
of California, several prisoners granted furloughs had escaped and committed murders. In a celebrated 1972 case, one of these furloughed prisoners murdered Los Angeles police officer Phillip J. Riley. In spite of the
murder, Reagan defended the state program as a "model in correctional
systems for the whole nation" that has "had great success."[61]

The pervasiveness of these furlough programs did not preclude the
Bush campaign from deploying racial fear to depict Dukakis as soft on
crime. Years later, Jane Mayer of the *New Yorker* described Bush's use of
Willie Horton as "the political equivalent of an improvised explosive de-
vice demolishing the electoral hopes of Dukakis."[62] In the crucial weeks
after the Republican convention, Dukakis's lead evaporated as Bush used
Horton as a staple in his campaign speeches, contrasting his own support of the death penalty with Dukakis's endorsement of weekend furloughs for murderers. Bush never mentioned the fact that Horton was
African American—he did not have to: the Republican Party whipped
out pamphlets that paired Horton's ominous photograph with Dukakis
and the words "Is This Your Pro-Family Team for 1988?"[63]

In September, a purportedly independent conservative organization called the National Security Political Action Committee released
a low-budget political ad titled "Weekend Passes" detailing Horton's
crime. It appeared nationally on cable television for twenty-eight days
in the fall. The spot featured a mug shot of a scowling Horton sporting
a disheveled Afro alternating with a picture of Dukakis. The ad's cre-
ator, Larry McCarthy, said that when he first saw Horton's mug shot,
he thought the man had the look of a caged animal and said to himself, "This is every suburban mother's greatest fear."[64] The combustible
mixture of race, sex, and violence was so provocative that it garnered a
lot of free press—further cementing the connection between Dukakis
and Horton. Another independent PAC with ties to the Bush campaign
raised $2 million to finance a speaking tour for Cliff Barnes, the fiancé

of the woman raped by Horton. Barnes appeared on several popular TV talk shows, including those hosted by Oprah Winfrey and Geraldo Rivera, where he blamed Dukakis for the grisly crime.[65]

On October 5, 1988, the Bush campaign began to air its own television advertisements linking Dukakis with the now infamous Willie Horton. One, titled "Revolving Door," showed grainy black-and-white images of men bleakly entering and exiting prison through a turnstile as the narrator explained that Dukakis was soft on crime and opposed the death penalty. Most of the actors playing the inmates were white, but the widespread public awareness of the Willie Horton story led virtually all observers to the mistaken perception that the majority of inmates in the ad were African American.[66] In the public imagination, Dukakis and Horton had become synonymous. A CBS News/New York Times poll indicated that "Revolving Door" was the most effective political ad of the entire 1988 election cycle.[67]

In the closing weeks of the campaign, the ubiquity of the Horton ad prompted the *New York Amsterdam News* to accuse the Republicans of relentlessly running a Jim Crow campaign.[68] Bush and his political operatives vociferously denied any racial animus, alleging that the ad was accurate and concerned only crime, not race. They claimed that the ad had been the brainchild of an independent organization, but its creators had previously worked for Roger Ailes, and they supposedly had the tacit support of senior officials in the Bush campaign.[69] Neither Bush nor Reagan ever stood up to douse the flames of racism that permeated the Willie Horton issue. In a postmortem interview, Dukakis's campaign manager, Susan Estrich, sighed and said, "Look, you can't find a stronger metaphor, intended or not, for racial hatred in this country than a black man raping a white woman."[70]

In addition to fomenting palpable racial fears over the prospect of a Dukakis presidency, Bush's advisors succeeded in caricaturizing Dukakis as an unpatriotic liberal for vetoing a bill requiring teachers to lead their classes in reciting the Pledge of Allegiance.[71] Dukakis temporarily halted his slide in the polls when he performed well in the first debate, but he floundered in the second debate when Bernard Shaw, an African American journalist, asked him whether he would favor the death penalty if someone murdered his wife, Kitty. His passionless, cold response explaining his opposition to capital punishment astonished viewers and corroborated the view that he was soft on crime. Although Dukakis displayed some pluck in the closing days of the campaign, Bush defeated him in a landslide. For the first time since the 1920s, the Republicans were victorious in three successive elections.

Ironically, Dukakis, who was so lackluster on racial issues and had survived the strongest challenge ever mounted by a Black man (Jackson) in a presidential primary, would be eviscerated by his link to an African American convicted felon. Bush rewarded Atwater's role in masterminding his victory by naming him chair of the Republican National Committee. The following year, the thirty-nine-year-old Atwater would be diagnosed with an inoperable brain tumor. In his final weeks, the dying Atwater apologized to Dukakis for the "naked cruelty" of his comment about making Willie Horton his running mate.[72]

As Reagan was poised to depart the presidency, he basked in the approval of white America. Until the very end, however, African Americans continued to be Reagan's most bitter detractors. A *Los Angeles Times* headline noted African Americans' anger at the Reagan presidency, and a Harris poll reported that almost 80 percent of Blacks considered the administration oppressive to members of their race.[73]

As he had throughout his political career, Reagan professed bewilderment, incredulity, and anger over the criticism from African Americans. In a final parting shot on CBS's *60 Minutes*, Reagan lashed out at civil rights leaders: "Sometimes I wonder if they really want what they say they want, because some of those leaders are doing very well leading organizations based on keeping alive the feeling that they're victims of prejudice."[74] Reagan's petty remarks unleashed a torrent of anger from civil rights leaders, who called his statement vacuous, reflecting his tendency to fantasize about civil rights problems. In the final days of Reagan's presidency, John Jacobs of the National Urban League condemned the Reagan era as a period when American society became more racially polarized than ever and argued that it was "no accident that recent years have seen a rise in violent racial incidents or that anti-Black attitudes appear to be strong."[75]

Reagan's spiteful, demeaning comment directed at critics of his civil rights record in the final days of his presidency was a fitting coda to his malign neglect of racial issues. It was consistent with his pettiness toward any criticism of his civil rights policies, which always saw him defending himself from the infrequently made charge that he was a bigot. Reagan's vindictiveness differed markedly from his reputation as a genial figure who "spoke to the better angels of our nature." Likewise, with respect to the homeless epidemic that ballooned during the Reagan administration, he enraged critics by denying responsibility, stating that the homeless "make their own choice for staying out there."[76]

Over the years, Reagan supporters have bristled over Blacks' critiques of the Reagan presidency and have contended that Black America benefited from the economic prosperity of the 1980s. David Stockman, the foremost architect of Reaganomics, attributed the economic success of the 1980s to the actions of Federal Reserve chief Paul Volcker in fighting inflation and stated that it had "almost nothing to do with our original supply-side doctrine."[77] Indeed, the cumulative effects of the Reagan administration's assaults on labor unions, tax cuts for the wealthy, and slashing of federal funds for low-income housing and other social programs such as food stamps and Medicaid contributed to the widening socioeconomic disparities between Blacks and whites. In 1987, the US Census Bureau reported that, since the beginning of Reagan's presidency, the Black poverty rate rose to 33.1 percent, while the white rate fell to 10.5 percent.[78] Perhaps the most emblematic statistic is that the Reagan years ushered in the declining fortunes of American cities. In the late 1970s, urban budgets received about 22 percent of their revenue from the federal government. By the end of the Reagan administration, it had been slashed to 6 percent. These consequences were devastating to urban schools, libraries, and police, fire, and sanitation departments, which never fully recovered from the descent that began during Reagan's presidency. The widening disparities were exacerbated by the racially disparate impact of the War on Drugs, which would not be discernible until after Reagan left office.

In looking forward, African Americans unanimously agreed on one point: it was inconceivable that George H. W. Bush could be worse than Reagan—even though the vice president had run the most racially polarizing campaign in recent US history.

REAGAN'S RACIAL LEGACY AND THE ROAD TO TRUMP

Donald Trump is a conservative populist and the direct descendant and rightful heir to Ronald Reagan.
—Patrick Buchanan (2017)[1]

On January 20, 1989, the seventy-eight-year-old Reagan returned to Los Angeles riding a crest of personal popularity among white America. He had the highest approval of a departing president since FDR's death ended his wartime presidency.[2] After a generation of wrenching turmoil over the Vietnam War, Watergate, and the economic woes and national malaise of the 1970s, millions of white Americans across the political spectrum hailed Reagan's inspirational leadership and gentle mirth for restoring the nation's confidence during the roaring 1980s.

Amid the slew of valedictory articles about Reagan's consequential presidency, there was little mention of Reagan's controversial record on civil rights. For example, longtime Reagan chronicler Lou Cannon's lengthy article in the *Washington Post* touted Reagan's "legacy of surprises," but his sole reference to civil rights was a sentence quoting the conservative columnist George Will's approving assessment that "the civil rights era ended in the Reagan years."[3] Cannon's piece also provoked Ralph Neas of the LCCR, an unsung civil rights leader of the 1980s, to write to Cannon, chiding him for failing to note how Reagan's reactionary policies forced civil rights advocates "to devote an inordinate amount of resources to refighting old battles" and diverting energy from the fight for economic justice.[4]

The Reagans retired to a 7,192 square foot ranch-style home on a 1.5-acre lot in the exclusive Bel Air neighborhood of Los Angeles. Eighteen of Reagan's wealthy friends, including longtime Kitchen Cabinet member Holmes Tuttle, had purchased the gated $2.5-million home for the Reagans with an option to buy.[5] In the first years of his retirement, critics assailed Reagan for receiving $50,000 per speech. His receipt of an astounding $2 million honorarium for two twenty-minute speeches he made in Japan in October 1989 also created a media firestorm.[6] The *New York Times* faulted the president for sullying the presidency. The paper noted that former presidents had not always comported themselves with dignity after leaving the Oval Office, but that "none have plunged so blatantly into pure commercialism."[7] The economic recession of the early 1990s, anxiety over spiraling budget deficits, and continued revelations around the Iran-Contra Affair all cast a shadow over Reagan's presidency. By the time he gave his primetime speech at the 1992 Republican convention, a New York Times/CBS poll found that 50 percent of Americans disapproved of his performance as president.[8]

For many Reagan critics, Simon and Schuster's publication of Reagan's memoir in November 1990, titled *An American Life*, corroborated suspicions that Reagan had been "sleepwalking through history."[9] Reagan's rendition of his storied American life overlooked the civil rights revolution that convulsed the country during his political rise. Given the centrality of Dr. Martin Luther King Jr. to Reagan's twentieth-century America, his failure to mention King seems astounding. Nor did he mention Nelson Mandela or his support of the South African apartheid regime that plagued his presidency. He also made no mention of the deadly AIDS crisis that likely killed many more people because of his administration's dilatory response to what his political advisors considered a "gay" disease. Such omissions were in keeping with Reagan's predilection to look away from unpleasant things that might cause him to rethink his life or the America he revered. The memoir, of course, returned to the narrative of racial innocence, that he was raised in a home where there was "no more grievous sin than racial bigotry."[10] After all of these years, whether consciously or not, he was still unable to distinguish between what he took to be his lack of personal bigotry and the racially discriminatory impact of his policies as president.

By the early 1990s, African Americans were dispirited over the political triumph of Reagan's conservatism, especially its success in shifting the narrative away from remedying centuries of structural racism toward a discourse of personal responsibility and "color blindness." While many commentators lauded the improving relationships between whites and African Americans, political scientist Andrew Hacker came to a grim conclusion in his 1992 book *Two Nations: Black and White, Separate, Hostile, Unequal*: "A huge racial chasm remains, and there are few signs that the coming century will see it closed."[11] Reagan's successor, George H. W. Bush, escalated the War on Drugs, further locking the country into the intolerant and punitive policy that would disproportionately ensnare millions of nonviolent African Americans into the burgeoning prison-industrial complex.[12]

In the wake of the Willie Horton ad in the 1988 campaign, Democratic presidential hopeful Arkansas governor Bill Clinton took notice of how the Republicans had won elections by exploiting the wedge issues of crime, welfare, and taxes to pry working-class whites away from the Democratic Party.[13] To counter the perception that Democrats were soft on crime, Clinton interrupted his 1992 campaign to return to Arkansas to witness the execution of an African American man convicted of murder who was so severely mentally disabled that he was unable to comprehend his fate.[14] Positioning himself as a "New Democrat," Clinton succeeded in wooing back large swaths of whites with his tough talk on crime, support for the death penalty, and his mantra-like campaign promise to end welfare "as we know it."

Shortly after Clinton wrapped up the Democratic nomination, Los Angeles erupted in riots after a jury in Simi Valley, the home of Reagan's presidential library, acquitted three policemen in the vicious beating of an unarmed Black man named Rodney King. Bigger than the urban riots of the 1960s, the 1992 LA riots testified to the unresolved relationship between the city's police and its Black residents. It also dramatized African Americans' bitterness at how their expectations of the 1960s had not been fulfilled. The riots transpired against the backdrop the Los Angeles Police Department's deployment of SWAT teams and the militarization of policing and the arrests and incarceration of Black and Latino people in furtherance of the War on Drugs.[15]

Around this time, reports of Reagan's mental deterioration began to emerge. On November 5, 1994, Reagan made the poignant announcement that he was afflicted with Alzheimer's and was now beginning "the journey that will lead me into the sunset of my life."[16] For years, observers had wondered whether his stumbling over words, falling asleep in public, difficulty speaking extemporaneously, and poor memory were symptomatic of his being stricken with dementia during his presidency.[17] By early 1987, not long after the shocking revelations of the Iran-Contra Affair, White House advisors were so concerned about Reagan's mental state that they considered invoking the Twenty-Fifth Amendment, which calls for the removal of a president in the event of his incapacitation.[18] In 2011, Ron Reagan Jr. wrote that he had been alarmed over his father's deteriorating mental condition as early as 1984.[19] Debates persist over whether Reagan had early-onset Alzheimer's while president.

Reagan's departure from public life did not dim his influence. He endured as the dominant figure in the conservative imagination, and his immediate successors, H. W. Bush and Clinton, continued his federal crime-control policies of targeting racially and ethnically marginalized urban youth under the guise of a war on drugs. Most notably, President Clinton signed the 1994 omnibus crime bill, which imposed automatic life sentences for certain felony offenses if a person already had two convictions on their record. Known as the "three strikes, you're out" law, it accelerated the process of mass incarceration and continued to decimate communities of color.

Meanwhile, wrapping himself in the mantle of Reagan, Georgia congressman Newt Gingrich engineered the 1994 Republican takeover of the House of Representatives, ending forty-two years of Democratic control over the lower chamber. Even while this new class of House Republicans adopted Reagan's visceral hostility to government, they dispensed with Reagan's penchant for compromise, negotiation, and comity. In the fall of 1995, House Republicans initiated a six-week government shutdown, inaugurating a new era of gridlock and hyperpartisanship that has often paralyzed the legislative process. The growing extremism of the rank-and-file Republican Party led a frail eighty-seven-year-old Barry Goldwater to jest to the presidential nominee Bob Dole in 1996: "We're the new liberals of the Republican Party."[20]

As mentioned, Reagan's death, in 2004, occasioned an outpouring of grief and affection in the political class and the media that revolted Reagan's critics, especially African Americans and the civil rights community. As a testament to Reagan's prestige as a conservative icon, Republican George W. Bush, Clinton's successor, modeled himself after Reagan, rather than his own father. Unlike his father, who signed a budget deal that broke his pledge not to raise taxes, George W. Bush made tax cuts the foundation of his fiscal policies. To concerns that a second round of tax cuts would ignite trillions of dollars in deficits, Vice President Richard B. Cheney responded that Reagan had proved "deficits don't matter."[21]

Though George W. Bush named two African Americans, Colin Powell and then Condoleezza Rice, as his secretaries of state, and talked about being a "compassionate conservative," Bush was a political protégé of Lee Atwater's and familiar with the efficacy of the old Republican playbook of using wedge issues around race for his political advantage. Most dramatically, during his 2000 primary campaign, Bush's campaign spread rumors that Senator John McCain's adopted daughter from Bangladesh was really a "Negro" child his fellow candidate had fathered out of wedlock.[22]

Following the federal government's failure to respond adequately to Hurricane Katrina in New Orleans, in 2005, Bush's approval ratings plummeted. African Americans were particularly incensed over Bush remaining on vacation in Texas while the hurricane slammed New Orleans. From the beginning of the crisis, the tragedy had a strong racial component, as the nation was bombarded with searing images of mostly Black New Orleans residents desperately stranded on rooftops or trapped in the crowded, fetid conditions of the Superdome crying for food and water. Critics charged that Federal Emergency Management Agency's response reflected the federal government's indifference to African Americans and was a by-product of Reagan's contempt for the federal government. In the aftermath of Katrina, many in the conservative media and right-wing bloggers portrayed the storm victims as criminals and looters.[23] Barbara Bush, the president's mother, declared the Katrina evacuees were "underprivileged anyway," so the fact that they had shelter in the Superdome was "working well for them."[24] Along with the Iraq War, Katrina inflicted a fatal blow on Bush's presidency. After the outbreak of the Great Recession in 2008, the Republican Party sustained devastating electoral losses. For a brief moment, historians wrote the obituary for the Age of Reagan, and one prominent scholar proclaimed the death of conservatism.[25]

For millions of Americans, the election of Barack Obama as the first African American to the presidency in 2008 sparked a wave of national euphoria. Obama's election fulfilled one of the great dreams of the civil rights movement: that an African American could attain the nation's highest office. Despite the persistence of decades of intractable structural racism exacerbated by spiraling levels of mass incarceration as a result of the ill-conceived and racist War on Drugs, Obama's victory was seen by some as evidence that the US had become a "post-racial" society.[26] Within a matter of weeks, however, this triumphalism was deflated by the Republicans' wall of opposition to Obama's policies and the unleashing of the Tea Party's racially tinged cries of "Let's take our country back." The backlash against the first African American president intensified during Obama's first term, culminating in racist conspiratorial theories that Obama was a Muslim, a socialist, and not an American citizen. The most distressing aspect was the failure of Reagan's Republican heirs to repudiate these scurrilous rumors.[27]

Obama's 2012 reelection failed to "break the fever" of intransigence and obstruction in Washington. In fact, Obama's second term witnessed further racial strife.[28] The 2012 shooting death of Trayvon Martin, an unarmed teenager, by an armed vigilante was followed by a series of other high-profile deaths of young African American men, women, and boys at the hands of law enforcement, which highlighted the horror of police brutality and violence inflicted on people of color. The rage over the murders of Trayvon Martin and Michael Brown in Ferguson, Missouri, lead to a new generation of civil rights activism under the hashtag Black Lives Matter, which clamored for an end to the War on Drugs and mass incarceration.

Then, a conservative majority on the Supreme Court set back the civil rights movement decades. Back in 2005, President George W. Bush had appointed John G. Roberts, the young lawyer in Reagan's Justice Department who had been such a zealous advocate for eviscerating the Voting Rights Act, to replace his mentor, Chief Justice Rehnquist. In Roberts's 2003 confirmation hearing for a seat on the distinguished DC Circuit Court of Appeals, he denied writing the memoranda outlined earlier, in which he expressed his vehement opposition to Congress' extension of the VRA.[29] In June 2013, Chief Justice Roberts wrote the decision in the case of *Shelby v. Holder*, which struck down the VRA's Section 5 pre-clearance as unconstitutional. The ruling drove a stake through the heart of the crowning achievement of the civil rights movement of the 1960s and led to a number of states passing laws that made it more onerous for African Americans and others to vote.[30]

Throughout the Obama presidency, the Republican Party continued to tout itself as the "Party of Reagan." Republican candidates vying for the presidential nomination all made a pilgrimage to the Reagan Presidential Library in Simi Valley, California, for one of the presidential primary debates. There, they jockeyed with each other to assume the crown as Reagan's heir. Not long after he announced his candidacy for the Republican nomination in 2015, Wisconsin governor Scott Walker quipped that he told his wife, "I know our wedding anniversary because it's Ronald Reagan's birthday."[31] In 2016, Florida senator Marco Rubio remarked, "It's time for children of the Reagan Revolution to assume the mantle of leadership."[32]

The ascension of Donald J. Trump in the 2016 Republican presidential primary battle removed whatever sliver of hope a number of conservative reformers harbored of moderating the Republican Party's harsh, mean-spirited image on racial issues. On June 16, 2015, the real estate developer turned reality-television star had announced his quixotic candidacy for the presidency by excoriating Mexican immigrants in profanely xenophobic language: "They are bringing drugs. They are bringing crime. They're rapists. Some, I assume, are good people."[33] Interestingly enough, when Trump initially flirted with running for president, in 2000, William F. Buckley Jr. perceptively observed, "When he looks at a glass, he is mesmerized by its reflection."[34]

With respect to African Americans, Trump had a long, sordid history of racism.[35] He first appeared on the front page of the *New York Times* on October 16, 1973, when the Justice Department charged the Trump family's real estate company with refusing to rent to African Americans in violation of the 1968 Fair Housing Act.[36] Throughout his rise to fame as a brash, wealthy real estate developer and the embodiment of the 1980s Reagan era decade of greed, Trump was dogged by allegations of racism. In 1989, after five young Black and Latino teenagers were accused of raping a young, white female jogger in Central Park, Trump spent $85,000 placing full-page ads in four New York City newspapers calling for the return of the death penalty in New York State. After DNA evidence exonerated the so-called Central Park Five in 2003, and a serial rapist confessed to the crime, the City of New York settled a civil rights lawsuit over their arrests and imprisonment in the sensational crime.[37] Trump, however, refused to accept that they were innocent, let alone apologize to the young men who had wrongly spent from seven to thirteen years in prison.[38]

Most egregiously, Trump laid the groundwork for his 2016 presidential campaign by becoming the most visible proponent of the "birther" conspiracy theory, which held that President Obama was born in Kenya, rather than Hawaii, and was therefore ineligible for the presidency. While claiming he was "the least racist person," Trump propagated demeaning jabs at Obama. He called Obama, the first African American editor of the prestigious *Harvard Law Review*, "a terrible student, terrible"; demanded that Obama release his college and law school transcripts; and even leveled the racist trope that he was a "lazy" president. As a celebrity known to millions of Americans, Trump made spurious attacks on Obama that exploited white anxieties over their loss of status amid looming demographic shifts and the profound challenges of globalization. Trump's angry ethno-nationalist populism, framed by the Reaganesque slogan "Make America Great Again," harkened back to a 1950s white, Christian, male nation before the Mexicans, African Americans, and other interlopers destroyed the American idyll.

Despite Trump's many patently racist, misogynist, demeaning, and mendacious statements during the 2016 presidential primary campaign, Trump still won nearly 45 percent of the Republican Party vote, nearly twice as many as his closest rival, Senator Ted Cruz. The bombastic reality-television star shockingly emerged in the spring of 2016 as the presumptive nominee of the party of Reagan. In an eerie resemblance to Nixon's in the late 1960s, Trump's acceptance speech at the Republican convention in July struck an authoritarian tone as he declared himself the candidate of "law and order," promising to keep the nation safe from violent crime and acts of terrorism, especially those committed by "illegal immigrants."[39]

Although many former Reagan administration officials and political supporters refused to endorse Trump, a number of high-level Reagan supporters and officials threw their support to the Trump campaign, such as 1984 campaign manager Ed Rollins; Paul Manafort, who was the Southern coordinator for Reagan's 1980 campaign; Ed Meese; and Jeffrey Lord, a Reagan political advisor.[40] Less than ten days before the election, Trump announced the formation of the "Reagan Alumni Advisory Council for Trump-Pence," composed of 240 former Reagan advisors who supported Trump for president.[41] Furthermore, the conservative Heritage Foundation, Reagan's favorite think tank and one of the most ardent purveyors of Reagan's legacy, played a pivotal role in staffing Trump's administration with conservatives.[42]

Trump's upset victory over Hillary Clinton was a devastating blow to African Americans and the civil rights communities, but one of the most underreported stories of the 2016 election was the missing African American voter. Turnout among Black voters in 2016 declined substantially.[43] The 2016 election was the first presidential contest to occur without the full protections of the Voting Rights Act. Research by a distinguished team of political scientists determined the impact of racially discriminatory Voter ID laws, racially motivated polling-place closures, and the impact of registration barriers had significantly depressed Black turnout.[44] Another reason for the decrease in Black turnout was the lingering impact of Reagan's War on Drugs, whereby nearly one in thirteen African Americans of voting age were disenfranchised due to a felony conviction, often for nonviolent drug offenses.[45] Finally, simmering resentment over the Clinton legacy from the 1990s, including Hillary Clinton's 1996 use of the term "superpredators" to describe some young Black people, further depressed Black turnout.

Shortly after Trump was elected, the party of Reagan completely morphed into the party of Trump.[46] Fox News's many segments flashing pictures of Reagan and Trump indicated a campaign among the conservative media to link Reagan with the new president. Trump's tax cuts on behalf of the wealthy, despite the effect they had on the deficit, was indeed very Reaganesque.[47] Like Reagan, Trump delegated the Federalist Society the task of rubber-stamping very conservative federal judges. Trump's judicial nominees were united in their embrace of Meese and Bork's doctrine of originalism, which prior to the Reagan era was derided as a fringe philosophy.[48] Despite their rather tepid criticisms of Trump's boorish behavior, his serial lying, and his bigotry, especially after he claimed a moral equivalence between clashing neo-Nazis and counterdemonstrators in Charlottesville, Virginia, in August 2017, Trump still managed to dominate the Republican Party.

Still, a number of conservative pundits, such as George Will, William Kristol, David Frum, David Brooks, and Bret Stephens, insisted that Trump was an aberration, a usurper of Reagan's noble legacy. These never-Trump Republicans seemed oblivious to Reagan and the conservative movement having been on the wrong side of history on so many issues, especially civil rights. A number of former Reagan political officials and supporters recoil at any insinuation that Reagan had any similarities with Trump.[49] One conservative "Never Trumper," Peggy Noonan, a Reagan speechwriter who had written a gushing book on Reagan, shuddered at the comparisons between Trump and Reagan: "Donald Trump is no Ronald Reagan." Not only is Trump not Reagan, she argued, but in saying so, one sounded "desperate and historically illiterate."[50]

Noonan and the others are only partially correct; Trump and Reagan have a number of discernable differences, but Trump's rise to become the face of the conservative movement is not a complete rupture from the overall trajectory of the Republican Party and the conservative movement since Goldwater. Granted, Trump and Reagan differed substantially on vital issues like immigration, free trade, and foreign policy. While Reagan thrilled crowds with his clarion calls to tear down the Berlin Wall, Trump made building a "big beautiful wall" at the Mexican border the focal point of his campaign. Reagan signed into law a comprehensive immigration bill in 1986, which mandated that any immigrant who entered the US prior to 1982 would be eligible for amnesty. Trump's propitiation to Russian president Vladimir Putin, an ex-KGB officer, would have appalled Reagan. Whereas Reagan imparted an irenic, sunny vision of America as a Shining City on a Hill, Trump has a relentlessly dark, apocalyptic vision of the US, best evidenced by his talk of "American carnage" in his inaugural address. Above all, Reagan came from humble roots, was a patriot, and was endowed with good manners, and would likely have been revolted by Trump's insulting and bullying manner.

All of that said, there are a number of important parallels between Reagan and Trump. The self-proclaimed "Errol Flynn of the B's," and the reality-television host both began their public lives in the entertainment industry. Even if Reagan had served two terms as governor of California,

he, like Trump, was not well-versed in the details of domestic or foreign policy and did not have much interest in becoming better versed.
Both men ran for the presidency as "Washington outsiders." Furthermore, both the Reagan and Trump administrations were marred by rampant corruption. By the end of his presidency, the Reagan White House
was mired in a miasma of corruption that enveloped a whopping 138
members of his administration, who faced investigation, indictment, or
convictions for their roles in the numerous scandals that beset the administration.[51] Perhaps it is no accident that Trump became a cultural
icon during the Reagan era, the 1980s, "the decade of greed."

While the term "fake news" may have only recently entered the political lexicon, Reagan was a serial fabulist. He was an avid reader of the
sensational right-wing *Human Events* and *Reader's Digest*, which were
often the source of his fictitious stories on welfare queens and other of
his preposterous assertions, such as trees contributing more to air pol-
lution than cars. Reagan cared less that a story was accurate than if it
carried the right message. Political scientist James David Barber fittingly
observed that "Reagan was the first modern presidency whose contempt
for facts was treated as a charming idiosyncrasy."[52] Both Trump and Reagan were septuagenarians when they took office, both engineered a hostile takeover of the Republican Party, and both molded the conservative
movement in their image by appealing to a mythic American past with
their own takes on making America great again.

Most significantly, however, the most racially infused parts of
Trumpism—its calls to ban Muslims and build a wall, locking thousands
of Latino children in cages, and its conspiratorial claims that the first
African American president was not really American—did not suddenly
emerge when Donald Trump descended his golden escalator in June
2015. They were the product of a long progression that began back in
1964, when Reagan delivered his iconic "A Time for Choosing" speech
and the party of Lincoln nominated Barry Goldwater as their presidential nominee, and when the conservative movement rose to power in
part by exploiting whites' racial anxieties. While Trump and Reagan
were never personally acquainted, Trump honed his racist rhetoric and
unvarnished law and order views in the political and intellectual milieu
of the Reagan era of greed in the 1980s. Trump is not *sui generis* but
rather the culmination of the putrefaction of American conservatism

into racism, isolationism, xenophobia, and an embrace of conspiratorial theories. Although these tendencies have not always dominated the conservative movement, since Obama's election in 2008, they have metastasized into a dangerous cancer on the American body politic.[53] Reagan was neither an isolationist nor a xenophobe, but Trump has followed Reagan's playbook in stacking the federal courts with judges opposed to civil rights enforcement and to civil rights themselves. Reagan's and Ed Meese's troubling statements on race and civil rights never rose to the overt racism of Trump's tweets, but Reagan's hostility to civil rights and civil rights enforcement eerily anticipated the policies of Trump and his administration.

Though the pro-civil rights Rockefeller wing of the Republican Party waged a fierce struggle in the 1960s and 1970s to combat the party's rightward, racially conservative drift, Reagan's capture of the Republican Party nomination in 1980 marked the triumph of "states' rights" conservatism. Reagan's "polite racism" betrayed the fact that he perfected the art of the politics of white supremacy. From the beginning of his career as a Barry Goldwater conservative, Reagan chose states' rights over human rights. Instead of allying himself with Martin Luther King Jr., Nelson Mandela, and other contemporaries who risked their lives in the pursuit of racial justice and equality, Reagan cozied up to Strom Thurmond and Jesse Helms, and as president opposed the imposition of sanctions against the apartheid regime. The recent revelations of Reagan's racist statement slurring African diplomats as "monkeys" still "uncomfortable wearing shoes" suggests Reagan's sinister, racist motives for his support of Pretoria. Though he vociferously and angrily denied any racist intent, his acute sensitivity to being called a racist conveyed the impression that the man "doth protest too much."

The Republican Party's ultimate embrace of Trump was a product of the "wrong turn" it made when it chose Reagan and Goldwater's brand of states' rights conservatism that stood "athwart history" to oppose the struggle for racial justice.[54] Reagan's racially coded dog whistles pale in comparison to Trump's racist barks, such as his tweeting that the "squad," four US congresswomen of color should all "go back and help fix the totally broken and crime infested countries where they came from," and his attacks on US representative Maxine Waters as having a "low I.Q.," just to name a few.[55] Nonetheless, Reagan was more sinister than Trump because he was able to mask his heinous policies on race behind his amiable façade and convince the American public that he was a great man.[56]

Reagan's communications director Patrick Buchanan said it best: "Donald Trump is a conservative populist and the direct descendant and rightful heir to Ronald Reagan."[57] Reagan's legacy survives in the form of crushing poverty, prisons overflowing with poor people of color, and a nation plagued by profound racial strife and socioeconomic inequities. In reconsidering Reagan and the conservative movement that emerged in tandem with the civil rights movement, Reagan's racist politics and policies cast a blight on his legacy, and have ensured that the color line will continue to be a central problem of American life well into the twenty-first century. This legacy is something Reagan's acolytes can no longer ignore.

ACKNOWLEDGMENTS

This book is the product of years of thinking, reading, and researching about Ronald Reagan, the conservative movement, African American history, and the civil rights movement. It was also informed by my searing exposure to the racial inequities of the criminal justice system during my years as a legal and criminal defense attorney. I have incurred many debts in writing this book. First, I would like to thank the numerous people I have talked to about this book. So many people provided me with unflagging enthusiasm about this project and fortified my determination to complete it. During the many difficult and frustrating days, weeks, months, and years when I wearied over this arduous task, your words furnished me with the determination and energy to finish this. There are too many of you to thank here, but I could not have done it without you.

Whatever contribution I make to this timely discussion has been facilitated by the pathbreaking work of many brilliant scholars, journalists, and others who have written about these issues. As such, I am standing on the shoulders of many giants. I would like to thank my mentor, the Pulitzer Prize–winning historian Leon Litwack for his passion, support, and commitment to excellence. During a critical phase of the book, Robin Einhorn, another Berkeley professor and mentor, invited me to give a paper at a political history seminar, which helped crystalize many of these issues. I would also like to thank Kerwin Klein, another brilliant Berkeley professor, for graciously taking the time to read the manuscript and providing valuable feedback.

Writing history is often a lonely and isolating endeavor, but it could not have been written without the support and assistance of family, friends, librarians, and archivists who generously took time out of their busy lives to read my manuscript or offer their valuable assistance and suggestions. The staff at the Ronald Reagan Presidential Library in Simi Valley were always helpful and made research there a delight. Jennifer Mandel, in particular, was most helpful. The respective archivists and staffs at the Hoover Institute at Stanford University, the Bancroft Library at the University of California at Berkeley, the Library of Congress, and the Richard Nixon Presidential Library in Yorba Linda, California, were also helpful.

A number of historians whose work I have admired but had never met responded to my unsolicited emails and gave me encouragement and suggestions and read portions of my manuscript. I would like to thank Mary Frances Berry, Doug Rossinow, Laura Kalman, Geoffrey Kabaservice, and Matthew Dallek, all of them brilliant historians, for making this book better.

A number of Reagan's supporters and political aides generously agreed to share their recollections and thoughts about Reagan. Even though they were skeptical about my project and motivations, they were kind and generous with their time, which shows that even in our current political milieu, we can disagree without being disagreeable. Their portraits of Reagan enriched my perspective. I would like to thank Thomas C. Reed, Stuart Spencer, Annelise Anderson, and William Brock for taking the time to talk with me.

Thanks also to journalist Bill Boyarsky, former Republican assemblyman William T. Bagley, and the late assemblyman and former US congressman Anthony Beilenson. Bagley's and Beilenson's exemplary years of public service in the California legislature are a testament to the legacy of bipartisan cooperation that made California great in the postwar years. Their insightful comments and perspectives on Reagan during his gubernatorial years deepened my understanding of Reagan.

I am especially grateful to a number of close friends and family members who provided invaluable assistance and emotional support during the long gestation of this book. I would like to thank Tracy O'Callaghan Gage, who, at an early stage of this project, provided me unstinting support, for which I am eternally grateful. Susan Fitzpatrick-Behrens read an early proposal of this project and gave support and encouragement. Nadine Bopp graced me with her hospitality during my short trips from Los Angeles to Carlsbad. I am still in touch with my junior high social studies teacher Larry Hays, who nourished my passion for history at a young age, and we are now good friends. He read drafts of the manuscript and provided me encouragement. I would also like to thank my neighbor and friend R. Lawrence Tripp and my cousins Gary Lucks, Lisa Gibson, and Dylan Lucks for their hospitality during the times I travelled up to the Bay Area to interview subjects and spend time at the Hoover Institute and Bancroft Library.

Friends and family in New York City also graced me with their hospitality during my frequent trips to the East Coast. I would like to thank my friends Nancy and Dr. David Payne, and Elizabeth Gaffney, and my nephews Joshua, Zachary, Jacob, and Bryan Meisel.

I could not have been luckier to meet my editor, Gayatri Patnaik, at the Organization of American Historians meeting in New Orleans in April 2017. Gayatri's enthusiasm and dedication to this book has continued unabated. Along with Gayatri, Maya Fernandez, and Susan Lumenello, the dedicated staff at Beacon Press have all displayed a dedication to excellence and a unique commitment to publishing books that make a difference. I would also like to thank Jeanne Theoharis for her brilliant suggestions for improving my introduction. During the final stages of my book, a dear friend and brilliant editor Mary Murrell read the entire manuscript, and her efforts made the book much better.

My family has been a source of support throughout my entire life. My sister-in-law Gail Kiefer Lucks has also been a fountain of support during tough times, as have my two nieces, Emily Lucks and Ilana Lucks, and my nephew Alexander Lucks. My mother, Sheila Lucks, as always, has been my biggest supporter, and her life has set an example.

My brother-in-law Dr. Lee Meisel and sister Dr. Deborah Lucks Meisel have been most gracious and generous. It is to them that I devote this book.

NOTES

INTRODUCTION

1. Thurmond, quoted in Joseph Crespino, *Strom Thurmond's America* (New York: Hill and Wang, 2012), 287.

2. Kiron K. Skinner, Annelise Anderson, and Martin Anderson, eds., *Reagan: A Life in Letters* (New York: Free Press, 2003), 339.

3. For works periodizing an era of Reagan, see Sean Wilentz, *The Age of Reagan: A History, 1974–2008* (New York: Harper Perennial, 2008); Gil Troy, *Morning in America: How Ronald Reagan Invented the 1980s* (Princeton, NJ: Princeton University Press, 2005); Steven F. Hayward, *The Age of Reagan: The Conservative Counterrevolution, 1980–1989* (New York: Crown Forum, 2009); Doug Rossinow, *The Reagan Era: A History of the 1980s* (New York: Columbia University Press, 2015); Jacob Weisberg, *Ronald Reagan: The American President Series, the 40th President, 1981–1989* (New York: Times Books, 2016).

4. Bosman, "Edwards Attacks Obama for View of Reagan."

5. On the Ronald Reagan legacy project, see Will Bunche, *Tear Down This Myth: The Right-Wing Distortion of the Reagan Legacy* (New York: Free Press, 2009); Niels Bjerre-Poulsen, "The Road to Mount Rushmore: The Conservative Commemoration Crusade for Ronald Reagan," in *Ronald Reagan and the 1980s: Perceptions, Policies, Legacies*, ed. Cheryl Hudson and Gareth Davies (New York: Palgrave MacMillan, 2008), 209–28.

6. "Dr. King Calls Race Top in Issue in Voting," *New York Times*, November 10, 1966, 30.

7. Glenn Frankel, "Limited Sanctions Imposed on South Africa," *Washington Post*, September 10, 1985, A1, A12.

8. Jeff R. Woods, *Black Struggle, Red Scare: Segregation and Anti-Communism in the South, 1948–1968* (Baton Rouge: LSU Press, 2003); George Lewis, *The White South and the Red Menace: Segregationists, Anti-Communism, and Massive Resistance, 1945–1965* (Gainesville: University Press of Florida, 2004).

9. This is an exhaustive but not a complete list of Reagan biographies; none of these studies are exclusively devoted to Reagan's policies on race and civil rights: Bill Boyarsky, *The Rise of Ronald Reagan* (New York: Random House, 1968); Joseph Lewis, *What Makes Reagan Run? A Political Profile* (New York: McGraw Hill, 1968); Lee Edwards, *Reagan: A Political Biography* (New York: Viewpoint Books, 1968); Lou Cannon, *Ronnie & Jesse: A Political Odyssey* (New York: Doubleday,

1969); Bill Boyarsky, *Ronald Reagan: His Life & Rise to the Presidency* (New York: Random House, 1980); Lou Cannon, *Reagan* (New York: G. P. Putnam & Sons, 1982); Ronnie Dugger, *On Reagan: The Man and His Presidency* (New York: McGraw Hill, 1983); Laurence I. Barrett, *Gambling with History: Ronald Reagan in the White House* (New York: Doubleday, 1983); Garry Wills, *Reagan's America: Innocents at Home* (New York: Penguin Press, 1987); Anne Edwards, *Early Reagan: The Rise to Power* (New York: William Morrow, 1987); Michael Rogin, *Ronald Reagan, the Movie: And Other Episodes in Political Demonology* (Berkeley: University of California Press, 1987); Mark Hertsgaard, *On Bended Knee: The Press and the Reagan Presidency* (New York: Farrar, Straus & Giroux, 1988); Sidney Blumenthal and Thomas Byrne Edsall, eds., *The Reagan Legacy* (New York: Pantheon, 1988); Jane Mayer and Doyle McManus, *Landslide: The Unmaking of the President, 1984–1988* (New York: Houghton Mifflin, 1988); Sidney Blumenthal, *Our Long National Daydream: A Political Pageant of the Reagan Era* (New York: Harper Collins, 1990); Haynes Johnson, *Sleepwalking through History: America in the Reagan Years* (New York: W. W. Norton, 1991); Theodore Draper, *A Very Thin Line: The Iran-Contra Affair* (New York: Hill and Wang, 1991); Michael Schaller, *Reckoning with Reagan: America and Its President in the 1980s* (New York: Oxford University Press, 1992); Stephen Vaughn, *Ronald Reagan in Hollywood: Movies and Politics* (New York: Cambridge University Press, 1994); Beth Fischer, *The Reagan Reversal: Foreign Policy and the End of the Cold War* (Columbia: University of Missouri Press, 1997); William Pemberton, *Exit with Honor: The Life and Presidency of Ronald Reagan* (New York: Routledge, 1997); Dinesh D'Souza, *Ronald Reagan: How an Ordinary Man Became an Extraordinary Leader* (New York: Free Press, 1997); Edmund Morris, *Dutch: A Memoir of Ronald Reagan* (New York: Random House, 1999); Matthew Dallek, *The Right Moment: Ronald Reagan's First Victory and the Decisive Turning Point in American Politics* (New York: Free Press, 2000); Frances Fitzgerald, *Way Out in the Blue: Reagan, Star Wars, and the End of the Cold War* (New York: Simon & Schuster, 2000); Peggy Noonan, *When Character Was King: A Story of Ronald Reagan* (New York: Viking, 2001); Michael Deaver, *A Different Drummer: My Thirty Years with Ronald Reagan* (New York: Harper, 2001); Peter Schweizer, *Reagan's War: The Epic Story of His Forty-Year Struggle and Final Triumph over Communism* (New York: Doubleday, 2002); Lou Cannon, *Governor Reagan: His Rise to Power* (New York: Public Affairs, 2003); W. Eliot Brownlee and Hugh Davis Graham, eds., *The Reagan Presidency: Pragmatic Conservatism and Its Legacies* (Lawrence: University Press of Kansas, 2003); Peter Robinson, *How Ronald Reagan Changed My Life* (New York: Harper Perennial, 2003); Troy, *Morning in America*; John Ehrman, *The Eighties: America in the Age of Reagan* (New Haven, CT: Yale University Press, 2005); Craig Shirley, *Reagan's Revolution: The Untold Story of the Campaign That Started It All* (Nashville: Thomas Nelson, 2005); Richard Reeves, *President Reagan: The Triumph of Imagination* (New York: Simon & Schuster, 2005); Robert Collins, *Transforming America: Politics and Culture in the Reagan Years* (New York: Columbia University Press, 2006); Thomas Evans, *The Education of Ronald Reagan: The General Electric Years and the Untold Story of His Conversion to Conservatism* (New York: Columbia University Press, 2006); Paul Kengor, *The Crusader: Ronald Reagan and the Fall of Communism* (New York: Harper, 2006); John Patrick Diggins, *Ronald Reagan: Fate, Freedom,*

and the Making of History (New York: W. W. Norton, 2007); William F. Buckley
Jr., The Reagan I Knew (New York: Basic Books, 2008); John W. Sloan, FDR and
Reagan: Transformative Presidents with Clashing Visions (Lawrence: University
Press of Kansas, 2008); Wilentz, The Age of Reagan; Hayward, The Age of Reagan;
Bunche, Tear Down This Myth; Martin Anderson and Annelise Anderson, Reagan's
Secret War: The Untold Story of His Fight to Save the World from Nuclear Disaster
(New York: Crown Archetype, 2009); William Kleinknecht, The Man Who Sold
the World: Ronald Reagan and the Betrayal of Main Street America (New York:
Nation Books, 2009); Ron Reagan, My Father at 100 (New York: Viking, 2011);
Mary Beth Brown, The Faith of Ronald Reagan (Nashville: Thomas Nelson, 2011);
Joseph McMartin, Collision Course: Ronald Reagan, the Air Traffic Controllers,
and the Strike that Changed America (New York: Oxford University Press, 2011);
Rick Perlstein, The Invisible Bridge: The Fall of Nixon and the Rise of Reagan (New
York: Simon & Schuster, 2014); Thomas C. Reed, The Reagan Enigma: 1964–1980
(Los Angeles: Figueroa Press, 2014); Gerard DeGroot, Selling Ronald Reagan: The
Emergence of a President (London: I. B. Tauris, 2015); Craig Shirley, Last Act: The
Final Years and Emerging Legacy of Ronald Reagan (Nashville: Thomas Nelson,
2015); H. W. Brands, Reagan: The Life (New York: Doubleday, 2015); Rossinow,
The Reagan Era; Weisberg, Ronald Reagan; Iwan Morgan, Reagan: An American
Icon (London: I. B. Taurus, 2016); Gene Kopelson, Reagan's 1968 Dress Rehearsal:
Ike, RFK, and Reagan's Emergence as a World Statesman (Los Angeles: Figueroa
Press, 2016); James Rosebush, True Reagan: What Made Ronald Reagan Great and
Why It Matters (New York: Center Street, 2016); Weisberg, Ronald Reagan; Henry
Olsen, The Working Class Republican: Ronald Reagan and the Return of Blue-Collar
Conservatism (New York: Broadside Books, 2017); Craig Shirley, Reagan Rising:
The Decisive Years, 1976–1980 (New York: Broadside Books, 2017); Bob Spitz,
Reagan: An American Journey (New York: Penguin, 2018); David T. Byrne, Reagan:
An Intellectual Biography (Lincoln, NE: Potomac Books, 2018); Robert Mann, Be-
coming Reagan: The Rise of a Conservative Icon (Lincoln, NE: Potomac Press, 2019).

10. For scholarly articles, book chapters, and other treatments of Reagan and
race, see Mary Frances Berry, History Teaches Us to Resist: How Progressive Movements Have Succeeded in Challenging Times (Boston: Beacon Press, 2018), 59–86;
Ibram X. Kendi, Stamped from the Beginning: The Definitive History of Racist Ideas
in America (New York: Bold Type Books, 2016), 424–39; Kenneth Osgood and
Derrick E. White, Winning While Losing: Civil Rights, the Conservative Movement,
and the Presidency from Nixon to Obama (Tallahassee: University Press of Florida,
2014); Emily Zuckerman, "EEOC Politics and Limits on Reagan's Civil Rights
Legacy," in Freedom Rights: New Perspectives on the Civil Rights Movement, ed.
Danielle L. McGuire and John Dittmer (Lexington: University Press of Kentucky,
2011); Robert C. Smith, Conservativism and Racism, and Why in America They Are
the Same (Albany: SUNY Press, 2010); Mary Frances Berry, And Justice for All: The
United States Commission on Civil Rights and the Continuing Struggle for Freedom
in America (New York: Random House, 2009); Denise M. Bostdorff and Steven R.
Goldzwig, "History, Collective Memory, and the Appropriation of Martin Luther
King, Jr.'s Rhetorical Legacy," Presidential Studies Quarterly 35, no. 4 (December
2005): 661–90; Jeremy Mayer, "Reagan and Race: Prophet of Color Blindness, Baiter

of the Backlash," in *Deconstructing Reagan: Conservative Mythology and America's Fortieth President*, ed. Kyle Longley, Jeremy Mayer, Michael Schaller, and John M. Sloan (New York: Routledge, 2006), 70–89; Stephen Tuck, "African American Protest during the Reagan Years: Forging New Agendas, Defending Old Victories," in Hudson and Davies, *Ronald Reagan and the 1980s*, 119–34; Kurt Schuparra, *Triumph of the Right: The Rise of the California Conservative Movement, 1945–1966* (Armonk, NY: M. E. Sharpe, 1998); Kenneth O'Reilly, *Nixon's Piano: Presidents and Racial Politics from Washington to Clinton* (New York: Free Press, 1995), 355–406; "Looking Back: Ronald Reagan, a Master of Racial Polarization," *Journal of Blacks in Higher Education* 58 (Winter 2007–08): 33–36; "Black America Has Overlooked the Racist Policies of Ronald Reagan," *Journal of Blacks in Higher Education* 64 (Summer 2009): 13–14; Jeremy D. Mayer, *Running on Race: Racial Politics in Presidential Campaigns, 1960–2000* (New York: Random House, 2002), 152–56, 164–70, 174–78, 192–94; Thomas Byrne Edsall and Mary Byrne Edsall, *Chain Reaction: The Impact of Race, Rights, and Taxes on American Politics* (New York: W. W. Norton, 1991); Stephen Shull, *A Kinder, Gentler Racism? The Reagan-Bush Civil Rights Legacy* (Armonk, NY: M. E. Sharpe, 1993); and Norman C. Amaker, *Civil Rights and the Reagan Administration* (Washington, DC: Urban Institute Press, 1988). For a defense of Reagan's racial policies, see Nicholas Laham, *The Reagan Presidency and the Politics of Race: In Pursuit of Colorblind Justice and Limited Government* (New York: Praeger, 1998); Raymond Wolters, *Right Turn: The Reagan Administration and Black Civil Rights* (New Brunswick, NJ: Transaction, 1996); and Robert R. Dethlefsen, *Civil Rights under Reagan* (Washington, DC: ICS, 1991). On Reagan's racist War on Drugs, see Heather A. Thompson, "Why Mass Incarceration Matters: Rethinking Crisis, Decline, and Transformation in Post-War American History," *Journal of American History* 97, no. 3 (December 2010): 703–34; Michelle Alexander, *The New Jim Crow: Mass Incarceration in the Age of Colorblindness* (New York: New Press, 2010); Jimmie L. Reeves and Richard Campbell, *Cracked Coverage: Television News, the Anti-Cocaine Crusade, and the Reagan Legacy* (Durham, NC: Duke University Press, 1994).

    11. Dallek, *The Right Moment*, 187.

    12. Jackie Robinson, "Ronald Reagan, Just Another Goldwater, Hollywood Style," *Philadelphia Tribune*, June 14, 1966, 6.

    13. "Satisfying the Bigots," *Los Angeles Sentinel*, October 27, 1966, A6.

    14. In 2018, Kay Cole James, the new president of the conservative Heritage Foundation, expressed this sentiment. Tim Alberta, *American Carnage: On the Front Lines of the Republican Civil War and the Rise of President Trump* (New York: Harper Collins, 2019), 501.

    15. "1980 Ronald Reagan/Jimmy Carter Presidential Debate," October 28, 1980, http://www.reagan.utexas.edu/archives/reference/10.28.80debate, accessed May 9, 2015.

    16. James Baldwin, *The Fire Next Time* (New York: Dial Press, 1963), 115.

    17. Shirley, *Last Act*.

    18. Bunche, *Tear Down This Myth*, 189.

    19. Julian Borger, "Ronald Reagan: Reagan Was His Lifelong Hero," *Guardian*, June 11, 2004, 3. See, also, Bunche, *Tear Down This Myth*, 190; Tim Harper,

"Reagan Era Tough for Blacks, Many Choose to Sit Out Memorials for Late U.S. Leader," *Toronto Star*, June 11, 2004, A10.

20. Reggie Williams, "Americans Mourn, but Not African Americans," *Afro American Red Star*, June 19, 2004, A1; "Why Many Americans Didn't Adore Reagan," *Oakland Tribune*, June 14, 2004, 1.

21. Betty Winston Baye, "The Adulation of Ronald Reagan Ignores His Other, More Reprehensible Side," *Louisville Courier-Journal*, June 24, 20–24, A6; "Blacks Do Not Reflect Fondly on Reagan's Leadership," *USA Today*, June 9, 2004, A10. On the War on Drugs, See Alexander, *The New Jim Crow*.

22. Dorothy E. Roberts, "The Social and Moral Costs of Mass Incarceration in African American Communities," *Stanford Law Review* 56, no. 4 (April 2004).

23. Kelly Brewington, "For Blacks, a Different Legacy," *Baltimore Sun*, June 13 2004, 4A; George E. Curry, "Reagan Made Racism Respectable," *Los Angeles Sentinel*, June 10, 2004, A1.

24. Nancy Reagan (with William Novak), *My Turn: The Memoirs of Nancy Reagan* (New York: Random House, 1989), 107.

25. Gladwin Hill, "Reagan Pressed 'Noncandidacy' in Visits to Florida and Chicago," *New York Times*, May 22, 1968, 1, 28; Richard Corrigan, "Reagan Stars in Screen Test," *Washington Post*, May 26, 1968, A8; "Negress Chides Reagan at Florida GOP Lunch," *Boston Globe*, May 22, 1968, 22.

26. Deaver quoted in Bernard von Bothmer, *Framing the Sixties: The Use and Abuse of a Decade from Ronald Reagan to George W. Bush* (Amherst: University of Massachusetts Press, 2009), 65.

27. "I Was for Civil Rights Before It Was 'Civil Rights': Reagan," *Los Angeles Times*, September 5, 1984, A2.

28. Kyle Longley, "Why Trump Is Just Following in Reagan's Footsteps on Race," *Washington Post*, August 5, 2019.

29. See Jesse Curtis, "'Will the Jungle Take Over?': *National Review* and the Defense of Western Civilization in the Era of Civil Rights and Age of African Decolonization," *Journal of American Studies* (Spring 2018): 1–27.

30. Karen R. Miller, *Managing Inequality: Northern Racial Liberalism in Interwar Detroit* (New York: NYU Press, 2015).

31. Robin DiAngelo, *White Fragility: Why It's So Hard for White People to Talk About Racism* (Boston: Beacon Press, 2018).

32. For a lackluster defense of Reagan's civil rights policies, see Laham, *The Reagan Presidency and the Politics of Race*, and Hayward, *The Age of Reagan*, 219–29.

33. See Rick Perlstein, *Before the Storm: Barry Goldwater and the Unmaking of the American Consensus* (New York: Hill and Wang, 2001).

34. For an indictment of Buckley's racial views, see Nicholas Buccola, *The Fire Is Upon Us: Baldwin, William F. Buckley Jr., and the Debate over Race in America* (Princeton, NJ: Princeton University Press, 2019).

35. Larry Kramer, "Reagan and AIDS," *New York Review of Books*, April 12, 2007.

36. Cannon, *Ronnie & Jesse*; Cannon, *Reagan*; Cannon, *President Reagan*; Cannon, *Governor Reagan*.

37. Lou Cannon, "Reagan's Southern Stumble," *New York Times*, November 18, 2007; Lou Cannon, email to author, April 3, 2016.

38. See Matt Dallek, "Not Ready for Mt. Rushmore: Reconciling the Myth of Ronald Reagan with the Reality," *American Scholar* (June 1, 2009).

39. Ronald Reagan quoted in Kurt Schuparra, "A Great White Light," in *The Conservative Sixties*, ed. David Farber and Jeff Roche (New York: Peter Lang, 2003), 100; Carl Greenberg, "Reagan Accused of Signing 'Caucasians Only' Covenant," *Los Angeles Times*, September 13, 1966, 3, 26.

40. An exception is Kopelson, *Reagan's 1968 Dress Rehearsal.*

41. William A. Link, *Righteous Warrior: Jesse Helms and the Rise of Modern Conservatism* (New York, St. Martin's Press, 2008), 148.

42. Geoffrey Kabaservice, *Rule and Ruin: The Downfall of Moderation and the Destruction of the Republican Party from Eisenhower to the Tea Party* (New York: Oxford University Press, 2012).

43. O'Reilly, *Nixon's Piano*, 355.

44. Black Issues Polling, January 1982, Melvin Bradley Files, Box 2, Black Issues 1982, Ronald Reagan Presidential Library (RRPL); "Mr. Reagan and Black America," *New York Times*, May 7, 1982, A30.

45. Terrel H. Bell, *The Thirteenth Man: A Reagan Cabinet Memoir* (New York: Free Press, 1988), 104.

46. Marc Morjé Howard, *Unusually Cruel: Prisons, Punishment and the Real American Exceptionalism* (New York: Oxford University Press, 2017), 1.

47. Marc Mauter, *Race to Incarcerate: The Sentencing Project* (New York: Free Press, 2006), 1–2.

48. See Michael Tonry, *Punishing Race: A Continuing American Dilemma* (New York: Oxford University Press, 2011).

49. Alexander, *The New Jim Crow*, 49.

50. H. R. Haldeman, *The Haldeman Diaries: Inside the Nixon White House* (New York: G. P. Putnam's Sons, 1994), 53; Dan Baum, "Legalize It All: How to Win the War on Drugs," *Harpers*, April 2016, 22.

51. Elizabeth Hinton, *From the War on Poverty to the War on Crime: The Making of Mass Incarceration in America* (Cambridge, MA: Harvard University Press, 2016), 5.

52. Mary Frances Berry, "Ronald Reagan and the Leadership Conference on Civil Rights," in Osgood and White, *Winning While Losing*, 82–120.

53. Mary McGrory, "A Hostile Legacy for Blacks," *Washington Post*, January 17, 1989, A2.

54. Rossinow, *The Reagan Era*, 8.

55. Max Boot, "The GOP Is America's Party of White Nationalism," *Foreign Policy*, March 14, 2017; Michelle Goldberg, "Trump Is a White Nationalist Who Inspires Terrorism," *New York Times*, August 5, 2019.

56. "Half Century of US Civil Rights Gains Have Stalled or Reversed, Report Finds," *Guardian*, February 27, 2018.

CHAPTER 1: EARLY REAGAN

1. Patti Davis, *The Way I See It: An Autobiography* (New York: Putnam, 1992), 23.

2. John Meroney, "Ron Reagan: Growing Up as the Son of a President—and a Movie Star," *Atlantic*, January 18, 2011.

3. Quoted in Ronald Reagan (with Richard G. Hubler), *Where's the Rest of Me? The Autobiography of Ronald Reagan* (New York: Karz, 1965), 13.

4. Reagan, *Where's the Rest of Me?*, 7.

5. Cannon, *President Reagan*, 8; Reagan, *Where's the Rest of Me?*, 40.

6. Robert E. Gilbert, "Reagan's Presidency: The Impact of an Alcoholic Parent," *Political Psychology* 29, no. 2 (2008): 737–65.

7. Author interview with Stuart Spencer, March 28, 2016, Palm Desert, CA.

8. Reagan, *Where's the Rest of Me?*, 17.

9. Edwards, *Early Reagan*, 48, 53.

10. Linda Gordon, *The Second Coming of the KKK: The Ku Klux Klan of the 1920s and the American Political Tradition* (New York: Liveright, 2017); Vaughn, *Ronald Reagan in Hollywood*, 11.

11. Ronald Reagan, *An American Life* (New York: Simon and Schuster, 1990), 30.

12. Edwards, *Early Reagan*, 53.

13. Reagan, *An American Life*, 30.

14. Wills, *Reagan's America*, 18.

15. Reagan, *An American Life*, 30.

16. Vaughn, *Ronald Reagan in Hollywood*, 11.

17. Wills, *Reagan's America*, 37.

18. "Closest Friend Was Reagan Teammate," *Washington Post*, January 16, 1986, C4.

19. "I Was for Civil Rights before It Was 'Civil Rights,'" A2.

20. Quoted in Vaughn, *Reagan in Hollywood*, 27.

21. Reagan, *Where's the Rest of Me?*, 81.

22. Edwards, *Early Reagan*, 203–5.

23. Vaughn, *Ronald Reagan in Hollywood*, 40–42, 172.

24. Seth Rosenfeld, *Subversives: The FBI's War on Student Radicals and Reagan's Rise to Power* (New York: Picador, 2012), 118; Vaughn, *Reagan in Hollywood*, 106–7.

25. Vaughn, *Reagan in Hollywood*, 118.

26. *Reagan in Hollywood*, 174.

27. Reagan, *Where's the Rest of Me?*, 139, 141.

28. Rosenfeld, *Subversives*, 120.

29. Perlstein, *Invisible Bridge*, 354–59; Edwards, *Early Reagan*, 306.

30. Quoted in Vaughn, *Reagan in Hollywood*, 171.

31. See Larry Ceplair and Steven Englund, *The Inquisition in Hollywood: Politics in the Film Community* (Urbana: University of Illinois Press, 1980).

32. Quoted in Vaughn, *Reagan in Hollywood*, 172.

33. Vaughn, *Reagan in Hollywood*, 172.

34. See John Sbardellati, *J. Edgar Hoover Goes to the Movies: The FBI and the Origins of Hollywood's Cold War* (Ithaca, NY: Cornell University Press, 2012), 3.

35. Reagan, *Where's the Rest of Me?*, 169–70. In Reagan's 1990 ghostwritten memoir, he claims only *two* agents knocked on his door. Reagan, *An American Life*, 111.

36. Sbardellati, *J. Edgar Hoover Goes to the Movies*, 3–8, 66–68, 97–105.

37. See Neil Reagan, *Private Dimensions and Public Images: The Early Political Campaigns of Ronald Reagan*, interview conducted by Stephen Stern, 1981, University of California, Regional Oral History Project.

38. Rosenfeld, *Subversives*, 122.

39. Reagan, *Where's the Rest of Me?*, 169–70.

40. Reagan, *An American Life*, 109.

41. See Rosenberg, *Subversives*.

42. Kenneth O'Reilly, *Racial Matters: The FBI's Secret File on Black America, 1960–1972* (New York: Free Press, 1989).

43. Rosenfeld, *Subversives*, 123.

44. Reagan, *Where's the Rest of Me?*, 166–69.

45. Reagan, *Private Dimensions and Public Images*; Rosenfeld, *Subversives*, 124.

46. Reagan, *An American Life*, 113–14.

47. Reagan, *An American Life*, 109.

48. See George Lipsitz, *Rainbow at Midnight: Labor and Culture in the 1940s* (Urbana: University of Illinois Press, 1994).

49. Vaughn, *Reagan in Hollywood*, 134–35; Gerald Horne, *Class Struggle in Hollywood, 1930–1950: Moguls, Mobsters, Stars, Reds, and Trade Unionists* (Austin: University of Texas Press, 2001), 24–26.

50. Quoted in Horne, *Class Struggle in Hollywood*, 17.

51. "AFL Unions Fight Paralyzes Studios," *Los Angeles Times*, March 13, 1945, 1, 2.

52. "Film Strike Continues Despite WLB Order," *Atlanta Constitution*, March 23, 1945, 22.

53. Vaughn, *Regan in Hollywood*, 134–36; Edwards, *Early Reagan,* 308–10; Wills, *Reagan's America*, 224–40; "Hollywood Riot Flares in Strike," *New York Times*, October 6, 1945, 3.

54. See Horne, *Class Struggle in Hollywood*, 153–90.

55. "Reds Blamed for Strike; Warren Urged to Act," *Los Angeles Times*, October 9, 1945, 2.

56. Herbert Sorrell, "You Don't Choose Your Friends: The Memoirs of Herbert Knott Sorrell," 1963, Special Collections, UCLA Oral History Project, 20–50.

57. Whether Sorrell was a Communist remains controversial. At times, his militancy might have endeared him to the Communists, but he was fiercely independent. Horne, *Class Struggle in Hollywood*, 15–20; Sbardellati, *J. Edgar Hoover Goes to the Movies*, 110–11.

58. Reagan, *Where's the Rest of Me?*, 161–63.

59. Jack Dales, "Pragmatic Leadership: Ronald Reagan as President of the Screen Actors Guild," interview conducted by Mitch Tuchman, 1981, UCLA Oral History Project.

60. Reagan, *Where's the Rest of Me?*, 157.

61. "Jane Wyman Found Ex-Husband Reagan 'A Bore,'" UPI, November 26, 1982.

62. Cannon, *Governor Reagan*, 74.

63. Quoted in Vaughn, *Reagan in Hollywood*, 141.

64. Spitz, *Reagan*, 244.

65. Eric Pace, "George Dunne, 92, Priest and Ecumenist Dies," *New York Times*, July 14, 1998.

66. George H. Dunne, SJ, "Christian Advocacy and Labor Strife in Hollywood," Oral History Collection, interview conducted by Mitch Tuchman, 1981, UCLA Oral History Project, 28.

67. Quoted in Vaughn, *Reagan in Hollywood*, 143; Rosenfeld, *Subversives*, 125–26.

68. Perlstein, *The Invisible Bridge*, 378.

69. Rosenfeld, *Subversives*, 125–26.

70. Rosenfeld, *Subversives*, 127–28, 145–47.

71. Edwards, *Early Reagan*, 350; Vaughn, *Reagan in Hollywood*, 206–18; Wills, *Reagan's America*, 55.

72. Reagan, *Where's the Rest of Me?*, 169–70.

73. Stephen Vaughn, "Ronald Reagan and the Struggle for Black Dignity in Cinema, 1937–1953," *Journal of African American History* 77, no. 1 (Winter 1992): 88; on the Hollywood blacklist, see Thomas Doherty, *Show Trial: Hollywood HUAC and the Birth of the Blacklist* (New York: Columbia University Press, 2018).

74. Trumbo quoted in Vaughn, *Reagan in Hollywood*, 151–52.

CHAPTER 2: ON THE WRONG SIDE OF HISTORY

1. Martin Luther King Jr., "Goldwater's Nomination," *New York Amsterdam News*, August 1, 1964, 18.

2. On Reagan's display of awards from Faubus and Barnett, see Joseph Roddy, "Ronnie to the Rescue," *Look*, November 1, 1966, 54.

3. Quoted in Dan E. Moldea, *Dark Victory: Ronald Reagan, MCA, and the Mob* (New York: Viking, 1986), 3.

4. Cannon, *Governor Reagan*, 104.

5. Connie Bruck, *When Hollywood Had a King: The Reign of Lew Wasserman, Who Leveraged Talent into Power and Influence* (New York: Random House, 2003), 120–23.

6. Dennis McDougal, *The Last Mogul: Lew Wasserman, MCA, and the Hidden History of Hollywood* (New York: Crown, 1998), 261–65.

7. Moldea, *Dark Victory*, 142.

8. Quoted in Wills, *Reagan's America*, 277.

9. Howard Kohn and Lowell Bergman, "Ronald Reagan's Millions," *Rolling Stone*, August 26, 1976; Bruck, *When Hollywood Had a King*, 265–68; Charles R. Babcock, "Seed of Reagan's Wealth Planted in Land Sale," *Washington Post*, September 20, 1984.

10. Cannon, *Governor Reagan*, 106; Wills, *Reagan's America*, 265, 271–78.

11. Bruck, *When Hollywood Had a King*, 360.

12. Evans, *The Education of Ronald Reagan*.

13. Evans, *The Education of Ronald Reagan*, 38.

14. Kim Phillips-Fein, *Invisible Hands: The Businessmen's Crusade against the New Deal* (New York: W. W. Norton, 2009), 104.

15. Evans, *The Education of Ronald Reagan*, 40.

16. On Loyal and Edith Davis's racism, see Cannon, *Ronnie & Jesse*, 158; Bob Colacello, *Ronnie & Nancy: Their Path to the White House, 1911 to 1980* (New York: Warner Books, 2004), 127–31; Kitty Kelley, *Nancy Reagan: The Unauthorized Biography* (New York: Simon & Schuster, 1991), 39–41.

17. See Patrick Allitt, *The Conservatives: Ideas & Personalities throughout American History* (New Haven, CT: Yale University Press, 2009), 2; George H. Nash, *The Conservative Intellectual Movement in America* (New York: Intercollegiate Studies Institute, 1976), xv.

18. Lionel Trilling, *The Liberal Imagination: Essays on Literature and Society* (New York: Viking, 1950), ix.

19. See Buccola, *The Fire Is Upon Us*.

20. William F. Buckley, "Our Mission Statement," *National Review*, November 19, 1955.

21. For the impact of the *Review*, see Nash, *The Conservative Intellectual Movement in America Since 1945*, 140. According to Nash, "If *National Review* . . . had not been founded there would have been no cohesive intellectual force on the right in the 1960s and 1970s."

22. John B. Judis, *William F. Buckley, Jr.: Patron Saint of Conservatism* (New York: Simon & Schuster, 1988); Carl T. Bogus, *William F. Buckley, Jr. and the Rise of American Conservatism* (New York: Bloomsbury Press, 2011).

23. Kim Mills, "Reagan Praises Conservative Magazine for Intellectual, Political Influence," AP, December 6, 1985.

24. On Buckley and Reagan's friendship, see Buckley, *The Reagan I Knew*; see, also, Alvin Felzenberg, *A Man and His Presidents: The Political Odyssey of William F. Buckley Jr.* (New Haven, CT: Yale University Press, 2017).

25. Lou Cannon interview with William F. Buckley, May 10, 1989, Lou Cannon–Ronald Reagan Papers, Box 22, Special Research Collections, University of California, Santa Barbara, Library; Buckley, *The Reagan I Knew*, 37.

26. Buckley, *The Reagan I Knew*, 79–80.

27. Douglas Martin, "William F. Buckley, Champion of Conservatism, Dies at 82," *New York Times*, February 27, 2008.

28. Judis, *William F. Buckley, Jr.*, 24.

29. Judis, *William F. Buckley, Jr.*, 27–28.

30. Crespino, *Strom Thurmond's America*, 10.

31. See Joe Lowndes, *From the New Deal to the New Right: Race and the Southern Origins of Modern Conservatism* (New Haven, CT: Yale University Press, 2008); see, also, Nancy MacLean, "Neo-Confederacy Versus the New Deal: The Regional Utopia of the American Right," in Matthew D. Lassiter and Joseph Crespino, *The Myth of Southern Exceptionalism* (New York: Oxford University Press, 2009), 308–39.

32. Richard H. King, "The Struggle against Equality: Conservative Intellectuals in the Civil Rights Era, 1954–1975," in *The Role of Ideas in the Civil Rights South*, ed. Ted Ownby (Jackson: University Press of Mississippi, 2002), 113–36.

33. Marc Elliot, *Reagan: The Hollywood Years* (New York: Crown, 2008), 222–23, 233–36, 238, 243.

34. Bradley J. Birzer, *Russell Kirk: American Conservative* (Lexington: University Press of Kentucky, 2015), 47–51.

35. George H. Nash, "The Conservative Mind in America," *International Collegiate Review* 30, no. 1 (Fall 1994): 27.

36. Russell Kirk, "Norms, Conventions, and the South," *Modern Age* 2 (Fall 1958): 334–38; MacLean, "Neo-Confederacy Versus the New Deal," 316.

37. Richard Weaver, "Integration Is Communization," *National Review*, July 13, 1957, 68–69.

38. Richard Weaver, *The Southern Tradition at Bay: A History of Postbellum Thought* (Washington, DC: Regnery Books, 1989), 167–68; Richard M. Weaver, "The Regime of the South," *National Review*, March 14, 1959, 587–89.

39. "Segregation and Democracy," *National Review*, January 25, 1956, 5.

40. Forest Davis, "The Right to Nullify," *National Review*, April 25, 1956, 9.

41. "The South Girds Its Loins," *National Review*, February 29, 1956; Kevin Schultz, "William F. Buckley's and National Review's Vile Race Stance: Everything You Need to Know about Conservatives and Race," *Slate*, June 7, 2015, https://www.salon.com/2015/06/07/william_f_buckley_and_national_reviews_vile_race_stance_everything_you_need_to_know_about_conservatives_and_civil_rights.

42. "Why the South Must Prevail," editorial, *National Review*, August 24, 1957, 148–49.

43. "Why the South Must Prevail."

44. L. Brent Bozell, "Open Letter: Mr. Bozell Dissents from Views Expressed in the Editorial, 'Why the South Must Prevail,'" *National Review*, September 7, 1957, 209.

45. "A Clarification," *National Review*, September 7, 1957, 199.

46. On Kilpatrick, see William P. Hustwit, *James J. Kilpatrick, Salesman for Segregation* (Chapel Hill: University of North Carolina Press, 2013).

47. Quoted in Nancy MacLean, *Freedom Is Not Enough: The Opening Up of the American Workplace* (Cambridge, MA: Harvard University Press, 2006), 46.

48. James J. Kilpatrick, *The Sovereign States: Notes of a Citizen of Virginia* (Chicago: Henry Regnery, 1957).

49. Hustwit, *Kilpatrick*, 68–70.

50. "Conservative Commentator James J. Kilpatrick Remembered," *Tulsa World*, August 17, 2010. https://www.tulsaworld.com/obituaries/conservative-commentator-james-j-kilpatrick-remembered/article_c51cfc11-2065-5010-9324-e2288d87be18.html.

51. Ernest Van den Haag, "Intelligence or Prejudice?," *National Review*, December 1, 1964, 1059–63.

52. John P. Jackson Jr., *Science for Segregation: Race Law, and the Case against Brown v. Board of Education* (New York: NYU Press, 2005), 143.

53. "Ernest Van den Haag Dead at 87," UPI, March 21, 2002.

54. William F. Buckley Jr., "Obituary: Ernest Van den Haag: R.I.P.," *National Review*, April 22, 2002, 16–18.

55. William F. Buckley Jr., *Up from Liberalism* (New York: McDowell, 1959), 155.

56. William F. Buckley Jr. "Crucial Steps in Combating the AIDS Epidemic; Identify All of the Carriers," *New York Times*, March 18, 1986.

57. James Carney, "10 Questions for William F. Buckley," *Time*, April 5, 2004.

58. Curtis, "'Will the Jungle Take Over?'"

59. "Doctors Hear Medical Insurance Plan Scored," *Los Angeles Times*, February 13, 1962, 17; "Encroaching Control," speech, Annual Meeting, Phoenix Chamber of Commerce, March 30, 1961, Clotworthy Papers, Box 1, RRPL.

60. Bob Spitz, *Reagan, An American Journey* (New York: Penguin Press, 2018), 239, 269; Rick Perlstein, *The Invisible Bridge*, 377; Rosenfeld, *Subversives*, 142.

61. Reagan, *Where's the Rest of Me?*, 245.

62. Rosenfeld, *Subversives*, 148–49; Seth Rosenfeld, "Reagan's Personal Spy Machine," *New York Times*, September 1, 2012, SR4.

63. Quoted in Cannon, *Reagan*, 65.

64. Cannon, *Governor Reagan*, 109.

65. "Ronald Reagan Says Reds Active in Hollywood," *Boston Globe*, March 5, 1961, 20.

66. Quoted in Steven J. Ross, *Hollywood Left and Right: How Movie Stars Shaped American Politics* (New York: Oxford University Press, 2011), 163; Louis Fleming, "15,700 at Anti-Red School Rally," *Los Angeles Times*, August 31, 1961, B1.

67. Quoted in Rosenfeld, *Subversives*, 293; "Testimonial Dinner to Honor Rousselot," *Los Angeles Times*, August 16, 1962.

68. See Nicole Hemmer, *Messengers of the Right: Conservative Media and the Transformation of American Politics* (Philadelphia: University of Pennsylvania Press, 2016).

69. Perlstein, *Before the Storm*, 48; Robert Alan Goldberg, *Barry Goldwater* (New Haven, CT: Yale University Press, 1995), 142; Hemmer, *Messengers on the Right*, 137–41; "Manion Wants GOP to Pick Goldwater in '60," *Los Angeles Times*, May 3, 1960, B7.

70. "13 Votes to Goldwater: South Carolina Republicans Pledge Delegation," *New York Times*, March 27, 1960.

71. Goldberg, *Barry Goldwater*, 27–33.

72. Quoted in Perlstein, *Before the Storm*, 431; see, also, Nadine Cahodas, *Strom Thurmond and the Politics of Southern Change* (New York: Simon & Schuster, 1993).

73. Quoted in Timothy N. Thurber, *Republicans and Race: The GOP's Frayed Relationship with African Americans* (Lawrence: University Press of Kansas, 2013), 123.

74. Goldberg, *Barry Goldwater*, 138–39.

75. Frank S. Meyer, "A Man of Principle," *National Review*, April 23, 1960, 269–70.

76. Barry Goldwater, *The Conscience of a Conservative* (Shepardsville, KY: Victor Publishing, 1960), 35.

77. Quoted in Joshua D. Farrington, *Black Republicans and the Transformation of the GOP* (Philadelphia: University of Pennsylvania Press, 2016), 94.

78. Perlstein, *Before the Storm*, 92–95.

79. Edward T. Folliard, "South Carolina Crowds Sing to New Hero—Nixon: Carry Confederate Flags," *Washington Post*, November 4, 1960, 12.

80. Quoted in Lisa McGirr, *Suburban Warriors: The Origins of the New American Right* (Princeton, NJ: Princeton University Press, 2001), 189.

81. Quoted in Thomas C. Reed, *The Reagan Enigma, 1964-1980* (Los Angeles: Figueroa Press, 2014), 88.

82. Author interview with Thomas C. Reed, April 3, 2016, Los Angeles.

83. Chesly Manly, "Goldwater, Rockefeller Clash Over Strategy," *Chicago Tribune*, December 28, 1962, 7; Goldberg, *Barry Goldwater*, 115.

84. Gary Younge, "1963: The Defining Year of the Civil Rights Movement," *Guardian*, May 7, 2013; "How Whites Feel about Negroes: A Painful American Dilemma," *Newsweek*, October 21, 1963, 44–47; George H. Gallup, *The Gallup Poll: Public Opinion, 1935-1971, Vol. 3* (New York: Random House, 1972), 1812, 1842.

85. Ross, *Hollywood Left and Right*, 284–85.

86. Dallek, *The Right Moment*, 38; DeGroot, *Selling Ronald Reagan*, 28.

87. Quoted in Perlstein, *Before the Storm*, 363; see, also, Goldberg, *Barry Goldwater*, 196–97.

88. Charles Mohr, "Goldwater Says He'll Vote 'No' on the Rights Measure," *New York Times*, June 19, 1964, 1, 18.

89. Quoted in Thurber, *Republicans and Race*, 171.

90. Anthony Lewis, "Arizonan Target of GOP Leader," *New York Times*, June 20, 1964, 1.

91. E. W. Kenworthy, "Dirksen Shaped Victory for Civil Rights Forces," *New York Times*, June 20, 1964, 11.

92. Bill D. Moyers, "What a Real President Was Like," *Washington Post*, November 13, 1989, 89.

93. Leah Wright Rigueur, *The Loneliness of the Black Republican: Pragmatic Politics and the Pursuit of Power* (Princeton, NJ: Princeton University Press, 2014), 57.

94. Wallace Turner, "40,000 in Parade Against Arizonan," *New York Times*, July 13, 1964, 1, 18.

95. Richard Nixon, *RN: The Memoirs of Richard Nixon* (New York: Simon & Schuster, 1990), 260.

96. Taylor Branch, *Pillar of Fire: America in the King Years, 1963–1965* (New York: Simon & Schuster, 1998), 403–4.

97. *Pittsburgh Courier*, July 23, 1964, 1. See, also, Jackie Robinson (with Alfred Duckett), *I Never Had It Made: An Autobiography of Jackie Robinson* (New York: Ecco Press, 1972), 181.

98. Rosemary Tyler Brooks, "GOP Convention, 1964 Recalls Germany, 1933," *Chicago Defender*, July 18, 1964, 1, 2.

99. Manfred Berg, *The Ticket to Freedom; The NAACP and the Struggle for Black Political Integration* (Tallahassee: University Press of Florida, 2005), 211.

100. Robert E. Baker, "Goldwater Woos Dixie Democrats," *Washington Post*, September 17, 1964, A6.

101. Richard H. Rovere, "The Campaign: Goldwater," *New Yorker*, October 3, 1964.

102. "Barry Backers Heckle Mrs. LBJ in Dixie," *Hartford Courant*, October 8, 1964, 12A. See, also, Perlstein, *Before the Storm*, 463–70.

103. "A Two-Party South," *Chicago Tribune*, September 18, 1964, 12; Lewis Lord, "One of South's Worst Racists Backs Barry, Quits the Democrats," *Chicago Defender*, September 17, 1964, 2.

104. Quoted in Crespino, *Strom Thurmond's America*, 182. See, also, Joseph Crespino, "Goldwater in Dixie: Race, Region and the Rise of the Right," in *Barry Goldwater and the Remaking of the American Political Landscape*, ed. Elizabeth Tandy Shermer, (Tucson: University of Arizona Press, 2013), 144–69.

105. Carl Greenberg, "Thurmond Visit Irks States' GOP Chairman," *Los Angeles Times*, September 25, 1964, 8.

106. Perlstein, *Before the Storm*, 498–500; Charles Mohr, "Attacks Provoke Goldwater Camp," *New York Times*, May 30, 1964, 6.

107. Reagan, *An American Life*, 143.

108. Gene Kopelson, "The Speech," *National Review*, April 30, 2016, https://www.nationalreview.com/2016/04/ronald-reagan-dwight-eisenhower-1964-time-choosing-barry-goldwater; Mann, *Becoming Reagan*, 178–89.

109. F. Clifton White and William J. Gill, *Why Reagan Won: A Narrative History of the Conservative Movement, 1964–1981* (Chicago: Regnery Gateway, 1981), 24.

110. David Broder and Stephen Hess, *The Republican Establishment: The Present and Future of the GOP* (New York: Harper & Row, 1967), 253.

111. Harvard Sitkoff, *The Struggle for Black Equality, 1954–1992*, rev. ed. (New York: Hill and Wang, 1993), 172.

112. Ron Walters, *Black Presidential Politics* (Albany: State University of New York Press, 1988), 28.

113. Lott quoted in Godfrey Hodgson, *The World Turned Right Side Up: A History of the Conservative Ascendancy in America* (New York: Houghton Mifflin, 1996), 108.

114. Richard Hofstadter, "A Long View: Goldwater in History," *New York Review of Books*, October 8, 1964.

115. Anthony Lewis, "White Backlash Doesn't Develop," *New York Times*, November 4, 1964, 1, 26.

116. "Backlash Shows Up in California and Ohio Vote on Laws," *Washington Post*, November 6, 1964, 2.

117. King quoted in Mark Brilliant, *The Color of America Has Changed: How Racial Diversity Shaped Civil Rights Reform in California, 1941–1978* (Berkeley: University of California Press, 2010), 190; Paul Weeks, "Dr. King Sees Tragedy If Prop. 14 Is Approved," *Los Angeles Times*, October 28, 1964, 16; C. Marie Hughes, "Housing Foes Picket King, CRB Banquet," *California Eagle*, February 20, 1964, 1; Dallek, *The Right Moment*, 60.

118. "California Proposition 14," *Time*, September 25, 1964, 23.

119. "The Republican Party and the Conservative Movement," *National Review*, December 1, 1964, 1053–56.

120. Cannon, *Governor Reagan*, 132.

121. Seymour Korman, "Reagan's Political Star Rises," *Chicago Tribune*, December 14, 1964, 12.

CHAPTER 3: REAGAN'S FIRST CAMPAIGN

1. Ronald Reagan quoted in Kurt Schuparra, "A Great White Light," in *The Conservative Sixties*, ed. David Farber and Jeff Roche (New York: Peter Lang, 2003), 100; Carl Greenberg, "Reagan Accused of Signing 'Caucasians Only' Covenant," *Los Angeles Times*, September 13, 1966, 3, 26.

2. "Dr. King Calls Race Top Issue in Voting," 10.

3. John Lewis quoted in Harvard Sitkoff, *King: Pilgrimage to the Mountaintop* (New York: Hill and Wang, 2009), 168.

4. Sitkoff, *King*.

5. Daryl E. Lembke, "N. California Drive Started with Reagan: Candidate Talks with Negro Questions in S.F.," *Los Angeles Times*, January 23, 1966; "Reagan Hit Civil Rights Rule, Calls Some Laws Grandstand Stunt," *Washington Post*, June 17, 1966, A2.

6. "Mixed Couple Tests Coasts Housing Law," *New York Times*, January 4, 1965; "NAACP Vies for Open Housing in CA," *New York Amsterdam News*, December 19, 1964, 10.

7. Richard Bergholz, "Young GOP Affirms Support of Goldwater," *Los Angeles Times*, November 11, 1964, 11; "Reagan Hits 'Moderates' Among G.O.P.," *Chicago Tribune*, November 11, 1964, 14.

8. Hale Champion, "Oral History Interview with Hale Champion," Bancroft Regional Oral History Program University of California, Berkeley, July 25, 1978, 58.

9. Carl Greenberg, "Reagan Announces He's Candidate for Governor," *Los Angeles Times*, January 5, 1966, 35.

10. Milton Viorst, *Fire in the Streets: America in the 1960s* (New York: Simon & Schuster, 1979), 309.

11. Quoted in Jeanne Theoharis, *A More Beautiful and Terrible History: The Uses and Misuses of Civil Rights History* (Boston: Beacon Press, 2018), 66.

12. See Josh Sides, *L.A. City Limits: African American Los Angeles from the Great Depression to the Present* (Berkeley: University of California Press, 2003), 169–76.

13. Peter Bart, "Watts Riot Panel Warns of Danger of New Violence," *New York Times*, December 7, 1965, 1, 26. On the connection between Prop. 14 and Watts, see Jeanne Theoharis, "Alabama on Avalon: Rethinking the Watts Uprising and the Character of Black Protest in Los Angeles," in *The Black Power Movement: Rethinking the Civil Rights Movement*, ed. Peniel E. Joseph (New York: Routledge, 2006), 27–54.

14. See Gerald Horne, *Fire This Time: The Watts Uprising and the 1960s* (Charlottesville: University of Virginia Press, 1995), 3.

15. Joseph A. Califano. Jr., *The Triumph & Tragedy of Lyndon Johnson: The White House Years* (New York: Atria Books, 2014), 52;

16. Robert Dallek, *Flawed Giant: Lyndon Johnson and his Times, 1961–1973* (New York: Oxford University Press, 1998), 222–25.

17. Gladwin Hill, "Los Angeles Rioting Is Checked," *New York Times*, August 16, 1965, 1, 8.

18. Dallek, *The Right Moment*, 136.

19. Dallek, *The Right Moment*, 141.

20. Quoted in Rick Perlstein, *Nixonland: The Rise of a President and the Fracturing of America* (New York: Scribner, 2008), 71.

21. Richard Bergholz, "Reagan to Decide Soon on Running for Office," *Los Angeles Times*, January 22, 1965, 22; Gladwin Hill, "Reagan Weighing a New Role in Gubernatorial Campaign on Coast," *New York Times*, January 23, 1965, 10.

22. Quoted in Joshua Zeitz, *Building the Great Society: Inside Lyndon Johnson's White House* (New York: Penguin Books, 2018), 253.

23. Pete Hamill, "Brown Reagan Clash Test of White Backlash: The Key Issue is Race," *Boston Globe*, August 22, 1966, 17.

24. Lawrence E. Davies, "California Issue for '66 Emerges," *New York Times*, August 16, 1965, 1, 17; "Riots Give California Election a New Look," *Washington Post*, September 19, 1965, M4.

25. Schuparra, *Triumph of the Right*, xix, 146.

26. See Edmund G. Brown Sr., "Years of Growth, 1939–1966: Law Enforcement, Politics, and the Governor's Office," Regional Oral History, Bancroft Library, University of California, Berkeley, 266.

27. Mark Brilliant, *The Color of America Has Changed: How Racial Diversity Shaped Civil Rights Reform in California, 1941-1978* (Berkeley: University of California Press, 2010), 61.

28. Ethan Rarick, *California Rising: The Life and Times of Pat Brown* (Berkeley: University of California Press, 2005), 258–59; Earl C. Behrens, "Brown Hit for Help to Riders," *San Francisco Chronicle*, June 27, 1961, 7.

29. Edmund G. Brown Sr., "Years of Growth," 544.

30. Brown quoted in Rarick, *California Rising*, 267.

31. Tom Cameron, "State Realtors Declare War on New Housing Law," *Los Angeles Times*, September 27, 1963, A1.

32. Brilliant, *The Color of Race*, 190.

33. Earl C. Behrens, "Brown's View of Fight for Passage of Prop 14," *San Francisco Chronicle*, August 12, 1964, 14.

34. "Public Opinion on Civil Rights: Reflections on Civil Rights Act of 1964," blog, Roper Center, July 2, 1964, https://ropercenter.cornell.edu/blog/public-opinion -civil-rights-reflections-civil-rights-act-1964-blog.

35. For a discussion of the fight to preserve these Los Angeles neighborhoods from racial diversity, see Becky N. Nicolaides, *My Blue Heaven: Life and Politics in the Working-Class Suburbs of Los Angeles, 1920–1965* (Chicago: University of Chicago Press, 2002); see, also, Robert O. Self, *American Babylon: Race and the Struggle for Postwar Oakland* (Princeton, NJ: Princeton University Press, 2005).

36. Quoted in Lewis, *What Makes Reagan Run?*, 103.

37. Everett Andrews to Ronald Reagan, undated, Ronald Reagan Gubernatorial Campaign, Box C31, RRPL.

38. Gene Blake, "Proposition 14: The Cases for and Against," *Los Angeles Times*, September 20, 1964, K1, K2.

39. Quoted in Joshua D. Farrington, *Black Republicans and the Transformation of the GOP* (Philadelphia: University of Pennsylvania Press, 2016), 162.

40. "Reagan Cheered on U.C. Ideas," *Oakland Tribune*, April 2, 1966.

41. Robert Cohen, *Freedom's Orator: Mario Savio and the Radical Legacy of the 1960s* (New York: Oxford University Press, 2009), 43, 49–72.

42. See C. Michael Otten, *University Authority and the Student: The Berkeley Experience* (Berkeley: University of California Press, 1970), 112–27.

43. Peter Bart, "Reagan Enters Gubernatorial Race in California," *New York Times*, January 5, 1966.

44. George Goodman, "Reagan Dodges Stand on Prop 14," *Los Angeles Sentinel*, January 6, 1966, A2; Carl Greenberg, "Reagan Announces He's Candidate for Governor," *Los Angeles Times*, January 5, 1966, 35.

45. Quoted in Cannon, *Governor Reagan*, 153.

46. Paul T. Miller, *The Postwar Struggle for Civil Rights: African Americans in San Francisco, 1945–77* (New York: Routledge, 2009), 58.

47. For the most extensive treatment of the NNRA, see Rigueur, *The Loneliness of the Black Republican*, 55–92.

48. Dallek, *The Right Moment*, 198–204; Cannon, *Governor Reagan*, 142–44; Rigueur, *The Loneliness of the Black Republican*, 81–83; DeGroot, *Selling Ronald Reagan*, 167–71; "Reagan's Basic Plan: Ignore Negro Voters," *Los Angeles Sentinel*, July 21, 1966, A6.

49. Dallek, *The Right Moment*, 200.

50. Dallek, *The Right Moment*, 200–201.

51. Quoted in Boyarsky, *The Rise of Ronald Reagan*, 97; DeGroot, *Selling Ronald Reagan*, 167.

52. Carl Greenberg, "Christopher Sees GOP Losing Votes over Reagan Outburst," *Los Angeles Times*, March 11, 1966, 3.

53. Paul Beck, "Reagan Storms from Meeting of Negro GOP Unit," *Los Angeles Times*, March 6, 1966; "Reagan's Exit Stirs Negro G.O.P. Parley," *New York Times*, March 7, 1966, 53.

54. Dallek, *The Right Moment*, 199–202.

55. Citizens Committee to Elect Ronald Reagan Governor news release, March 6, 1966, Box 31C, Folder 1, 1966 Gubernatorial Campaign, RRPL.

56. On Reagan's rage at Conrad's cartoon, see Lyn Nofziger, *Nofziger* (Washington, DC: Regnery, 1992), 39–40; Carl Greenberg, "Reagan Walkout Led to Ire at Christopher," *Los Angeles Times*, March 10, 1966, 29.

57. Carl Greenberg, "Christopher Again Blasts Reagan," *Los Angeles Times*, March 29, 1966, 3.

58. Dave Hope, "Even Nice Guys Get Mad," *Oakland Tribune*, March 18, 1966; RR to Jack R. Rudder, Box 31C, Folder 2, 1966 Gubernatorial Campaign, RRPL; "Reagan Says Inaccuracies on Walkout," *Los Angeles Sentinel*, March 17, 1966.

59. "Prayers and Work," *Los Angeles Times*, March 16, 1966, 3; "Reagan Raps Handling of Watts Riots," *Chicago Defender*, April 2, 1966, 7.

60. Peter Bart, "Watts Riots Stirs Political Battle," *New York Times*, March 18, 1966, 24.

61. Reitman v. Mulkey, 64 Cal. 2d 877 (1966).

62. Bob Jackson, "Mixed Reaction to High Court Ruling," *Los Angeles Times*, May 11, 1966, 20.

63. Tom Wicker, "Reagan Shuns Image of Goldwater in Coast Race," *New York Times*, June 1, 1966, 38.

64. "California Primaries," *New York Times*, June 9, 1966, 46; quoted in Dallek, *The Right Moment*, 210–11.

65. Jackie Robinson, "Re[a]gan's Victory in California," *New York Amsterdam News*, June 18, 1966, 17.

66. "Ronald Reagan's New Tune," *Baltimore Afro-American*, July 2, 1966, 4.

67. "White Backlash Aided His Rivals, Brown Declares," *Los Angeles Times*, June 17, 1966, 3.

68. Dallek, *The Right Moment*, 226.

69. Rowland Evans and Robert Novak, "Inside Report: Watts in Cement," *Washington Post*, July 18, 1966, A17.

70. Darren Dochuk, *From Bible Belt to Sunbelt: Plain Folk Religion, Grass-Roots Politics, and the Rise of Evangelical Conservatism* (New York: W. W. Norton, 2010); see, also, McGirr, *Suburban Warriors*.

71. "Most Whites Found Oppose Civil Rights Demonstrations," *New York Times*, August 16, 1966, 24.

72. "Election 1966," *Saturday Evening Post*, November 15, 1966.

73. On Black Power, see Peniel E. Joseph, *Waiting 'Til the Midnight Hour: A Narrative History of Black Power in America* (New York: Henry Holt, 2006), 146.

74. "Civil Rights: The New Racism," *Time*, July 1, 1966, 11.

75. Gene Roberts, "Civil Rights: A Turning Point," *New York Times*, September 19, 1966, 1, 36.

76. Quoted in Ira Katznelson, *Fear Itself: The New Deal and the Origins of Our Time* (New York: Liveright, 2013), 15.

77. Quoted in Edsall and Edsall, *Chain Reaction*, 58.

78. John Herbers, "G.O.P. Will Press Racial Disorders as Election Issues," *New York Times*, October 4, 1966, 1.

79. "Backlash Is Found at a 4-Year Peak," *New York Times*, September 30, 1966, 39.

80. William Brink and Louis Harris, *Black and White: A Study of U.S. Racial Attitudes Today* (New York: Simon & Schuster, 1967), 21; "The White Backlash," *Newsweek*, October 10, 1966.

81. "Reagan Wins Demand," *Los Angeles Sentinel*, August 11, 1966, A6; Richard Bergholz, "GOP Calls for Revision on Housing," *Los Angeles Times*, August 7, 1966, B1, B12.

82. "White Consensus: They're Trying to Go Too Fast," *Newsweek*, August 22, 1966, 24–26.

83. Lawrence E. Davies, "Reagan Wooing the Farm Voters: On 3-Day Tour, He Charges Brown Broke Promises," *New York Times*, September 16, 1966, 27.

84. Rarick, *California Rising*, 356; Dallek, *The Right Moment*, 226; "Governor Signs Controversial Anti-Riot Measure, Negro Assemblyman Protests," *Sacramento Bee*, July 22, 1966, 4; "Brown Seeks Overhaul of Rumford Act," *Sacramento Bee*, August 13, 1966.

85. Rarick, *California Rising*, 358.

86. Quoted in Boyarsky, *The Rise of Ronald Reagan*, 101–2; Bill Boyarsky interview with author, Los Angeles, April 11, 2016.

87. Dallek, *The Right Moment*, 189; Michael Harris, "Reagan's View of the Riots," *San Francisco Chronicle*, September 30, 1966, 14; "Candidates Clash over Coast Riots," *New York Times*, October 2, 1966, 55.

88. "The San Francisco Riot," *Newsweek*, October 10, 1966, 28–29.

89. "Ronald Reagan for Real," *Time*, October 7, 1966, 31–35.

90. "Governor Brown Slips in Polls with Reagan," *Washington Post*, October 12, 1966, A2.

91. Lawrence E. Davies, "'White Backlash' Becomes a Major Coast Issue," *New York Times*, September 28, 1966, 28.

92. "Reagan Urges Carmichael Not to Speak at UC," *Los Angeles Times*, October 19, 1966, 25; Michael Flamm, *Law and Order: Street Crime, Civil Unrest, and the Crisis of Liberalism in the 1960s* (New York: Columbia University Press, 2005), 74.

93. Quoted in Rosenfeld, *Subversives*, 344; Seymour Korman, "Brown and Reagan Clash Over S.N.C.C.," *Chicago Tribune*, October 22, 1966, 10.

94. Stokely Carmichael, *Stokely Speaks: From Black Power to Pan Africanism* (Chicago: Chicago Review Press, 2007), 53; Lawrence E. Davies, "Carmichael Asks Draft's Defiance: Ridicules Johnson and Rusk at Rally in Berkeley," *New York Times*, October 30, 1966, 62.

95. "Transcript of Joint Conference by President, McNamara, and General Wheeler," *New York Times*, November 11, 1966, 18.

96. Johnson quoted in Taylor Branch, *At Canaan's Edge: America in the King Years, 1965–1968* (New York: Simon & Schuster, 2006), 548–49.

97. "Ronald Reagan on the Unrest on College Campuses, 1967," History Now, Gilder Lehrman Institute of American History, https://www.gilderlehrman.org /history-now/spotlight-primary-source/ronald-reagan-unrest-college-campuses -1967, accessed December 11, 2019.

98. Brink and Harris, *Black and White*, 111; John J. Goldman, "Pollsters Call Backlash Big Factor in Elections," *Los Angeles Times*, November 6, 1966, 2.

99. "Brown Assesses Backlash," *New York Times*, December 29, 1966, 14.

100. Quoted in Flamm, *Law and Order*, 70; Brown quoted in Rarick, *California Rising*, 357.

101. Minorities Division, Republican National Committee, Republicans and the Black Vote 1966, [1967], Folder Republican Party—RNC—Correspondence, 1967.

102. Earl Warren quoted in Miriam Pawel, *The Browns of California: The Family Dynasty that Transformed a State and a Nation* (New York: Bloomsbury, 2018), 173.

103. "Politics: The White Backlash, 1966," *Newsweek*, October 10, 1966, 27; "Backlash Is Found at a 4-Year Peak," *New York Times*, September 30, 1966, 39.

CHAPTER 4: REAGAN'S 1968 RACE FOR THE PRESIDENCY

1. "Dr. King Slashes Vietnam as Boon to Extreme Right," *Hartford Courant*, November 12, 1967, 7B.

2. Gladwin Hill, "Reagan Emerging in 1968 Spotlight," *New York Times*, November 10, 1966, 1, 29.

3. Wills, *Reagan's America*, 308; Stanley Plog, 1981, interview conducted with Stephen Stern, Special Collections, UCLA Oral History Project, 6.

4. Theodore H. White, *The Making of the President 1968* (New York: Athenaeum, 1969), 35; Thomas C. Reed, interview with author, April 1, 2016, Los Angeles.

5. Cannon, *Governor Reagan*, 258; White and Gill, *Why Reagan Won*, 88.

6. Quoted in Collins, *Transforming America*, 44; "Reagan Rules Out Race in '67: "I Have a Four-Year Contract,"" *Washington Post*, November 21, 1966, A9.

7. Wallace Turner, "Reagan Doubts He'll Be Drafted: But Says He Won't Tell the Party to 'Get Lost,'" *New York Times*, June 27, 1967, 24.

8. "Reagan Flying to Dixie to Counter Wallace Bid," *Washington Post*, July 20, 1968, A2; Gladwin Hill, "Reagan Compares Hecklers to Nazis," *New York Times*, July 29, 1968, 23.

9. Quoted in Diggins, *Ronald Reagan*, 116.

10. Quoted in Lewis, *What Makes Reagan Run?*, 163.

11. William T. Bagley, *California's Golden Years: When Government Worked and Why* (Berkeley, CA: Institute of Government Studies Press, 2009); William T. Bagley, interview with author, July 1, 2016, San Rafael, CA.

12. Nofziger, *Nofziger*, 60–61; Steven V. Roberts, "White House Confirms Reagan Followed Astrology, Up to a Point," *New York Times*, May 4, 1988, 1, B9.

13. Quoted in Johnson, *Sleepwalking through History*, 71.

14. Reagan, *My Turn*, 135.

15. Poll cited in Cannon, *Governor Reagan*, 209.

16. "Reagan Reluctantly Signs Bill Easing Abortions," *New York Times*, June 16, 1967, 24.

17. Cannon, *Governor Reagan*, 194; Bruce Bartlett, "Reagan's Forgotten Tax Record," *Capital Gains and Games*, February 22, 2011, http://capitalgainsandgames .com, accessed October 23, 2015; "Lawrence E. Davies, "California Gets Billion Tax Rise," *New York Times*, July 30, 1967, 26; "Reagan Wins $1 Billion Hike in Taxes," *Atlanta Journal and the Atlanta Constitution*, July 30, 1967, 6B.

18. "Cannon, *Governor Reagan*, 201; Carl Greenberg, "Reagan Appoints Rumford Act Foe Real Estate Chief: Smith," *Los Angeles Times*, January 17, 1967, 3; "Rumford Act Foe New Realty Chief," *Los Angeles Sentinel*, March 30, 1967, A2; "Smith's Confirmation Represents a Setback," *Los Angeles Sentinel*, April 6, 1967, A6.

19. Ronald Reagan, press conference transcript, April 18, 1967, Box 31, Press Unit, Speech and Press Conferences, RRPL; Seymour Korman, "Reagan Backs Lt. Governor on 1968 Ticket," *Chicago Tribune*, April 19, 1967, C1.

20. Reitman v. Mulkey, 387 U.S. 369 (1967); Fred Graham, "High Court Voids Fair-Housing Ban in California," *New York Times*, May 30, 1967, 1, 8.

21. Seymour Korman, "Reagan Seeks Changes in Fair Housing Law," *Chicago Tribune*, May 30, 1967, 12; Ray Zeman, "Rumford Up to Legislature, Reagan Asserts," *Los Angeles Times*, May 30, 1967, 3.

22. Cannon, *Governor Reagan*, 202; author interview, William T. Bagley, July 1, 2016, San Rafael, CA.

23. Jerry Gillam, "Rumford Act Revision Fails: Rumford Act Revision Killed By Legislature," *Los Angeles Times*, August 7, 1967, 1; Cannon, *Governor Reagan*, 204–5; Jerry Gillam, "Rumford Bill Remains in Doubt," *Los Angeles Times*, August 6, 1967; "Reagan Urges Senate to Pass Rumford Act Modification Bill, "*Los Angeles Times*, August 4, 1967.

24. Howard Seelye, "Legislators Gauge Reagan's Performance," *Los Angeles Times*, August 13, 1967.

25. "Reagan Denounces Open Housing Laws as Rights Violation," *New York Times*, September 27, 1967, 35.

26. Ronald Reagan, "On Becoming Governor," in *Governor Ronald Reagan and His Cabinet: An Introduction*, Oral History Office, Bancroft Library, University of California at Berkeley, January 19, 1979, 15; Cannon, *Governor Reagan*, 204.

27. On Reagan's receipt of information from Hoover's FBI, see Rosenfeld, *Subversives*, 1–8, 370–72. See, also, Daryl E. Lembke, "Kerr Fired as UC President in Surprise Vote by Regents: Reagans Sides With Majority in a 14 to 8 Decision," *Los Angeles Times*, January 21, 1967, 1.

28. Gladwin Hall, "Berkeley Faculty Rebukes Regents: Kerr Ouster Is Denounced as Betrayal of Trust," *New York Times*, January 25, 1967, 33.

29. "Reagan Presidential Chance Seen by Kerr," *Los Angeles Times*, March 30, 1967, A11.

30. Julius Duscha, "Reagan Succeeds with '67 Legislature," *Washington Post*, August 6, 1967, A11; Muchmore quoted in "California Fast Starts," *Time*, August 11, 1967, 17.

31. Warren Weaver Jr., "Reagan Asks Delay in Support of Nixon," *New York Times*, August 22, 1967, 1, 18.

32. On the Detroit riots, see Sidney Fine, *Violence in the Model City: The Cavanaugh Administration, Race Relations, and the Detroit Riots of 1967* (Lansing: Michigan State University Press, 2007).

33. See Richard Rothstein, *The Color of Law: A Forgotten History of How Our Government Has Segregated America* (New York: Liveright, 2017); on Detroit, see Thomas J. Sugrue, *The Origins of the Urban Crisis: Race and Politics in Post War Detroit* (Princeton, NJ: Princeton University Press, 1996).

34. Lawrence E. Davies, "Reagan Brands Those in Riots 'Mad Dogs against People,'" *New York Times*, July 26, 1967, 19; press conference of Governor Ronald Reagan, July 25, 1967, Box P1, Ronald Reagan Gubernatorial Papers (RRPG), 1966–1974, RRPL; "Reagan Sees Negroes to Forestall Disorder," *Washington Post*, July 20, 1967, A6.

35. "After the Riots: A Survey," *Newsweek*, August 21, 1967, 18–19.

36. Harris, *The Harris Survey*, September 11, 1967.

37. Martin Luther King Jr., *Where Do We Go from Here: Chaos or Community?* (Boston: Beacon Press, 1967), 107.

38. "Republicans: Anchors Aweigh," *Time*, October 20, 1967, 20; Gladwin Hall, "Reagan Aids G.O.P. in South Carolina; Wins Enthusiastic Reception at Fund-Raising Dinner," *New York Times*, September 30, 1967, 13; "Excerpts of Speech by Governor Ronald Reagan to South Carolina Republican State Committee," September 29, 1967, Box P17, RRPG, RRPL.

39. "Reagan Off and Running," *Baltimore Afro-American*, October 14, 1967, 4.

40. Brooke quoted in Rigueur, *The Loneliness of the Black Republican*, 99.

41. See Kabaservice, *Rule and Ruin*, 202.

42. "Romney Alone in GOP Shown Leading Johnson," *Washington Post*, November 20, 1966, A2.

43. Warren Weaver Jr., "Romney Assails Racial Injustice: He Urges Citizen Drive in Talk to Mormon Church," *New York Times*, February 20, 1967, 30.

44. John Herbers, "Romney Attacked Goldwater as Keyed to South," *New York Times*, November 29, 1966, 1, 35.

45. "The Bell Tolls for a Galloping Ghost," *Newsweek*, September 25, 1967, 27; Robert B. Semple Jr., "Romney Sees Need for a Major Effort to Prevent Rioting," *New York Times*, September 13, 1967, 1, 32; Kabaservice, *Rule and Ruin*, 215–16.

46. "Romney Claims He Was 'Brainwashed' on Vietnam Visit," *Los Angeles Times*, September 5, 1967, 1; Russell Baker, "The Sentencing of George Romney," *New York Times*, September 12, 1967, 46.

47. William Borders, "Reagan Keeps Smiling at Yale Despite Sneers and Hostile Air: Bitterness Noted," *New York Times*, December 7, 1967, 30.

48. Smith quoted in Kabaservice, *Rule and Ruin*, 240. For more on Michael C. Smith's 1968 report for the Ripon Society, see Johnson, *Sleepwalking through History*, 86–87; Michael C. Smith, "Here's the Rest of Him," *Ripon Forum*, June 1968, 13–32.

49. "Reagan's Racism Seen Underneath Ambiguous Talk," *Los Angeles Sentinel*, November 9, 1967, A8.

50. On Reagan's influence over Nixon, see Perlstein, *Nixonland*, xii, 94, 306, 747.

51. Joe McGinniss, *The Selling of the President, 1968* (New York: Trident Press, 1969), 190.

52. Lawrence E. Davies, "Reagan Disavows Primary Plan: Says He Has No Intention to Campaign in Election," *New York Times*, January 11, 1968, 23.

53. David S. Broder, "Reagan Banks Prairie Fire," *Washington Post*, January 14, 1968, B1; Stuart Spencer interview with author, March 28, 2016, Palm Desert, CA.

54. Thomas C. Reed, interview with author, April 1, 2016, Los Angeles.

55. Louis Harris, "Reagan Appeal to Voters Seems Weaker," *Washington Post*, January 15, 1968, A2.

56. Quoted in Martin Luther King Jr., "Beyond Vietnam—A Time to Break Silence," *Freedomways* 7, no. 2 (Spring 1967): 103–17.

57. On the fractious debates within the civil rights movement over the war, see Daniel S. Lucks, *Selma to Saigon: The Civil Rights Movement and the Vietnam War* (Lexington: University Press of Kentucky, 2014).

58. Reagan quoted in Timothy N. Thurber, "Goldwaterism Triumphant? Race and the Republican Party, 1965–1968," *Journal of Historical Society*, 7, no. 3 (August 2007): 369; Tom Wicker, "Reagan Questions Warren's Motive," *New York Times*, June 24, 1968, 1, 17; Ronald Goetz, "Reagan and the Poor," *Christian Century* (June 12, 1968): 776–77.

59. See Steven M. Gillon, *Separate and Unequal: The Kerner Commission and the Unraveling of American Liberalism* (New York: Basic Books, 2018); *Report of the National Advisory Commission on Civil Disorders* (New York: Bantam Books, 1968), 1.

60. Tom Goff, "Reagan Disputes Conclusion of U.S. Report on Disorders," *Los Angeles Times*, March 6, 1968; "Press Conference of Governor Ronald Reagan," March 5, 1968, Box P02, Ronald Reagan's Gubernatorial Papers 1966–1975, RRPL; "Reagan Interview," *U.S. News & World Report*, March 25, 1968.

61. Clay Risen, *A Nation on Fire: America in the Wake of the King Assassination* (New York: Wiley, 2009).

62. "Reagan to Address Capital Unit Today," *New York Times*, April 5, 1968, 33.

63. Ward Just, "The City Besieged: A Study in Ironies and Contrasts," *Washington Post*, April 6, 1968, A14.

64. "Press Release, April 5, 1968," Box P17, RRPG, 1966–1975, RRPL.

65. Lyndon B. Johnson, *The Vantage Point: Perspectives of the Presidency, 1963–1968* (New York: Holt, Rinehart and Winston, 1971), 176.

66. "120 Million Watched Funeral Service on TV," *New York Times*, April 10, 1968, 95.

67. "Nation: King's Last March," *Time*, April 19, 1968, 18.

68. "Press Release, Governor's Schedule, April 6, 1968 through April 14, 1968," Box P08, RRPG, 1966–1974, RRPL.

69. Gladwin Hill, "Reagan Not Sure Johnson Had Quit," *New York Times*, April 10, 1967, 20.

70. Thurmond quoted in Flamm, *Law and Order*, 145.

71. On the loathing of King, see Jason Sokol, *The Heavens Might Crack: The Death and Legacy of Martin Luther King, Jr.* (New York: Basic Books, 2018), 89–111; Ariel Edwards-Levy, "In 1968, Nearly a Third of Americans Said MLK Brought His Assassination on Himself," *Huffington Post*, April 4, 2018.

72. Gladwin Hill, "Reagan Steps Up a 'Noncandidacy,'" *New York Times*, April 14, 1968, 50; "Republicans: Rocky's Return," *Time*, April 19, 1968.

73. R. W. Apple, "'Choice' Offered by Rockefeller as He Joins Race," *New York Times*, May 1, 1968, 1, 30.

74. Quoted in White and Gill, *Why Reagan Won*, 109; Gladwin Hill, "Reagan Condemns Protests," *New York Times*, May 20, 1968, 39.

75. Jack Bass and Marilyn W. Thompson, *Ol' Strom: An Authorized Biography of Strom Thurmond* (Atlanta: Longstreet, 1998), 214–16; Tom Wicker, *One of Us: Richard Nixon and the American Dream* (New York: Random House, 1991), 342–43; Perlstein, *Nixonland*, 283–85; Crespino, *Strom Thurmond's America*, 209; Harry S. Dent, *The Prodigal South Returns to Power* (New York, Wiley, 1978), 82–83.

76. Robert B. Semple Jr., "Nixon Building Up Support in the South; G.OP.," *New York Times*, June 2, 1968, 27; "Mississippi for Nixon," *New York Times*, June 2, 1968, 26.

77. "Race Unrest Is Seen as Helping Reagan," *New York Times*, May 22, 1968, 31.

78. Hill, "Reagan Pressed 'Noncandidacy' in Visits to Florida and Chicago," 1, 28; Richard Corrigan, "Reagan Stars in Screen Test," *Washington Post*, May 26, 1968, A8; "Negress Chides Reagan at Florida GOP Lunch," *Boston Globe*, May 22, 1968, 22.

79. White and Gill, *Why Reagan Won*, 100; author interview with Thomas C. Reed, August 16, 2016, San Diego, CA.

80. Jack Newfield, *Robert Kennedy: A Memoir* (New York: E. P. Dutton, 1969), 250–51.

81. Author interview with Thomas C. Reed, August 16, 2016, San Diego, CA.

82. A. S. "Doc" Young, "Gov. Reagan Meets Minority 'Press,'" *Los Angeles Sentinel*, July 18, 1968, A1.

83. David S. Broder, "Reagan Would Be Beneficiary If Nixon Fails on 1st Ballot," *Washington Post*, July 16, 1968, A13.

84. "Press Conference of Governor Ronald Reagan Held June 25, 1968," RRPG, Box P2, RRPL.

85. Cannon, *Governor Reagan*, 265; "Reagan Flies to Dixie to Counter Wallace Bid," *Washington Post*, July 20, 1968, A2; "Reagan Says Wallace Bloc Should Vote Republican," *New York Times*, July 17, 1968, 30; "Press Conference of Governor Ronald Reagan Held July 16, 1968," Box P2, RRPG, RRPL; "Reagan Says Swing Is Aimed at Wallace," *New York Times*, July 16, 1968, 26; "Governor Ronald Reagan Visits Wallace Country," *Norfolk Journal and Guide*, July 20, 1968, B23.

86. Broder, "Reagan Would Be Beneficiary If Nixon Fails on 1st Ballot"; Gladwin Hall, "Reagan Looking to Later Ballots," *New York Times*, July 21, 1968, 46.

87. Lou Cannon, "Support for Reagan Grows in the South," *Washington Post*, November 18, 1973; A2; John Dillion, "Reagan Favorite of South GOP," *Christian Science Monitor*. December 11, 1973.

88. Warren Weaver Jr., "Wallace Gains Disturb Governors of Both Parties," *New York Times*, July 24, 1968, 25.

89. Carl Greenberg, "The Reagan Story: Anything Can Happen," *Los Angeles Times*, August 4, 1968, E2.

90. David S. Broder, "Reagan Stock Rises," *Washington Post*, July 29, 1968, A1, A2.

91. "Nixon Slips to 591," *Newsweek*, August 5, 1968, 22–23; "Nixon Votes in South Shift to Reagan, Survey Finds," *Chicago Tribune*, August 1, 1968, 20.

92. Perlstein, *Nixonland*, 785; Jules Witcover, *The Resurrection of Richard Nixon* (New York: G. P. Putnam's Sons, 1970), 326; "The Convention Countdown," *Newsweek*, August 12, 1968, 20; John W. Finner, "Nixon and Reagan Ask War on Crime," *New York Times*, August 1, 1968. 1, 20.

93. Fred P. Graham, "Warren Says All Share Crime Onus," *New York Times*, August 2, 1968, 1, 13.

94. Warren Weaver Jr., "Nixon Said to Want Rockefeller, Lindsay or Percy for 2nd Place," *New York Times*, August 5, 1968, 1, 24.

95. David S. Broder, "Nixon Backers Struggle to Hold South," *Washington Post*, August 6, 1968, A1.

96. White and Gill, *Why Reagan Won*, 117.

97. Quoted in Lewis Chester, Godfrey Hodson, and Bruce Page, *An American Melodrama: The Presidential Campaign of 1968* (New York: Viking, 1969), 437.

98. Dent, *Prodigal Son*, 89; Crespino, *Thurmond*, 219; Cahodas, *Strom Thurmond*, 398–400.

99. Rowland Evans and Robert Novak, "Thurmond Helped Nixon Forces Prevent Fla. Bolt," *Washington Post*, August 9, 1968, A21.

100. White and Gill, *Why Reagan Won*, 117–29.

101. William Chapman, "Reagan Pitch for Delegates Never Let Up," *Washington Post*, August 8, 1968, A6.

102. White and Gill, *Why Reagan Won*, 128.

103. "How Nixon Put It Together," *Newsweek*, August 19, 1968, 24–25.

104. Lawrence E. Davies, "Politics: Reagan, Denying 'Presidential Bug' Hints at Running for Governor Again," *New York Times*, August 14, 1968, 26.

105. RR to Francis H. Parkard, August 1, 1975, Citizens for Reagan, Box 9, Hoover Institution Archives, Stanford, CA (hereafter HIA).

106. Thomas C. Reed, interview with author, April 3, 2016. Reagan told journalist Elizabeth Drew in 1976 that he "never once lifted my finger" to run for the presidency in 1968. Elizabeth Drew, *An American Journal: The Events of 1976* (New York: Random House, 1977), 54.

107. See Kopelson, *Reagan's 1968 Dress Rehearsal*.

CHAPTER 5: THE PERFECT TARGETS

1. Steven V. Roberts, "Ronald Reagan Is Giving 'Em Heck," *New York Times Magazine*, October 25, 1970, SM22.

2. Michelle Reeves, "'Obey the Rules or Get Out': Ronald Reagan's 1966 Gubernatorial Campaign and the 'Trouble in Berkeley,'" *Southern California Quarterly* 92, no. 3 (Fall 2010): 275–305.

3. The uprising of Black students in the late 1960s and early 1970s was a national phenomenon. See Martha Biondi, *The Black Revolution on Campus* (Berkeley: University of California Press, 2012).

4. "Rights Campaign Begun in San Jose," *New York Times*, October 3, 1967, 33.

5. Arnold Hano, "The Black Rebel Who 'Whitelists' the Olympics," *New York Times*, May 21, 1968; "Olympic Boycott by Negroes Hit by Ronald Reagan," *Hartford Courant*, November 29, 1967, 53b.

6. Biondi, *The Black Revolution on Campus*, 43.

7. Steve Harvey, "20 Negro Students Seize Building at UC Santa Barbara," *Los Angeles Times*, October 15, 1968, 1, 20.

8. Gladwin Hill, "300 Seize College Building in Los Angeles Suburb," *New York Times*, November 5, 1968, 20.

9. "College Upsets Pact on Protest: Coast Aide Says Amnesty Was Vowed under Duress," *New York Times*, November 6, 1968, 30.

10. For accounts of the San Francisco State College strike, see Joshua Bloom and Waldo E. Martin, *Black against Empire: The History and Politics of the Black Panther Party* (Berkeley: University of California Press, 2013), 269–87, and Biondi, *The Black Revolution on Campus*, 43–78.

11. "The Demands of the Black Students Union," RRPG, undated, GO75, RRPL.

12. Biondi, *The Black Revolution on Campus*, 56.

13. Daryl Lembke, "Panther-Teacher Suspended by S.F. State College Chief," *Los Angeles Times*, November 9, 1968, 1, 14; Ron Moscowitz, "Dumke Orders Murray

Suspended," *San Francisco Chronicle*, November 1, 1968, 1, 12; Robert Rawitch, "Stormy Negro Students Force San Francisco State to Close," *Los Angeles Times*, November 7, 1968, B1; Robert Rawitch, "Small Explosion, Fires Hit S.F. College Campus," *Los Angeles Times*, November 8, 1968, 3.

14. "S.F. State Students, Cops in Wild Fight: Classes Suspended by Smith," *San Francisco Chronicle*, November 14, 1968, 1, 10–11; Wallace Turner, "College Closed after Protests: San Francisco State Will Be Shut Down Indefinitely," *New York Times*, November 14, 1968, 28.

15. "Reagan Is 'Shocked' at Closing of San Francisco State College," *New York Times*, November 15, 1968, 29.

16. Nancy Adler, "Head of San Francisco State Resigns," *New York Times*, November 27, 1968, 25.

17. Wallace Turner, "Classes Resume after Protest at College on Coast," *New York Times*, December 3, 1968, 29.

18. Wallace Turner, "Two Radical Students Seized as Reagan Urges 'Hard Line,'" *New York Times*, December 13, 1968, 14.

19. Steven V. Roberts, "Reagan Reaps Political Profit from Student Revolts on Coast," *New York Times*, February 10, 1969, 25; E. W. Kenworthy, "Reagan Confounds Critics with Growing Strength," *New York Times*, February 23, 1969, 44.

20. "Reagan Backs Officials," *New York Times*, January 6, 1969, 31; "Campus Fascists Rapped," *Chicago Defender*, January 8, 1969, 3; Lawrence E. Davies, "Reagan Promises to Rid Campuses of 'Anarchists,'" *New York Times*, January 8, 1969, 36; "Ronald Reagan Press Conference, January 8, 1969," Box P02, RRPL.

21. Gerard J. DeGroot, "Ronald Reagan and the Student Unrest in California," *Pacific Historical Review* 65, no. 1 (February 1996): 115–16.

22. Tom Goff, "Reagan May Ask Stiff Rules for Professors," *Los Angeles Times*, January 15, 1969, A3; John Dreyfuss, "Reagan Ties Faculty Jobs to Ideology," *Los Angeles Times*, March 27, 1969, 1, 32.

23. Steven V. Roberts, "Reagan Reaps Political Profit from Student Revolts on Coast," *New York Times*, February 10, 1969, 45; "Poll Finds Reagan at Popularity Peak," *New York Times*, February 28, 1969, 27; "Students: California Backlash," *Time*, March 14, 1969, 60; "Now, Wait a Minute," *Los Angeles Sentinel*, January 23, 1969, B4.

24. "University of Calif. Slates Panthers Cleaver Lectures, Stirs Storm," *Pittsburgh Courier*, September 28, 1968, 2; Bloom and Martin, *Black against Empire*, 136–38.

25. John Kifner, "Eldridge Cleaver, Black Panther Who Became GOP Conservative Is Dead at 62," *New York Times*, May 2, 1998, 1, 24.

26. On Cleaver and Berkeley, see Julie A. Reuben, "The Limits of Freedom: Students Activists and Educational Reform at Berkeley," in *The Free Speech Movement: Reflections on Berkeley in the 1960s*, ed. Robert Cohen and Reginald E. Zelnik (Berkeley: University of California Press, 2002), 485–505.

27. "Bid to Cleaver Scored by Reagan and Unruh," *New York Times*, September 18, 1968, 56.

28. Reagan quoted in Rosenfeld, *Subversives*, 425.

29. Lawrence E. Davies, "Cleaver Derides Reagan and 3 Candidates in Lecture at Stanford," *New York Times*, October 3, 1968, 22.

30. Rosenfeld, *Subversives*, 425.

31. Gladwin Hill, "Cleaver to Give Talk at Berkeley," *New York Times*, September 21, 1968, 14.

32. "Berkeley Faculty Says Regents Infringe on Academic Freedom," *New York Times*, October 4, 1968, 16.

33. "Black Conference Threatens Campaign against University," *Daily Californian*, October 3, 1968, 3; Bloom and Martin, *Black against Empire*, 137–38.

34. "Berkeley Campus Faces New Strife: Cleaver Issue Is Foremost as Fall Classes Begin," *New York Times*, September 29, 1968, 54; Lawrence E. Davies, "Races: Professor on Ice," *Time*, September 27, 1968, 19–20.

35. Lawrence E. Davies, "Cleaver to Give Berkeley Talks," *New York Times*, October 8, 1968, 75.

36. "Cleaver Lectures Class at UC Berkeley," *New York Times*, October 9, 1968, 94; "Cleaver Omits Obscenities in 'Scholarly' First UC Lecture," *Los Angeles Times*, October 9, 1968, 6; "Cleaver Stays Clean and Calm in U. of Cal. Talk," *Washington Post*, October 9, 1968, A3.

37. Rosenfeld, *Subversives*, 466–84.

38. "The Nation Deserves Better," *Oakland Tribune*, January 25, 1984.

39. "Nation: Occupied Berkeley," *Time*, May 30, 1969, 22–23.

40. DeGroot, "Ronald Reagan and Student Unrest in California," 117.

41. Cannon, *Governor Reagan*, 295.

42. Mervyn D. Field, "State Poll: Reagan's Rating," *San Francisco Chronicle*, August 27, 1974, 8.

43. William Trombley, "Admitted Red Fired from UCLA Faculty," *Los Angeles Times*, September 20, 1969, 1, 14; Lawrence E. Davies, "U.C.L.A. Teacher Is Ousted as Red," *New York Times*, September 20, 1968, 23, "Battle over Academic Freedom at U.C.L.A.," *New York Times*, October 12, 1969, 229.

44. "Hard on Communism," *Newsweek*, October 6, 1969, 101.

45. "Academic Freedom: The Case of Angela the Red," *Time*, October 17, 1969, 64.

46. Kenneth Reich, "UCLA Red Lays Ouster Proceedings to Racism," *Los Angeles Times*, September 24, 1969, 3.

47. Kenneth Reich, "2,000 Jam UCLA Hall to Hear First Lecture by Angela Davis," *Los Angeles Times*, October 7, 1969, 1.

48. "Angela Safe—for Awhile," *Los Angeles Sentinel*, October 23, 1969, A1; Rudy Villasenor, "Judge Pacht Upholds Rights of Individual," *Los Angeles Times*, October 21, 1969, 22.

49. Kendi, *Stamped from the Beginning*, 412.

50. Wallace Turner, "California Regents Drop Communist from Faculty," *New York Times*, June 20, 1970, 32; William Trombley, "Regents Refuse to Renew Miss Davis' UCLA Contract," *Los Angeles Times*, June 20, 1970, 1, 15.

51. Noel Greenwood, "Regents Reported in Agreement to Fire Angela Davis," *Los Angeles Times*, June 9, 1970, 1, 22.

52. "UCLA Regents Fire Militant Teacher," *Baltimore Afro-American*, June 27, 1970, 12.

53. "Education: The Governor v. the University," *Time*, March 30, 1970; Wallace Turner, "Reagan, Campus Critic, Gains Control of California Colleges," *New York Times*, August 11, 1970, 1, 26; William Trombley, "Conservatives Now Control Regents Board," *Los Angeles Times*, June 23, 1969, 1.

54. "Angela Davis: Black Revolutionary," *Newsweek*, October 26, 1970; "Crime: The Professor's Guns," *Time*, August 24, 1970, 13; "Angela Davis Is Indicted for Murder and Conspiracy on Coast," *New York Times*, November 12, 1970, 20.

55. "Chief Justice Burger," *Chicago Defender*, June 25, 1969, 15.

56. On the Haynsworth nomination, see Dean J. Kotlowski, "Trial by Error: Nixon, the Senate, and the Haynsworth Nomination," *Presidential Studies Quarterly* 26, no. 1 (Winter 1996): 71–91.

57. "Civil Libertarians Hit Haynsworth Selection," *Washington Post*, August 19, 1969, A6.

58. "Haynsworth Member of Jim Crow Richmond Club," *Baltimore Afro-American*, September 27, 1969, 27; "Haynsworth Casts Shadow Over Court," *Baltimore Afro-American*, October 4, 1969, 4.

59. Warren Weaver, "Roll-Call Is Tense: Dissidents of G.O.P. Join 38 Democrats in the Rejection," *New York Times*, November 22, 1969, 1, 20.

60. "Reagan Raps Rejection of Haynsworth," *Chicago Tribune*, November 22, 1969, W22; "Reagan Backs Nixon," *New York Times*, November 22, 1969, 20.

61. Hugh Graham Davis, "Richard Nixon and Civil Rights: Explaining an Enigma," *Presidential Studies Quarterly* 26, no. 1 (Winter 1996): 93–106.

62. Peter Kihss, "'Benign Neglect' on Race Proposed by Moynihan," *New York Times*, March 1, 1970, 1, 69.

63. For the most authoritative view on Nixon's complicated civil rights record, see Dean Kotlowski, *Nixon's Civil Rights: Politics, Principle and Policy* (Cambridge, MA: Harvard University Press, 2001); on Nixon's suburban strategy, see Matthew D. Lassiter, *The Silent Majority: Suburban Politics in the Sunbelt South* (Princeton, NJ: Princeton University Press, 2006), 1.

64. See Brilliant, *The Color of America Has Changed*, 234–38; Jack McCurdy, "L.A. Schools Given Integration Order," *Los Angeles Times*, February 12, 1970, 1, 22.

65. Reagan quoted in Charles M. Wollenberg, *Deliberate Speed: Segregation and Exclusion in California Schools, 1855–1975* (Berkeley: University of California Press, 1976), 178.

66. "Reagan to Fight Busing," *New York Times*, February 18, 1970, 26.

67. Tom Goff, "State to Support L.A. Schools Plea: Reagan Orders Full Help for Board in Integration Battle," *Los Angeles Times*, February 18, 1970, 1, 23.

68. Brilliant, *The Color of America Has Changed*, 237.

69. George Skelton, "Reagan Signs Bill Banning Busing," *Chicago Defender*, September 15, 1970, 2; "'Anti-Busing' Bill Gets Calif. Governors' OK," *Chicago Defender*, October 3, 1970, 31; Jerry Gillam, "Anti-Busing Bill Signed by Reagan," *Los Angeles Times*, September 15, 1970, 1, 22.

70. "NAACP Director Hits Gov.'s Anti-Busing Bill," *Los Angeles Sentinel*, September 24, 1970, A2.

71. On the 1970 campaign, see Cannon, *Governor Reagan*, 336–47.

72. Jack Thomas, "Reforming Welfare in the Reagan Style," *Boston Globe*, March 16, 1975, A1, A4; Wallace Turner, "Reagan Assailed on Tax Liability," *New York Times*, May 9, 1971, 41.

73. Ronald Reagan speech, July 10, 1967, RRPG 1966–75, Box GO19, Folder: Fraud, RRPL.

74. See, for example, Mrs. John Castanguay to Governor Reagan, July 29, 1970, RRGP 1966–75 GO153, RRPL.

75. Harold J. to Governor Reagan, September 15, 1970, Correspondence Unit, Administrative Box 1970/79½, RRPL.

76. Quoted in Steven V. Roberts, "Ronald Reagan Is Giving 'Em Heck," *New York Times Magazine*, October 25, 1970, SM22.

77. Earl Caldwell, "Hearst Abductors Score Food Plan in a New Tape," *New York Times*, March 10, 1974, 28.

78. Cannon, *Governor Reagan*, 342.

79. "Reagan Tells Plans to Reform Welfare System in California," *Chicago Tribune*, January 13, 1971, B6; Tom Goff, "Reagan Calls for Cuts in Welfare, Medicaid," *Washington Post*, January 13, 1971, A2.

80. Cannon, *Governor Reagan*, 349–52.

81. "Reagan Seeks Relief Cuts to Balance Peak Budget," *New York Times*, February 3, 1971, 1, 44; "$6.7 Billion Budget Proposed by Reagan," *Washington Post*, February 3, 1971, A2.

82. Steven V. Roberts, "Reagan: Critics Calls His Budget 'Political and Inhumane,'" *New York Times*, February 21, 1971, 221.

83. "Reagan Rebuffed on Bid to Unveil Welfare Reform," *New York Times*, February 27, 1971, 14.

84. Burton quoted in Garin Burbank, "Governor Reagan and California Welfare Reform: The Grand Compromise of 1971," *California History* 70, no. 3 (Fall 1991): 282.

85. William T. Bagley, interview with author, July 1, 2016, San Rafael, CA.

86. Leroy F. Aarons, "Reagan Proposes Virtual Freeze on State's Welfare, Health Aid," *Washington Post*, March 4, 1971, 1, A9.

87. Robert Fairbanks, "Governor's Welfare Proposals Scored by Democratic Leaders," *Los Angeles Times*, March 4, 1971, 1, 33.

88. On FAP, see Brian Steensland, *The Failed Welfare Revolution: America's Struggle over Guaranteed Federal Income* (Princeton, NJ: Princeton University Press, 2007).

89. Wallace Turner, "Reagan Proposes a Huge Reduction in California Welfare Rolls," *New York Times*, March 4, 1971, 1, 23.

90. Ronald Reagan," Welfare Is a Cancer," *New York Times*, April 1, 1971, 41; Wallace Turner, "Reagan Is Beset with Problems," *New York Times*, May 30, 1971, 30; Anthony Beilenson, February 25, 2016, Los Angeles.

91. Robert Fairbanks, "'True' Reform of Welfare Is Reagan Hope," *Los Angeles Times*, July 23, 1971, 27.

92. Tom Goff, "Senate Committee Kills Reagan Program for Welfare Reform," *Los Angeles Times*, June 10, 1971, 1; Cannon, *Governor Reagan*, 353.

93. Anthony C. Beilenson, *California Years*, vol. II of *Looking Back: A Memoir* (self-published, 2012), 147–48.

94. "Legislative Panel Kills Reagan Plan on Welfare Reform," *New York Times*, June 11, 1971, 14; Beilenson, *Looking Back*, 148–52.

95. Cannon, *Governor Reagan*, 354–63; Bill Stall, "How Moretti, Reagan Ironed Out Bill on Welfare Reform," *Los Angeles Times*, August 14, 1971, 1, 14; "California Legislature Approves Welfare Reform Bill after Compromise with Reagan," *New York Times*, August 12, 1971, 24.

96. Miller quoted in Steven V. Roberts, "Welfare Reform Is This Year's 'Ecology,'" *New York Times*, August 15, 1971, E7.

97. Leo Rennert, "Reagan Expected to Use Reform Plan as Springboard," *Sacramento Bee*, September 13, 1974.

98. John Balzar, "Reagan Was Lucky: Two Other Factors, Not Reform, Responsible for Welfare Decrease," *Los Angeles Sentinel*, February 21, 1974, C7; Beilenson, *Looking Back*, 162–63.

99. Anthony Beilenson, interview with author, February 25, 2016, Los Angeles, CA.

100. David Broder, "GOP Left Speechless by Agnew Headlines," *Washington Post*, August 8, 1973, A1, A9.

101. Stephen Badrich, "Innocent Until Proven?," letter to the editor, *Washington Post*, August 11, 1973, A17.

102. Neil Mehler, "Pardon for Nixon Won't Help G.O.P., Reagan Says Here," *Chicago Tribune*, September 12, 1974, 3; Cannon, *Governor Reagan*, 386.

103. Reed, *The Reagan Enigma*, 204.

104. "Reagan Reveals He Was Not Consulted by Ford on VP," interview with Jeffrey St. John, TVN NewsService, August 24, 1974, Citizens for Reagan Records, Box 13, Folder 3, HIA.

105. On Proposition 1, see Cannon, *Governor Reagan*, 369–79; Garin Burbank, "Governor Reagan's Only Defeat: The Proposition 1 Campaign in 1973," *California History* 72, no. 4 (Winter 1993/94): 360–73; Jerry Gillam, "$436,452 Spent in Qualifying Reagan Tax Measure for Ballot," *Los Angeles Times*, August 1, 1973, 3C.

106. "No on Prop. 1," *Los Angeles Sentinel*, November 1, 1973, A6.

107. Mervin D. Field, "Reagan's Rating," *San Francisco Chronicle*, August 27, 1974, 8.

108. Michael Coakley, "Gov. Reagan Left His Mark in California," *Chicago Tribune*, February 18, 1976, 1, 4.

109. Bagley, *California's Golden Years*, 59.

110. Quoted in Joan Liebman, "Keeping Busy Won't Be a Problem for Ronald Reagan," *Wall Street Journal*, January 15, 1975, 1, 28.

111. Tom Goff, "Reagan Never Got His Act Together: Reagan Thwarted as Governor," *Los Angeles Times*, November 21, 1975, A12.

112. Johnson, *Sleepwalking through History*, 56.

113. William T. Bagley, Reagan Gubernatorial Oral History Project, Bancroft Library, University of California, Berkeley, December 21, 1981, interview conducted by Gabrielle Morris, 20a; author interview with William T. Bagley, July 1, 2016. San Rafael, CA.

114. O'Reilly, *Nixon's Piano*, 357.

115. "Bob Keyes, Governor's 'Trouble Shooter,'" *Sacramento Observer*, March 25, 1971, B1.

116. Jim Cleaver, "Political Potpourri," *Los Angeles Sentinel*, October 2, 1975, A2; A. S. "Doc" Young, "A 'Dangerous' Political Year," *Los Angeles Sentinel*, June 17, 1976, A7.

117. Nofziger, *Nofziger*, 244; Kenneth Reich, "Reagan Again Clarifies Rhodesia Remark," *Los Angeles Times*, June 7, 1976, 5.

118. "Lockheed Director Dies at Home," *Los Angeles Sentinel*, July 20, 1978, A20; on Keyes, see, also, Mayer, *Running on Race*, 164–65.

CHAPTER 6: REAGAN'S NEAR MISS IN 1976

1. Lou Cannon, "Support for Reagan Grows in South," *Washington Post*, November 18, 1973, A2.

2. Reston quoted in Jules Witcover, *Marathon: The Pursuit of the Presidency, 1972–1976* (New York: Viking Press, 1977), 64.

3. Christopher Lydon, "G.O.P. Right Wing Seems to Rule Out Support for Ford for 1976 Campaign," *New York Times*, February 10, 1975, 18.

4. "G.O.P. Role Sought by Conservatives; Some at Conference Back Forming a Third Party," *New York Times*, March 2, 1975, 42; William Rusher, "Speculation on a New Party . . . Under the Banner of a Conservative Party," *Human Events*, November 9, 1974, 12; Drummond D. Ayers, "Wallace Is Close to G.O.P.-Oriented Group," *New York Times*, June 22, 1975, 34; William A. Rusher to Ronald Reagan, October 7, 1975, Citizens for Reagan, Box 11, HIA.

5. Robert Shogan, "Dream of Reagan-Wallace Ticket: Right-Wing, Populist Coalition Sought," *Los Angeles Times*, June 1, 1975, A1, 18; Kevin B. Phillips, "Which Way for Conservatives? Reagan and Wallace in 1976," *Human Events*, November 9, 1974, 12.

6. R. W. Apple Jr., "Study of 3d Party for '76 Approved by Conservatives," *New York Times*, February 16, 1975, 1, 12.

7. Rigueur, *The Loneliness of the Black Republican*, 224–25.

8. Lou Cannon, "Support for Reagan Grows in South," *Washington Post*, November 18, 1973, A2.

9. William A. Link, *Righteous Warrior: Jesse Helms and the Rise of Modern Conservatism* (New York: St. Martin's Press, 2008). 147.

10. Link, *Righteous Warrior*, 51; Ernest B. Furgurson, *Hard Right: The Rise of Jesse Helms* (New York: W. W. Norton, 1986), 51.

11. "Thunder from the Right," *New York Times*, February 8, 1981.

12. Link, *Righteous Warrior*, 148.

13. "Black Solons Cool to Ford," *Chicago Defender*, December 8, 1973, 1; see, also, Simeon Booker, "Blacks View Vice President," *Ebony*, November 1, 1973.

14. Roy Wilkins with Tom Mathews, *Standing Fast: The Autobiography of Roy Wilkins* (New York: Da Capo Press, 1982), 339.

15. Jon Nordheimer, "Reagan Enters Campaign Seeks a Curb on Spending," *New York Times*, November 21, 1975, 1, 20.

16. Witcover, *Marathon*, 95.

17. Lou Cannon, "Reagan: Sense of Purpose," *Washington Post*, November 23, 1975, A1, A14, A15; "Reagan Pledges to Keep GOP Together," *Daily Times-News*, November 22, 1975, 1.

18. Witcover, *Marathon*, 95; Perlstein, *Invisible Bridge*, 554.

19. Reagan quoted in Witcover, *Marathon*, 95; see, also, Lou Cannon, "Reagan: Sense of Purpose," *Washington Post*, November 23, 1975, A1, A14, A15; Richard Bergholz, "Reagan Returns from Whirlwind 2-Day Trip to Launch Presidential Campaign," *Los Angeles Times*, November 22, 1975, 28; "Reagan on Protest," *Baltimore Sun*, November 24, 1975, A1.

20. Lou Cannon, *President Reagan: The Role of a Lifetime* (New York: Simon & Schuster, 1991), 486; see, also, James Kahn, "Blumenthal, Reagan, and the Big Lie,"

American Thinker, May 30, 2010; Christine Knauer, *Let Us Fight as Free Men: Black Soldiers and Civil Rights* (Philadelphia: University of Pennsylvania Press, 2014).

21. Cannon, *Reagan*, 428–31; see, also, James Kahn, "Blumenthal, Reagan, and the Big Lie," *American Thinker*, May 30, 2010.

22. "'Welfare Queen' Becomes Issue in Reagan Campaign," *New York Times*, February 15, 1976, 51.

23. Julilly Kohlman-Hausman, "Welfare Crises, Penal Solution, and the Origins of the 'Welfare Queen,'" *Journal of Urban History* 41 no. 2 (2015): 756–71.

24. Quoted in Drew, *An American Journal*, 52.

25. Perlstein, *Invisible Bridge*, 603–4; Josh Levin, "The Welfare Queen," *Slate*, December 19, 2013.

26. "The Reagan Record," Citizens for Reagan, Box 11, Folder 9, HIA.

27. Louis Harris, "Majority Ambivalent on Welfare," *Chicago Tribune*, June 10, 1976, A4.

28. John Fialka, "Reagan's Stories Don't Always Check Out," *Washington Star*, February 9, 1976.

29. "'Welfare Queen' Becomes Issue in Reagan Campaign," *New York Times*, February 15, 1976, 51.

30. Investigative reporter Josh Levin recently uncovered salacious evidence that Linda Taylor was not merely a welfare cheat but also a con artist, a kidnapper, and possibly a murderer. In spite of her transgressions, Reagan provided a playbook to demonize and racially caricaturize present and future welfare recipients. See Josh Levin, *The Queen: The Forgotten Life Behind an American Myth* (New York: Little, Brown, 2019).

31. John Fialka, "Reagan's Stories Don't Always Add Up," *Washington Star*, February 9, 1976; Benjamin Taylor, "Ronald Reagan: The Rhetoric vs. the Record," *Boston Globe*, January 4, 1976, A1.

32. Witcover, *Marathon*, 389.

33. Witcover, *Marathon*, 389.

34. John Fialka, "Reagan's Stories Don't Always Add Up," *Washington Star*, February 9, 1976; Perlstein, *The Invisible Bridge*, 604.

35. John Nordheimer, "Reagan Is Picking His Florida Spots: His Campaign Aides Aim for New G.O.P. Voters in Strategic Areas," *New York Times*, February 5, 1976, 24.

36. Witcover, *Marathon*, 410.

37. Nofziger quoted in Furgurson, *Hard Right*, 117; Lyn Nofziger, Miller Center of Public Affairs, University of Virginia, Oral History Project, March 6, 2003, 16; Nofziger, *Nofziger*, 179–80; Drew, *American Journal*, 237.

38. "Jesse Helms Direct Mail Letter," Citizens for Reagan, Box 31, HIA; Link, *Righteous Warrior*, 148–49.

39. Bill Peterson, "Reagan Nominee Details Segregationist Activities," *Washington Post*, July 27, 1983, A3.

40. "Helms Is Named Chairman of the North Carolina Reagan Committee," October 27, 1975, Citizens for Reagan, Box 31, HIA.

41. Kevin Sack, "As Helms Exits, a Conservative Crusader Will Carry On," *New York Times*, August 25, 2001; Link, *Righteous Warrior*, 152.

42. "Excerpts by the Hon. Ronald Reagan at Florida Appearances," March 7, 1976, Citizens for Reagan, Box 39, HIA.

43. Ferrel Guillory, "Ford Says Brooke Prospect for No. 2 Post," *News and Observer*, November 15, 1975, clipping found in Citizens for Reagan, Box 31, HIA.

44. James M. Naughton, "Reagan Halts a Pamphlet Linking Ford to Brooke," *New York Times*, March 21, 1976, 43.

45. Ferrel Guillory, telephone interview with author, June 7, 2016.

46. Link, *Righteous Warrior*, 152–53. See, also, Shirley, *Reagan's Revolution*, 163.

47. "Reagan Cancels Flyers Having Racial Overtones," *Boston Globe*, March 22, 1976, 6.

48. Shirley, *Reagan's Revolution*, 163–64; William Bennett, *From a World at War to the Triumph of Freedom*, vol. II, *America: The Last Best Hope* (Nashville: Thomas Nelson, 2007), 455.

49. Perlstein, *Invisible Bridge*, 647.

50. R. W. Apple Jr., "Reagan Tops Ford in N. Carolina for First Triumph in a Primary," *New York Times*, March 24, 1976, 1, 20; Mary McGrory, "Reagan Stunned by N.C. Win," *Boston Globe*, March 27, 1976, 6; "Reagan Spurts Back into Race against All the Odds," *Guardian*, March 25, 1976, 2.

51. Lou Cannon, "Reagan Stuck to Battle Plan for Victory," *Washington Post*, March 24, 1976, A6; Cannon, *Governor Reagan*, 426.

52. "Helms-Reagan Victory," *Raleigh Times*, March 25, 1976; Cannon, *Reagan*, 426.

53. William Safire, "Whole New Ball Game," *New York Times*, March 25, 1976, 35; "Reagan Gets a New Life," *Newsweek*, April 5, 1976, 15.

54. John Chamberlain, "North Carolina Results Show the Effectiveness of a Change in Tactics," Citizens for Reagan, Box 33, Folder 5, HIA.

55. Kenneth Reich, "Reagan Short on Money. Gives up Jet: Halt in U.S. Campaign Funds Blamed," *Los Angeles Times*, April 3, 1976, A6; R. W. Apple, "Uphill Fight for Reagan, Carter Despite North Carolina Victories," *New York Times*, March 25, 1976, 30.

56. Lou Cannon, "Reagan Seeking New Start in Texas," *Washington Post*, April 5, 1976, A1.

57. Rowland Evans and Robert Novak, "In Texas, a Wallace-to-Reagan Switch," *Washington Post*, April 21, 1976, A15.

58. "Busing in Dallas Is Set by Judge," *New York Times*, March 11, 1976, 30; Mark Siebel, "Appeal of Mixing Order Expected," *Dallas Morning News*, March 11, 1976, 1.

59. Lou Cannon, "Reagan Takes Aim at 'Forced Busing,'" *Washington Post*, June 3, 1976, A16.

60. Shirley, *Reagan's Revolution*, 191.

61. "Carter Leads Wallace in the South, Poll Indicates," *New York Times*, March 3, 1976, 17; B. Drummond Ayers Jr., "His Health Problem Erodes Even-Hard Core Support: For Wallace, It's All Over but the Exit," *New York Times*, April 11, 1976, 143; see, also, Dan T. Carter, *The Politics of Rage: George Wallace, the Origins of the New Conservatism, and the Transformation of American Politics* (New York: Simon & Schuster, 1995), 458–59; Witcover, *Marathon*, 255–73.

62. Millirons quoted in Gilbert Garcia, *Reagan's Comeback: Four Weeks in Texas That Changed American Politics Forever* (San Antonio, TX: Trinity University Press, 2012), 60–61; Witcover, *Marathon*, 419.

63. Bill McAllister, "U.S. School Suits Hit by Reagan," *Washington Post*, April 30, 1976, A9.

64. "Earl Lively Memo," undated, Peter Hannaford Papers, Box 6, HIA.

65. James P. Sterba, "Democratic Vote Propels Reagan to Texas Sweep; Large Crossover Is Cited," *New York Times*, May 2, 1976, 1, 36; Kenneth Reich, "Reagan Sweeps Texas Primary," *Los Angeles Times*, May 2, 1976; Carolyn Barta, "GOP Voting Strong: Heavy Cross-Over of Democrats Suspected," *Dallas Morning News*, May 2, 1976, 1.

66. Bill Montgomery, "Crossovers Key in GOP Primary," *Atlanta Constitution*, May 1, 1976, 1, 22.

67. "Reagan Holds Edge," *Atlanta Constitution*, May 2, 1976, 22.

68. Frederick Allen, "Reagan Stuns Ford in Georgia," *Atlanta Constitution*, May 5, 1976, 1, 6A.

69. Witcover, *Marathon*, 419–21.

70. Kenneth Reich, "Reagan Wins Indiana, Georgia and Alabama," *Los Angeles Times*, May 5, 1976, 5, 10; Shirley, *Reagan's Revolution*, 199.

71. David Nyhan, "The Possible Catastrophe for the Ford Candidacy," *Boston Globe*, May 13, 1976, 1.

72. Jonathan Steele, "Smell of Defeat in the Ford Camp," *Guardian*, May 13, 1976, 1.

73. William K. Stevens, "Wallace Voters Lean Reagan in Michigan," *New York Times*, May 11, 1976; Saul Friedman, "Wallace Voters Hold the Key," *Detroit Free Press*, May 16, 1976, 1A, 12A.

74. On Dewey Burton, see Jefferson Cowie: *Staying' Alive: The 1970s and the Last Days of the Working Class* (New York: New Press, 2011), 1–19; Nan Robertson, "Michigan 'Primary Jumper' Explains Why He Is Planning to Vote for Reagan," *New York Times*, May 18, 1976, 18.

75. Witcover, *Marathon*, 423.

76. Remer Tyson, "Ford Breezes Past Reagan," *Detroit Free Press*, May 19, 1976, 1A, 5A.

77. David Nyhan, "The Possible Catastrophe for the Ford Candidacy," *Boston Globe*, May 13, 1976, 1, 20.

78. Witcover, *Marathon*, 425–26; Joe Rosenbloom, "Carter and Reagan Tell It as South Wants to Hear It," *Boston Globe*, May 24, 1976, 1, 10.

79. Michael T. Kaufman, "Kissinger Begins His Tour in Kenya," *New York Times*, April 25, 1976, 5; "Kissinger Pressures Rhodesia to Yield to Rule by Blacks," *Boston Globe*, April 28, 1976, 1; "Kissinger in Africa," *Newsweek*, May 10, 1976, 50–51.

80. Curtis, "'Will the Jungle Take Over?,'" 1–27.

81. Jon Nordheimer, "Reagan Attacks Kissinger for His Stand on Rhodesia," *New York Times*, May 1, 1976, 10; "Talk of Rhodesian War Greets Kissinger Tour," *Dallas Morning News*, April 27, 1976, 6; Stewart Davis, "Africa 'Adventure' Unsettles Reagan," *Dallas Morning News*, May 1, 1976, 24A.

82. See Neil R. McMillen, *The Citizens' Council: Organized Resistance to the Second Reconstruction, 1954–1964*, new ed. (Urbana: University of Illinois Press, 1994), xiii.

83. "A President in Jeopardy," *Newsweek*, May 17, 1976, 26.

84. Witcover, *Marathon*, 430–31; Perlstein, *Invisible Bridge*, 698–99; Shirley, *Reagan's Revolution*, 235–36.

85. Simon Winchester, "Reagan in a Mess over Rhodesia," *Guardian*, June 4, 1976, 1.

86. Michael Harris, "Reagan Would Send GIs to Avert Rhodesia War: New Issue Injected," *San Francisco Chronicle*, June 3, 1976, 1, 22; "Shooting from the Hip Again," *San Francisco Chronicle*, June 4, 1976, 44.

87. Robert Lindsay, "Rhodesia Remark Is Dogging Reagan," *New York Times*, June 4, 1976, 12.

88. Lou Cannon, "Reagan Clarifies His Stance on U.S. Troops in Rhodesia," *Washington Post*, June 4, 1976, A6; Michael Harris, "Reagan Says He Didn't Mean GIS Should Fit in Rhodesia," *San Francisco Chronicle*, June 4, 1976, 1, 28; Witcover, *Marathon*, 431.

89. "Reagan in Disneyland," *New York Times*, June 8, 1976, 31.

90. Kenneth Reich, "Reagan Again Clarifies Rhodesia Remark," *Los Angeles Times*, June 7, 1976, 5.

91. "Reagan's Rhodesian Expeditionary Force," *Time*, June 14, 1976, 15–16.

92. Author interview with Stuart Spencer, March 28, 2016, Palm Desert, CA.

93. Andy Cooper, "One Man's Opinion: Brooklyn Political Scene," *New York Amsterdam News*, June 19, 1976, B1.

94. "Reagan and Rhodesia," *Pittsburgh Courier*, May 22, 1976, 6.

95. "Setback for Reagan Is Reported by Poll," *New York Times*, July 18, 1976, 38; Lou Cannon, "Reagan's Camp: An Air of Resignation," *Washington Post*, July 19, 1976, A1, A5; Dennis Farney, "An Uphill Battle: Reagan Forces Beset by Reverses," *Wall Street Journal*, July 19, 1976, 1.

96. On the racist elements of Carter's 1970 primary campaign against Carl Sanders, see Betty Glad, *Jimmy Carter: In Search of the Great White House* (New York: W.W. Norton, 1980), 132–35.

97. Barbara Reynolds, "Black Vote Responds to Carter," *Chicago Tribune*, May 14, 1976, 4; A. S. "Doc" Young, "Convention Comments," *Los Angeles Sentinel*, July 15, 1976, A7; "Carter for President," *Oakland Post*, May 26, 1976, 4; "Andrew Young to Visit Bay on Carter's Behalf," *Oakland Post*, May 5, 1976, 1.

98. Ethel Payne, "From Where I Sit: Barbara Jordan Is Truly a Woman for All Seasons," *Tri-State Defender*, July 24, 1976, 5.

99. "Reflections of the Democratic Convention," *San Francisco Sun Reporter*, July 24, 1976, 1.

100. Benjamin E. Mayes, "My View: Black and White Democrats Unite on Issues at Convention," *Tri-State Defender*, August 14, 1976, 5; "Carter's Margin in Gallup Poll Now 2–1 over Ford or Reagan," *New York Times*, August 1, 1976, 28; Louis Harris, "Carter Polls 'Massive' Lead on Ford, Reagan," *Chicago Tribune*, July 26, 1976, A4.

101. "Ford and Reagan," *Pittsburgh Courier*, August 7, 1976, 6.

102. Witcover, *Marathon*, 465–68.

103. "A Bold Move, But," *Birmingham World*, July 31, 1976, 4; Reagan's 'Coup,'" *Baltimore Afro-American*, August 7, 1976, 4.

104. B. Drummond Ayers, "Schweiker Bids for Votes of the 76 Black Delegates," *New York Times*, August 15, 1976, 25; Vernon Jarrett, "Schweiker Woos Black Delegates," *Chicago Tribune*, A4.

105. Vernon Jarrett, "Reagan Courts Black Delegates," *Chicago Tribune*, August 18, 1976, B3.

106. Vernon Jarrett, "Could Reagan Be Sold to Blacks?," *Chicago Tribune*, August 15, 1976, A6.

107. "The Plight of the GOP," *Time*, August 23, 1976, 12.

108. On the import of Reagan's 1976 bid, see Shirley, *Reagan's Revolution*; see, also, E.J. Dionne Jr., *Why the Right Went Wrong: American Conservatism—from Goldwater to the Tea Party and Beyond* (New York: Simon and Schuster, 2016), 78–81.

CHAPTER 7: LET'S MAKE AMERICA GREAT AGAIN

1. "Martin Luther King, Sr. Sees 'A Long Way to Go,'" *Indianapolis Recorder*, March 15, 1980, 1.

2. Ethel Payne, "The Real Ronald Reagan," *Baltimore Afro-American*, April 5, 1980, 5.

3. Gary Wills, "Scene 3: Ron and Destiny," *Esquire*, August 1980, 36.

4. David Broder, "Carter Wins a Narrow Victory with Near Sweep of the South," *Washington Post*, November 3, 1976, A1; Jack Bass, "Jimmy Carter: Off on a Southern Tide," *Los Angeles Times*, November 17, 1976, D7.

5. Austin Scott, "Study Shows Carter's Share of the Black Vote at 94 Percent," *Washington Post*, November 5, 1976, A10; "94 Pct. of Black Vote Went to Carter, Study Reports," *Washington Post*, November 11, 1976, A22; "Carter Harvests Black Vote," *Pittsburgh Courier*, November 13, 1976, 1.

6. "The Election; Jimmy's Debt to Blacks—and Others," *Time*, November 22, 1976, 16; Rigueur, *The Loneliness of the Black Republican*, 263.

7. "Could Have Beaten Carter—Reagan: Watergate Wouldn't Have Been Issue," *Los Angeles Times*, December 6, 1976.

8. Murray Kempton, "Born-Again Republicans," *Harper's*, November 1976, 43.

9. See Cannon, *Governor Reagan*, 437–42.

10. Rowland Evans and Robert Novak, "Another Round for Reagan?," *Washington Post*, March 2, 1977, A19; "Reagan Plans Discussions on TV to Raise Money and Followers," *New York Times*, April 28, 1977, 95.

11. Kiron Skinner, Annelise Anderson, and Martin Anderson, eds., *Reagan's Path to Victory: The Shaping of Ronald Reagan's Vision; Selected Writings* (New York: Free Press, 2004), 103.

12. Mary McGrory, "Congress Baffled by Aloof Carter," *Chicago Tribune*, June 17, 1977, B4.

13. Hedrick Smith, "Problems of a Problem Solver," *New York Times*, January 8, 1978, S8.

14. On the 1970s, see Bruce J. Schulman, *The Seventies: The Great Shift in American Culture, Society, and Politics* (New York: Free Press, 2001).

15. "Born Again: 'The Year of the Evangelicals,'" *Newsweek*, October 25, 1976, 68–78.

16. William Martin, *With God on Our Side: The Rise of the Religious Right in America* (New York: Broadway, 1996), 168–73; Hodgson, *The World Turned Right Side Up*, 171–72.

17. See Robert Freedman, "The Religious Right and the Carter Administration," *Historical Journal* 48, no. 1 (March 2005): 231–60.

18. See Joseph Crespino, "Civil Rights and the Religious Right," in *Rightward Bound: Making America Conservative in the 1970s*, ed. Bruce J. Schulman and Julian Zelizer (Cambridge, MA: Harvard University Press, 2008), 90–105; Russell

Chandler, "'Christian Voice' Political Action Group Plans Massive Drive on Reagan's Behalf," *Los Angeles Times*, March 6, 1980, B10.

19. William Brock, telephone interview with author, October 24, 2016.

20. See Joseph Crespino, *In Search of Another Country: Mississippi and the Conservative Counterrevolution* (Princeton, NJ: Princeton University Press, 2007), 228, 237–66.

21. Mondale quoted in Crespino, *In Search of Another Country*, 229–30.

22. Fred P. Graham, "Federal Judges Rule Out Benefit for Segregated 'Academies,'" *New York Times*, January 14, 1970, 1, 26.

23. "A Brief for Injustice," *New York Times*, May 18, 1970, 28.

24. Crespino, *In Search of Another Country*, 252–56.

25. Edsall and Edsall, *Chain Reaction*, 131–32; Peter Skerry, "Christian Schools Versus the IRS," *Public Interest* 61 (Fall 1980): 18–41; Steven Rattner, "Washington Watch: Private Schools and I.R.S. Test," *New York Times*, December 4, 1978, D2.

26. Crespino, *In Search of Another Country*, 252–56.

27. Edsall and Edsall, *Chain Reaction*, 132; A. O. Sulzberger Jr., "Private Academies Protest Tax Plan," *New York Times*, December 11, 1978, A20.

28. Weyrich quoted in Dominic Sandbrook, *Mad as Hell: The Crisis of the 1970s and the Rise of the Populist Right* (New York: Knopf, 2011), 357.

29. Billings quoted in Edsall and Edsall, *Chain Reaction*, 133.

30. Russell Chandler, "IRS Reconsiders Plan on School Taxing: Storm of Protest Hits Proposal to Remove Religious Exemption," *Los Angeles Times*, December 16, 1978, C18.

31. William J. Eaton, "IRS Private School Plan 'Repulsive,' Senator Says," *Los Angeles Times*, December 6, 1978, 13.

32. Mitchell quoted in Skerry, "Christian Schools Versus the I.R.S.," 19.

33. Crespino, *In Search of Another Country*, 254; "Private Schools Practice Bias but Pay No Taxes," *Baltimore Afro-American*, March 3, 1979, 6.

34. Kiron K. Skinner, Annelise Anderson, and Martin Anderson, eds., *Reagan in His Own Hand: The Writings of Ronald Reagan That Reveal His Revolutionary Vision for America* (New York: Free Press, 2001), 354–55.

35. "83% in Poll Oppose Reverse Bias Plans," *New York Times*, May 1, 1977, 33.

36. "A Coast Court Bars Special Admissions," *New York Times*, September 17, 1976, 87; William Trombley, "College Racial Quotas Barred: State High Court Voids Preferential Admissions," *Los Angeles Times*, September 17, 1976, 1, 23.

37. Bakke v. Regents of the University of California 438 US 265 (1978).

38. Marquis Childs, "Reagan: More Serious Than Ever," *Washington Post*, May 16, 1978, A13.

39. Bill Peterson, "Ronald Reagan: A Sense of Timing. Some Backscratching," *Washington Post*, September 24, 1978, A3.

40. "A Royal Progress?" *Newsweek*, November 26, 1979, 50, 52; Robert Lindsey, "Reagan Entering Presidency Race, Calls for North American 'Accord,'" *New York Times*, November 14, 1979, 25; "The 1980 Model Reagan: Strident Campaign Tone Is Gone," *New York Times*, November 14, 1979, 25; Alan Baron, "Reagan Trumpets Traditional Verities in a New Key," *Los Angeles Times*, November 18, 1979, F1.

41. Adam Clymer, "Crisis in Iran Alters '80 Race," *New York Times*, December 13, 1979, 22.

42. Falwell quoted in Paul Boyer, "The Evangelical Resurgence in 1970s American Protestantism," in Schulman and Zelizer, *Rightward Bound*, 44.

43. Randall Ballmer, "Real Origins of the Religious Right," *Politico*, May 27, 2014.

44. Falwell quoted in Max Blumenthal, "Agent of Intolerance," *Nation*, May 16, 2007; Carol Howard Merrit, "Liberty University: Your Roots Are Showing," *Christian Century*, May 15, 2017.

45. For the transcript of the "Minister and Marches" speech, see Perry Deane Young, *God's Bullies: Native Reflections on Preachers and Politics* (New York: Holt, Rinehart and Winston, 1982), 310–17.

46. Grace Elizbeth Hale, *A Nation of Outsiders: How the White Middle Class Fell in Love with Rebellion in Postwar America* (New York: Oxford University Press, 2011), 263–64.

47. John Dart, "'New Face' Emerging in Protestant Fundamentalism," *Los Angeles Times*, October 13, 1979, A31; Russell Chandler, "'Christian Voice' Political Action Plans Massive Drive on Reagan's Behalf," *Los Angeles Times*, March 6, 1980, B10.

48. Martin, *God on Our Side*, 193.

49. Martin, *God on Our Side*, 172.

50. Nofziger quoted in Daniel K. Williams, *God's Own Party: The Making of the Christian Right* (New York: Oxford University Press, 2010), 189.

51. "Bob Jones University: A Boot Camp for Bigots," *Journal of Higher Education* 27 (Spring 2000): 15–16.

52. Crespino, "Civil Rights and the Religious Right," in Schulman and Zelizer, *Rightward Bound*, 104.

53. Robert Lindsay, "Reagan to Debate His G.O.P. Rivals in South Carolina," *New York Times*, January 31, 1980, 33.

54. "The Bumpy Campaign Trail," *Newsweek*, December 17, 1979, 51.

55. Richard Ciccone, "Reagan's Dominance Weakened," *Chicago Tribune*, January 22, 1980, 1, 7; Bella Stumbo, "On the Campaign Trail with Reagan: Access Limited, Spontaneity Lacking," *Los Angeles Times*, February 4, 1980, B1, B14, B16; Lou Cannon, "After First Blush Reagan Loosing Bloom," *Washington Post*, January 25, 1980, A3; Colman McCarthy, "Reagan: Not His Age, His Staleness," *Washington Post*, January 20, 1980, E5.

56. Reagan appeared at a debate with his primary foes in Nashua, New Hampshire, on February 23 1980, where Reagan turned off the moderator's microphone and thundered, "I am paying for this microphone, Mr. Green!"

57. "Reagan Is Back in the Saddle," *Newsweek*, March 10, 1980, 26, 34.

58. Adam Clymer, "Approval of Carter's Foreign Policy Declines in Poll to 20%," *New York Times*, June 25, 1980, 1, A20.

59. Frank Viviano, "Depressed, Desperate, and Poor: Letter from Detroit," *Los Angeles Times*, July 13, 1980, F1, F2; Robert A. Jordan, "GOP Blacks Few, Uncertain of Role," *Boston Globe*, July 15, 1980, 6; Ethel Payne, "Blacks Not Wanted at GOP Convention?," *Baltimore Afro-American*, July 26, 1980, 5.

60. Adam Clymer, "Detroit Chosen by G.O.P. for Its Convention in 1980," *New York Times*, January 24, 1979, 1.

61. Theodore H. White, *America in Search of Itself: The Making of the President, 1956–1980* (New York: Harper & Row, 1982), 314.

62. Sandbrook, *Mad as Hell*, 380–81.

63. Quoted in Timothy J. Minchin and John A. Salmond, *After the Dream: Black and White Southerners since 1965* (Lexington: University Press of Kentucky, 2011), 226.

64. "Mrs. Harris Quotes Klan in Its Backing of Reagan," *New York Times*, August 7, 1980, 27.

65. Brooks Jackson, "Reagan's Road: GOP Nominee Pledges Prosperity and Stresses Old-Fashioned Values," *Wall Street Journal*, July 18, 1980, 2.

66. "Reagan Bush Give GOP Strong Ticket," *Atlanta Daily World*, July 18, 1980, 1; Mary McGrory, "For 6 Hours, It Was Paradise for the GOP," *Boston Globe*, July 18, 1980, 14.

67. Adam Clymer, "G.O.P. Seeks Wider Reach," *New York Times*, July 18, 1980, 1, 11.

68. Keith Richburg, "Black Delegates from D.C. Lead on G.O.P. Issues," *Washington Post*, July 16, 1980, C1, C5; Manning Marable, "From the Grassroots Symbols without Substance," *Norfolk Journal and Guide*, July 30, 1980, 6; Ethel Payne, "Blacks Not Wanted?," *Baltimore Afro-American*, July 26, 1980, 5.

69. Louis Harris, "The Harris Survey: Convention Polished Reagan's Image," *Newsday*, August 2, 1980, 2.

70. Howell Raines, "Reagan's Vacation Becomes a 'Retreat,'" *New York Times*, July 2, 1980, 17.

71. Sheila Rule, "Reagan Turns Down Invitation to Address N.A.A.C.P.," *New York Times*, July 1, 1980, 26; "Hooks Finds Little Support for Reagan among Blacks," *New York Times*, June 30, 1980, 33.

72. Charles Pickering to Senator Paul Laxalt, June 16, 1980, Box 277, RRPL; Michael Retzer to Senator Paul Laxalt, July 1, 1980, Box 277, RRPL; Senator Paul Laxalt to Charles Tyson, July 11, 1980, Box 277, RRPL.

73. Cannon, *Governor Reagan*, 476; "Reagan Wins Endorsement of a Major Klan Group," *New York Times*, July 31, 1980, 30; Ken Klinge to Bill Timmons and Chuck Tyson, memo, undated, Box 264, Ronald Reagan 1980 Campaign Papers, RRPL.

74. Cannon, *Governor Reagan*, 478; Mayer, *Running on Race*, 168.

75. "Louisiana Gov. David Treen's Efforts to Woo Black Voters," UPI, September 6, 1983; "David Treen, 81, Louisiana's Governor Loosened Democrats' Grip on LA," *Washington Post*, November 4, 2009.

76. Douglas E. Kneeland, "Reagan Campaigns at Mississippi Fair: Nominee Tells Crowd of 10,000 He Is Backing States' Rights—Attacks Inflation Policy," *New York Times*, August 4, 1980, 11; William Endicott, "Reagan Opens Campaign at a Dixie County Fair," *Los Angeles Times*, August 4, 1980, 1, 6; "Reagan Opens Bid in Visit to the South," *Boston Globe*, August 4, 1980, 8; David Hampton, "Reagan Addresses Enthusiastic Supporters," *Jackson Daily News*, August 4, 1980.

77. Crespino, *In Search of Another Country*, 1.

78. Andrew Young, "Reagan, 'States' Rights,' and Blacks," *Newsday*, August 11, 1980, 39.

79. Andrew Young, "Chilling Words in Neshoba County," *Washington Post*, August 11, 1980, A19.

80. "Reagan Chats with Jordan; Plans Major Speech Today," *New York Times*, August 5, 1980, A17.

81. Reagan's Address to the Annual Convention of the National Urban League, August 5, 1980, Box 384, Ronald Reagan 1980 Campaign Papers, RRPL.

82. Douglas E. Kneeland, "Reagan Urges Blacks to Look Past Labels and to Vote for Him," *New York Times*, August 6, 1980, A1, 16; Draft Speech to the NUL, July 10, 1980, Box 126, Ed Meese Files, Ronald Reagan 1980 Campaign Papers, RRPL.

83. Cannon, *Governor Reagan*, 478–79.

84. Alison Mitchell, "Reagan Is Heckled by Crowd in Bronx," *Newsday*, August 6, 1980, 3.

85. Lou Cannon, "Reagan Makes Appeal for Black Votes: Don't Pigeonhole Me," *Washington Post*, August 6, 1980, A1, A3; "Reagan Booed in Bronx Slum: Gets into Shouting Match with Poor: Told to 'Go Home,'" *Los Angeles Times*, August 5, 1980, A1.

86. Rachelle Patterson, "Reagan Pays Visit to Slum, Is Jeered," *Boston Globe*, August 6, 1980, 10.

87. David Wood, "Reagan Tastes Flavor of Decay in South Bronx," *Washington Star*, August 6, 1980, A1, A3.

88. Benjamin Taylor, "Poll Shows Carter Trailing Reagan in the South," *Boston Globe*, August 14, 1980, 10; Sandbrook, *Mad as Hell*, 376.

89. Ethel Payne, "Reagan Cloud Hovers over Carter," *Baltimore Afro-American*, August 23, 1980, 1, 2.

90. Herbert Denton, "Carter Begins His Campaign by Appealing to Black Voters," *Washington Post*, August 16, 1980, A11.

91. Martin Schram, "Reagan Beats a Retreat on the Klan: Under Heavy Fire," *Washington Post*, September 3, 1980, A1.

92. Terrence Smith, "Carter Assails Reagan Remark about the Klan as an Insult to the South," *New York Times*, September 3, 1980, 28; "The Mood of the Voter," *Time*, September 15, 1980.

93. "Reagan Criticism Fails to Alienate Klansman," *New York Times*, September 3, 1980, B15.

94. Martin Schram, "Carter Says Reagan Injects Racism into the Campaign," *Washington Post*, September 17, 1980, A1.

95. Francis X. Clines, "Carter Suggests Turn to Racism in Reagan's Views," *New York Times*, September 17, 1980, B10; Cannon, *Governor Reagan*, 487; Ed Davis, "Carter Says Reagan Stirs Racial Hate," *Los Angeles Sentinel*, September 18, 1980, A1.

96. White, *America in Search of Itself*, 389.

97. Steven R. Weissman, "Bush Assails Carter on 'Ugly' Insinuations' of Racism," *New York Times*, September 18, 1980, B10; "Carter Stoops to a 'New Low,' Bush Says," *Washington Post*, September 18, 1980, A4; "Running Mean," *Washington Post*, September 18, 1980, A18.

98. Eleanor Randolph and Richard Bergholz, "Carter Denies Suggesting Reagan is Racist," *Los Angeles Times*, September 19, 1980, 1, 17; "Carter Defensive at Politics-Laden News Conference," *Washington Post*, September 19, 1980, A1, A3.

99. Terence Smith, Terence Smith, "Carter Says He Isn't Terming Reagan Racist," *New York Times*, September 19, 1980, B4; Helen Thomas, "Racism Remark," *Los Angeles Times*, September 20, 1980, A28.

100. "Reagan Calls Carter's Statement on Racism 'Harmful, Shameful,'" *Independence Examiner*, September 17, 1980; Josh Levin, "Being Right about Reagan's Racism Was Bad for Jimmy Carter," *Slate*, August 1, 2019, https://slate.com/news-and-politics/2019/08/ronald-reagan-richard-nixon-racism-monkeys-tape-jimmy-carter.html.

101. Hedrick Smith, "Reagan in Shift, Agrees to Debate," *New York Times*, October 18, 1980, 1, 8.

102. Drew, *Portrait of an Election*, 321–22.

103. Ronald Reagan, "1980 Ronald Reagan/Jimmy Carter Presidential Debate," October 28, 1980, accessed May 9, 2015, http://www.reagan.utexas.edu/archives /reference/10.28.80debate; "Transcript of Presidential Debate between Carter and Reagan in Cleveland, " *New York Times*, October 29, 1980, A26.

104. Bernard Weinraub, "Area Panel's Scorecard on the Debate: Reagan Won It by a Wide Margin," *New York Times*, October 30, 1980, B20; "It's Reagan 2 to 1 in Poll by ABC after the Debate," *Chicago Tribune*, October 29, 1980, 10; White, *America in Search of Itself*, 405.

105. Lou Cannon, "A Buoyed Reagan Raps Carter on Record," *Washington Post*, October 30, 1980, A3; Cannon, *Governor Reagan*, 506.

106. "Poll on Election," *New York Amsterdam News*, November 1, 1980.

107. Conor O'Clery, "Blacks See Little to Like in Reagan," *Irish Times*, November 1, 1980, 6.

108. Julius Nicholas, "Blacks See Reagan Win as Setback," *Philadelphia Tribune*, November 7, 1980, 10; Pete Earley and Janet Cooke, "Reagan's Victory Brings Little Rejoicing in D.C.'s Neighborhoods," *Washington Post*, November 5, 1980, A23.

109. Austin Scott and Lee May, "Blacks View Reagan's Term with Fear, Some Optimism," *Los Angeles Times*, December 8, 1980, B1, B7; Edward A. Gargan, "Black Leaders Express Concerns About Reagan," *New York Times*, November 23, 1980, 27.

110. "Our Opinion: Civil Rights Gains Under the Gun," *Philadelphia Tribune*, November 18, 1980, 8; Gerald Horne, "Racism Recurring," *Pittsburgh Courier*, December 13, 1980, 6.

111. "NAACP Message to Reagan," *Baltimore-Afro American*, December 6, 1980, 1.

112. David E. Rosenbaum, "Black Leaders Declare Differences Remain After a Talk with Reagan," *New York Times*, December 12, 1980, A31; Herbert Denton, "Reagan Assures Blacks He'll Defend Civil Rights," *Washington Post*, December 12, 1980, 1, 26.

113. Daniel Leon, "Reagan, Violence, Create Widespread Fear," *Baltimore Afro-American*, December 27, 1980, 6.

114. Herbert Denton, "A Different Look at Old Problems," *Washington Post*, December 15, 1980, A1, A8.

115. Sheila Rule, "Jordan Expresses Alarm at 'Erosion' in Blacks' Status," *New York Times*, January 15, 1981, A18; Lee May, "League Warns of Racial Tensions," *Los Angeles Times*, January 15, 1981, B6.

116. Goldwater quoted in Leslie Bennetts, "Nancy Reagan, with a New First Lady, a New Style," *New York Times*, January 21, 1981, B1; Johnson, *Sleepwalking through History*, 16.

117. James H. Cleaver, "Pompous Inaugural Raises Questions," *Los Angeles Sentinel*, January 22, 1981, A1, A13; James Fleming "Reagan Regime Takes Over," *Baltimore Afro-American*, January 31, 1981, 16; Alfreda L. Madison, "Only the Rich Could Afford It," *Washington Informer*, January 29, 1981.

118. Carter quoted in O'Reilly, *Nixon's Piano*, 376.

CHAPTER 8: LAUNCHING A COUNTERREVOLUTION IN CIVIL RIGHTS

1. Leland quoted in Howell Raines, "Reagan and Blacks: News Analysis," *New York Times*, September 17, 1982, B6.

2. Juan Williams, "In His Mind but Not His Heart," *Washington Post*, January 10, 1988, SM10.

3. Quoted in Carol Anderson, *White Rage: The Unspoken Truth of Our Racial Divide* (New York: Bloomsbury, 2016), 101.

4. O'Reilly, *Nixon's Piano*, 355.

5. Jacqueline Trescott, "Is Social Racism Now Becoming 'Acceptable'?," *Los Angeles Times*, June 12, 1981, G2; "'Renewed Racism' Facing New President, Jordan Declares," *Atlanta Daily World*, January 23, 1981, 3.

6. Alexandra Topping, "Nancy Reagan Refused to Help Dying Rock Hudson," *Guardian*, February 3, 2015.

7. Memo, LCCR Papers, Box 51, Part II, Folder 5, Library of Congress (hereafter LOC).

8. Robert E. Taylor, "Expected Choice to Head Civil Rights Unit Is Said to Have Little Experience in the Field," *Wall Street Journal*, May 12, 1981, 12; Robert Pear, "Reagan's Choice for Civil Rights Post: William Bradford Reynolds," *New York Times*, June 8, 1981, B10.

9. See Wolters, *Right Turn*, 6.

10. Robert Pear, "Civil Rights and Reagan," *New York Times*, August 31, 1981, A15; Herbert Denton, "Civil Rights Movement Has Reached a Dead End," *Chicago Tribune*, September 27, 1981, A1, 5; Howell Raines, "Reagan Sends Mixed Signals on Civil Rights," *New York Times*, July 16, 1981, A1, A18.

11. Terry H. Anderson, *The Pursuit of Fairness: A History of Affirmative Action* (New York: Oxford University Press, 2004), 162.

12. Simon Anekwe, "Pierce Stands Firm Behind Reagan," *New York Amsterdam News*, June 13, 1981, 4, 55.

13. David J. Garrow, *The FBI and Martin Luther King, Jr.: From "Solo" to Memphis* (New York: Penguin, 1981), 106.

14. Kleinknecht, *The Man Who Sold the World*, 189–203.

15. Gwen Ifill, "Pierce Invokes Fifth Amendment," *Washington Post*, September 27, 1989; Johnson, *Sleepwalking through History*, 183–84.

16. Eric Foner, "Lincoln, Bradford, and the Conservatives," *New York Times*, February 13, 1982, 23.

17. Bill Peterson, "GOP Chairman Is Abolishing Ethnic Liaison Groups," *Washington Post*, February 19, 1981; author interview with William Brock, October 24, 2016.

18. David S. Broder, "Still Learning to Be the Opposition," *Washington Post*, February 15, 1981, C7; Cannon, *President Reagan*, 457; Simon Anekwe, "Reagan Meets Black Caucus," *New York Amsterdam News*, February 7, 1981, 3.

19. "Reagan and Blacks," *Newsweek*, July 13, 1981, 20.

20. David Stockman, *The Triumph of Politics: Why the Reagan Revolution Failed* (New York: Harper & Row, 1986) 26.

21. Stockman, *The Triumph of Politics*, 9, 192.

22. Keith B. Richburg, "Reagan's Ax: Cutting Ties That Bind," *Washington Post*, April 9, 1981, DC1.

23. Robert D. McFadden, "Comments by Meese over Hunger Produce a Storm of Controversy," *New York Times*, December 10, 1983, 12.

24. Ira Katznelson, *When Affirmative Action Was White: An Untold History of Racial Inequality in America* (New York: W. W. Norton, 2005).

25. Robert Lakachman, "Reagan's Economic Message: His Policies Promise a Bleak Future for the Poor," *Los Angeles Times*, February 8, 1981, F2; Michael Harrington, "Will Reagan's Budget Leave the Poor Empty Handed? Yes: But Corporations and the Rich Will Prosper," *Los Angeles Times*, February 15, 1981, F3; "Unleashing Greed," *Nation*, February 21, 1981, 197–98; Reagan's Cruel Budget," *Baltimore Afro-American*, February 28, 1981, 4.

26. Pamela Smith, "Reagan's Chopping Block: Poor Being Abandoned for the Rich," *Philadelphia Tribune*, February 20, 1981, 1, 6.

27. "A Constructive Alternative Budget: An Address by Walter E. Fauntroy, Chairman of the Congressional Black Caucus," March 18, 1981, Dan Smith Files, Box 4 OA8610, RRPL.

28. "From the Grassroots: 'Chickens Come Home to Roost,'" *Pittsburgh Courier*, June 20, 1981, 6.

29. Simeon Booker, "Ticker Tape U.S.A.," *Jet*, April 16, 1981, 11.

30. Howell Raines, "Political Drama Surrounds First Speech Since Attack," *New York Times*, April 29, 1981, A1, A23.

31. Martin Tolchin, "It's Reagan's Strong Suit: Against the Odds It Takes a President," *New York Times*, May 3, 1981, E1; Kleinknecht, *The Man Who Sold the World*, 33.

32. Quoted in Chris Matthews, *Tip and the Gipper: When Politics Worked* (New York: Simon & Schuster, 2013), 122.

33. John A. Farrell, *Tip O'Neill and the Democratic Century* (New York: Little, Brown, 2001), 167.

34. Farrell, *Tip O'Neill and the Democratic Century*, 169.

35. Lou Ranson, "At NAACP Dinner: Rowan Sings Out," *Pittsburgh Courier*, May 16, 1981, 1, 7.

36. Stephanie Lee-Miller to Ed Meese, memo, May 18, 1981, Ed Meese Files, Box 34, OA9545, RRPL.

37. Dan J. Smith to Martin Anderson, memo, "The President's NAACP Address," June 3, 1981, Ed Meese Files, Box 34, OA9454, RRPL.

38. Quoted in Troy, *Morning in America*, 93.

39. Remarks in Denver at annual NAACP Conference, June 29, 1981, http://www.presidency.ucsb.edu/ws/index.php?pid=44016&st=NAACP&st1=Denver.

40. Kenneth Cribb through Craig Fuller to Edwin Meese III, memo, "Timing of the Voting Rights Position," June 10, 1981, Ed Meese Files, Box 20, Voting Rights Act Materials (1), RRPL; Lou Cannon, "Reagan Dodges Voting Rights Issue," *Washington Post*, June 30, 1981 A1, A7.

41. Sheila Rule, "Reagan Greeted Politely but Coolly by N.A.A.C.P.," *New York Times*, June 30, 1981, D21; Gwen McKinney, "NAACP Not Persuaded by Reagan," *Pittsburgh Courier*, June 30, 1981, 1, 23; Vernon Jarrett, "Reagan No Hit with NAACP," *Chicago Tribune*, July 3, 1981, 18.

42. "Bondage and the Social Safety Net," *New York Times*, July 1, 1981, A1.

43. On OBRA and ERTA, see Morgan, *Reagan*, 180–82.

44. A. S. "Doc" Young, "Blacks Give Reagan All-Time Low Ranking," *Los Angeles Sentinel*, July 30, 1981, A1, A7, A15, A17; Howell Raines, "Blacks Shift to Sharper Criticism on Civil Rights," *New York Times*, July 26, 1981, E4.

45. Bill Peterson, "Detroit Soup Kitchen's Crowded Holidays—with 'New Poor,'" *Washington Post*, December 29, 1982, A3; Sheila Rule, "Hunger Found to Grip Rising Number in City," *New York Times*, October 24, 1982, 1, 34.

46. John Herbers, "Poverty Rate, 14%, Termed Highest Since '67," *New York Times*, July 20, 1982, A1, A18.

47. Tip O'Neill (with William Novak), *Man of the House: The Life & Political Memoirs of Speaker Tip O'Neill* (New York: Random House, 1987), 346.

48. Harry Bernstein and William J. Eaton, "260,000 Protest Reagan Policies: AFL-CIO and 200 Other Groups Launch Counterattack in Capital," *Los Angeles Times*, September 20, 1981, A1, 4.

49. Interview with Ralph Neas and William Taylor, Michael Pertschuk Papers, Box 1: Folder 108, LOC.

50. Quoted in Michael K. Honey, *To the Promised Land: Martin Luther King and the Fight for Economic Justice* (New York: W.W. Norton, 2018), 97.

51. "Attendance—Voting Rights Meeting," January 7, 1981, Records of the Leadership Conference on Civil Rights, LCCR, Box 68, Folder 7, LOC ; Vernon Jordan, "New Era: Civil Rights Issues Coming Up," *Los Angeles Sentinel*, January 29, 1981, A7, A15.

52. James C. Cobb, "The Voting Rights Act at 50: How It Changed the World," *Time*, August 6, 2015.

53. Reagan quoted in Barrett, *Gambling with History*, 428.

54. "Voting Rights Law Has Met Its Goals," *State*, May 22, 1981; "Water under the Bridge," *Augusta Chronicle-Herald*, April 7, 1981, clippings found in Ed Meese Files, Box 20, Voting Rights Act Materials (1), RRPL; "Statement of Strom Thurmond," June 24, 1981, Ed Meese Files, Box 20, Voting Rights Materials (1), RRPL.

55. Sheila Rule, "Blacks and Reagan's Goal on States: Rights," *New York Times*, March 11, 1981, B20; Howell Raines, "Reagan and States' Rights," *New York Times*, March 4, 1981, 1, 24.

56. "NAACP Places Top Priority on Voting Rights Act," *Baltimore Afro-American*, May 2, 1981, 6; Robert Pear, "Major Fight Expected over Efforts to Extend Voting Rights Measure," *New York Times*, March 9, 1981, A1, B6.

57. City of Mobile, Alabama, et. al v. Bolden, et al., 446 U.S. 55 (1980).

58. Robert Pear, "Congress Begins Fight over Extension of the Voting Rights Act," *New York Times*, April 8, 1981, A10; Eleanor Randolph, "Battle on Extension of Voting Act Starts," *Los Angeles Times*, April 8, 1981, A4; "On the Hill: Voting Wrongs," *New Republic*, June 27, 1981, 8–10.

59. Interview with Neas and Taylor, July 18, 1982, 3, Michael Pertschuk Papers, Part 1: Box 108, LOC.

60. Adam Clymer, "Don Edwards, Congressman Who Championed Civil Rights, Dies at 100," *New York Times*, October 2, 2015.

61. Hearings Before the Subcommittee on Civil and Constitutional Rights of the House Committee on the Judiciary, 97th Cong.,1st Session Part 1 at 1–2 (1981).

62. Robert Pear, "Civil Rights and Labor Leaders Urge a 10-Year Extension of Voting Act," *New York Times*, May 7, 1981, A24; William Raspberry, "New Ways in the Old South," *Washington Post*, June 3, 1981, A23.

63. See Ari Berman, *Give Us the Ballot: The Modern Struggle for Voting Rights in America* (New York: Farrar, Strauss & Giroux, 2015), 140; Robert Pear, "Campaign to Extend Voting Rights Act Gains Support: Hyde Shifts Position," *New York Times*, July 2, 1981, D17; Henry Hyde to the President, memo, August 5, 1981, ID# 03322855, HU015, WHORM, Subject File, RRPL; Henry Hyde, "Why I Changed My Mind on the Voting Rights Act," *Washington Post*, July 26, 1981, D7.

64. "Extending the Voting Rights Act," *Washington Post*, July 31, 1981, A20.

65. Attorney General Smith to President Reagan, memo, October 2, 1981, Melvin L. Bradley Files, Box 37, Voting Rights Act (3), OA 11746, RRPL.

66. Trent Lott to Attorney General Smith, September 16, 1981, Ed Meese Files, Box 20, Voting Act Materials (1), RRPL; Ed Thomas to Ed Meese, memo, August 27, 1981, Ed Meese Files Box 20, Voting Rights Act Materials (1), OA 9460, RRPL.

67. Bill Peterson, "House Backs Vote Rights Extension," *Washington Post*, October 6, 1981, A1, A8.

68. Steven V. Roberts, "House Vote Backs Keeping Key Parts of 1965 Voting Act," *New York Times*, October 6, 1981, 1, D31.

69. "Late Entrance on Voting Rights," *New York Times*, November 4, 1981, A1, A8.

70. *Conference Report: Preliminary Strategy on Voting Rights*, October 8, 1981, Ed Meese Files, Box 20, Voting Rights Act Materials (1), RRPL.

71. Berman, *Give Us the Ballot*, 141; Wolters, *Right Turn*, 56.

72. George Skelton, "An Angry Smith Won Voting Act Concession," *Los Angeles Times*, November 8, 1981, A1, A6.

73. Robert L. Jackson, "President Endorses Voting Rights Act," *Los Angeles Times*, November 7, 1981, A2; Robert Pear, "Reagan Backs Voting Rights Act but Wants to Ease Requirements," *New York Times*, November 7, 1981, A1, A30; Wolters, *Right Turn*, 54; Berman, *Give Us the Ballot*, 141–43.

74. Reginald Stuart, "Voting Rights Backers Assail Reagan's Stand," *New York Times*, November 8, 1981, 22; "President Gags on Voting Rights," *New York Times*, November 10, 1981, A22; "NAACP Raps Voting Rights Changes," *Los Angeles Sentinel*, November 19, 1981, A8.

75. "Voting Rights: Be Strong," *Washington Post*, January 26, 1982, A18.

76. Glazer quoted in Berman, *Give Us the Ballot*, 143.

77. Berman, *Give Us the Ballot*, 51.

78. See Ari Berman, "John Roberts' Decades-Long Crusade against the Voting Rights Act," *Politico*, August 10, 2015, http://www.politico.com/magazine/story/2015/08/john-roberts-voting-rights-act-121222?o=2; Robin Toner and Jonathan D. Glater, "Roberts Helped Shape 80s Civil Rights Debate," *New York Times*, August 4, 2005.

79. Berman, *Give Us the Ballot*, 155.

80. John Herbers, "Reagan's Changes on Rights Are Starting to Have an Impact," *New York Times*, January 24, 1982, 1.

81. Mary Thornton, "Reagan Administration Attacked as Voting Rights Hearings Begin," *Washington Post*, January 28, 1982, A4.

82. "Reagan Bid to Soften Civil-Rights Laws," *Chicago Tribune*, January 28, 1982, 8.

83. "Wronged on Voting Rights," *New York Times*, January 29, 1982, A26.

84. "Voting Rights Are Not Quotas," *New York Times*, March 19, 1982, A30; "Who Wants Quotas," *Washington Post*, March 20, 1982, A16.

85. "Voting Rights March Clarion Call For Nation," *Pittsburgh Courier*, March 13, 1982, A2; "3,000 Demand Extension of Voting Rights Act," *Los Angeles Times*, February 19, 1982, 18.

86. Mary Thornton, "White House Wins in Voting Rights Act Fight," *Washington Post*, March 25, 1982, A5.

87. Dole quoted in Steven Lawson, *In Pursuit of Power: Southern Blacks & Electoral Politics, 1965-1982* (New York: Columbia University Press, 1987), 290.

88. "Finally, Hope for Voting Rights," *New York Times*, May 2, 1982, E20; Mary McGrory, "Sen. Dole: Voting Rights Make Strange Bedfellows," *Washington Post*, May 9, 1982, D1, D4; Steven Roberts, "Voting Law Compromise Clears Senate Panel," *New York Times*, May 5, 1982, A23.

89. Steven V. Roberts, "President Backs Bipartisan Plan on Voting Law," *New York Times*, May 4, 1982, clipping found in Ed Meese Files, Box 37, Voting Rights Act, RRPL.

90. Link, *Righteous Warrior*, 259-61; Steven V. Roberts, "Senators Debate Voting Rights Act," *New York Times*, June 10, 1982, A27.

91. "Reagan Signs Extension of '65 Voting Act," *Los Angeles Times*, June 29, 1982, A2; Ronald Reagan Signing Statement, June 29, 1982, Ed Meese Files, Box 37, Voting Rights Act (1); Contrast to LBJ noted in Berman, *Give Us the Ballot*, 157. See, also, Lawson, *In Pursuit of Power*, 292.

92. Howell Raines, "Voting Rights Act Signed by Reagan," *New York Times*, June 30, 1982, A16.

93. James Nathan Miller, "Ronald Reagan and the Techniques of Deception," *Atlantic Monthly* 65 (February 1984): 65.

94. Stuart Taylor, "When Goals of Boss and Staff Lawyers Clash," *New York Times*, June 22, 1984, A14.

95. Michael Wines, "Administration Says It Merely Seeks a 'Better Way' to Enforce Civil Rights," *National Journal*, March 27, 1982, 539.

96. Jesse Rhodes, *Ballot Blocked: The Political Erosion of the Voting Rights Act* (Stanford, CA: Stanford University Press, 2017), 109-10.

97. Robert Pear, "Voting Rights Law Provokes Dispute," *New York Times*, November 14, 1982, 37.

98. David Gergen to Ed Meese, Jim Baker, Fred Fielding, memo, January 8, 1982, M. B. Ogelsby Jr. Files, Box 4, OA8610, RRPL; see, also, Barrett, *Gambling with History*, 416-21.

99. Quoted in "Justices to Rule on Tax Break Issue," *Los Angeles Times*, April 19, 1982, A1, A2.

100. Cannon, *President Reagan*, 459-60; Trent Lott to Don Regan, December 21, 1981, William P. Barr Papers, Box 2, RRPL.

101. Haynes Johnson, "Reagan Contribution to Race Bias Can't Be Explained Away," *Washington Post*, January 17, 1982, A3.

102. "U.S. Tax Rule Shift Applauded and Attacked," *New York Times*, January 9, 1982; Fred Barbash, "Tax Penalty on School Bias Ended," *Washington Post*, January 9, 1982, A1, A10; Paul Houston, "Tax Break for Biased Schools Sure to Draw Fire," *Los Angeles Times*, January 9, 1982, 1, 18; Barrett, *Gambling with History*, 416.

103. Tom Wicker, "Subsidizing Racism," *New York Times*, January 12, 1982, A15.

104. Dugger, *On Reagan*, 214; "Justice Dept. Lawyers Protest Tax Status of Biased Schools," *Los Angeles Times*, February 3, 1982, B15; Aaron Haberman, "Into The Wilderness: Ronald Reagan, Bob Jones University, and the Political Education of the Christian Right," *Historian* 67, no. 2 (Summer 2005): 244.

105. Michael Wines, "Administration Says It Seeks a Better Way to Enforce Civil Rights," *National Journal*, March 27, 1982.

106. Barrett, *Gambling with History*, 415; Chris Benson, "Blacks in the White House," *Ebony*, April 1982.

107. Parable recounted in Cannon, *President Reagan*, 460; and Barrett, *Gambling with History*, 416.

108. Statement by the President, January 12, 1982, Elizabeth Dole Files, Box 6, RRPL.

109. Announcement, Rostenkowski to Hold Hearings, January 12, 1982, M. B. Ogelsby Files, Box 4, OA8610; Martin Schram and Charles R. Babcock, "Reagan Advisers Missed School Case Sensitivity," *Washington Post*, January 17, 1982, A1.

110. Barry Sussman, "Poll Finds Most Think Recovery Program Hurts," *Washington Post*, February 5, 1982, A4; William Raspberry, "Reagan's Problem with Blacks," *Washington Post*, February 22, 1982, A11.

111. Cannon, *President Reagan*, 459.

112. Robert L. Jackson, "Tax Favor Denied for Biased Schools," *Los Angeles Times*, February 20, 1982, A12, A13.

113. Linda Greenhouse, "Rights Officials Defend Tax Break for Racially-Biased Schools," *New York Times*, October 13, 1982, A19.

114. Bob Jones University v. United States 461 U.S.574 (1983).

115. "Tax-Exempt Hate, Undone," *New York Times*, May 25, 1983, A26.

116. Quoted in *Baron Report*, September 27, 1982, clipping found in Elizabeth Dole File, Box 6, Blacks: July–Dec. 1982 (3 of 3), RRPL.

117. Troy, *Morning in America*, 94.

118. Joann S. Lublin, "Senate Panel Postpones Vote on Nominee to Head EEOC as Foes Grow More Vocal," *Wall Street Journal*, November 13, 1981, 14; Telegram from National Urban Coalition to Ronald Reagan, Re Withdrawal of Bell, November 5, 1981, FG123, Box 52, OA046581, RRPL; Diana Lozano to Elizabeth Dole, November 9, 1981, Elizabeth Dole Files Box 6, RRPL.

119. "Minorities: Drive Thrown into Reverse?," *U.S. News & World Report*, September 27, 1982, 40–42.

120. Elizabeth Dole to Edwin Meese, James A. Baker III, and Michael Deaver, memo, May 5, 1982, Edwin Meese Files, Box 29, OA9449, RRPL; "Damage: Decline of Equal Employment Enforcement Under the Reagan Administration, Women Employed," November 1982, Thelma P. Duggin Files, Box 7, RRPL.

121. Adam Clymer, "Republicans Worry about Eroding Black Support," *New York Times*, April 14, 1982, A20.

122. Quoted in "Firing of a Fighter," *Time*, November 30, 1981, 29.

123. Black Issues Polling, January 1982, Melvin Bradley Files, Box 2, Black Issues 1982, RRPL; "Reagan and Black America," A30.

124. Hedrick Smith, "Black Vote a Factor in Increased Turnout in Off-Year Election," *New York Times*, November 10, 1982, A1, A28.

125. Haley Barbour to James H. Baker III, memo, December 1, 1982, Ed Meese Files, Box 34, RRPL.

126. Robert Pear, "Reagan Is Rebuked by 33 State Heads of Rights Panels," *New York Times*, September 12, 1982, 1, 34; Stuart Taylor, "How Resolute Is Reagan on Civil Rights?," *New York Times*, October 10, 1982, E2.

127. Eric Foner, "Redemption II," *New York Times*, November 7, 1981, 23.

CHAPTER 9: CONTROLLING THE CIVIL RIGHTS COMMISSION
AND IGNITING OLD CONSERVATIVE BATTLES

1. Peter Appelbome, "Dueling with the Heirs of Jefferson Davis," *New York Times*, December 27, 1998, 1.

2. Walker poem, "Each One, Pull One," quoted in Rossinow, *The Reagan Era*, 140.

3. "Reagan Gaining Control of Federal Judiciary," *CQ Almanac*, https://library.cqpress.com/cqalmanac/document.php?id=cqal84-1152666, accessed October 14, 2017.

4. Chester J. Finn, "'Affirmative Action' Under Reagan," *Commentary*, April 1982, clipping found in Thelma P. Duggin Files, Box 1, RRPL; "83% Oppose Reverse Bias Plans," *New York Times*, May 1, 1977, 33.

5. President's News Conference, January 29, 1981, available at http://www.presidency.ucsb.edu/ws/?pid=44101.

6. "American Can't Be Colorblind Yet," *New York Times*, June 10, 1981, clipping found in Edwin Meese Files, Box 20, RRPL.

7. Katznelson, *When Affirmative Action Was White*; see, also, Michael K. Brown, Martin Carney, Elliott Currie, Troy Duster, David B. Oppenheimer, Marjorie M. Shultz, and David Wellman, *Whitewashing Race: The Myth of a Color-Blind Society* (Berkeley: University of California Press, 2003).

8. Testimony of Reynolds to Subcommittee on Education and Labor Subcommittee, House of Representatives, September 23, 1981, Thelma P. Duggin Files, Box 1, Folder-Affirmative Action II, RRPL.

9. "Hawkins Condemns Administration's Affirmative Action Policies," September 23, 1981, Thelma P. Duggin Files, Box 1, RRPL.

10. "Civil Rights Head Will Seek Supreme Court Ban on Affirmative Action," *Wall Street Journal*, December 8, 1981, 4.

11. Daniel Seligman, "Affirmative Action Is Here to Stay," *Fortune*, April 1982.

12. Thelma Duggin to Elizabeth Dole, memo, December 16, 1981, Elizabeth Dole Files, Box 6, RRPL. OFCCP is part of the Department of Labor and ensures that parties doing business with the US government comply with antidiscrimination laws.

13. "President's News Conference," December 17, 1981, http://www.presidency.ucsb.edu/ws/index.php?pid=.

14. Robert Pear, "Aides Say President Opposes Quotas in Affirmative Action," *New York Times*, January 4, 1982, A1, A15.

15. Elizabeth Dole to Meese and Baker, memo, March 9, 1982, Elizabeth Dole Files, Box 1, Affirmative Action 1982 (2 of 6), RRPL.

16. Michael Putzel, "Civil Rights Claims Disputed by Report," AP, September 27, 1982, clipping found in Thelma P. Duggin Files, Box 1, Affirmative Action II (5 of 6), RRPL; Anderson, *Pursuit of Fairness*, 177–78.

17. Quoted in Berry, *And Justice for All*, 3.

18. John Herbers, "Hesburgh Quits Civil Rights Panel at the Request of the White House," *New York Times*, November 17, 1972, 1, 22.

19. Flemming to Attorney General Smith, December 8, 1981, Records of the Justice Department, Box 216, Folder Civil Rights Division (1 of 3), National Archives.

20. "Affirmative Action in the 1980s: Dismantling the Process of Discrimination," Proposed Statement of the US Commission on Civil Rights, January 1981, Clearing House Publications, https://www.law.umaryland.edu/marshall/usccr /documents/cr11065.pdf; Berry, *And Justice for All*, 183.

21. "Firing a Fighter," *Time*, November 30, 1981, 29; Howell Raines, "Reagan Dismisses Civil Rights Chief, Busing Supporter," *New York Times*, November 17, 1981, A1, A26.

22. Flemming to Reagan, May 13, 1981, White House Subject Files, FG O93, Commission on Civil Rights, RRPL; Flemming to AG Smith, RG General Files, Records of DOJ, Box 216, National Archives.

23. Quoted in Nadine Cahodas, "Reagan Miscues Cost Him on Rights Battle," *Congressional Quarterly Weekly Report*, November 26, 1983, 2518.

24. "Q&A: Arthur S. Flemming: On Affirmative Action and Deeds and Words," *New York Times*, December 8, 1981, A24.

25. "Former Federal Officials Form Civil Rights Monitoring Group," July 19, 1982, Thelma P. Duggin Files, Box 5, RRPL; Penny Chorlton, "Group to Monitor 'Regressive' Civil Rights Actions," *Washington Post*, July 20, 1982, A15.

26. Vernon Jordan, "A Step Back on Civil Rights," *Chicago Tribune*, November 20, 1981, 23.

27. Judith Cummings, "FBI Opens Background Check of Nominee for Civil Rights Post," *New York Times*, March 4, 1982, 18; Richard C. Paddock, "Urban League Probing Pendleton," *Los Angeles Times*, January 29, 1982, SD—A1; Richard C. Paddock, "Pendleton to Return Money for 'Vacation,'" *Los Angeles Times*, April 9, 1982, SD—A1.

28. Berry, *And Justice for All*, 199–201.

29. Nomination of B. Sam Hart, February 9, 1982, American Presidency Project, http://www.presidency.ucsb.edu/ws/?pid=42065.

30. Lois Romana, "Jill Ruckelshaus, Back in the Fishbowl," *Washington Post*, May 18, 1983.

31. Statement of LCCR Opposition to B. Sam Hart, February 21, 1982, LCCR Papers, Box 61, Part II, Folder 3, LOC.

32. Hart quoted in James Reston Jr., "United States Commission on Civil Rights: We Shall Undermine," *Rolling Stone*, March 13, 1986; Lee Lescaze, "Rights Nominee Speaks Out," *Washington Post*, February 11, 1982, A1, A10.

33. "Strangling a Voice for Civil Rights," *New York Times*, March 2, 1982, A22.

34. Jack Nelson, "Reagan Orders Change on Rights Appointees," *Los Angeles Times*, March 24, 1982, B17; William Raspberry, "Taming the Civil Rights Commission," *Washington Post*, February 17, 1982, A23.

35. Nominations, May 20, 1982, https://www.reaganlibrary.archives.gov/archives /speeches/1982/52082b.htm.

36. Destro quoted in Reston, "United States Commission on Civil Rights," *Rolling Stone*, March 13, 1986.

37. Althea Madison, "Civil Rights Movement to Right," *Skanner*, November 17, 1982, 5.

38. "Civil Rights Commissioners," *Baltimore-Afro American*, October 23, 1982, 4.

39. Robert Pear, "Rights Panel Criticizes President on Two Affirmative Action Stands," *New York Times*, January 12, 1983, A19; Felicity Barringer, "Civil Rights Commission Gets Tough," *Washington Post*, December 6, 1982, A9.

40. Ogelsby and Scruggs to Meese and Baker, memo, March 21, 1983, Ed Meese Files, Box 58, OA11839, RRPL.

41. Ken Cribb to Mike Horowitz, memo, March 31, 1983, Michael Uhlmann Files, OA9441, RRPL.

42. Civil Rights Commission Reauthorization Act of 1983, April 6, 1983, John G. Roberts Files, Box 11, JGR/Civil Rights Commission, RRPL.

43. "President Draws Heavy Criticism over His Choice for Civil Rights Panel," *New York Times*, May 27, 1983, A11; Murray Saltzman, "Watchdog without Bark," *Los Angeles Times*, March 27, 1983, clipping found in Edwin Meese Files, Box 58, OA11839, RRPL.

44. "President Draws Heavy Criticism over His Choices for Rights Panel," A11.

45. Berry, *And Justice for All*, 209–10; Ben Wattenberg, "Commissioner Berry," *Baltimore Sun*, September 15, 1983, A21; Albert Shanker to Metzenbaum, July 15, 1983, Edwin Meese Files, Box 58, OA11839, RRPL.

46. "Suddenly It Was All Action," *Time*, July 25, 1983, 24; Robert Pear, "Reagan Rights Nominees Touch Off a Heated Clash in the Senate," *New York Times*, July 14, 1983, A1.

47. Robert Pear, "Republican Joins Civil Rights Fray," *New York Times*, July 27, 1983, 16.

48. James Worsham, "House Acts to Curb Rights Panel Firings," *Chicago Tribune*, August 5, 1983, 1, 16.

49. Mike Horowitz to Ken Cribb, memo, September 19, 1983, Edwin Meese Files, Box 58, OA11839, RRPL; Ellen Elsasser, "White House Rejects Deal on Civil Rights Panel," *Chicago Tribune*, October 1, 1983, 8; "A Way out of the Civil Rights Feud," *New York Times*, September 15, 1983, 26.

50. Robert Pear, "Deadlock Clouds Fate of U.S. Rights Agency," *New York Times*, October 1, 1983, 1, 12.

51. Robert Dole to Ed Meese, memo, October 3, 1983, Edwin Meese Files, Box 58, OA11839, RRPL.

52. Berry, *History Teaches Us to Resist*, 59.

53. Press release, October 25, 1983, Sherri M. Cooskey Files, Box 1, OA11722, RRPL.

54. Robert Pear, "Reagan Ousts 3 from Civil Rights Panel," *New York Times*, October 26, 1983; Berry, *And Justice for All*, 186–87; Glen Elasser, "Firing of 3 on Rights Panel Shocks Congress," *Chicago Tribune* October 26, 1983, 1, 2; "Storm over Civil Rights," *Newsweek*, November 7, 1983.

55. Opinion in *Mary Frances Berry, et. al. v. Ronald Reagan*, November 14, 1983, Sherri M. Cooksey Files, Box 1, OA11722, RRPL.

56. George Lardner Jr., "Compromise Apparently Reconstitutes Civil Rights Commission," *Washington Post*, November 11, 1983, A1, A14; Robert Pear, "Accord Reported on Appointment of Rights Panel," *New York Times*, November 11, 1983, A1, A23.

57. Martin Tolchin, "Senate Approve Rights Panel Bill," *New York Times*, November 15, 1983, A26.

58. Statement of the President, November 30, 1983, Edwin Meese Files, Box 58, OA11839, RRPL; David Stockman to Ronald Reagan, memo, November 25, 1983, Edwin Meese Files, Box 58, OA11838, RRPL.

59. "Baker Puts Tennessean on Civil Rights Panel," *New York Times*, December 13, 1983, 8; Bill Kekirk, "Jill Ruckelshaus Bypass by GOP for Rights Panel," *Chicago Tribune*, December 8, 1983, N1; Margaret Shapiro, "Rights Leaders Charge 'Double-Cross' by White House and GOP," *Washington Post*, December 9, 1983, A3.

60. Sara Fritz, "Reagan's Refusal to Rename Rights Aide Irks Critics," *Los Angeles Times*, December 7, 1983, B6; Steven V. Roberts, "And One Who Is Disappointed," *New York Times*, January 25, 1984, 16.

61. Robert Pear, "President, Naming 3 to Rights Unit, Bars Critic of His Policies," *New York Times*, December 7, 1983, A1; Juan Williams, "Mary Louise Smith Dropped from Rights Panel," *Washington Post*, December 2, 1983; "Baker Puts Tennessean on Civil Rights Panel," *New York Times*, December 13, 1983, 8B.

62. Bill Kekirk, "Jill Ruckelshaus Bypass by GOP for Rights Panel," *Chicago Tribune*, December 8, 1983, N1; Shapiro, "Rights Leaders Charge 'Double-Cross' by White House and GOP."

63. Barbara Rosewicz, "How the Civil Rights Commission Deal Blew Up," UPI, December 21, 1983, clipping found in Edwin Meese Files, Box 58, OA11839, RRPL.

64. Ronald Reagan, *The Reagan Diaries*, ed. Douglas Brinkley (New York: Harper Perennial, 2007), 197; Berry, *And Justice for All*, 212.

65. Neas quoted in Berry, *And Justice for All*, 213.

66. Robert Pear, "Commission Intends to Reassess Rights," *New York Times*, January 8, 1984, clipping found in Edwin Meese Files, Box 58, OA 11839, RRPL.

67. Juan Williams, "Rights Panel Agenda Recast," *Washington Post*, January 9, 1984.

68. Robert Pear, "Rights Commission Abandons Use of Racial Quotas," *New York Times*, January 18, 1984; Walter Goodman, "New U.S. Panel Narrows Definition of Civil Rights," *New York Times*, February 2, 1984, B25.

69. "Civil Rights, Reagan Style," *Newsweek*, January 30, 1984, 18.

70. "The Civil Rights Commission as a Parrot," *New York Times*, January 25, 1984; "The Nation: Rights Panel Echoes Reagan Point of View," *New York Times*, January 23, 1984.

71. Berry, *And Justice for All*, 216.

72. Berry quoted in "Declaration of Independence: Conservatives Change the Course of a Federal Panel," *Time*, January 30, 1984, 15.

73. Pendleton quoted in "The Rise and Fall of the United States Commission on Civil Rights," *Harvard Law Review* 22 (1987): 504.

74. "Civil Rights, Reagan Style," *Newsweek*, January 30, 1984; "New Panel Narrows Definition of Civil Rights," *New York Times*, February 2, 1984, B24.

75. Steven A. Holmes, "With Glory of Past Only a Memory, Rights Panel Searches for New Role," *New York Times*, October 10, 1991, B16.

76. "King's Widow Charges Reagan Ignoring Poor," *Clarion-Ledger*, August 28, 1983.

77. Kenneth B. Noble, "Marchers Ask New Coalition for Social Change," *New York Times*, August 28, 1983, 1, 30; Eleanor Randolph, "Reagan Assailed at Rally of 250,000," *Los Angeles Times*, August 28, 1983, A1.

78. Kenneth B. Nobel, "March on Capital Is Seen Spurring Vast Coalition," *New York Times*, August 29, 1983, 12.

79. See David L. Chappell, *Waking from the Dream: The Struggle for Civil Rights in the Shadow of Martin Luther King, Jr.* (New York: Random House, 2014), 91–123; House Committee on Post Office and Civil Service Judiciary Committee, Joint Hearings, 96th Cong., 1st Sess., "Martin Luther King, Jr. S. 25," March 27, 1979, and June 21, 1979, 1–169.

80. Gail Gregg, "Holiday Bill Facing Strong Attack in Congress," *Atlanta Daily World*, June 24, 1979, 1; "Conservatives Use Old Tact to Oppose Holiday for Dr. King," *Baltimore Afro-American*, June 26, 1979, 1, 2.

81. "King Bill Fails," *New York Amsterdam News*, November 17, 1979, 4.

82. Statement on the Anniversary of the Birth of Martin Luther King Jr., January 15, 1982, http://www.presidency.ucsb.edu/ws/index.php?pid=42365.

83. See Bostdorff and Goldzwig, "History, Collective Memory, and the Appropriation of Martin Luther King, Jr.'s Rhetorical Legacy," 661–90.

84. Coretta Scott King to Ronald Reagan, May 11, 1982, WHORM Subject File, IV, 079024, RRPL; "Reagan Sympathetic, but Cautious on a King Day," *New York Times*, May 11, 1982.

85. Skinner, Anderson, Anderson, and Schultz, *Reagan in His Own Hand*, 634.

86. "Remarks Stir Hearing on Holiday for King," *Washington Post*, February 24, 1982, A4.

87. Coretta Scott King quoted in Chappell, *Waking from the Dream*, 110–11.

88. Juan Williams and Lou Cannon, "President to Support King Holiday," *Washington Post*, August 6, 1983, A1, A5.

89. Mel Bradley from Edwin L. Harper, memo, January 18, 1983, WHORM Subject Files, HO114010, RRPL; "Reagan and Bush Praise Kings," *Atlanta Daily World*, January 18, 1983, 1.

90. House Committee on Post Office and Civil Service Judiciary Committee, Joint Hearings, 98th Cong., 1st Sess., "Martin Luther King, Jr. S. 25," June 7, 1983, 1–169.

91. House Committee on Post Office and Civil Service Judiciary Committee, 8; Sandra Evans Teeley, "O'Neill Urges King Holiday," *Washington Post*, June 8, 1983, A8.

92. Chappell, *Waking from the Dream*, 114–16; "House Votes Holiday for King Who Evoked 'Conscience of U.S.,'" *Chicago Tribune*, August 3, 1983, 10.

93. Tom Gibson to Craig Fuller, memo, undated, WHORM Subject Files, FG, Box 52 RRPL; Morning Briefing, August 4, 1983, WHORM Subject Files, FG, Box 52, RRPL; Joe Wright to Ed Meese, memo, August 31, 1983, Martin Luther King Jr. Holiday, OA 9417, RRPL.

94. Steven R. Weisman, "Aides Assert Reagan May Shift to Support Holiday for Dr. King," *New York Times*, August 7, 1983, 1, 20.

95. James F. Clarity and Warren Weaver Jr., "Briefing: Dr. King Holiday Opposed," *New York Times*, September 29, 1983, B12; Sandy Grady, "Smearing Dr. King," *Hartford Courant*, October 3, 1983, B11.

96. Helms quoted in Link, *Righteous Warrior*, 80.

97. Congressional Record, 98th Congress, 1st Sess., Senate, "Birthday of Martin Luther King Jr, as a Federal Holiday," October 3, 1983, 26868; Steven V. Roberts, "King Holiday Bill Faces a Filibuster," *New York Times*, October 4, 1983, A17.

98. Helen Dewar, "Helms Stalls King's Day in Senate," *Washington Post*, October 4, 1983, A1.

99. "Filibuster by Helms on Dr. King Is Dropped in the Senate," *New York Times*, October 5, 1983, A16; "King Bill Approval Is Virtually Assured," *Washington Post*, October 6, 1983, A14.

100. "Writer Says Helms Can't Prove King Was Communist," *Baltimore Sun*, October 17, 1983, A3; Haynes Johnson, "Smear: A Generation-Old Crusade to Destroy King's Name at Any Cost," *Washington Post*, October 16, 1983, A3.

101. Link, *Righteous Warrior*, 264–68; Steven V. Roberts, "Senators Are Firm on King Holiday," *New York Times*, October 19, 1983, A18.

102. Dorothy Collin, "King Bill Passes Test, Sparks Teddy-Helms Tiff," *Chicago Tribune*, October 19, 1983, 12; Congressional Record, 98th Congress, 1st Sess., October 18, 1983, 28073.

103. Congressional Record, 98th Congress, 28075.

104. Helen Dewar, "Solemn Senate Votes for National Holiday Honoring Rev. King," *Washington Post*, October 20, 1983, A1.

105. Steven V. Roberts, "Senators Are Firm on King Holiday," *New York Times*, October 19, 1983, 18.

106. "Senate's Roll Call Vote on King Holiday," *New York Times*, October 20, 1983, B9.

107. Juan Williams, "President Reluctantly Promises to Sign King Holiday Bill," *Washington Post*, October 20, 1983, A11.

108. President's News Conference, American Presidency Project, October 19, 1983, http://www.presidency.ucsb.edu/ws/?pid=40666.

109. "Not a 35-Year Question," *New York Times*, October 21, 1982, A34.

110. "Anthony Lewis, Abroad at Home: The Real Reagan," *New York Times*, October 24, 1983, A19.

111. Cannon, *President Reagan*, 524; Lou Cannon interview with David Gergen, March 6, 1989, Lou Cannon Papers, Box 22, Folder 93, Gergen, David, University of California, Santa Barbara Special Collections.

112. Skinner, Anderson, Anderson, and Schultz, *Reagan in His Own Hand*, 634.

113. Francis X. Clines, "Reagan's Doubts on Dr. King Disclosed," *New York Times*, October 22, 1983, 7.

114. "Reagan Apologizes for King Insult," *Baltimore Afro-American*, October 29, 1983, 1.

115. "Ronald Reagan Signing Statement," November 2, 1983, James Jenkins Files, Box 2, RRPL.

116. Robert Pear, "President, Signing Bill, Praises Dr. King," *New York Times*, November 3, 1983, A1.

117. Ronald Smothers, "Jackson Declares Formal Candidacy," *New York Times*, November 4, 1983, B5.

118. "2 Million More Black Voters Seen in '84," *Boston Globe*, November 4, 1983, 12; "Black Registration Alarms G.O.P. Leaders," *New York Times*, June 7, 1984, B12.

119. Gerald M. Boyd, "Reagan and Congress Assailed on Plight of Poor Blacks," *New York Times*, January 20, 1984, B4.

120. Spencer Rich, "Cutbacks 'Crushing' Blacks," *Washington Post*, January 20, 1984, 1, A8.

121. Joyce Purnick and Michael Orestes, "Jesse Jackson Aims for the Mainstream," *New York Times*, November 29, 1987, Section 6, 28.

122. Ellen Hume, "Jackson Galvanizes Black Voters," *Wall Street Journal*, March 27, 1984, 62.

123. Ronald Smothers, "Beyond the Jackson Bid: Some Gains for Blacks," *New York Times*, July 1, 1984, 16.

124. Steven R. Weisman, "Will the Magic Prevail?," *New York Times*, April 29, 1984, SM39.

125. Stanley Cohen, "A Spectacle Stirs a Jumble of Nationalism," *New York Times*, August 26, 1984, Section 5, 2.

126. "For Blacks, Reagan's Words Spell Out a Gloomy Future," *Philadelphia Tribune*, August 28, 1984, 4; Marilyn Milloy, "Civil Rights Took Back Seat in '84," *Newsday*, November 5, 1984, 11.

127. Francis X. Clines, "Reporter's Notebook: Few Blacks in Reagan Crowds," *New York Times*, September 8, 1984, 9; Betty Pleasant, "Blacks Absent from Reagan's Gala," *Los Angeles Sentinel*, November 8, 1984, A1.

128. Carter quoted in Mike Wallace and Gary Paul Gates, *Between You and Me: A Memoir* (New York: Hyperion, 2005), 49–50.

129. Carl T. Rowan, "The Real Shame," *Washington Post*, October 30, 1984, A19.

130. Jordan quoted in Anderson, *The Pursuit of Fairness*, 170.

131. Simon Anekwe, "Massive Black Vote Fails to Stop Reagan," *New York Amsterdam News*, November 10, 1984, 1, 20.

132. Mayer and McManus, *Landslide*, 18.

133. Ashley Hasley III, "Reagan's Coattails Called the Difference in Helms' Victory," *Philadelphia Inquirer*, November 8, 1984, A17.

134. Marilyn Milloy, "Civil Rights Took Backseat in '84," *Newsday*, November 5, 1984, 11, 14; John E. Jacob, "The Reagan Landslide and the Black Vote," *Pittsburgh Courier*, December 1, 1984, 4.

135. Quoted in Alexander P. Lamis, "Mississippi," in *The 1984 Presidential Election in the South: Patterns of Southern Party Politics*, ed. Robert B. Steed, Laurence W. Moreland, and Tod A. Baker (New York: Praeger, 1986), 45.

136. Ronald Smothers, "Election Results Troubling Blacks," *New York Times*, November 9, 1984, A20.

CHAPTER 10: SOUTH AFRICA

1. Glenn Frankel, "Limited Economic Sanctions Imposed on South Africa." *Washington Post*, September 10, 1985, A1, A12.

2. Leslie Phillips, "Rights Groups Take Aim at Reagan Today," *USA Today*, June 4, 1985, 1A, 2A.

3. See Francis Njubi Nesbitt, *Race for Sanctions: African Americans Against Apartheid, 1946–1994* (Bloomington: Indiana University Press, 2004).

4. See Nicholas Grant, *Winning Our Freedoms Together: African Americans and Apartheid, 1945–1960* (Chapel Hill: University of North Carolina Press, 2017).

5. Lewis Baldwin, "Martin Luther King, Jr., a 'Coalition of Conscience' and Freedom in South Africa," in *Freedom's Distant Shores: American Protestants and*

Alliances with Post-Colonial Africa, ed. R. Drew Smith (Waco, TX: Baylor University Press, 2006), 67–68, quoted in Sokol, *The Heavens Might Crack*, 160–61.

6. Piero Gleijeses, *Visions of Freedom: Havana, Washington, Pretoria, and the Struggle for South Africa, 1976–1991* (Chapel Hill: University of North Carolina Press, 2013), 139–65; Alex Thompson, "'The Diplomacy of Impasse': The Carter Administration and Apartheid South Africa," *Diplomacy and Statecraft* 21, no. 1 (2010): 107–24; see, also, Nancy Mitchell, *Jimmy Carter and Africa: Race and the Cold War* (Palo Alto, CA: Stanford University Press, 2016).

7. Gary Thatcher, "How the World Reacts to Reagan's Massive Victory," *Christian Science Monitor*, November 1980, 6, 52; Nesbitt, *Race for Sanctions*, 113.

8. Nesbitt, *Race for Sanctions*, 103–11.

9. Chester A. Crocker, "South Africa: Strategy for Change," *Foreign Affairs* 59, no. 2 (Winter 1980): 328.

10. From an interview with Walter Cronkite, March 3, 1981, American Presidency Project, www.presidency.ucsb.edu/ws/?pid=43497.

11. Joseph Lelyveld, "Reagan's Views on South Africa Praised by Botha," *New York Times*, March 5, 1981, A15; Clayton Fritchey, "A Worrisome Tilt Toward South Africa," *Washington Post*, March 16, 1981, A19; June Kronholz, "South Africa Sees a Friend in Reagan," *Wall Street Journal*, March 27, 1981, 33.

12. For example, see Steven F. Hayward, Paul Kengor, Craig Shirley, and Kiron K. Skinner, "What 'The Butler' Gets Wrong about Race," *Washington Post*, August 29, 2013.

13. See, for example, William F. Buckley, Jr., "Deadend [*sic*] in South Africa," *National Review*, April 23, 1960, 254–55; William F. Buckley Jr., "Will the Jungle Take Over?," *National Review*, July 30, 1960, 39–40; William F. Buckley Jr., "Must We Hate Portugal?," *National Review*, December 18, 1962, 448.

14. "Why the South Must Prevail," *National Review*, August 24, 1957, 148–49.

15. "Black Legislators Urge Dismissal of Mrs. Kirkpatrick," *New York Times*, March 27, 1981, A8.

16. John Conyers to Reagan, May 13, 1981, WHORM Subject Files, South Africa, RRPL.

17. Juan de Onis, "6 African Leaders Criticize Administration Policies," *New York Times*, April 17, 1981, 8.

18. Gleijeses, *Visions of Freedom*, 179.

19. Robert A. Manning, "Appeasing Pretoria Won't Pay: Unrealpolitik on Africa," *New Republic*, June 13, 1981, 14–16.

20. Edward Walsh, "'Time Is Running Out,' South Africa Study Says," *Washington Post*, May 22, 1981, A29.

21. Robert McFadden, "Tutu Assails U.S. on Pretoria Ties," *New York Times*, October 28, 1984, 19.

22. Ronald V. Dellums (with H. Lee Alterman), *Lying Down with the Lions: A Public Life from the Streets of Oakland to the Halls of Power* (Boston: Beacon Press, 2000), 126–27.

23. "Capital's House Delegate Held in Embassy," *New York Times*, November 22, 1984, B10.

24. Courtland Milloy, "Blacks Form 'Free S. Africa Movement,'" *Washington Post*, November 24, 1983, C1, C4; Berry, *History Teaches Us to Resist*, 88–91.

25. Karlyn Barker and Michel Marriott, "Protest Spreads to Other U.S. Cities," *Washington Post*, December 4, 1984, A1, A8; Karlyn Barker and Michel Marriott, "1960s Tactics Revived for Embassy Sit-ins," *Washington Post*, November 29, 1984, A1, A12; Barbara A. Gamarekian, "Apartheid Protest Takes Page from 60's History," *New York Times*, November 30, 1984, A13.

26. "Debating Race and Politics," *Newsweek*, December 17, 1984, 58, 59; "Reagan's S. Africa Policy 'Immoral,' Tutu Says," *Los Angeles Times*, December 4, 1984, A2.

27. Memorandum of conversation of meeting with Bishop Desmond Tutu, December 7, 1984, Executive Secretariat, NSM, Contents M, Box 17, RRPL; "Fresh Anger over Apartheid," *Time*, December 17, 1984; Gerald M. Boyd, "Reagan Rejects Tutu's Plea for Tough Policy on Pretoria," *New York Times*, December 8, 1984, 1.

28. Reagan, *The Reagan Diaries*, 285.

29. Sandra Evans, "Moves Against Apartheid Urged," *Washington Post*, December 10, 1984, A8.

30. Sanford Ungar, "Disengaging a Failed Policy," *Chicago Tribune*, December 26, 1984, 23.

31. Nesbitt, *Race for Sanctions*, 132; Allister Sparks, "Tens of Thousands Make Political Rally of S. African Funeral," *Washington Post*, April 14, 1985, A29.

32. Jonathan Fuerbringer, "House Votes Sanctions against South Africa," *New York Times*, June 6, 1985, A1, A17; Nesbitt, *Race for Sanctions*, 133–34.

33. "Not a Black and White Issue," *Time*, June 17, 1985, 32.

34. Jonathan Fuerbringer, "Senate Approves Economic Moves Against S. Africa," *New York Times*, July 12, 1985, 1, 6.

35. "Principle of Vital Importance," *Time*, August 5, 1985, 33; Francis X. Clines, "Fledgling Protest Movement Gathers Steam," *New York Times*, August 5, 1985, B4.

36. Joanne Omang, "Veto of Sanctions Unlikely," *Washington Post*, July 30, 1985.

37. Telephone interview with Bob Mohan of WSB Radio in Atlanta, Georgia, August 24, 1985, https://www.reaganlibrary.gov/82485c.

38. "Manifesto for Disappointment," *Time*, August 26, 1985, 27, 28; "Leaving Reagan High and Dry," *U.S. News and World Report*, August 26, 1985, 22, 24, Bernard Weinraub, "Reagan Apologizes for Asserting that Pretoria Segregation Is Over," *New York Times*, September 7, 1985, 1, 5.

39. "Reagan's Abrupt Reversal," *Time*, September 16, 1985, 42–44.

40. Bernard Weinraub, "President Adopts Most of the Economic Steps Asked by Congress," *New York Times*, September 10, 1985, A1, 12; Frieserdorf and McFarlane to Reagan, memo, September 9, 1985, WHORM Subject Files, Box 166, RRPL.

41. Frankel, "Limited Sanctions Imposed on South Africa," A1, A12.

42. "President's News Conference on Foreign and Domestic Issues," *New York Times*, April 10, 1986, 22.

43. Anthony Lewis, "Wringing Our Hands," *New York Times*, June 19, 1986, A27.

44. Gleijeses, *Visions of Freedom*, 290; Allister Sparks, "Botha Cites Raids on Libya as Example for South Africa," *Washington Post*, May 20, 1986, A1, A41; Allen Cowell, "State of Emergency Imposed throughout South Africa," *New York Times*, June 13, 1986, 1, 13.

45. Dellums and Halterman, *Lying Down with Lions*, 134–35; Nesbitt, *Race for Sanctions*, 140–41.

46. Lou Cannon and David B. Ottaway, "Reagan Pressured on Apartheid," *Washington Post*, June 28, 1986, A18.

47. "Transcript of Talk by Reagan on South Africa and Apartheid," *New York Times*, July 23, 1986, 12.

48. Text of Remarks by the President to Members of the World Affairs and the Foreign Policy Association, July 22, 1986, Mari Maseng Files, Box 2, OA14573, RRPL.

49. Memo to Gwendolyn King, July 24, 1986, Gwendolyn S. King Files, Box 2, OA16166, RRPL.

50. Sara Fritz, "GOP Fear of Racist Image on S. Africa Stand Grows," *Los Angeles Times*, July 26, 1986, 1, 10.

51. Jon Margolis, "Reagan's Best Friends Won't Join Apartheid Stance," *Chicago Tribune*, July 22, 1986, 8.

52. Alan Cowell, "Pretoria Praises Reagan's Speech," *New York Times*, July 24, 1986, A4.

53. Chester A. Crocker, *High Noon in Southern Africa: Making Peace in a Rough Neighborhood* (New York: W. W. Norton, 1993), 323.

54. Steven V. Roberts, "House Passes Pretoria Sanctions; President Is Expected to Veto Bill," *New York Times*, September 13, 1986, 1, 5; Reagan to Robert Michel, September 29, 1986, Alton Keel Files, Box 3, RRPL.

55. "'Eyeball to Eyeball,' Reagan, Congress and the Sanctions Veto," *Time*, October 6, 1986, 36, 37; Talking Points, Meeting with Senators Dole and Lugar on September 15/16, 1986, Alton Files, Box 3, RRPL.

56. Veto Message, September 26, 1986, Dean C. McGrath Files, Box 6, OA 15548, RRPL.

57. Edward Walsh, "House Easily Overrides Veto of South Africa Sanctions," *Washington Post*, September 30, 1986, A1.

58. Desson Howe, "Cheers for Sanctions," *Washington Post*, October 4, 1986, G1.

59. Mandela quoted in Steven G. N. Tuck, *We Ain't What We Ought to Be: The Black Freedom Struggle from Emancipation to Obama* (Cambridge, MA: Harvard University Press, 2010), 382.

60. Kate Coleman, "The Roots of Ed Meese," *Los Angeles Times*, May 4, 1986.

61. "Dangerous Attorney General," *Chicago Tribune*, January 24, 1984, 14.

62. "The Nation Deserves Better," *Oakland Tribune*, January 25, 1984, B6.

63. "Memo on Meese," February 29, 1984, LCCR Papers, Part II, Box 61, LOC; "NAACP Opposes Meese Nomination," February 1984, LCCR Papers, Part II, Box 61, LOC; Carl Ingram, "Meese Ties ACLU to 'Crime Lobby,'" *Los Angeles Times*, May 12, 1981, B12.

64. "Counsel Is Named for Meese Inquiry," *New York Times*, April 3, 1984, 1, 21.

65. "Meese Confirmed after a Delay of 13 Months," *Congressional Quarterly*, https://library.cqpress.com/cqalmanac/document.php?id=cqal85-1147784, accessed November 2, 2017.

66. Stuart Taylor Jr., "Memo Cites Meese over Ethics Rules," *New York Times*, January 29, 1985, B5.

67. Stuart Taylor Jr., "Ethics Chief Found to Have Wavered on 'Violation' by Meese," *New York Times*, January 30, 1985, 22.

68. "Meese Confirmed after Delay of 13 Months," *Congressional Quarterly*, https://library.cqpress.com/cqalmanac/document.php?id=cqal85-1147784.

69. Philip Shenon, "High Justice Aides Quit Amid Meese's Role," *New York Times*, March 30, 1988, 1, 16.

70. "Highlights of Meese's Legal Problems," AP, July 5, 1988.

71. Leslie Maitland Werner, "Busing and Quotas Assailed by Meese," *New York Times*, March 16, 1985, 40.

72. Testimony of Ralph Neas Opposing Reynolds, June 5, 1985, LCCR Papers, Part II: Box 62, Folder 5, LOC.

73. Testimony of Ralph Neas Opposing Reynolds.

74. Neil Lewis, "Hostile Questions Greet Nominee for Justice Dept. Post Hearing," *New York Times*, June 5, 1985, B6; Confirmation of William Bradford Reynolds to Be Associate Attorney General of the United States, June 4, 1985, Congressional Record, 99th Cong., 1st Sess., 51.

75. Berman, *Give Us the Ballot*, 167.

76. Howard Kurtz, "Reynolds to Lay Error to Faulty Recollection," *Washington Post*, June 18, 1985, A3; Robert Pear, "Reynolds Apologizes for Senate Testimony Errors," *New York Times*, June 19, 1985, 20; Declaration of Charles Victor McTeer, LCCR Papers, Part II: Box 62, Folder 5, LOC.

77. Robert Pear, "Senate Committee Rejects Reynolds for Justice Post," *New York Times*, June 28, 1985, A1, A13.

78. Howard Kurtz, "Reynolds' Nomination Voted Down," *Washington Post*, June 28, 1985, A1, A5.

79. Glen Elsasser, "Reagan's Nominee Rejected," *Chicago Tribune*, June 28, 1985.

80. Reynolds quoted in Juan Williams, "In His Mind but Not His Heart," *Washington Post*, January 10, 1988.

81. Anderson, *Pursuit of Fairness*, 185; MacLean, *Freedom Is Not Enough*, 301; Robert Pear, "Reagan Aides Map Repeal of Rules on Bias in Hiring," *New York Times*, August 15, 1985, A1, A20; Juan Williams, "Reagan Considers Stance on Affirmative Action," *Washington Post*, July 11, 1985, A7.

82. George Gilder, "The Myths of Racial and Sexual Discrimination," *National Review*, November 14, 1980, 1381–90.

83. "The New Rights War," *Newsweek*, December 30, 1985; Robert Pear, "Goals for Hiring Split Reagan Aides," *New York Times*, October 23, 1985, A1, B5.

84. "Secretary Brock's Pledge," *Washington Post*, June 27, 1985, A22; William H. Brock, telephone interview with author, October 24, 2016.

85. Howard Kurtz, "Minority Hiring Battle Illustrates Policy Stalemate," *Washington Post*, January 11, 1986, A3.

86. Ronald Reagan, Radio Address to Nation on Martin Luther King Jr., January 18, 1986, http://www.presidency.ucsb.edu/ws/?pid=37302.

87. Quoted in Honey, *To the Promised Land*, 162.

88. Roger Wilkins, "A Dream Still Deferred," *Los Angeles Times*, January 19, 1986, G1.

89. Paul Houston, "Administration Asks Court to Limit Affirmative Action," *Los Angeles Times*, February 26, 1986, 21.

90. Quoted in Anderson, *The Pursuit of Fairness*, 192.

91. Quoted in MacLean, *Freedom Is Not Enough*, 302.

92. Robert A. Jordan, "Southern Strategy Backfires," *Boston Globe*, November 9, 1986, 129; Dorothy Gilliam, "Celebrating Black Margins of Victory," *Washington Post*, November 6, 1986, C3.

CHAPTER 11: THE BATTLE FOR THE JUDICIARY

1. William T. Coleman, "Why Judge Bork Is Unacceptable," *New York Times*, September 15, 1987, A35.

2. "Reagan Seeks Judges with 'Traditional Approach,'" *U.S. News & World Report*, October 14, 1985, 67.

3. Philip Shenon, "Reagan Judges Gets Lower Bar Rating," *New York Times*, May 25, 1986, 25; Herman Schwartz, *Packing the Courts: The Conservative Campaign to Rewrite the Constitution* (New York: Scribner's, 1988), 54, 61–62.

4. See Steven M. Teles, *The Rise of the Conservative Legal Movement: The Battle for Control of the Law* (Princeton, NJ: Princeton University Press, 2008).

5. Remarks of Thurgood Marshall, May 6, 1987, Leadership Conference of Civil Rights, Part II: Box 50, Folder 2, LOC.

6. "Judges with Their Minds Right," *Time*, November 4, 1985, 77.

7. Ethan Bronner, *Battle for Justice: How the Bork Nomination Shook America* (New York: Union Square Press, 1988), 32.

8. "Judging the Judges: The Courts Are Being Re-created in Reagan's Image," *Newsweek*, October 14, 1985, 73.

9. Lena Williams, "Race Issues Key to Judicial Nominee," *New York Times*, March 14, 1986, A36.

10. Statement of Thomas Figures, LCCR Papers, Part II: Box 63, Folder 1, LOC; Phillip Shenon, "Senator Urges Withdrawal of Judicial Nomination," *New York Times*, March 20, 1986, A22.

11. Memo from Ralph Neas re Sessions, March 27, 1986, LCCR Papers, Part II: Box 63, Folder 2, LOC; "Record, Not Racism Taints Judge Choice," *Atlanta Constitution*, March 22, 1986.

12. John Brinkley, "Sessions Admits Being 'Loose with My Tongue' Sometimes," *Birmingham Post-Herald*, (undated), LCCR Papers, Part II: Box 62, Folder 7, LOC.

13. Irvin Molotsky and Robin Toner, "Eyes on Senator Heflin," *New York Times*, June 7, 1986, 7.

14. Lena Williams, "Senate Panel Hands Reagan First Defeat on Nominee for Judgeship," *New York Times*, June 6, 1986, 13; Philip Hager, "Reagan's Judicial Nominee Rejected," *Los Angeles Times*, June 6, 1986, A4.

15. Teles, *The Rise of the Conservative Legal Movement*, 140.

16. A. S. "Doc" Young, "Matters of Fact & Opinion," *Los Angeles Sentinel*, June 26, 1986, A7.

17. Quoted in John A. Jenkins, "The Partisan: A Talk with Justice Rehnquist," *New York Times Magazine*, March 3, 1985.

18. "Memo from Rehnquist," *Newsweek*, December 13, 1971, 32, 37.

19. Fred P. Graham, "Rehnquist Says '52 Memo Outlined Jackson's Views," *New York Times*, December 9, 1971, 26; Laura Kalman, *The Long Reach of the Sixties: LBJ, Nixon, and the Making of the Contemporary Supreme Court* (New York: Oxford University Press, 2017), 302.

20. UPI, "Rehnquist's View on Memos Disputed by Aide to Jackson," *New York Times*, August 11, 1986, A14.

21. Adam Liptak, "New Look at an Old Memo Casts More Doubt on Rehnquist," *New York Times*, March 19, 2012, A18; Hutchison quoted in Jenkins, "The Partisan," *New York Times Magazine*, March 3, 1985.

22. John Dean, *The Rehnquist Choice: The Untold Story of the Nixon Appointment That Redefined the Supreme Court* (New York: Free Press, 2001), 277–78.

23. Congressional Record, Nominations of William H. Rehnquist and Lewis F. Powell Jr., 92nd Cong., 1st Sess., November 3, 1971, 70.

24. "Rehnquist Accused of Harassment," *Pittsburgh Courier*, November 27, 1971, 37; "Reject Nominee Rehnquist," *Chicago Daily Defender*, December 2, 1971.

25. Fred Graham, "Rights Aides Call Rehnquist Racist," *New York Times*, November 10, 1971, 29.

26. Ronald J. Ostrow and Robert L. Jackson, "Bias, Candor Again Issues as Rehnquist Faces Senate," *Los Angeles Times*, July 29, 1986; "Through the Wringer: A Senate Panel Questions Rehnquist on Race and His Past," *Time*, August 11, 1986.

27. The Case against William Rehnquist, undated, LCCR Papers, Part II: Box 61, Folder 6, LOC; Rick Black, "'Anti-Black' Rehnquist Confirmed," *New York Amsterdam News*, August 23, 1986, 1, 22.

28. Stuart Taylor Jr., "Opposition to Rehnquist Hardens," *New York Times*, July 27, 1986, 18.

29. Nomination of William H. Rehnquist to Be Supreme Court Justice of the United States, *Congressional Record*, August 1, 1986, 987–1078; Ronald Ostrow and James Gerstenzang, "Four Witnesses Dispute Word of Rehnquist," *Los Angeles Times*, August 2, 1986; Affidavit of Ruth Finn, August 12, 1986, LCCR Papers, Part II: Box 61, Folder 8, LOC.

30. Robert Andrews, "Former Prosecutor Says He Saw Rehnquist in Voter Confrontation Effort," AP, August 1, 1986.

31. Ronald J. Ostrow, "100 Law Professors Question Rehnquist's Ethics," *Los Angeles Times*, September 11, 1986, 20.

32. Al Kame, "Senate Opens Debate on Rehnquist Nomination," *Washington Post*, September 12, 1986, A10.

33. Linda Greenhouse, "Senate, 65 to 33, Votes to Confirm Rehnquist as 16th Chief Justice," *New York Times*, September 18, 1986.

34. Gerald M. Boyd, "Bork Nomination to Court Weighted by President," *New York Times*, June 30, 1987, A1, B20.

35. Remarks of the President at Nomination of Judge Bork, July 1, 1987, Alan C. Rauh Files, Box 9, OA19157, RRPL; Dewayne Wickham, "Bork—He's Bad News for Blacks," *Des Moines Register*, August 5, 1987.

36. Quoted in Schwartz, *Packing the Courts*, 3.

37. See Bronner, *The Battle for Justice*.

38. Lou Cannon and Edward Walsh, "Reagan Nominates Appeals Judge Robert Bork to the Supreme Court," *Washington Post*, July 2, 1987, A1, A17.

39. Linda Greenhouse, "Senators' Remarks Portend a Bitter Debate over Bork," *New York Times*, July 2, 1987, 22.

40. Sarah Raper, "NAACP Chief Vows Battle over Bork," *Pittsburgh Courier*, July 18, 1987, 2; Robert H. Bork, "Neutral Principles and Some First Amendment Problems," *Indiana Law Journal* 47, no. 1 (Fall 1971): 1–35.

41. Robert Bork, "Civil Rights—A Challenge," *New Republic*, August 31, 1963, 21–24.

42. "Civil Rights—A Reply," *New Republic*, August 31, 1963, 24; see, also, Perlstein, *Before the Storm*, 363. See, also, Christopher W. Schmidt, "Defending the Right to Discriminate: The Libertarian Challenge to the Civil Rights Movement," in *Signposts: New Directions in Southern Legal History*, ed. Sally Hadden and Patricia Minter (Athens: University of Georgia Press, 2013), 417–46.

43. Senate Judiciary Committee Hearings on Bork, LCCR Papers, Part II: Box 54, Folder, 1, LOC.

44. Peter K. Keisler to Kenneth Cribb Jr., memo, July 31, 1987, Alan C. Rauh Files, Box 9, OA19157, RRPL; William T. Coleman Jr., "Why Judge Bork Is Unacceptable," *New York Times*, September 15, 1987, 35.

45. Alden Whitman, "Earl Warren, 83, Who Led the High Court in Time of Vast Social Change Is Dead," *New York Times*, July 10, 1974.

46. Robert H. Bork, "Neutral Principles and Some First Amendment Problems," *Indiana Law Journal* 47, no. 1 (Fall 1971): 1–35.

47. Summary of Some of the Major Arguments against the Nomination of Bork, undated, NAACP Papers, Part 8: Box 311, Folder 7, LOC; Joe Rodota to Frank Donatelli, memo, August 27, 1987, Public Affairs, WHORM, Box 29, OA16024, RRPL; Philip B. Kurland, "The Transformation of a Conservative Constitutionalist," *Chicago Tribune*, August 18, 1987, 6, 7.

48. Quoted in Lanny Davis, *Scandal: How "Gotcha" Politics Is Destroying America* (New York: Palgrave MacMillan, 2006), 111.

49. Janet Cawley, "Delay on Vote Threatened in the Senate," *Chicago Tribune*, September 29, 1987.

50. Wendy Zentz, "Brennan Calls on Judges to Remain True to Founding Fathers," UPI, September 16, 1987, clipping found in Patricia Mack Bryan Files, Box 6, OA19247, RRPL.

51. Jordan quoted in Bronner, *Battle for Justice*, 253–54.

52. Kenneth Noble, "Fervor over Bork Nomination Intensifies as Start of Senate Hearing Nears," *New York Times*, September 12, 1987.

53. David Lauter and Donald J. Ostrow, "Fears of Blacks, ABA Dissenters on Bork Told," *Los Angeles Times*, September 22, 1987, B1, 16.

54. "Bork's Credentials Get Mixed Review from Panel," *Baltimore Sun*, September 10, 1987, 1A; Bronner, *Battle for Justice*, 175.

55. "Groups Voice Opposition to Bork's Nomination," UPI, September 11, 1987.

56. Tom Shales, "The Bork Turnoff; On Camera, the Judge Failed to Save Himself," *Washington Post*, October 9, 1987, B1, B6.

57. Stuart Taylor, "The Bork Hearings: Bork Backs Away from His Stances on Rights Issues," *New York Times*, September 17, 1987; Al Kamen and Edward Walsh, "Senators Increase Pressure over Bork's Shifting Opinions," *Washington Post*, September 18, 1987.

58. Kennedy quoted in Bronner, *Battle for Justice*, 193.

59. Testimony of William T. Coleman, September 21, 1987, Patricia Mack Bryan Files, Box 9, OA19247, RRPL; David Lauter and Ronald J. Ostrow, "Fears of Blacks, ABA Dissenters on Bork Told," *Los Angeles Times*, September 22, 1987, B1, 16.

60. John Hanrahan, "Opponents Say Bork an Extremist," UPI, September 21, 1987; "Barbara Jordan Returns," *Baltimore Afro-American*, October 3, 1987, 1, 2.

61. "The Strength of Black Voters," *Baltimore Afro-American*, October 17, 1987, 4; Edward Walsh, "Bork's Foes Built Strategy on South," *Washington Post*, October 4, 1981, A1, A10.

62. Steven V. Roberts, "9–5 Panel Vote Against Bork Sends Nomination to Senate Amid Predictions of Defeat," *New York Times*, October 7, 1987.

63. Alan Dershowitz, "Reagan's Litmus Tests for All Judges Doomed Bork," *Los Angeles Times*, October 19, 1987, C7.

64. Nat Hentoff, "What Robert Bork Never Understood," *Washington Post*, October 11, 1987.

65. Al Kamen and Edward Walsh, "Black Leaders, GOP Senator Voice Opposition to Bork," *Washington Post*, September 22, 1987; Young quoted in Bronner, *Battle for Justice*, 254.

66. Marshall quoted in Juan Williams, *Thurgood Marshall: American Revolutionary* (New York: Crown, 1998), 384.

67. Thurgood Marshall Address, May 6, 1987, LCCR Papers Part II: Box 50, Folder 2, LOC.

68. Stuart Taylor Jr., "Marshall Puts Reagan at 'Bottom' among Presidents on Civil Rights," *New York Times*, September 9, 1987, 1, 22.

69. Reagan, *Reagan Diaries*, 549.

70. Reagan, *Reagan Diaries*, 549.

71. Fred P. Graham, "Marshall Is Questioned on Fine Points of the Law," *New York Times*, July 20, 1967, 17.

72. Wil Haygood, *Showdown: Thurgood Marshall and the Supreme Court Nomination That Changed America* (New York: Knopf, 2015), 243–55.

73. A. Leon Higginbotham, "The Case of the Missing Black Judges," *New York Times*, July 29, 1992, 21.

74. Berry, *History Teaches Us to Resist*, 84.

CHAPTER 12: THE WAR ON DRUGS, WILLIE HORTON, AND THE CRIMINALIZATION OF BLACKNESS

1. Ronald Reagan, "Remarks in New Orleans, Louisiana, at the Annual Meeting of the International Chiefs of Police, September 28, 1981," American Presidency Project, http://www.presidency.ucsb.edu/ws/?pid=44300.

2. Quoted in Roger Simon, *Road Show: In America Anybody Can Become President, It's One of the Risks We Take* (New York: Farrar, Straus & Giroux, 1990), 203.

3. Lou Cannon, "Why the Band Has Stopped Playing for Ronald Reagan," *Washington Post*, December 21, 1986.

4. Grove City Veto Message, March 16, 1988, David M. McIntosh Files, Box 3, RRPL; Helen Dewar, "Congress Overrides Civil Rights Law Veto," *Washington Post*, March 23, 1988, A1, A2.

5. See Hugh Davis Graham, "The Storm over Grove City College: Civil Rights Regulation, Higher Education, and the Reagan Administration," *Higher Education Quarterly* 38, no. 4 (Winter 1998): 407–29.

6. Grove City College v. Bell, 465 U.S. 555 (1984).

7. Ronald Reagan, "Federal Harassment Worsening," *Denver Post*, January 7, 1977.

8. Reagan to Robert Michel, March 1, 1988, David McIntosh Files, Box 2, RRPL.

9. Alexander, *The New Jim Crow*, 6.

10. Julilly Kohler-Hausmann, *Getting Tough: Welfare and Imprisonment in 1970s America* (Princeton, NJ: Princeton University Press, 2017), 11.

11. Flamm, *Law and Order*, 22.

12. H. R. Haldeman, *The Haldeman Diaries: Inside the Nixon White House* (New York: G. P. Putnam's Sons, 1994), 53.

13. Dan Baum, "Legalize It All: How to Win the War on Drugs," *Harpers*, April 2016, 22.

14. "Ronald Reagan: 'Marijuana . . . is probably the most dangerous drug,'" posted September 4, 2014, https://www.youtube.com/watch?v=VxHBx6H-xFo.

15. Peter G. Bourne, "'Just Say No': Drug Abuse Policy in the Reagan Administration," in Hudson and Davies, *Ronald Reagan and the 1980s*, 41–56.

16. "Reagan Aide: Pot Can Make You Gay," *Newsweek*, October 27, 1986, 95.

17. Remarks on Signing Executive Order 12368, June 24, 1982, American Presidency Project, http://www.presidency.ucsb.edu/ws/index.php?pid=42671.

18. Howell Raines, "Reagan Proposes Revisions of Laws to Combat Crime," *New York Times*, September 29, 1981, 1, 19.

19. Radley Balko, *Rise of the Warrior Cop: The Militarization of America's Police Forces* (New York: Public Affairs, 2013), 145–47. See Hinton, *From the War on Poverty to the War on Crime*, 310–14.

20. Clyde Haberman, "The Rise of the SWAT Team in American Policing," *New York Times*, September 7, 2014.

21. Alexander, *The New Jim Crow*, 49.

22. See Michael Tonry, "Race and the War on Drugs," *University of Chicago Legal Forum*, no. 1 (1994): 29–37.

23. William Overend, "First Lady's Drug War Hit," *Los Angeles Times*, March 30, 1982, OC–D1.

24. Stuart Taylor Jr., "New Crime Act a Vast Sea Change, Officials Assert," *New York Times*, October 15, 1984, 1, 26.

25. Dan Baum, *Smoke and Mirrors: The War on Drugs and the Politics of Failure* (New York: Little, Brown, 1996), 203–5.

26. Baum, *Smoke and Mirrors*, 220.

27. "Kids and Cocaine," *Newsweek*, March 17, 1986; Baum, *Smoke and Mirrors*, 219–21; "Crack and Crime," *Newsweek*, June 16, 1986, 16; see, also, Reeves and Campbell, *Cracked Coverage*.

28. Alexander, *The New Jim Crow*, 52–53.

29. "Rolling Out the Big Guns," *Time*, September 22, 1986, 25.

30. Loretta Tofani, "Meese Seeks Press Help in Drug Fight," *Washington Post*, March 21, 1985, A4; Address of Meese, May 1, 1985, https://www.justice.gov/sites/default/files/ag/legacy/2011/08/23/05-01-1985.pdf.

31. Baum, *Smoke and Mirrors*, 214–15.

32. Clarence Page, "Bias's Unintended Legacy," *Baltimore Sun*, June 23, 2006.

33. Quoted in Baum, *Smoke and Mirrors*, 225; Eric E. Sterling and Julie Stewart, "Undo This Legacy of Len Bias's Death," *Washington Post*, June 24, 2006.

34. "Defense Demurs," *Time*, September 29, 1986, 36.

35. See James Forman Jr., *Locking Up Our Own: Crime and Punishment in Black America* (New York: Farrar, Straus & Giroux, 2017).

36. Tracie Reddick, "Communities Move against Drug Dealers," *Washington Times*, March 1, 1988.

37. Gerald M. Boyd, "Reagans Advocate 'Crusade' on Drugs," *New York Times*, September 15, 1986, A1.

38. Judith Havemann, "Reagan Signs Antidrug Bill," *Washington Post*, October 28, 1986, A3.

39. Ronald Reagan, "Remarks on Signing the Anti-Drug Abuse Act of 1986," October 27, 1986, http://www.presidency.ucsb.edu/ws/?pid=36654; "War on Drugs: More Than a 'Short-Term High'?," *U.S. News and World Report*, September 29, 1986, 28.

40. H.R. 5484, Anti-Drug Abuse Act of 1986, 99th Cong., Public Law No. 99–570.

41. Hinton, *From the War on Poverty to the War on Crime*, 317; David Sklansky, "Cocaine, Race and Equal Protection," *Stanford Law Review* 47 (1995): 1291.

42. Danielle Kurtzleben, "Data Shows Racial Disparity in Crack Sentencing," *U.S. News & World Report*, August 3, 2010.

43. "Cracks in the System: 20 Years of the Unjust Federal Crack Cocaine Law," ACLU, October 2006, https://www.aclu.org/other/cracks-system-20-years-unjust -federal-crack-cocaine-law. See, also, Marc Mauer, *Race to Incarcerate* (New York: New Press, 2006), 158–74.

44. "Targeting Blacks: Drug Law Enforcement and Race in the United States," Human Rights Watch, May 4, 2008, https://www.hrw.org/report/2008/05/04 /targeting-blacks/drug-law-enforcement-and-race-united-states.

45. Alexander, *The New Jim Crow*, 100–106.

46. Tony Platt, *Beyond These Walls: Rethinking Crime and Punishment in the United States* (New York: St. Martin's Press, 2019), 215.

47. Haynes Johnson and Gwen Ifill, "Jackson Stirs White Underdogs," *Washington Post*, April 2, 1988, A1, A5.

48. E. J. Dionne Jr., "Jackson Share of Votes by Whites Triples in '88," *New York Times*, June 13, 1988, B7.

49. "Taking Jesse Seriously," *Time*, April 11, 1988; Lewis quoted in Mayer, *Running on Race*, 207.

50. Robin Toner, "Battle for the Black Vote Is Over before It Started," *New York Times*, February 28, 1988, 29.

51. Jefferson Morley, "Bush and Blacks: The Unknown Story," *New York Review of Books*, January 16, 1992.

52. Margaret Garrard Warner, "Bush Battles the 'Wimp Factor,'" *Newsweek*, October 19, 1987.

53. Jack W. Germond and Jules Witcover, *Whose Broad Stripes and Bright Stars: The Trivial Pursuit of the Presidency, 1988* (New York: Grand Central Publishing, 1989), 157–59.

54. Margorie Williams, "The New Lee Atwater Lies Low," *Washington Post*, November 19, 1989, 22.

55. Bob Herbert, "Impossible, Ridiculous, Repugnant," *New York Times*, October 6, 2005, 37.

56. Dirk Kirchten, "How the Furlough Issue Grew and Dominated the Campaign," *National Journal*, October 29, 1988, 2718–19.

57. Quoted in Simon, *Road Show*, 203; Rossinow, *The Reagan Era*, 247.

58. Sidney Blumenthal, "Willie Horton and the Making of an Election Issue," *Washington Post*, October 28, 1988, D1.

59. Richard Stengel, "The Man behind the Message," *Time*, August 22, 1988, 29.

60. T. R. Reid, "Most States Allow Furloughs from Prison," *Washington Post*, June 24, 1988.

61. David Lauter, "Prison Furloughs: Campaigns Obscuring Complex Issue," *Los Angeles Times*, July 22, 1988, 15.

62. Jane Mayer, "Attack Dog," *New Yorker*, February 13 and 20, 2012.

63. Rossinow, *The Reagan Era*, 256.

64. Rossinow, *The Reagan Era*, 256.

65. Keith Love, "Bush Backers Have Horton Victims Speak," *Los Angeles Times*, October 8, 1988, 23; Mayer, *Running on Race*, 219.

66. See Kathleen Hall Jamieson, *Dirty Politics, Distraction, and Democracy* (New York: Oxford University Press, 1993).

67. Inside Politics, http://www.insidepolitics.org/ps111/candidateads.html.

68. "Jim Crow for President," *New York Amsterdam News*, November 5, 1988, 15; "George Bush and Willie Horton," *New York Times*, November 4, 1988, A34.

69. "Bush, His Disavowed Backers and a Very Potent Attack Ad," *New York Times*, November 3, 1988, A1, B20.

70. Stephen Chapman, "Would It Matter If Willie Horton Were White?," *Chicago Tribune*, October 27, 1988, 23.

71. "Taking the Pledge," *Time*, September 5, 1988, 14–15.

72. "Atwater Apologizes for '88 Remarks about Dukakis," *Washington Post*, January 13, 1991, A6.

73. Lee May, "Blacks Look Back with Anger at Reagan Years," *Los Angeles Times*, January 20, 1989, B1.

74. Andrew Rosenthal, "Reagan Hints Leaders Exaggerate Racism to Preserve Cause," *New York Times*, January 14, 1989, 8.

75. John E. Jacobs, "The Reagan Era Ends," *Los Angeles Sentinel*, January 19, 1989, A7.

76. Steven V. Roberts, "Reagan on Homeless: Many Choose to Live Out There," *New York Times*, December 23, 1988, A26.

77. Stockman, *The Triumph of Politics*, 396.

78. May, "Blacks Look Back with Anger," *Los Angeles Times*, January 20, 1989.

CONCLUSION

1. Pat Buchanan, "Is Trump the Heir to Reagan?," Townhall, October 13, 2017, https://townhall.com/columnists/patbuchanan/2017/10/13/is-trump-the-heir-to-reagan-n2394415.

2. "The Reagan Years," *Washington Post*, January 20, 1989, A26; "Exit the Music Man," *New York Times*, January 20, 1989, A30.

3. Lou Cannon, "Reagan Leaves a Legacy of Surprises," *Washington Post*, January 15, 1989, A1, A15–17.

4. Ralph Neas to Lou Cannon, January 19, 1989, Lou Cannon Papers, Box 28, University of California Santa Barbara Library, Special Collections.

5. "Reagan Friends Buy Him a Place to Retire," *New York Times*, January 24, 1987, 8.

6. "Reagan Praises Japan in $1 Million Speech," UPI, October 25, 1989; Laurie Becklund, "Reagan Fee Per Speech, a Cool $50,000," *Los Angeles Times*, January 28, 1991, 31.

7. Spitz, *Reagan*, 743; David Sanger, "Reagan's Host: A Japan Media Giant," *New York Times*, October 19, 1989; "Striking It Rich in Japan," *New York Times*, October 26, 1989.

8. Robert Reinhold, "Republicans in Houston: The Reagan Speech," *New York Times*, August 17, 1992.

9. Johnson, *Sleepwalking through History*.

10. Reagan, *An American Life*, 150.

11. Andrew Hacker, *Two Nations: Black and White, Separate, Hostile, Unequal* (New York: Scribner's, 1992), 219

12. Matthew R. Pendleton, "George H. W. Bush Biggest Failure? The War on Drugs," *Washington Post*, December 6, 2018.

13. Edsall and Edsall, *Chain Reaction*.

14. Peter Appelbome, "The 1992 Campaign: Death Penalty; Arkansas Execution Raises Questions on Governor's Politics," *New York Times*, January 25, 1992, 8.

15. See Donna Murch, "Crack in Los Angeles: Crisis, Militarization, and Black Response to the Late Twentieth-Century War on Drugs," *Journal of American History* 102, no. 1 (June 2015): 162–75.

16. "Text of Letter Written by President Ronald Reagan Announcing He Has Alzheimer's Disease," November 5, 1994, https://www.reaganlibrary.gov/sreference/reagan-s-letter-announcing-his-alzheimer-s-diagnosis.

17. Laurence K. Altman, "Parsing Ronald Reagan's Words for Early Signs of Alzheimer's," *New York Times*, March 30, 2015.

18. Mayer and McManus, *Landside*, viii–xi.

19. "Ronald Reagan Had Alzheimer's While President, Says Son," *Guardian*, January 17, 2011; Reagan, *My Father at 100*, 203–5.

20. Katherine Q. Seelye, "Bob Dole in Visit to Goldwater Emphasizes Goldwater Roots," *New York Times*, February 26, 1996.

21. John Cassidy, "Taxing," *New Yorker*, January 18, 2004.

22. Jennifer Steinhauer, "Confronting Ghosts of 2000 in South Carolina," *New York Times*, October 19, 2007, A1.

23. Jacqueline Bacon, "Saying What They've Been Thinking: Racial Stereotypes in Katrina Commentary," Fair, November 1, 2005, https://fair.org/extra/8220saying-what-they8217ve-been-thinking8221.

24. "Barbara Bush Calls Evacuees Better Off," *New York Times*, September 7, 2005.

25. Sam Tanenhaus, *The Death of Conservatism: The Movement and Its Consequences* (New York: Random House, 2009); Wilentz, *The Age of Reagan*.

26. Daniel Schorr, "A New, Post-Racial Political Era in America," National Public Radio, January 28, 2008; Nikole Hannah Jones, "The End of the Post-Racial Myth," *New York Times*, November 15, 2016.

27. George Zornick, "Boehner, Like Cantor, Refuses to Repudiate Birther Conspiracy Theories," *ThinkProgress*, February 13, 2011, https://thinkprogress.org/boehner -like-cantor-refuses-to-repudiate-birther-conspiracy-theories-51eb941619cf.

28. Terrence Samuels, "The Racist Backlash Obama Has Faced during His Presidency," *Washington Post*, April 22, 2016.

29. Joan Biskupic, *The Chief: The Life and Turbulent Times of Chief Justice John Roberts* (New York: Basic Books, 2019), 134–35.

30. Carol Anderson, *One Person, No Vote: How Voter Suppression Is Destroying Our Democracy* (New York: Bloomsbury, 2018).

31. Patrick Healy, "How Is Scott Walker Like Reagan? He'll Tell You," *New York Times*, April 6, 2015.

32. Bradford Richardson, "Rubio Casts Himself as a Child of the Reagan Revolution," *Hill*, February 26, 2016.

33. "Here's Donald Trump's Presidential Announcement Speech," Time.com, June 16, 2015, http://time.com/3923128/donald-trump-announcement-speech.

34. William F. Buckley Jr., "On Donald Trump and Demagoguery," *National Review*, January 22, 2016, https://www.nationalreview.com/2016/01/william-f-buckley -donald-trump-demagoguery-cigar-aficionado.

35. German Lopez, "Trump's Long History of Racism, from the 1970s to 2019," *Vox*, February 14, 2019, https://www.vox.com/2016/7/25/12270880/donald-trump -racist-racism-history.

36. Morris Kaplan, "Major Landlord Accused of Anti-Black Bias in the City," *New York Times*, October 16, 1973.

37. Benjamin Weiser, "5 Exonerated in Central Park Jogger Case Agree to Settle Lawsuit for $40 Million," *New York Times*, June 19, 2014.

38. Benjy Sarlin, "Donald Trump Says Central Park Five Are Guilty, Despite DNA Evidence," *NBC News*, October 7, 2016, https://www.nbcnews.com/politics/2016 -election/donald-trump-says-central-park-five-are-guilty-despite-dna-n661941.

39. "Donald Trump Declares Himself to Be the Law and Order Candidate," *Guardian*, July 21, 2016.

40. Andrew Rastucia, "Sources: Former Trump Critic Ed Meese Joins Transition Team," *Politico*, September 26, 2016, https://www.politico.com/story/2016/09 /meese-trump-transition-228694.

41. Jennifer Harper, "Reagan Alumni Unite for Trump," *Washington Times*, October 30, 2016.

42. Jonathan Mahler, "How One Conservative Think Tank Is Stocking Trump's Government," *New York Times Magazine*, June 20, 2018.

43. Steven Shepard, "Missing Black Voter," *Politico*, May 10, 2017.

44. Bernard L. Fraga, Sean McElwee, Jesse Rhodes, and Brian F. Schaffner, "Why Did Trump Win? More Whites—and Fewer Blacks Actually Voted," *Washington Post*, May 8, 2017.

45. Melissa Franqui, "Felony Disenfranchisement: How the War on Drugs Impacted the 2016 Election," *Salon*, November 28, 2016, https://www.salon.com/2016 /11/28/felony-disenfranchisement-the-untold-story-of-the-2016-election_partner.

46. Daniel McCarthy, "There's No Going Back: The GOP Is Trump's Party," *New York Times*, November 1, 2018.

47. "How Trump Is Like Reagan," *Washington Post*, February 8, 2018.

48. Andy Kroll, "Inside Trump's Judicial Takeover," *Rolling Stone*, August 19, 2018.

49. Author interviews with Annelise Anderson, Thomas C. Reed, and Stuart Spencer.

50. Susan B. Glasser, "Is Trump the Second Coming of Reagan?," *New Yorker*, May 18, 2018; Noonan, *When Character Was King*.

51. Kleinknecht, *Man Who Sold the World*, 193.

52. James David Barber, "The Oval Office Aesop," *New York Times*, November 6, 1982, 213.

53. Dionne, *Why the Right Went Wrong*, 4.

54. See Corey Robin, *The Reactionary Mind: Conservatism from Edmund Burke to Sarah Palin* (New York: Oxford University Press, 2011); Max Boot, *The Corrosion of Conservatism: Why I Left the Right* (New York: Liveright, 2018); Perlstein, *Before the Storm*; Dionne, *Why the Right Went Wrong*; Kabaservice, *Rule and Ruin*; Lowndes, *From the New Deal to the New Right*.

55. Katie Rogers and Nicholas Fandos, "Trump Tells Congresswomen to "Go Back' to the Countries They Came From," *New York Times*, July 14, 2019.

56. Interview with Mary Frances Berry, April 6, 2019, Philadelphia.

57. Buchanan, "Is Trump the Heir to Reagan?"

INDEX